1996 Have a great time in Mexico! Merry Christmas! Love, Micah

Fodor's

EXPLORING MEXICO

FODOR'S TRAVEL PUBLICATIONS, INC.
NEW YORK • TORONTO • LONDON • SYDNEY • AUCKLAND

While every care has been taken to ensure the accuracy of the information in this guide, time brings change, and consequently the publisher cannot accept responsibility for errors that may occur. Prudent travelers will therefore want to call ahead to verify prices and other "perishable" information.

Published in the United States by Fodor's Travel Publications, Inc.
Published in the United Kingdom by AA Publishing.

ISBN 0–679–02821–8
First Edition

Fodor's Exploring Mexico

Author: **Fiona Dunlop**
Series Adviser: **Christopher Catling**
Joint Series Editor: **Susi Bailey**
Copy Editor: **Karen Kemp**
Cartography: **The Automobile Association**
Cover Design: **Louise Fili, Fabrizio La Rocca**
Front Cover Silhouette: **Melinda Berge/Photographers/Aspen**

Special Sales
Fodor's Travel Publications are available at special discounts for bulk purchases (100 copies or more) for sales promotions or premiums. Special editions, including personalized covers, excerpts of existing guides, and corporate imprints, can be created in large quantities for special needs, For more information, contact your local bookseller or write to Special Markets, Fodor's Travel Publications, 201 East 50th Street, New York, NY 10022.

Los Cabos Westin Regina resort, Baja California

MANUFACTURED IN ITALY
10 9 8 7 6 5 4 3 2 1

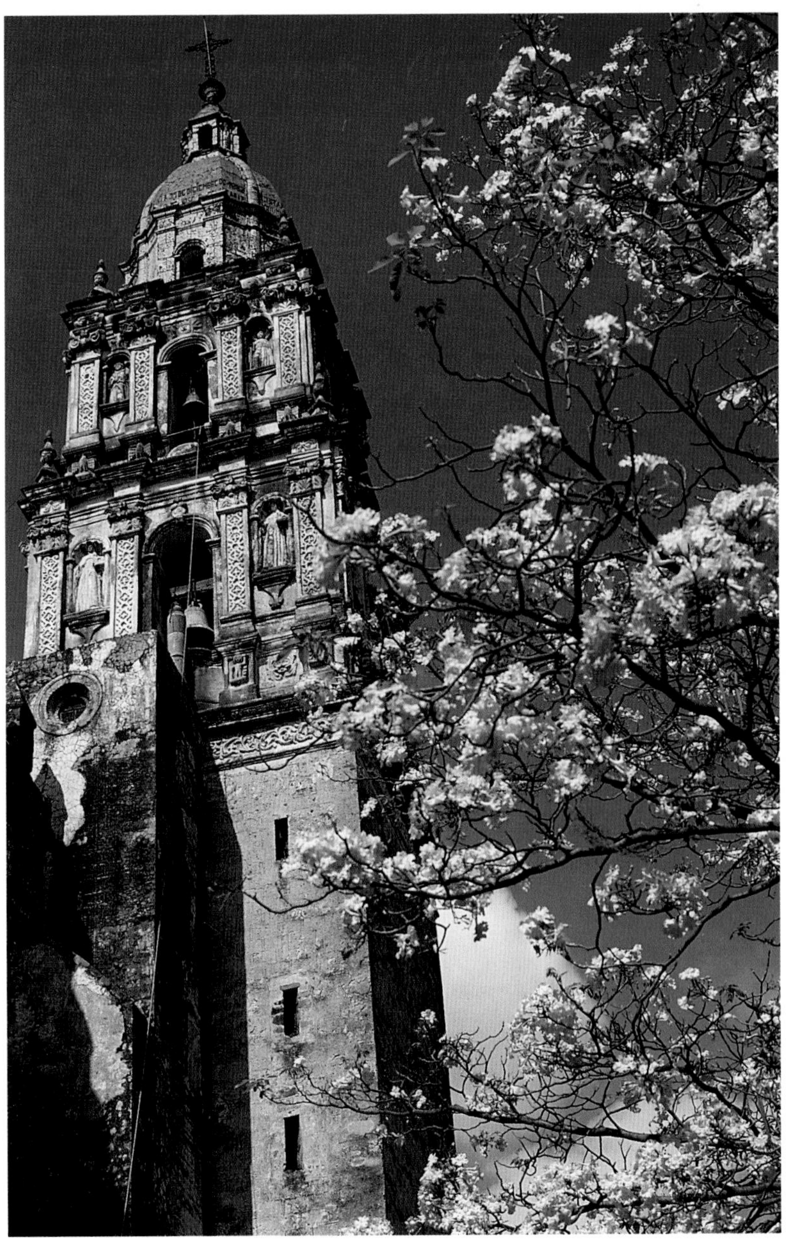

The cathedral, Cuernavaca

Fiona Dunlop lives and works in Paris where she has reported on the city's cultural life for newspapers and magazines such as *The Times*, the *Sunday Times*, the *European*, *Art International*, *Vogue Décoration* and *Elle Décoration*. She is the author of the *Paris Art Guide*, and of both *Paris* and *Singapore and Malaysia* in the Fodor's Exploring series. She has also contributed to several other guides, including the UK's *Time Out Guide to Paris*.

How to use this book

This book is divided into five main sections:

❑ **Section 1: *Mexico Is***
Discusses aspects of life and living today, from folk art to environmental problems

❑ **Section 2: *Mexico Was***
Places the country in its historical context and explores those past events whose influences are felt to this day

❑ **Section 3: *A to Z Section***
Breaks down into regional chapters, and covers places to visit, including walks and drives. Within this section fall the Focus-on articles, which consider a variety of subjects in greater detail

❑ **Section 4: *Travel Facts***
Contains the strictly practical information that is vital for a successful trip

❑ **Section 5: *Hotels and Restaurants***
Lists recommended establishments throughout Mexico, giving a brief summary of what they offer

How to use the star rating
Most of the places described in this book have been given a separate rating:

►►►	**Do not miss**
►►	**Highly recommended**
►	**Worth seeing**
	Not essential viewing

Map references
To make the location of a particular place easier to find, every main entry in this book is given a map reference, such as176B3. The first number (176) indicates the page on which the map can be found, the letter (B) and the second number (3) pinpoint the square in which the main entry is located. The maps on the inside front cover and inside back cover are referred to as IFC and IBC respectively.

Contents

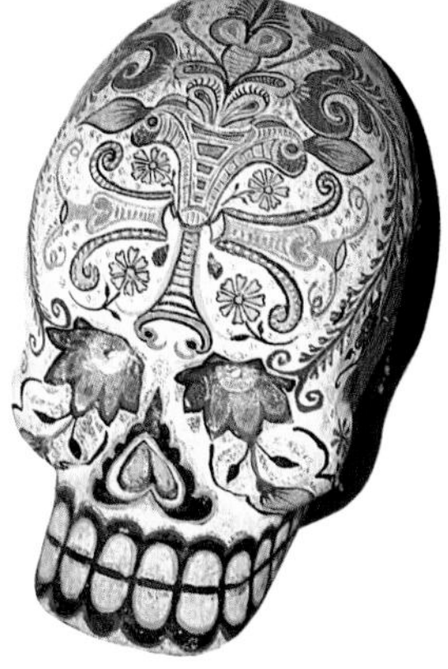

Quick reference

This quick-reference guide highlights the features of the book you will use most often: the maps; the introductory features; the Focus-on articles; the walk; and the drives.

Maps

Mexico Is

Mexico Was

Focus on

Walk

Drives

Travel Facts

Sunset over the Pacific Ocean at Ixtapa

Eduardo Mata
The Mexican conductor and composer Eduardo Mata spends much of his time traveling the world, fulfilling professional engagements with symphony orchestras in four continents. He was Principal Conductor of the Dallas Symphony Orchestra from 1977–93 and is a former Artistic Director of the National Opera in Mexico City. He is currently Principal Guest Conductor of the Simón Bolívar Symphony Orchestra in Caracas. In the American continent he flies his own plane and has his home outside Mexico City.

My Mexico

by Eduardo Mata

Being asked to write this short article titled 'My Mexico' set me thinking. My career has inevitably—and happily—made me an experienced traveler. However, when given the choice of where to spend free time, strictly for pleasure, I choose Mexico again and again.

Mexico is a country of diverse landscapes, of particular lights and shades, of archaeological ruins, and with a living colonial heritage. It has beaches, forests, deserts, mountains, outdoor markets, popular fairs, great food, and excellent beers.... It's a country with a complex sociological profile, perhaps more like a whole host of nations masquerading as one country—but it's precisely this cultural diversity that makes it so maddeningly attractive.

My advice to visitors would undoubtedly be: Drive Mexico! Try the local foods, and immerse yourself in that particular native sense of timing. Don't expect too much of the large cities, though if you are interested in the pulsating energy of a city with an enormous 20-million population, then Mexico City can't be beat. Make sure you don't miss the Sierra de Puebla or the gloriously beautiful countryside around Lake Pátzcuaro. Likewise, Oaxaca is one of the true highlights of any trip around Mexico. The museums in Villahermosa and the Mayan remains in Yucatán and Quintana Roo are unrivaled for beauty and atmosphere. And if you feel the need to laze on the beach, then you can make your choice by color of sand, by type of accommodation, by sea temperature—even by ocean, since the Caribbean, Atlantic, and Pacific are all available. I hope you enjoy the adventure!

Mariana Yampolsky
Photographer Mariana Yampolsky began her career as an engraver in the famed Taller de Grafica Popular. Photographing rural life she has traveled the length and breadth of Mexico. She has also worked as curator of exhibitions and editor of publications for children. Her latest book is *The Traditional Architecture of Mexico.*

My Mexico

by Mariana Yampolsky

Mexico, it is often said, is a land of contrasts. I suspect this must be true, for it's clear that the rich are filthy rich, and the poor are filthy poor; that the rain forests are wet and the deserts dry. But what is it that really intrigues and fascinates?

Is it the mix of splendor and sacrifice that the names Teotihuacán, Monte Albán, and Chichén Itzá evoke? Is it the churches, altars, and shrines that, as a result of the Spanish Conquest, sprang up in every city, town, and village? Is it the profusion of plants and animals, as diverse as the land itself? Is it the masterly murals of Rivera and Orozco, seen in and on public buildings across the country? Certainly there is enough variety in Mexico to satisfy every possible taste.

However, I am constantly amazed at the surprises! Most countries have their share of *contrasts,* but not all can offer such *surprises.* A hot-pink house front, trimmed in violet, surprises me. An old, empty passenger bus built into a city wall surprises me. Two small angels, feather wings bobbing as they run, surprise me. A sugar skull with marble eyes and a rock-star hairdo surprises me. Tombs like miniature houses surprise me. The list can go on forever...

Love of form and of color vanquishes the drabness of poverty. Inventiveness transforms the mundane factory product and imbues it with a different meaning. Here in Mexico, even death is honored with a touch of genius.

MEXICO IS

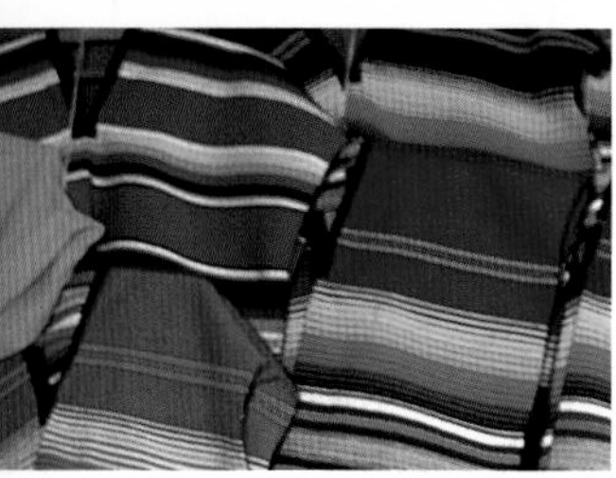

Throwing off their usual reserve, Mexicans spring into action for well over 4,000 *fiestas* and festivals every year. Whether taking place in a tiny village or on a national scale, *fiestas* verge on a sacred institution, offering the opportunity to dance, sing, eat, and drink intensively in an outburst of exuberance that mirrors the vibrant colors of this vast land.....

From the grand colonial cities of the central highlands to the more modest villages of the south, façades are brilliant pink, dense turquoise, saffron yellow, or deep red-ocher. Baroque churches resemble ornate Mexican pâtisseries, ice-cream parlors rival the rainbow and vibrant Indian costumes lend color to the whole. Yucatán *cenotes* (sinkholes) offer shades of emerald and jade, the Caribbean topaz and aquamarine, and the Pacific a deep cobalt. All reflect one aspect of the complex Mexican spirit—exuberance.

Typically colorful houses in Oaxaca

Viva Mexico Wherever you are, at whatever time of the year, day or night, you are likely to experience one of Mexico's myriad festivals. Birthdays of patron saints, anniversaries of obscure heroes, political and historical milestones (something that Mexico excels in), agricultural rites or Catholic festivals—all are celebrated with equal animation. In the political calendar the most important is Independence Day (September 15–16) when the zócalo (main square) of every town and village in the country becomes a heaving mass of humanity gathered to roar *Viva México!* Costumed processions and brass bands transform a formal occasion into an uninhibited communal exorcism—with the obligatory *tacos* and *tequila* and the sky-shattering spectacle of fireworks. Revolution (November 20) and the Battle of Puebla (May 5) offer equally intensive revelry.

Religious calendar After four centuries of Catholicism, church festivals are now deeply embedded in the Mexican psyche and calendar. Over 90 percent of the country is Catholic, dedicated to the cult of the Virgin of Guadalupe ever since this mysterious mirage appeared to an Indian in 1531 (see pages 64–65). On December 12 her feast is announced in churches all over the country, and celebrations are particularly lively in the town of Tequila, where two weeks of festivities culminate in bullfights, rodeos, music, and dancing. Prodigious and delirious Mardi Gras carnivals in the ports of Veracruz and Mazatlán announce the approach of Easter Week, highlight of the religious calendar. Candlelit processions and Passion plays can last over four days, and Taxco's famous week-long *fiesta* is comparable in scale to that of Seville in Spain. Countless other Christian celebrations pepper the calendar and include such oddities as the feast of San Antonio,

Traditional Indian dancers perform for tourists in Mexico City's Zócalo

when household pets (including pigs, chickens, and cows) are decked out in ribbons and flowers and taken to church for a blessing. At the other end of the scale are the strange Easter processions of the primitive Tarahumara, in the northern sierra.

Pre-Hispanic legacies Any excuse to pick up a mask and put on a brilliantly colored costume is sufficient. Mexicans indulge with gusto, along with countless itinerant traditional dance groups who perform pre-Hispanic fertility rites or act out the lives of patron saints at village festivals. *Voladores* (see pages 165 and 170) spin through the air in a breathtaking re-enactment of a Totonac ritual, "devils" are defeated by "priests" and "Christians" by "Moors."

❑ **"**During these ceremonies ... the Mexican opens himself up. They allow him to reveal himself and dialogue with a god, his homeland, friends or relatives. During these days, the silent Mexican whistles, shouts, sings, lights fireworks, fires his pistol into the air. Fires his soul." Octavio Paz: *The Labyrinth of Solitude*, 1950. ❑

Brilliantly colored and feathered Quetzal headdresses monopolize Pueblan dances, while in Oaxaca the two-week *Guelaguezta* dance festivities in late July have their roots in corn-god rituals. In Mexico All Saints' Day becomes the Day of the Dead (see pages 144–145), creating a unique combination of pagan and Christian worship.

Life and death

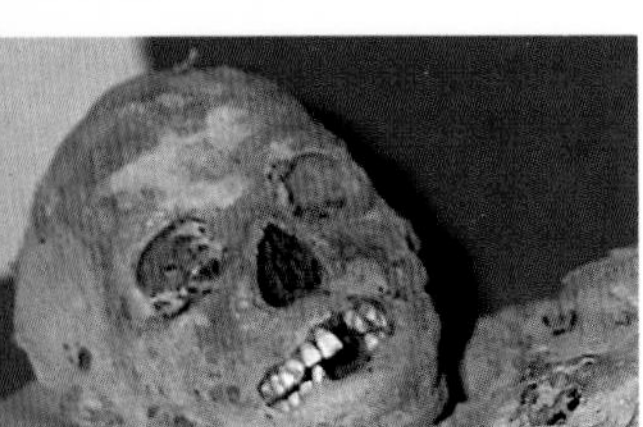

■ The Mexicans are fervent lovers of myths and legends, assimilating the cult of death into the cult of life. Their fascination with death is revealed in every aspect of their existence, from rattling *fiesta* skeletons to the soul-wrenching laments of *mariachi* singers and the often tragic vagaries of Mexican history.....■

For the Aztecs life and death were two sides of the same coin—the sun set only to rise again, just as dead souls would be reborn once more. This deeply-rooted belief also spelled their downfall when the Spanish conquistador Hernán Cortés was mistakenly welcomed as the reincarnation of the Aztec god Quetzalcóatl who, according to legend, had sailed towards the horizon of the rising sun, vowing to return. Even after over four centuries of Catholicism the kernel of this belief remains, embellished by other rituals, but essentially an unwavering serenity in the face of the great beyond.

Masochism Taken to its extreme, this attitude could be labeled masochistic. Joy in suffering, or the expectation of it, is often pushed to the brink in customs which defy normal survival instincts. The exploits of the famous divers plunging 130 ft. into the pounding Pacific at La Quebrada, Acapulco, may be inextricably linked with macho *bravura*, but they also reveal a fascination with challenging the ultimate—death. And as Papantla's *voladores* (flying dancers) spin head-first to earth in a ritual that dates from pre-Hispanic days, they too are toying with the infinite; casualties occur in both cases. More widespread is the Mexican addiction to transcending life through alcohol (usually *mezcal* or *tequila*) or

Many pilgrims to Guadalupe take the last few steps on their knees

the Indian use of the hallucinogenic *peyote*, mainly limited to the Huichols and the Tarahumara, which is an integral part of their spiritual rituals. But then comes the reverse, *fiesta*, an exuberant and chaotic expression of life.

Religion Behind these attitudes lies a unique fusion of two systems of belief which place the afterworld on an equal footing with life. Human sacrifice was common practice among most Mesoamerican (Mexican and Central American) civilizations, with victims becoming deified at the moment their hearts were torn from their bodies. Election for sacrifice was the ultimate reward as it trans-

ported a poor mortal from his fragile and insignificant place in the universe into a divine realm. The arrival of Spanish friars with their claims that salvation was only attainable through the worship of one Christian god may have changed certain aspects of their rituals and switched images of "idols" for those of the Virgin Mary and the saints, but it had hardly any impact on the deeply fervent nature and morbid obsessions of the Indians. Incense-choked ceremonies continued, and the Christian cross became combined with the Mayan symbol into the *axis mundi* (crossroads of the world). Draped in pine branches—a sign of enduring pagan beliefs—these crosses still dominate the plazas of certain villages in the Chiapas highlands. And what else is the Day of the Dead but an extension of the Indian worship of the dead, right down to skull and skeleton imagery and the bone-shaped bread rolls.

Catastrophes In a nation for whom the notion of death is so important, it is perhaps not surprising that natural disasters frequently occur. Volcanic eruptions, earthquakes, floods, and hurricanes hit the country with seemingly inexorable regularity, shattering the structure of daily existence and underlining the fragility of life. Dry inhospitable land, remoteness and inaccessibility have long been the lot of Mexico's *campesinos* (peasant farmers) when they are not fighting battles to reclaim land stripped from them by corrupt administrations. Decimated by disease and appalling working conditions within a century of the Conquest, the indigenous people are still fighting for their rights, producing extremes of protest that have often provoked a bloody response from the authorities.

These papier-mâché images for the Day of the Dead are on show in Mexico City's Anahuacalli Museum

Folk art, in a bewildering variety of colors, forms, and media, is present all over the country, as diverse as the landscapes and peoples from which it originates. Industrialized techniques may be creeping in to replace time-honored skills passed on down the generations, but little can change the imagination and flair of the craftspeople.....

Most regions of Mexico have specific craft traditions, whether pottery, woodcarving, basket-making, weaving, metalwork, or simple objects made from pine trees, maguey fiber and sisal. The markets of large towns generally offer the best selection for visitors, with the majority concentrated in the states of Michoacán, Jalisco, Puebla, Guerrero, Oaxaca, and Chiapas, but Mexico City and Guadalajara offer the widest and most varied selection from all over the country. Hard to resist, these beautifully crafted objects were once extensions of spiritual beliefs, a rapidly disappearing practice in the face of commercialism and large-scale demand.

Metalwork Silver and gold brought colonialism to Mexico, and their importance is still apparent today in the silver shops of Taxco, thronging with tourists bargaining for hammered, engraved, or inlaid jewelry and *objets d'art.* By law all silver items are stamped with "sterling" or .925 (the minimum silver content) so confusion with alloys is impossible. Gold jewelry, sometimes inlaid with precious or semi-precious stones, is usually crafted from 14- and 18-carat gold. Intricate designs (often cast using the lost-wax method with molds of clay and beeswax) remain a specialty of the Mixtecs in Oaxaca, while filigree, incorporating local pearls and coral, is a Yucatán tradition. Gleaming copperware has its ancestral home at Santa Clara del Cobre in Michoacán, where the Tarascans excel at creating flawless pitchers, pans, or platters. Most popular of all Mexican metals is tin, a cheap and malleable alloy that can be beaten or cast into countless quirky *milagros* (votive offerings to saints), ornamental boxes, lanterns, candelabra, mirror frames, or trees swarming with fruit and birds.

Wood Whether rustic "colonial" furniture or terrifying ceremonial masks, sleek Seri ironwood carvings, or vividly patterned Oaxacan fantasy animals, Mexican wood is cut, carved and colored into endless shapes and forms. Touchingly crude Tarahumara animal carvings contrast with sophisticated lacquering techniques used in Uruapan to decorate boxes or chests. The popular pre-Hispanic *equipale*, a curved-backed chair of leather and slatted wood, is made in Tlaquepaque, while ritual masks—in every macabre and garish form—are a national passion, reaching heights of fantasy in Guerrero and Michoacán. Sadly, the quality of this craft has been greatly affected by tourist demand.

Silversmith at work in Taxco. This fine colonial town is famous for its silverware, which is crafted locally and recognized for the originality of its designs

Interesting display of local crafts in Tzintzuntzán, Michoacán

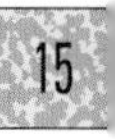

Pottery As closely linked to daily needs as to ceremonial purposes, pottery is a continuation of indigenous traditions which were strongly influenced by Hispanic-Moorish techniques. The Valley of Mexico is the main area where *barro* (terracotta) is produced, but these basic kitchen utensils are easily surpassed in the elaborate clay *arbol de la vida* ("tree of life") made in Metepec. Puebla and Guanajuato are home to ceramics which are renowned for their sophisticated glazed patterns, whether the *azulejos* (painted tiles) of Dolores Hidalgo, majolica-style objects from Guanajuato, or Puebla's famed *talavera poblana* (considered the *crème de la crème* of decorative *azulejos*) and superb ceramic tableware. Oaxaca is famous for its black pots from San Bartolomé, while the impoverished Tzotzil villages of Chiapas produce whimsical little clay animals (*animalitos*) sold for derisory amounts by child vendors. However, the extremes of fantasy lie in the state of Michoacán, where diabolical figures are conjured up by Ocumicho's women potters, and Patambán's green pineapple ceramics vie with the popularity of Tzintzuntzán's subtle cream-and-black designs.

❑ The most realistic masks are those fashioned out of wax. Their complex fabrication involves starching, molding and hardening cotton gauze which is painted and then coated with thin layers of wax. Before a dancer dons the mask he allows the wax to soften in the sun so that it will assume the contours of his own face. ❑

■ Colorful and exotic, Mexico's Indians, the most marginalized section of the population, reflect a strong continuity with the past which has been preserved by their rural isolation. Yet they are the victims of an agrarian system which unfortunately has not been a priority concern of this fast-developing nation.....■

Illustration depicting an Indian sacrifice in Mexico City's Museum of Anthropology

Mestizos (people of mixed Spanish and Mexican blood) form the majority of Mexico's population of 88 million, vastly outnumbering indigenous people who are estimated at just over 13 million. For the most part the latter lead impoverished lives as artisans or farmers within communal *ejidos*, a system that was instigated after the Revolution when the huge, hereditary estates were broken up and returned to local inhabitants to be farmed on a cooperative basis. Infertile land, severely limited resources, and no experience of modernized methods have propelled many of these farmers into insurmountable debt. With their land seized from them, their only escape is the inhospitable big city where social assistance is nonexistent and living conditions deteriorate. For many the last resort is begging.

Survivors Even the creation of the INI (National Institute for Indigenous People) has done little to modify this fate: 17 million Mexicans live on under $1 per day (a World Bank estimate). After the decimation brought about by the Spanish Conquest and what contemporary writer Octavio Paz has described as three centuries of "massive rape" under the rule of fortune-seeking Spaniards, it is a miracle that 56 Indian languages (and customs) survive. By far the biggest ethnic group is the Náhua, who speak the language of the Aztecs, followed by the Mayan groups of Chiapas and the Yucatán peninsula. Close at their heels, the Mixtecs and Zapotecs of Oaxaca, Otomís, Mazahua, Totonacs, Tarascans, and Huastecs still form substantial groups in central and eastern Mexico, while the only Indians of any numerical consequence in the north are the wild Tarahumara.

Revolt For writer Aldous Huxley, "the strength of the Indians is a strength of resistance, of passivity" and, although these words were written in 1934, the same could be repeated today. In 1993 *campesino* (peasant-farmer) movements intensified, provoked by government amendments made to *ejido* ownership status and the inflexibility of bank demands made against loans.

Timed to precede Independence celebrations, Mexico City's Zócalo (main square) was transformed into a 24-hour encampment for several weeks. The *campesinos* finally left armed with yet more government promises. In Cholula matters reached a head when 697 hectares of fertile *ejido* land were expropriated by the government for low-cost housing, part of Puebla's controversial Angelopolis development.

Far more spectacular—and bloodier—was the EZLN (Zapatista National Liberation Army) uprising in Chiapas, home to an estimated 800,000 Indians of Mayan descent. Again timing was impeccable and aimed to embarrass the inauguration of NAFTA (North Atlantic Free Trade Agreement) on January 1, 1994. Adopting the revolutionary Emiliano Zapata as their symbol, some 2,000 armed rebels, including women, denounced the non-respect of their land rights and "70 years of dictatorship" (by the PRI—Partido Revolucionario Institucional), as well as demanding the right to health care, education, and democracy. Morally supported by the *obispo rojo* (red bishop) of San Cristóbal de las Casas, Samuel Ruíz, their carefully prepared attack on San Cristóbal, Ocosingo, and three other towns soon bowed before 12,000 government troops and 15 Panzer tanks. The number of insurgents who died has been estimated by various sources as between 107 and 400.

❑ Eighty percent of Mexico's indigenous communities suffer from severe alcohol problems. In Oaxaca, the state with the largest concentration of Indians, about 50 percent of communities are assessed as "very marginalized" with no sewage disposal or electricity, their inhabitants often illiterate and undernourished. Chiapas, a rebellious *bête noire* since the 19th century, has never shaken off the rule of its landowners—despite the gains of the Revolution—who are often hand in glove with municipal authorities. ❑

Yautepec, in Morelos state: an old town with a lot of rural charm

Tacos and tortillas...

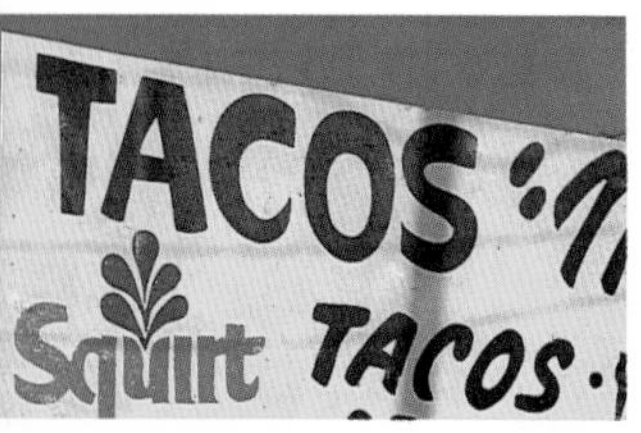

■ Mexican cuisine is a combination of traditional Indian dishes and later Spanish influences, often spicy and invariably accompanied by *tortillas* and red beans. Its famous *mole* (sauce), when cooked for three days according to tradition, is divine; when prepared in fast-food style it can be heavy, oily, tasteless, and depressing.....■

From north to south the basic ingredients in Mexican food remain much the same. Outside the main towns it is difficult to find restaurants of a high standard, but Pacific and Gulf regions compensate with a wealth of exquisitely fresh seafood (lobster, red snapper, abalone, clams ...) on often gargantuan scales or integrated into delicious soups. Resort towns offer a restricted choice of chain restaurants serving predictable fare, but are never without a sizzling street-corner *taco* stand: forget the infamous Montezuma's Revenge and indulge! Mexican eating habits require a shift from the usual Western pattern as breakfast (*desayuno*) is large and the main meal of the day is taken between 1 p.m. and 4 p.m. This is when restaurants offer *comidas corridas* (set menus) of three or four courses which are usually excellent value. Evening meals are lighter, often consisting of *antojitos* ("little whims") or *tortilla*-based snacks.

Tortillas A national passion, the *tortilla* (a flat, unleavened corn pancake) constitutes the basis of daily Mexican fare. Although traditionally made from distinctively-flavored cornmeal, blander wheat *tortillas* are making industrialized inroads in the north. But whatever its composition, the plain *tortilla* can be quickly transformed into a variety of more interesting dishes. A *burrito* is a stuffed *tortilla*. In its wrapping come infinite combinations of vegetables, beans, cheese, chicken, or meat seasoned with chilli sauce. *Tacos* may provide a crisper *tortilla* wrapping but essentially enclose the same range of ingredients. *Tamales* are southern euphemisms for *tacos* wrapped and steamed in corn husks or banana leaves, which sometimes have sweet fillings. The big difference with *enchiladas* is that here the *taco* is fried or baked in a cheese sauce, then served hot. Subtle comparisons can be made with the *quesadilla*, a principally cheese-filled *tortilla*. The ultimate variation is the *tostada*, a flat *tortilla* piled with meat, cheese, tomatoes, and the ubiquitous *frijoles* (red beans). And even the breakfast classic, *huevos rancheros*, consists of fried eggs and diced chilli in a tomato sauce, placed—where else?—on a *tortilla*.

❏ Of the 200 or more varieties of chilli, few actually blow the roof of your mouth off (though beware of the Yucatán's *habanero* or the *serrano*); most merely add spice to your life. However, recent public health studies indicate that frequent consumption can lead to gastric cancer—Mexico has one of the world's highest incidences of this disease. ❏

Give us our daily bread—tortillas *have been the staff of life for centuries of Mexicans*

Infinite ingredients *Mole poblano*, the nearest thing to a national dish, is a rich, dark sauce which comes straight out of Mexico's Baroque past. Legend has it that it was invented in a Pueblan convent to disguise a rather skinny turkey for an imminent visit from the Viceroy. Recipes vary immensely and a real *mole* is ideally cooked slowly over three days, but it basically incorporates numerous spices, herbs, chillies, cinnamon, and almonds with chocolate—a recipe inherited from the Aztecs who liked it frothy and spiked with chillies. Time is an essential ingredient in Mexican cuisine, whether 24-hour marinades in citrus juice (orange being the Yucatán special), Veracruz- and Acapulco-style *ceviche* (raw seafood marinated in lime), slow steaming of meat or vegetables wrapped in banana leaves, or the stewing of beef in *pulque* (maguey beer). Meat runs the gamut from iguana to suckling pig, lamb, beef, kid goat, and venison. The best beef comes from the cattle ranches of Chihuahua, while Monterrey is well-known for its *cabrito* (roast kid).

❑ They came, they saw and they conquered, but the conquistadors also brought with them apples, goats, chickens, pigs, wheat, garlic, and sugar. Reversing the process, Mexico gave the world chocolate, vanilla, potatoes, corn, pumpkins, avocados, and countless other fruits, seeds and nuts. ❑

■ The ultimate cliché—land of contrasts—is hard to avoid when describing Mexico's astonishing variety of climates, altitudes, vegetation, and landscapes. In a few hours you can move from cool, dry mountain air to steamy, tropical climes, from pine trees to banana palms, or from a palette of sandy yellows to one of lush greens.....■

Shaped like a funnel which links the U.S. with Central America, Mexico sweeps down the map from the arid, desert lands of the north to the tropical south, with a final twist as it turns east into the flat Yucatán peninsula. An area of almost 780,000 sq m offers a challenge to the most intrepid of travelers: even Baja California extends 800 miles from north to south. But distances are not the end of the story. Mexico is dominated by lofty mountain ranges which not only offer transitional contrasts in vegetation and climate but also spectacular canyons and waterfalls.

Three levels A common division of this vast land creates three climatic zones: *tierras calientes* (hot lands); *tierras templadas* (temperate lands); and *tierras frías* (cold lands). The latter covers the central highlands and plateau (including Mexico City) where altitudes averaging 6,500 ft. are sandwiched between the mighty *cordilleras* of the Sierra Madre. The highest, permanently snowcapped peaks tower to over 3 miles high in an east–west volcanic belt and create a fourth level—the *tierra helada* (frozen land). *Tierras calientes* cover the Gulf and the Pacific coastal regions, the Isthmus, most of Chiapas, and all of the Yucatán peninsula: these are Mexico's humid tropical zones where temperatures rarely drop below 68°F and can hit as high as 105°F. The last pockets of rain forest lie in the extreme south, in Chiapas on the Guatemalan border. Between the two extremes lie temperate regions of mountain slopes and the depressions of the central plateau with average altitudes of 4,000 ft.

In the oven-like northern plains rainfall is minimal and comes mainly in the fall, whereas coastal regions and the south, particularly Tabasco and Chiapas, experience year-round precipitation highlighted by heavy summer downpours.

What grows? Little can survive in the arid north and Baja California other than drought-resistant plants such as fast-growing shrubs, thorn bushes and cacti. But move south through the temperate zones to the humid coastal regions (bordering

The rugged peaks of the Sierra de la Giganta, west of Loreto, in Baja California Sur

The prickly pear cactus is cultivated for its fruit and leaves, both edible

Mexico's 5,720 miles of coastline) and you encounter many of the country's 20,000 species of flowering plants: cascading bougainvillaea, fragrant frangipani, jacaranda trees draped in blue flowers, poinsettias, hibiscus, clambering gold cups, and vivid clouds of orange flame-trees are interspersed with classic palm trees and feathery casuarinas. Cultivated crops include sugar-cane, cocoa, coffee, and fruits such as papayas, bananas, pineapples, limes, guavas, avocados, and mangoes. Savanna regions are home to a range of agaves, from the prickly-pear to the maguey, often towered over by spindly yuccas. In the wet regions of the *tierra templada* thrives Mexico's national tree, the *ahuehuete*, an imposing giant cypress which has reached mind-boggling proportions in Tule, Oaxaca, while in the mixed forests of higher altitudes Moctezuma pines are joined by oaks, cypresses, and an Australian immigrant, the eucalyptus.

❑ Lagoons and mangrove swamps dot Mexico's coasts from the Pacific to the Caribbean. These offer the best opportunities for birdwatching and are often within easy reach of resorts. Mazatlán has Teacapán, and Acapulco the lagoons of Coyuca and Papagayo. Puerto Escondido boasts those of Chicahua, Veracruz the marshes surrrounding the Río Papaloapán, Villahermosa the Usumacinta marshes, and the Yucatán the wetland reserves of Celestún, Río Lagartos and Sian Ka'an. On the Gulf coast virtually the entire coastline from Tampico north to the border is wetland. ❑

Environmental problems

■ Mexico is often cited as an example of wholesale environmental disasters. Industrial pollution, deforestation, toxic waste, clandestine waste-dumping, water depletion and ecologically unfriendly transportation have stained the nation, perhaps indelibly. Despite stringent government laws designed to put a brake on Mexico's notoriously bad environmental record, the problem remains one of ignorance.....■

In a country which has experienced an unprecedented industrial boom since the 1960s, together with an average annual population growth of 2.7 percent, little thought, let alone money has been given to preserving the environment. Thus rocketed into the industrial age, Mexico now shudders on the brink of ecological disaster.

A city in crisis Mexico City is the world's largest metropolis. Thermal inversions aggravate industrial and automobile emissions (particularly in the winter months) with dangerous levels of ozone, carbon dioxide, nitrogen dioxide and sulfur dioxide creating smog and provoking fatal respiratory illnesses.

Over 30,000 factories surround the city, of which 4,000 are considered to be significant hazards. Every year they pump out thousands of tons of sulfur dioxide, one of the worst air pollutants, but they also generate a third of Mexico's gross national product. Their chimneys were once seen as milestones on the way to the First World; today they are perceived as symbols of environmental degradation.

In 1992 it was announced that government and private industry would invest $5 billion over three years to meet minimum standards of pollution control. Twenty-five factories were moved out of the urban area and inspections of pollution-control equipment led to the shut-down of 109 plants. "Clean" industries (often owned by multi-national companies) are now setting the example in Monterrey, Guadalajara, and the capital. But enforcement of regulations remains lax, and officials even blithely ignore warning signals: the 1992 gas explosion in Guadalajara which killed 200 people could have been avoided if public health officials had investigated local complaints.

Depleted resources At the beginning of this century Mexico City stood more than 3 ft. above Lake Texcoco; it now lies 10 ft. below as its foundations gradually sink and continue to do so. Excessive industri-

Heavy traffic in Mexico City increases the pollution in the atmosphere and contributes to the overall problem

❑ "Mexico City is an omen, that jammed city of toxic air and leafless trees may be the first to know asphyxiation by progress ... Mexico City warns the rest of the species of all that has gone wrong with modernity's promised millenium of happiness."
Carlos Fuentes, contemporary Mexican writer. ❑

al and domestic water needs (excluding 8 million inhabitants without running water) have so depleted the lakes of the Valley of Mexico that water is now being pumped from 125 miles away. The surrounding agricultural regions are directly affected by this, as rainfall cannot replace the water that is transported to the capital. This major problem for farmers joins that of soil erosion, which affects about half the territory. Forests disappear at an alarming rate—the last remaining rain forest in Chiapas is estimated to have been reduced by half in the last 20 years—but ecological consciousness is at last increasing the area of biosphere and nature reserves.

Too late? For some the damage may be irreparable. A World Health Organization study recently found high levels of toxic lead in the blood of 70 percent of tested foetuses. Similar findings have emerged in the industrial north, where much of the blame has been laid at the door of *maquiladoras* (foreign-owned assembly plants) which profit from the laxity of Mexico's environmental controls. The American Medical Association has labeled the border area "a virtual cesspool and breeding ground for infectious diseases." Meanwhile, smoke billows out of stacks which, say some American environmentalists, could effect up to 16 U.S. national parks. With no natural gas in the north, power plants are fueled by coal, but even new plants are devoid of controls for sulfur dioxide emissions. One of NAFTA's provisions is to set up a jointly-financed development bank to help pay for the clean-up of the border. This new move may combine with growing public and government awareness (seen in the creation of biosphere reserves and the gradual replacement of urban bus engines with eco-friendly ones) in an effort to create a cleaner nation for the next generation.

Driving restrictions are enforced to reduce pollution

Boom or bust?

■ Following centuries of turbulence, Mexico is now considered the most stable country in Latin America. After riding out the storm of the early 1980s crisis, the PRI (Partido Revolucionario Institucional) initiated a development strategy that culminated on January 1, 1994 with the inauguration of NAFTA (North American Free Trade Agreement). The end? or just the beginning?.....■

As a result of NAFTA, Mexico—the world's 13th-largest economy—now finds itself inextricably linked to the economies of Canada and the U.S. on a 15-year path that will see the disappearance of all trade barriers and tariffs between the three countries. Initiated by former President Salinas de Gortari, NAFTA crowns a decade of profound economic change that has redefined the role of the state and transformed a highly regulated and protected economy into an open and market-oriented one. The turning point came with the 1982 foreign debt crisis, which marked the end of four decades of growth. Under Miguel de la Madrid's presidency (1982–1988) the nation rocked under soaring inflation (100 percent), devaluation, high unemployment, plummeting foreign investment, and a drastically reduced standard of living. Madrid introduced austerity measures and reforms, but not until Salinas' term (1988–1994) did the economy really start to look up.

Educated at Harvard, Salinas managed to restore confidence and bring growth back to 4 percent by 1990 by streamlining public finance, partly renegotiating the foreign debt and increasing exports. Through extensive privatization (banks, telephone, and mining companies) he also reversed the previous mold of nationalization which nurtured corrupt and inefficient management. At the same time, he ended protectionism by adhering to GATT (General Agreement on Tariffs and Trade), thus liberalizing trade and stimulating a flood of manufactured goods from across the border. As a result, Mexico's balance of payments is now in deficit with the U.S., which is $5 billion up on the exchange. But, within three years of the first talk of NAFTA foreign investment tripled and massive American telecommunications and agricultural, industrial, automobile, and tourism projects are now being launched. A positive picture? Not necessarily, as Mexico has not escaped world recession and this flood of investments will take years to affect unemployment, which is roughly estimated at 12–20 percent. And aside from the increased dependence on foreign structures (whether the International Monetary Fund or U.S. government and banks), Mexico is now undergoing massive cultural imperialism disguised as the "inevitable future" and promoted with the new catchword *modernidad* (modernity).

Mexico's former president, Carlos Salinas de Gortari

Social chasm Another element in Salinas's strategy was keeping wage increases below the 10 percent inflation level, and this, combined with reduced public spending on health, education, and housing, has widened the chasm between rich and poor, north and south. Over 47 percent of the nation lives in conditions of extreme poverty, and over half

occupy substandard dwellings and suffer from malnutrition. Add to this the 1992 modification of the Agrarian Reform Law which allows private sales of communal land, and you have an explosive social situation.

Corruption And explode it did, on January 1, 1994 with the Zapatistas' uprising in Chiapas—which soon spread to Oaxaca. With the August 1994 presidential elections looming, opposition parties seemed to be gaining popularity, whether the right-wing PAN (Partido de Acción Nacional) in the industrialized north, or the left-wing PRD (Partido Revolucionario Democrático) elsewhere. The latter was set up by a splinter group of the PRI (Partido Revolucianario Institucional) led by Cuauhtémoc Cárdenas (son of the heroic President Lázaro Cárdenas) just before the 1988 elections. A further *coup de théâtre* followed in March 1994 when Luis Donaldo Colosio, Salinas's designated successor, was assassinated in Tijuana, and replaced as candidate by Ernesto Zedillo, a 42-year-old Yale-educated economist. For some, convinced by Salinas's promises of a fraud-free election, hopes ran high that PRI's 65-year grip on power would be shattered. But this is Mexico; despite accusations of fraud toppling PRI governors-elect in previous state elections, the corruption habit seems ineradicable, and when the August results were declared Zedillo emerged as victor with 47 percent of the votes. "Massive fraud," declared both Cárdenas (awarded just 16 percent) and independent observers. Mexico's future thus remains in the balance, torn between the mirage of *modernidad* and the reality of widespread injustice and poverty. It is unlikely that the future path will be smooth.

Monterrey's quiet pedestrian area in the center of the city

Mexico shares a 2,079-mile border with the U.S. This vast strip has long been a testing-ground for two radically different cultures which meet, clash, and join economic forces. But interaction does not stop there and, with the advent of NAFTA (the North Atlantic Free Trade Agreement), every Mexican household is being sucked into a pop-culture vortex.....

There is nothing new about Mexican fears of a cultural takeover: the country has been under invasion from the U.S. in one form or another since the 1847 Mexican–American War that cost the nation half its territory. Since then, the arrival of each new fad or technology has been greeted by pessimists as heralding the end of tradition. Nor is extensive American investment new: in the late 19th century Porfirio Díaz' policies led to substantial American participation in profitable oil, mining, lumber, and transportation concerns. Today, with Mexican labor costs estimated at roughly a fifth of those in the States, *maquiladoras* (foreign-owned assembly plants) firmly implanted along the border are just the beginning of the story. Late 20th-century technology is speeding up the process and American influence is permeating every level of society in the name of progress.

Tijuana, Mexico's most famous border town, has a reputation for being brash and seedy

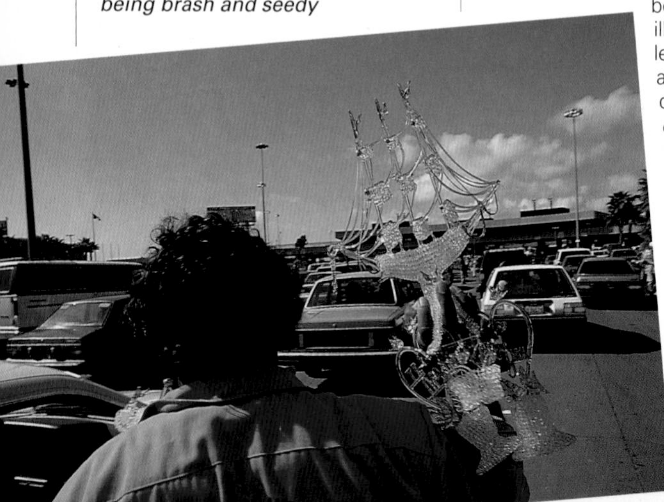

The border story Fears of "invasion" are no less strong on the other side of the border. For the last 50 years Mexican workers, legal and illegal, have flooded the labor markets of California and adjoining states in search of decent wages and a corresponding American lifestyle. As "wetbacks" (illegal immigrants) cross the dividing line of the Río Grande, American workers fear for their jobs and politicians stir up nascent xenophobia. In 1993 matters came to a head at the Ciudad Juárez/El Paso crossing when 600 armed Border Patrolmen (equipped with infra-red binoculars) massed there to prevent illegal immigrants and announced that it would be a permanent presence. Justification for this radical move included accusations of theft, burglary, and drug-trafficking. In protest, Mexican officials claimed that the estimated 11 million Mexican immigrants earned an annual total of $240 billion, paid U.S. taxes of $90 billion but only claimed $5 billion in public welfare assistance—mainly because of their illegal status. Far less talked about is another cross-border practice, *fayuca* (contraband). Once a flourishing concern for Mexican customs officials who cashed in on bribes, this practice has now been made unnecessary by the free-trade treaty.

❑ Economics aside, Mexico has long held a mythical fascination for certain Americans. John Steinbeck, Tennessee Williams, Saul Bellow, Jack Kerouac, William Burroughs, and Richard Brautigan are just some of the writers who were drawn to this land of freedom, cheap *tequila,* and indolence. "We'll go to Mexico and everything will be marvelous" utters Scarlett to Ashley in *Gone with the Wind.* But can the myth survive? ❑

Pop-culture Tomatoes grown in Sonora and Sinaloa already represent 60 percent of U.S. consumption, while cheap Mexican oranges are threatening the growers of Florida and California. But this hardly signifies a change in lifestyle. Far more insidious are MacDonalds, Taco Bell, Kentucky Fried Chicken, I Can't Believe it's Yoghurt, and Domino's Pizza, just some of the fast-food outlets that now sweeten the town centers of northern and central Mexico. The newest, priciest shopping-malls feature signs in English, and Mexicans have become the world's third greatest consumers of Coca-Cola (after Iceland and the U.S.), averaging 260 bottles a year per person.

Take a long-distance bus ride and you are bombarded with American films shown on TV monitors; switch on Mexican television and you might tune in to MTV. Cellular phones, automatic teller machines, new discos and aerobics classes have invaded upwardly mobile, middle-class habits. For the ultimate reverse of this cultural "exchange," Tijuana takes first prize. Seedy and full of dubious services and cheap souvenirs, it seems to embody the Mexican view of what the American consumer wants.

Downtown Tijuana

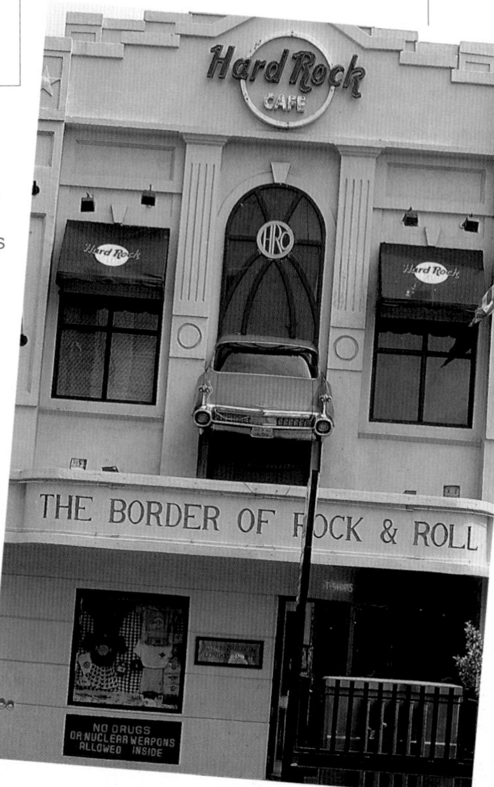

■ Mexico owes a great deal of its fate as the recurring victim of natural disasters to the expanding layers deep below the earth. Some of its highest peaks are active volcanoes, constant reminders of the seismic vulnerability of the nation.....■

Popocatépetl, whose name means "smoking mountain" in the Náhuatl language, is a sign that the Aztecs were only too aware of the true nature of this towering, snowcapped peak. Craters are an integral part of Mexico's magnificent landscape, but over the centuries earthquakes have destroyed city centers from Oaxaca to Guadalajara, culminating in the quake that struck Mexico City in 1985. Tremors continue, while almost a decade later the capital still licks its wounds.

Volcanic belt The Sierra Neovolcánica Transversal which forms the southern boundary of the central plateau is spiked by Mexico's highest peaks: Cofre de Perote, Pico de Orizaba (or Citlaltépetl—Mountain of the Star), La Malinche, Iztaccíhuatl (Sleeping Woman), and Popocatépetl.

To the west lies the volcanic zone of Michoacán, which has a long history of craters suddenly erupting out of flat fields. In 1943 the appearance of the Volcán de Paricutín led to nine years of lava flow coursing across the cornfields and engulfing the little village of Parangaricutiro with its hot lava.

The last puffing peak at the Pacific end is that of the active Volcán de Colima, off-balanced by the mighty and now inactive crater of the Nevado de Colima. The south is hardly spared—the 1982 eruption of El Chichon (Chiapas) left villages in darkness for two days and even the sky over Hawaii showed the effects.

Seismic chaos Respectively measuring 8.1 and 7.5 on the Richter scale, the earthquakes of September 19 and 20, 1985 not only succeeded in shattering Latin America's largest hospital, government buildings, hotels, and countless homes, but also put the final nail in the coffin of the image of municipal and federal organizations. Hopelessly inadequate in the face of such a calamity, their job of excavating the victims from the rubble was almost entirely undertaken by the inhabitants themselves, who formed spontaneous chains working around the clock in a desperate attempt to uncover survivors among the estimated 8,000 dead.

The Church of San Juan, in Parangaricutiro, rises forlornly from the lava that engulfed it in 1943

MEXICO WAS

■ The mysterious Olmecs, whose hierarchical society was said to function on fear, have only been recognized as Mexico's ancestral civilization in the last few decades. Their art, social organization, and astronomical and numerical achievements have profoundly influenced Mesoamerica's subsequent cultures—Zapotecs, Mixtecs, Toltecs, Teotihuacans.....■

Corn (maize) was the prosaic catalyst of ancient Mexican history. During the Ice Age (between 60,000 and 8,000BC) waves of nomadic hunters crossed the Bering Straits from Mongolia to Alaska and gradually moved south through Mesoamerica, shifting their base according to the laws of available food.

The earliest evidence of man in Mexico dates from around 20,000BC, but it was not until about 6,000BC that this "Desert Culture" commenced a sedentary existence, cultivating corn, pumpkins, beans, and chilli peppers. By the onset of what historians term the pre-Classic period (*ca.* 1,200BC) settlements had sprung up all over Mexico and included the mother of all Mesoamerican cultures, the Olmecs, now acknowledged as one of the most artistically advanced of Mexico's puzzling and still unresolved network of civilizations.

Rubber people Scattered across the sweltering, alluvial coastal regions of Veracruz and Tabasco, the vestiges of the Olmecs (meaning "people from the land of rubber") lay shrouded in jungle for some 3,000 years, only to be uncovered in the 1930s. This prompted a remake of the whole historical jigsaw.

❑ Scarcity of stone in the Veracruz/Tabasco region probably stimulated the Olmecs' inland advance, which led them through the Valley of Mexico and Morelos to the state of Guerrero. Olmec sites and cave paintings here date from about 1500BC, and their influence even extended through Oaxaca to Izapa on the Guatemalan border. ❑

❑ The Olmec's greatest achievement was their imposing carved monolithic basalt heads, measuring as much as 10 ft. and in some cases dragged or rafted from quarries 5 miles away. These noble heads, believed to be portraits of Olmec rulers, all wear headgear resembling helmets, probably protection for war and during ball games (*juegos de pelota*). ❑

Olmec head at Mexico City's Museum of Anthropology

Three main Olmec centers came to light: San Lorenzo, La Venta, and Tres Zapotes, each one spanning a specific epoch before being abandoned. During the zenith of La Venta (900–400BC) Olmec groups increased in number; earth mounds and platforms for houses and temples were arranged around patios to form ceremonial centers, but their architecture was poor in comparison to their advanced sculptural, calendric, and mathematical achievements.

Jaguar and colossus Jade, serpentine, obsidian, nephrite, and basalt were among the Olmecs' favorite materials, which they carved to create a fantastic range of sculptures from delicate jade heads, engraved stelae (stone slabs or pillars), figurines, stone masks and votive axes to monolithic altars and astonishing colossal basalt heads. A recurring theme is the jaguar, or were-jaguar (half-human, half-jaguar), the Olmec god of all gods, symbolizing day and night and depicted in stelae, masks, and figurines as a cleft-headed babe-in-arms, or in motifs used on pottery. Other sculptures portray the Olmecs themselves, their wide, flat noses and thick lips indicating some black African traits, as yet unexplained. They generally wore few or no clothes, and ornamentation ranged from mutilated teeth to earplugs, pendants, headbands, body tattoos, and breastplates. The use of wooden or clay masks representing jaguars, ducks, and mythological birds was restricted to shamans and priests during agricultural and religious festivities.

Structure and revolution The highly élitist society of the Olmecs reserved the center of their settlements for priests and rulers, while the outlying areas were left to corn-growing farmers, fishermen, tradesmen, and lesser craftsmen. Judicial, military, and religious power lay firmly in the hands of the former group who also benefited from higher grounds, less subject to floods and more liable to produce bumper crops.

Revolution was ever present and both San Lorenzo (*ca.* 900BC) and La Venta (*ca.* 400BC) underwent violent downfalls, their statues smashed and mutilated for, as yet, unknown reasons.

Olmec carving from the archeological site of La Venta, on show at the fascinating open-air museum of La Venta, near Villahermosa

■ Mexico's Classic era peaked in urban sophistication during the six centuries of Teotihuacán's domination. Meanwhile, in Oaxaca, Monte Albán flourished under the Zapotecs for an even longer period while, on the Gulf Coast, El Tajín became the focal-point for the artistically advanced Classic El Tajín culture.....■

Cast-iron dating for Mexico's Golden or Classic age is difficult, as the Zapotecs of Monte Albán were already laying the foundations for their empire in 300BC, four centuries before Teotihuacán started its climb to glory which soon overlapped with the Classic period of El Tajín. Although the basic farming economy and élitist social structures remained the same, innovations appeared in architecture, art, and science, resulting in an unprecedented cultural brilliance. The number of settlements was proportional to the population increase; it has been estimated that between 300BC and AD600 the population of the Valley of Mexico increased forty-fold, while improved communications resulted in an enrichening exchange of knowledge, food, and goods throughout Mesoamerica.

Teotihuacán This was the first planned metropolis of the Americas, laid out with innovatory geometric exactitude according to astronomical alignments. From its founding in the 1st century to its seemingly willful destruction by fire around AD700, it became the largest and possibly most powerful city of the western hemisphere, importing artisans and creating a vast trade network. Together with jade, green obsidian, pottery and clay figurines, the cosmopolitan Teotihuacános exported their gods (notably Quetzalcóatl, the plumed serpent, and Tláloc, the rain god) and their cosmic learning to regions as far away as Mayan Honduras, Guatemala, and Belize. These aggressive empire-builders probably financed their growing city with tributes from outlying peoples in the same way as the Aztecs later did. Writing, books, the numerical bar-and-dot system (already used by the Olmecs) and the 260-day sacred year all figured among their achievements (see pages 228–229).

❑ The importance of Teotihuacán is demonstrated by the fact that 500 years after its fall the Aztecs, including Moctezuma himself, worshipped at the ruined site and, even in the early 20th century, local Indians still practiced rites at its great pyramids. According to the Aztecs, Teotihuacán had given birth to the Fifth Sun, creator of the universe, at a meeting of all the gods (the four earlier ones having met catastrophic ends). Quetzalcóatl was sacrificed in order to create mankind. ❑

Monte Albán The Zapotecs, contemporaneous with the end of the Olmec civilization, and lasting through the Classic period until a major disruption in the 10th century, peppered the Valley of Oaxaca with some 200 sites, terraced and irrigated hillsides, and above all built the greatest of all Zapotec sites, Monte Albán (see pages 198–199). They

❑ The Totonacs produced sensitive, expressive clay figurines which reveal notable advances in clothing as well as a lyrical imagination exemplified by the laughing pottery figures found at Remojadas. ❑

were the writers of the first true literary texts in Mexico (found in glyphs on the Danzantes slabs) in the pre-Classic era, and used these symbols to decorate stuccoed and beautifully painted edifices alongside elaborately fashioned subterranean tombs, testimony to the great wealth of the lords of Monte Albán. Their frescos display a strong Teotihuacán influence, their pantheon shared many of the gods of Mesoamerica, and they also used the bar-and-dot numerical system. Although the city escaped the violent end meted out to other pre-Classic and Classic cities, its abandon around AD700 soon resulted in its ruin.

Los Danzantes (The Dancers)—mysterious Zapotec carvings of strangely deformed figures at Monte Albán, Oaxaca

Classic El Tajín Bridging the Olmec and Teotihuacán dynasties, but also generator of its own artistic techniques and forms, the Classic El Tajín civilization (presumed to be the ancestors of today's Totonacs) found its apogee in the city of the same name (see page 165) between AD300 and AD900. They were fervent addicts of ball games and obsessed with human sacrifice; many of their artifacts were connected with this practice, from the heavy stone *yugos* (yolks), replicas of ball-players' belts, and *hachas* (axes), to the finely chiseled, flat human profiles, possible emblems of the victors, linked to decapitation.

El Tajín's most striking structure is the famous Pyramid of the Niches. The building consists of six stories with a temple on top

The Maya are perhaps best noted for their complex systems of astronomy and mathematics, prolific city-building and architecture. This powerful civilization flourished for around 1,500 years. From Chiapas and the Yucatán to Central America, they constructed magnificent ceremonial centers, without the use of the wheel or beasts of burden, whose complexities still confound armies of archaeologists.....

Around 1500BC pre-Mayan groups started moving south and east from the Olmec heartland along the Gulf Coast, but the first rudimentary ceremonial centers of southeastern Mexico only appeared around 800BC. By the turn of the millennium, local artistic styles had developed: stelae bore glyphs with calendric calculations, and ceramics and images of deities demonstrated the genesis of Mayan form. By the end of this pre-Classic period a clear differentiation of social class had emerged. From AD300 construction on an unheard-of scale first produced the fine cities of Palenque, Yaxchilán, and Bonampak (as well as sites in Guatemala, Belize, and Honduras) before reaching a zenith between AD600 and AD900 with the building of Chichén Itzá, Uxmal, Kabah, Mayapán, and Cobá. By the end of the Classic period many of these centers were mysteriously abandoned. Overpopulation? the depletion of natural resources? drought? crop failure? invasion from central Mexico? internal warfare? plague?—hypotheses are many, and the search for an answer goes on.

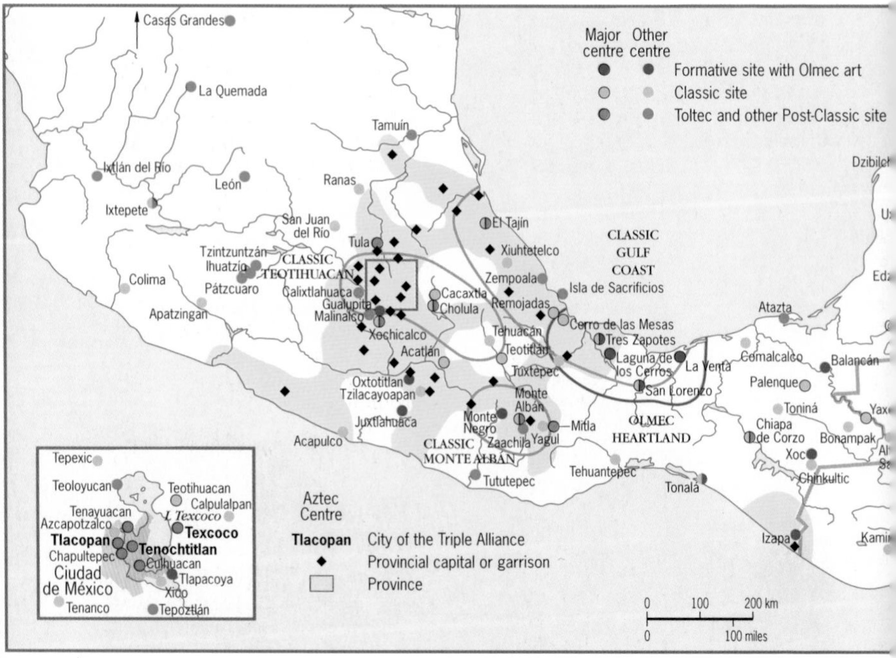

Major centre | Other centre
Formative site with Olmec art
Classic site
Toltec and other Post-Classic site

Aztec Centre
Tlacopan City of the Triple Alliance
◆ Provincial capital or garrison
Province

CLASSIC TEOTIHUACAN
CLASSIC GULF COAST
CLASSIC MONTE ALBÁN
OLMEC HEARTLAND

0 100 200 km
0 100 miles

Structure Though the Maya occupied a diverse climatic and geographic area covering humid rain forest, volcanoes, and dry plains, they were none the less dependent on agriculture, and the peasant class working the fields lay at the bottom of a strict hierarchical social structure. Each city was dominated by noble families (with the *halach uinic*, or king, at the top) who created a network of regional alliances and were supported by warriors and a priestly caste. Architects, scribes, traders, and artisans formed the middle class. Long thought to be a peaceful race, the Maya are now recognized as having used torture, mutilation, and human sacrifice for religious celebrations and sporting events, while skirmishes between city states later escalated into vicious, fully-fledged wars.

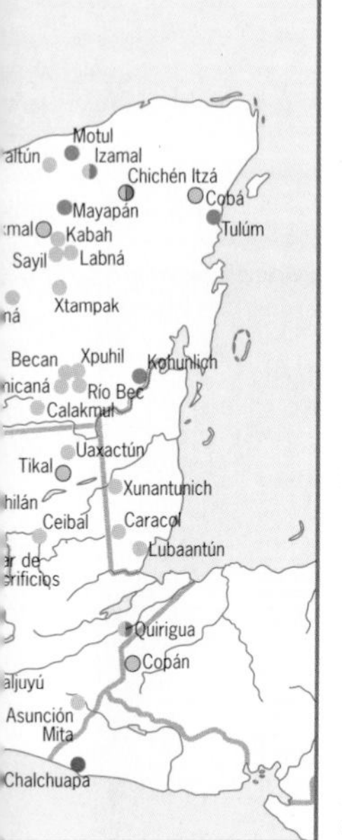

Achievements The fields in which the Maya excelled were those of mathematics and astronomy (see pages 228–229), backed up by a complex hieroglyphic system which has still not been deciphered fully. Their knowledge was recorded on stelae (stone slabs or pillars), façades, and codices (books of bark or deer-skin, of which only four have survived) filled with bar-and-dot numerals—including a glyph for zero. These detail past events, predict planetary movements and make calendar computations. The exact dates of eclipses, solstices, and equinoxes were calculated while buildings such as Uxmal's Governor's Palace and Chichén Itzá's Observatory were oriented according to the orbit of Venus. Using this knowledge of the heavens they developed a unique mythology encapsulated in sacred books such as the *Chilam Balam,* written by a Yucatecán priest a few decades before the Spanish Conquest.

Nor did the Maya die out with the conquest: even today Mayan communities speak the language of their ancestors and observe many of their customs, while the 260-day Sacred Almanac continues to be consulted by remote shamans.

Elaborately carved stonework detail on the Nuns' Quadrangle, Uxmal, exemplifies Puuc architecture, which is named after the surrounding hills

Rival states

■ The mysterious fall of Teotihuacán and the dispersal of the Maya, Totonacs, and Zapotecs from their respective ceremonial centers was followed by a new Mesoamerican culture—that of the militaristic Toltecs. In Oaxaca, the Mixtec invasion was more peaceful, while Michoacán later saw the arrival of the Purépechas.....■

The seemingly cataclysmic end of the Classic period between the 9th and 10th centuries is still unexplained, but what is certain is the arrival of strong new forces which conquered earlier races and imposed a new emphasis on war and the sacrificial spilling of human blood. Presumed to have been a branch of the barbarian Chichimecs from the north, the Toltecs, by the time they founded their capital at Tula, had appropriated (by force) "civilized" traits from Teotihuacán. Their controversial artistic and conceptual influence has been traced from the Veracruz area to Oaxaca and, above all, the Yucatán.

The real Quetzalcóatl Led by their ruler, Topiltzin, the Toltecs moved their capital to Tollan, present-day Tula ("City of God") in the 10th century. According to some accounts, Topiltzin was an intellectual priest-king dedicated to the cult of the feathered serpent Quetzalcóatl, whose pacifistic attitude stimulated a revolution of more bellicose Toltecs. Forced into exile, he made his way to the Gulf Coast where one of two fates befell him: either he set fire to himself, his ashes rising to become the Morning Star; or he set sail to the east on a raft of serpents, promising to return. He may have actually landed in the Yucatán, where his followers vanquished the Classic Maya and left the imprint of Kukulcán (the Toltec name for the Mayan feathered serpent).

Back in Tula, one of Mexico's most violent and bloodthirsty races blossomed into a prosperous civilization where the arts were so developed that the description *tolteca* came to mean "skilled, wise, dexterous." The rise of the warrior class over the priests led to Tula's destruction—by the late 12th century inner conflicts dispersed the Toltecs all over Mexico.

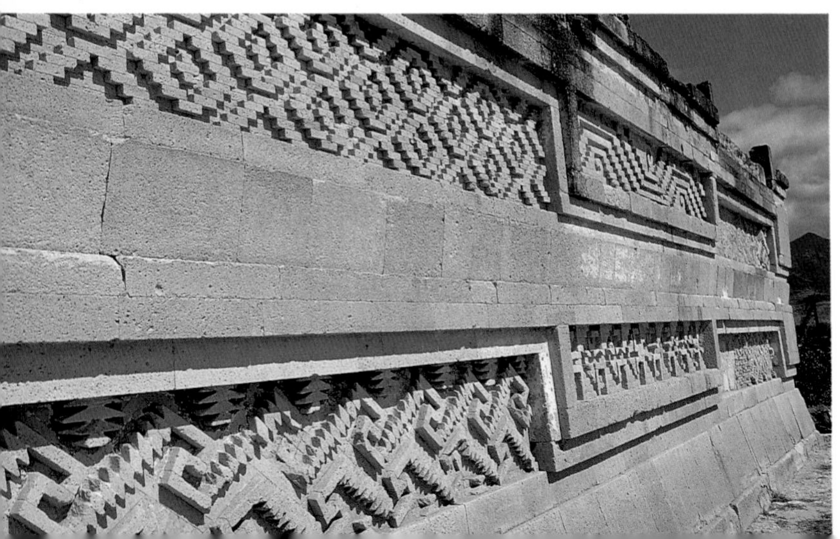

Detail of intricate Mixtec carving at Mitla, Oaxaca. The ruins rate among Mexico's major pre-Columbian centers

The Mixtecs Around the 9th century, the Mixtecs emerged from the mountainous, semi-desert region of northwestern Oaxaca, and by a series of astute intermarriages soon brought most of the Zapotec territory under their sway. Eight pre-Conquest codices (ancient scrolls) have survived, facilitating the task of tracing their evolution, although their origins remain as hazy as their name ("inhabitants of the land of the clouds"). They, too, were obsessed with the feathered serpent, claiming direct descent from Quetzalcóatl, and were under direct Toltec influence before the latter's dispersal. Yet their outstanding legacy of architectural detail (notably intricate stone fretwork exemplified at Mitla), their inventive polychrome pottery, and above all their advanced metalwork techniques were their own inventions. Allying with the Zapotecs, they were never completely conquered by the Aztecs and their descendants still inhabit the Valley of Oaxaca.

Purépechas Clustered around Lake Pátzcuaro in Michoacán, the Purépechas (later named Tarascans by the Spanish) were an isolated society who managed to escape Aztec domination. Worshippers of the sun and moon (one of several traits which could suggest links with Peru), their complex social structure was governed by priests, with the *kasonsi* at the summit, who acted as war chief and supreme judge. From their successive bases at Pátzcuaro, Ihuatzio and Tzintzuntzán, the Purépechas dominated most of the fertile region of Michoacán, leaving their unique *yácatas* (circular pyramid bases attached to a rectangular body) and advanced craftsmanship (ceramics, complex jewelry, lacquerwork, featherwork) as puzzling evidence of their cultural sophistication.

❑ Mixtec accomplishments included their lime-coated deerskin scrolls (codices) which, when unfolded, measured up to 40 ft. long. Historical events, royal births and marriages, place-names, and customs were recorded by superb illustrations and glyphs. Equally remarkable was their jewelry: turquoise mosaics and finely-wrought gold pieces cast with the lost-wax method surpass the artistry of any other Mesoamerican ornamentation. ❑

One of the many exquisite treasures from Monte Albán's Tomb 7, now on show at Oaxaca's Regional Museum

■ Hard on the heels of the expansionist Toltecs came the Aztecs, guided by the prophesies of their tribal god of war, Huitzilopóchtli, and set to become the last great Mesoamerican empire. They ably overcame numerous neighboring city-states with unpopular, sanguinary methods, and by the mid-14th century had laid the foundations of their capital.....■

Of dubious, but certainly Chichimec origin, the Aztecs were controlled in all matters by their god Huitzilopóchtli, whose voracious appetite for human hearts inspired much of the infamous Aztec ferocity. Raiding, killing, and sacrificing their neighbors, they finally settled on the swampy islands of the "Lake of the Moon," obeying a tribal prophecy which said their home would be announced by an eagle perched on a cactus with a snake in its mouth. Two adjoining capitals were founded: Tlatelolco and Tenochtitlán, later united under one king. By 1367 the Aztecs, calling themselves the México, were serving as mercenaries for the powerful Tepanecs to the north, and by 1428 their rapid grasp of political and military strategy left them victorious over this once-powerful tribe and ready to embark on building their own empire.

Consolidation Adept at rewriting history, the Aztecs set about destroying existing codices to create their own in which they supplanted their squalid past with glorious, cultured Toltec origins imbued with a divine mission. More pragmatically, they concentrated on constructing canals,

❑ The Aztecs developed a distinctive, rigid art style, much applied to monumental stone sculptures. One surviving masterpiece is the decapitated statue of Coatlicue, the earth goddess and mother of the moon and stars, who wears a necklace of human hearts and a skirt of serpents. ❑

The Aztec Calendar, unofficial symbol of Mexico, in the capital's National Museum of Anthropology

paths, dikes, and an aqueduct, reclaiming land with causeways, and adapting agriculture to the soggy terrain with *chinampas*, floating gardens whose plants eventually rooted themselves to the lake bed. At the heart of the great city stood the walled administrative and ceremonial center composed of the Great Pyramid, the Temple of Quetzalcóatl, the ball-court, and the skull rack. Beyond the enclosure were the palaces of nobles set in orchards and gardens, schools, market-places, temples, and more modest homes and farms.

Structure and expansion At the top of the Aztec hierarchy was a Council of State formed by nobles and elders who designated the king possessor of military, administrative, and judicial powers. Below him was the *cihuacóatl*, a kind of president, followed by the nobles and priests, the free citizens (mainly craftsmen)

Emperor Moctezuma II

organized into clans, and finally the serfs and porters. Aztec territorial expansion through military and economic subjugation was astounding, and their great market-places became the reflections of this far-reaching but unpopular dominion. Empire-building boomed, above all under the sixth Aztec king, Ahuítzotl (1486–1502), who conquered lands as far as the Guatemalan border and brought most of central Mexico under Aztec control.

Moctezuma II Greatest of all Aztec emperors was Moctezuma II (who ruled from 1502 to 1520), a philosophically-inclined character given more to meditation and learning than to warfare. His semi-divine status was such that nobody was allowed to look him in the face. His

❑ Twenty thousand war captives were said to have been sacrificed for the dedication of the Great Pyramid in 1487, their hearts torn from their bodies by the priests. ❑

elaborate pleasure gardens included a 10-room walk-in aviary. Guarded by 200 warriors, carried in a litter beneath a rich canopy of feathers, gold, and pearls, and preceded by lords who laid cloaks on the ground, Moctezuma seemed untouchable. Yet nothing could dissuade him from his conviction that Cortés was in reality the great Quetzalcóatl returning from the east, and this belief was to spell his tragic downfall. Tormented by indecision, Moctezuma was kidnapped by the Spaniards within his own city and killed (it is not known whether by his frustrated followers or by the conquistadors) just before the calamitous Spanish retreat of La Noche Triste (Sad Night) when the majority of Cortés' troops were either slaughtered or drowned under the weight of their plunder.

❑ By imposing tributes on conquered peoples, the Aztecs were supplied with exotic fruits and animals from tropical zones, gold and silver from Central America, jade from Guerrero, woven cloth from northern Veracruz, tortoiseshell from the Gulf, and liquid amber, tobacco, turquoise, and copal (resin from tropical trees) from numerous other vassal states. ❑

■ **Thirst for gold was the inspiration for the advance of Cortés and his men on the Aztec capital in 1519. Their destruction of Tenochtitlán laid the foundations of 300 years of Spanish rule which saw the decimation of the Indian population, the introduction of Catholicism, and the creation of a landowning system which has repercussions even today.....** ■

When Hernan Cortés sailed from Cuba to land at Villa Rica, near Veracruz on April 21, 1519 he was motivated above all by a lust for gold and silver. Single-minded, adept at double-dealing, and able to keep a straight face while offering simple glass beads as gifts in exchange for chest-loads of precious jewelry and cloth, Cortés even burned his boats to prevent his small army fleeing. During the eventful march on Tenochtitlán he allied himself with various tribes who resented the Aztec's domination (notably the Zempoalans and Tlaxcalans), thus vastly multiplying his forces and acquiring the redoubtable Indian princess La Malinche who was to become his consort and interpreter. After a prolonged siege, the Aztec capital finally fell on August 13, 1521. The young emperor Cuauhtémoc (Moctezuma's successor) was captured and eventually killed, signaling the end of Mesoamerican civilization and the beginning of a new colonial era.

❑ At the time of the Conquest the Indian population was estimated at 4.5 million; by the mid-17th century it had plummeted to 1.2 million, but by Independence in 1820 it had risen again to 3.5 million. The main causes of this decimation were European diseases such as smallpox, and exhaustion resulting from forced labor. ❑

Mural by Diego Rivera in the Palace of Cortés, Cuernavaca, depicting the brutality of the Spaniards against the Indians

Order and excess Justifying their presence by the need to stamp out human sacrifice, cannibalism, and sodomy, the Spaniards wasted no time destroying Indian temples and idols, using the stones of the pyramids to build cathedrals at the center of urban grid systems repeated in hundreds of towns. Cortés' soldiers were rewarded with vast tracts of land (*encomiendas*) over which they were given total ownership (including animals and Indians). Cortés himself was granted 22 *encomiendas*, and given the title Marqués del Valle de Oaxaca. The seeds were thus sown for the merciless land-grant system which left Indians virtual slaves work-

ing the estates and prolific mines of the great *hacendados* (estate owners). African slaves were even imported to swell the ranks of the workers.

Caste system Fearful of losing control over this profitable new colony, the Spanish Crown appointed an *audiencia*, a 12-man government-cum-court which from 1535 was headed by a Viceroy. A rigid social hierarchy was soon established: high government and church posts were reserved for *gachupines* ("pure" Spanish-born); educated *criollos* (creoles or Mexican-born Spanish) became wealthy landowners; *mestizos* (mixed Spanish and Mexican Indian blood) were restricted to lower middle-class roles, while at the bottom the Indians (*indígenas*) formed a diminishing work-force. The vice-regal period saw increasing discontent among creoles at their lack of political power and the heavy-handedness of distant Spain.

Mitla's red-domed church was built using stones taken from earlier Zapotec buildings

❑ Among enlightened churchmen who sought to protect the Indians were Bernardino de Sahagún, Bartolomé de Las Casas, Vasco de Quiroga, and Eusabio Francisco Kino. ❑

The Church The priests initially worked closely with the conquistadors and were a brake on their excesses, but later became an independently powerful force. Franciscans, Dominicans, and Jesuits carved up territory between them, building monasteries and missions in remote sierras and converting the Indian population. Although the Jesuits were expelled by the Crown in 1769, the rest of the Church amassed so much wealth that it became the greatest landowner and money-lender in Mexico. In 1804 all Church property was expropriated by the Crown, creating havoc. This, together with Napoléon's invasion of Spain in 1808, the spread of new revolutionary ideas from France and the U.S., and continuing social iniquities set the stage for the next turbulent chapter in Mexican history.

The 19th century, announced by the War of Independence, was to become the most confused period in Mexican history. Political systems veered from republicanism to monarchy and back again, foreign intervention became the norm and the nation was locked in a permanent state of civil war. When Miguel Hidalgo's *grito* (cry) of "*Mexicanos, Viva México!*" rang out on September 16, 1810 it sparked off a popular revolt which succeeded in dividing the church and set *mestizos* and Indians against the ruling classes.....

Land and social injustice were the motivation for the impromptu mob of 80,000 insurgents which rampaged across the countryside, massacring and pillaging. Even the capture and execution of the Creole priest Hidalgo could not stop this relentless movement, soon steered by the *mestizo* priest José María Morelos. Inspired by his revolutionary vision of a caste-free republic with all lands restored to the Indians, Morelos' small guerrilla army controlled most of the country by 1813, but he too was captured and the reins next passed to Vicente Guerrero. The catalyzing crunch came from the powerful creole population who, worried by the impact of new Spanish reforms, switched their allegiance to Guerrero, resulting in the former royalist General Agustín de Iturbide siding with the insurgents and marching on Mexico City in 1820. The following year the Plan de Iguala finally gave Mexico independence under a constitutional monarchy.

The Independence Bell on the Governor's Palace in Guadalajara—from here Hidalgo declared an end to slavery in 1810

❑ An estimated 600,000 lives were lost during the 11-year struggle for independence. ❑

Mexican–American War Iturbide declared himself Emperor, but this was only short-lived and power passed fitfully and eventfully into the hands of General Antonio López de Santa Ana, at the head of the new federal republic. Times remained troubled, separatist intrigues fermented and in 1836, despite Santa Ana's successful siege of the Alamo, Texas declared itself independent of Mexico. Nine years later U.S. expansionist policy led to the annexation of Texas, provoking a war which soon left Veracruz, Monterrey, and Mexico City in American hands. The Treaty of Guadalupe in 1848 ceded most of New Mexico, California and Texas to the U.S. for $15 million, followed by a further territorial cession in 1854 (for another $10 million into the Mexican coffers) which defined today's bor-

ders, altogether depriving Mexico of more than half its former territory.

Juárez versus Maximilian With Santa Ana ousted by a liberal movement headed by the Zapotec lawyer, Benito Juárez, Mexico plunged headlong into another bloody civil war between conservatives in Mexico City, backed by the reactionary Church, and liberals based in Veracruz. Priests were killed and churches sacked until in 1861 Juárez finally triumphed, imposing judicial reforms and anti-clerical legislation which shattered the power of the Church. Exhausted and torn apart, Mexico was not allowed to rest. The next threat came as a direct result of the nation's bankruptcy: payment of all foreign debts was suspended, leading to a concerted reprisal by Spain, France, and Britain, who attacked Veracruz. French troops, not content with a mere show of strength, proceeded to invade Mexico and, despite a major defeat at Puebla, by 1863 had occupied Mexico City.

The hapless Maximilian of Habsburg and his wife Carlota were hand-picked by Napoleon III as puppet Emperor and Empress, but their reign proved short-lived. Juárez, a

❑ For 30 years, between 1821 and 1851, Mexico teetered under more than 40 different governments. ❑

Maximilian of Habsburg, the ill-fated puppet Emperor of Mexico from 1862 to 1867. On his death Benito Juárez resumed office

fervent admirer of Abraham Lincoln, astutely obtained U.S. backing under the Monroe doctrine of "America for the Americans," and Napoleon III, already threatened on the home front, consented to withdraw most of his troops. Abandoned to his fate, isolated and outnumbered, finally Maximilian was executed in 1867 in Querétaro, leaving Carlota to end her days, insane, in Belgium. Back in power, Juárez set about implementing his Reform Laws, reconstructing the economy and developing public education, but his days, too, were numbered; in 1872 he died of a heart attack while still in office.

Dictatorship and revolution

■ Crowning the débâcle of the 19th century was the 34-year-long dictatorship of Porfirio Díaz, which brought comparative peace and prosperity but also a peak of repression and social injustice. Never ones to lie down, the Mexicans rebelled in 1910, initiating a decade of anarchy and yet further decimation of the population.....■

Commanding the troops that recaptured Mexico City for Juárez in 1867 was a *mestizo* (mixed Spanish and Indian blood) called Porfirio Díaz who, within 10 years, was sufficiently bitten by the attractions of political power to seize office for himself. Ruthless but efficient, he ruled in true dictatorial style with a handpicked clique, obliterating any opposition through a newly formed rural police force. Intent on rebuilding the nation, Díaz constructed roads and railroads, telephone and telegraph lines, and opened up remote towns to the march of modernization. Ultimate symbol of this progress was the grandiose architectural style, now called Porfiriato, which thrust itself on every city to stress the greatness of the regime. But none of this reconstruction came cheaply, and Díaz' policies included attracting outside investment: oil fields, mines, and railroads were soon all in foreign hands, provoking a rising xenophobia. More crucial was the fraudulent seizure of common land by voracious *hacendados* (estate owners); even whole villages were wiped out to extend plantations, and Indians found themselves yet again in a state of slavery, bound by debt to their exploitative employers and unable to escape due to the brutal methods of internal security forces.

On the boil When the liberal idealist Francisco Madero stood for election against Díaz in 1910 the dictator responded characteristically by throwing him into prison. But Madero escaped to Texas and from here called for a national insurrection. Several existing revolutionary groups responded, including forces led by Pancho Villa in the north and Emiliano Zapata in the south. By 1911 Madero had been elected President and Díaz was on the run to Europe. Reluctant to restore hacienda land to the people, Madero lost Zapata's support and soon had to confront a new protagonist, General Victoriano Huerta. After 10 days of vicious fighting in the capital, Huerta

❏ Zapata's stirring lines included "I'd rather die enslaved to my principles than to man" and "Rebels of the South! It is better to die on your feet than live on your knees!" ❏

Dictator Porfirio Díaz governed Mexico with an iron fist, exploiting the middle and lower classes

American aviator Hamilton carries out the first-ever aerial reconnaissance over Juárez, besieged by rebels, 1911

was installed as President, backed by American business interests, and soon recognized by foreign powers. Ineffective and unpopular, Huerta did nothing except ferment further conflicts, and in March 1913 the Plan of Guadalupe united three powerful revolutionary factions against him: Pancho Villa in Chihuahua, General Alvaro Obregón in Sonora, and Venustiano Carranza in Coahuila. Continuing his courageous struggle in the state of Morelos, Zapata also turned his forces against Huerta, and the final *coup de grâce* was given when the new American president, Woodrow Wilson, changed alliance and sent aid to the revolutionaries. In 1914 American troops occupied Veracruz, and Huerta's capitulation became inevitable.

Boiling Against a background of continuing civil war, Carranza formed a new government in alliance with Obregón. By 1916 it had set up a constitutional congress, and on February 5, 1917 proclaimed the new constitution which in theory recognized most of the revolutionary demands. The intervening years had witnessed anarchy on an unheard-of scale, with the uncompromising Villa skirmishing away in the north and Zapata even briefly occupying the capital in 1915. Rival factions issued their own currencies, railroad lines were blown up and armed ambushes became a daily occurrence. Millions of people died and the countryside was left in a state of total destruction. In 1919 the cowardly ambush of Zapata by one of Carranza's generals brought an end to Mexico's greatest defender of land rights and, although the 1920 Coahuila Pact marked the end of armed revolution, deadly rivalries did not fully abate until the next decade.

❑ **Revolutionary deaths**
1913—Madero executed
1919—Zapata assassinated
1920—Carranza assassinated
1923—Villa assassinated
1928—Obregón assassinated ❑

Reform and corruption

■ The chaotic aftermath of the Mexican Revolution settled into political stability in the 1930s, finally propelling the nation into the 20th century. But a booming economy and greatly developed infrastructure came together with a population explosion and spiraling corruption, making the path of progress a stony one.....■

When President Plutarco Elías Calles was sworn into office in 1924 he was faced with a nation in social and economic ruins, still fragmented by political allegiances, but by the end of his term he had formed the Partido Nacional Revolucionario (the precursor of today's PRI which has monopolized office ever since), a unifying force for the countless splinter groups. Education and land reforms were instigated and, once again, the Church became a target for attack, with the closure of monasteries and convents. Religious processions were forbidden and fanatical anti-clerical excesses were committed while masses were held secretly in private homes. The result was more civil unrest in the prolonged Cristero rebellion which, from 1927 to 1935, produced sporadic banditry as well as open warfare.

Former President Carlos Salinas de Gortari, who won widespread approval for his reforms

Reform It was only under President Lázaro Cárdenas (1934–1940) that Mexico finally entered a period of acknowledged prosperity and civil peace. Social injustices were partly solved by the redistribution of land to

❑ When Cárdenas left office in 1940 nearly 50 million acres of land had been redistributed to two million peasants. ❑

peasants which, under the *ejido* (communal holding) system, transferred hacienda land back into the hands of the *campesinos* (peasant farmers). Being Indian at last became a plus, promoted by the murals of Rivera, Orozco, and Siqueiros, which graphically glorified the indigenous role. The newly-born union movement was strengthened and the ruling party transformed from a tool of personal power into a corporate organization. In 1938 Cárdenas crowned this democratic approach by nationalizing all foreign oil companies and mines, a move which temporarily slowed growth by discouraging foreign investment but greatly boosted national confidence. At the onset of World War II Mexico was poised for profit. World demand for its natural resources, combined with domestic manufacture replacing imported goods, gave the economy an unprecedented boost.

Corruption The rapid expansion of the infrastructure and industrial landscape brought with it a new political lobby, that of the industrialists. To integrate this powerful new force, the ruling party was given the self-contradictory label of Partido Revolucionario Institucional (PRI) which remains to this day. Under President Miguel Alemán (1946–1952) Mexico saw the incipient rise of corruption and its rooting into the economic framework of nationalized companies, a practice which blossomed again under the Díaz Ordáz administration in the late 1960s and is still common. More visible was a population explosion that came hand in hand with improved social welfare during a period of stabilized growth which lasted from 1954 to 1970. In the two preceding decades the Mexican population had doubled and the chaotic, unregulated growth of industry appeared like a shining light on the horizon to the millions of still-deprived rural inhabitants. The great urban drift had begun.

Unrest and recession Increasing strains appeared by the late 1960s when inflation seriously started to take off and questioning of the legitimacy of the political system resulted in mounting dissent. Events came to a head in October 1968 when Mexico City staged the Olympic Games: university students descended on the Plaza de las Tres Culturas in Tlatelolco to protest against the injustices of Díaz Ordaz' regime (rigged elections, repression of liberals, corruption). In a merciless and bloody reprisal government troops shot hundreds of students, women, and children—the blackest moment in Mexico's post-revolutionary history. The 1970s saw continuing unrest, notably an armed uprising in 1974 in the state of Guerrero, and an economy that veered from an ephemeral, post oil-crisis boom to economic recession by the end of the decade. Accelerating inflation and a crippling foreign debt culminated in the announcement by President José López Portillo in 1982 of Mexico's inability to repay its foreign creditors.

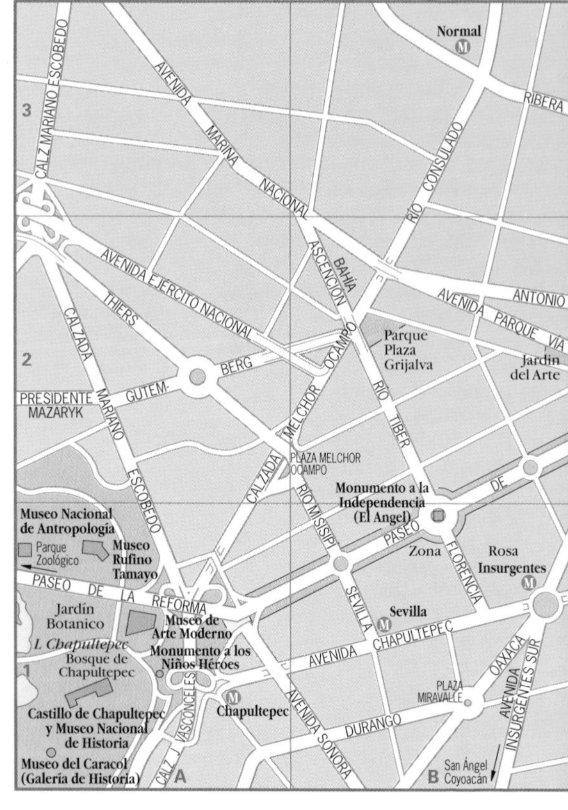
Normal
RIBERA
3
CALZ MARIANO ESCOBEDO
AVENIDA
MARINA
NACIONAL
RÍO CONSULADO
AVENIDA EJÉRCITO NACIONAL
ASCENCIÓN
BAHÍA
AVENIDA
ANTONIO
PARQUE
VIA
THIERS
CALZADA
Parque Plaza Grijalva
Jardín del Arte
2
BERG
GUTEM-
PRESIDENTE MAZARYK
MARIANO
MELCHOR
OCAMPO
RÍO
TIBER
ESCOBEDO
PLAZA MELCHOR OCAMPO
CALZADA
RÍO MISSIPI
Monumento a la Independencia (El Angel)
DE
Museo Nacional de Antropología
Parque Zoológico
Museo Rufino Tamayo
PASEO
Zona
FLORENCIA
Rosa
Insurgentes
PASEO DE LA REFORMA
SEVILLA
Jardín Botanico
Museo de Arte Moderno
Sevilla
CHAPULTEPEC
I. Chapultepec
Bosque de Chapultepec
Monumento a los Niños Héroes
AVENIDA
OAXACA
1
Chapultepec
PLAZA MIRAVALLE
AVENIDA INSURGENTES SUR
Castillo de Chapultepec y Museo Nacional de Historia
CALZ. J. VASCONCELOS
AVENIDA SONORA
DURANGO
Museo del Caracol (Galería de Historia)
A
B
San Ángel Coyoacán

MEXICO CITY

Mexico City At first sight Mexico City's vast expanse is daunting, blanketing its 7,350-ft.-high valley to the horizon. With a population currently hovering around the 22 million mark, pollution, uncontrollable traffic, severe water shortage, cheap buildings that crack at the slightest seismic shudder, cholera outbreaks on the outskirts, and highly visible imbalances in wealth, the capital's negative points are legion. Built over Lago de Texcoco, its foundations sink 6 inches every year while the edges creep inexorably outwards. A city out of control? Love it or hate it, this unique metropolis which somehow seems American to Europeans and European to Americans, is truly Mexican.

Whatever your reaction, Mexico City is a magnetic and essential starting point for exploring the rest of a richly diverse country and, despite its negative factors, remains the social, economic, cultural, and political pulse of the nation.

Early history It was the shores of Lago de Texcoco that attracted early settlers, forming the focal point for some of Mesoamerica's most powerful dynasties. After the ancient site of Cuicuilco was buried by volcanic lava

Mexico City (Ciudad de México), the oldest capital in the New World, sprawls across its valley floor. You get a good idea of its size when you fly over it

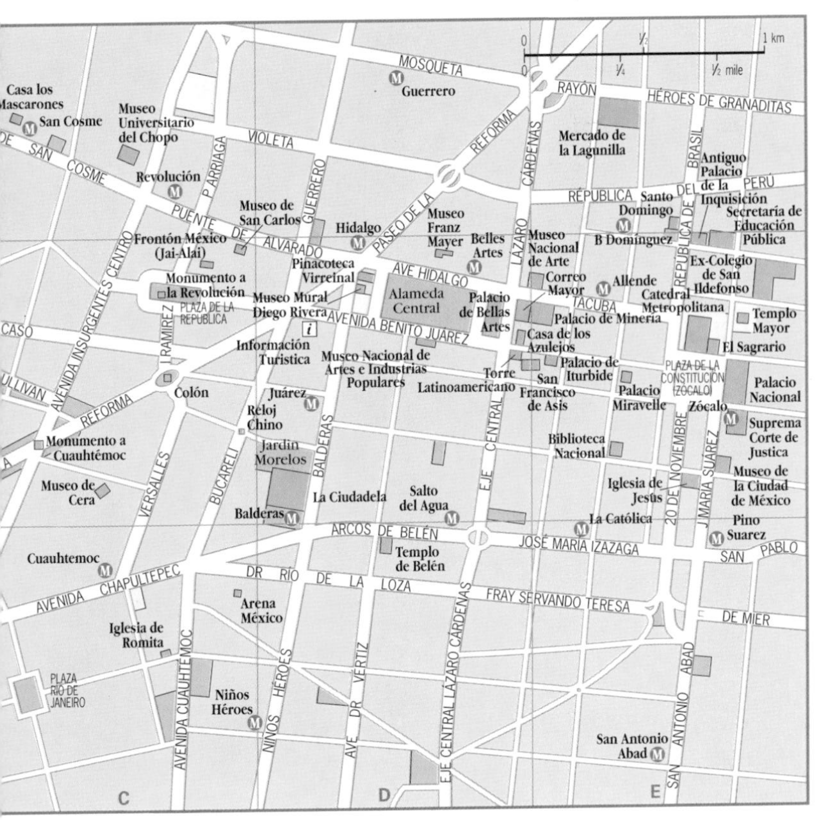

Sixteenth-century arrival
"Wide though the causeway was, it was so crowded with people that there was hardly room for them all ... For the towers and the cues were full, and they came in canoes from all parts of the lake. No wonder, since they had never seen horses or men like us before!

With such wonderful sights to gaze on we did not know what to say, or if this was real that we saw before our eyes. On the land side there were great cities and on the lake many more. The lake was crowded with canoes. At intervals along the causeway there were many bridges, and before us was the great city of Mexico."
Bernal Díaz del Castillo: *The Conquest of New Spain*, 1568.

around the 1st century AD came Teotihuacán, with its astonishing ceremonial structures and far-reaching influence. On the collapse of this civilization in 650, power moved to the equally dominant Toltecs at Tula who, in the 12th century, scattered to the Hill of Chapultepec and throughout Mexico. Then around 1300 came a tribe nourished by the prophesies of their god of war, Huitzilipóchtli: the Aztecs had arrived. They named their settlement Tenochtitlán ("place of the cactus"), dominated the neighboring tribes and, calling themselves the Méxica, occupied the island of Tlatelolco, and captured Coyoacán and Xochimilco to the south.

By the time Hernán Cortés arrived on the scene in 1519, Tenochtitlán's power and wealth had been consolidated and the lake city was deemed the "Venice of the New World." The defeat of the Aztecs in 1521 was followed by the total destruction of their magnificent city, a deliberate act by Cortés which made way for building the capital of Nueva España.

Recent developments After surviving centuries of adversity, riots inspired by racial divisions, floods, invasion by foreign powers, starvation and homelessness caused by Independence, Revolutionary chaos and, more recently, the 1968 bloodbath of Tlatelolco (see page 47), as well as the earthquake of 1985, the inhabitants of Mexico City have now to confront severe environmental problems. Thermal inversions trap smog in the valley, and industrial air-pollutants are magnified by around 15,000 antiquated buses, over 40,000 taxis and 3 million cars. Contaminated water has created severe health problems, and the underground lake is nearly pumped dry while tremors continue to

Juan O'Gorman's fine mosaics cover the walls of the university library

keep nerves on edge. Corruption is still a going concern, and public funds often miss their mark despite vociferous civic action following the 1985 earthquake which forced the government's hand in environmental matters. Wealthier classes move out to the healthier hills beyond the urban sprawl, while a weekly average of 10,000 poor from the surrounding rural areas continue to be sucked into the city's maelstrom. The population thus expands by approximately 3.5 percent annually, many living in an estimated 12 percent of homes which are basically cardboard-and-plank affairs.

Orientation The spruced-up historic heart of Mexico City lies in and around the Zócalo (main square), once the Plaza Mayor of Aztec Tenochtitlán. From here Avenida Madero and Calle Tacuba run parallel, west to Alameda Central, a small park flanked by numerous monuments and cut diagonally to the west by the Paseo de la Reforma. This majestic, broad avenue, more than 7 miles in length, sweeps southwest past the Zona Rosa, an exclusive commercial area, through Bosque de Chapultepec (Chapultepec Park), the recreational lungs of the city, to end in the residential area of Lomas. This entire area is, broadly, the city center, and a taxi ride from the Zócalo to Chapultepec will take no more than 20 minutes.

Insurgentes, a major north–south axis, starts north of Guadelupe and intersects with Paseo de la Reforma at the monument to Cuauhtémoc, the last emperor of Mexico, before continuing south to the suburb of San Ángel, the University and the Pyramid of Cuicuilco. Parallel to Insurgentes, to the east, is the other north–south axis, Calzada de Tlalpán, which runs south from the Zócalo to Coyoacán, finally joining up with Insurgentes beyond the *periférico* (ringroad).

Twentieth-century departure
Mexico City's long-distance bus stations are named according to the points of the compass, and all can be reached by metro. The largest, Terminal Norte (metro: Autobuses del Norte), covers northern and other destinations including Guadalajara, Mazatlán, Pachuca, and Papantla. Terminal Oriente (metro: San Lázaro) serves destinations east and south, including Puebla, Veracruz, and the states of Oaxaca, Chiapas, and the Yucatán. Terminal Sur (metro: Tasqueña) runs buses southeast to Cuernavaca, Taxco, Cuautla, and Acapulco. Terminal Poniente (metro: Observatorio) shuttles to Toluca as well as Morelia and Guadalajara. The airport, too, has its metro station, Terminal Aerea, but as bulky luggage is banned on the metro, you may have to use a taxi.

View from the Latin America Tower

Murals
More work by Mexico's muralists can be seen in public buildings around the Zócalo area. The courtyard and upper floor of the 1920s Secretaría de Educación Pública (Ministry of Public Education), 3½ blocks north of the Zócalo on Calle República de Argentina, boasts 235 early mural panels by Rivera which depict social and economic themes. Other muralists represented here include Juan O'Gorman, Carlos Merida, and Amado de la Cueva. At the Suprema Corte de Justicia, on the southeastern corner of the Zócalo, are grandiose works by Orozco. Located up the main staircase and along the second-floor walls, they pay homage to workers' rights, to national pride and—naturally enough—to justice.

Zócalo

►► Catedral Metropolitana (Metropolitan Cathedral) *49E2*

Metro: Zócalo, Allende
This massive cathedral, dominating the historic heart of Mexico City, was begun in 1563 to replace an earlier version built by Cortés, and incorporates stones from the ruins of the Temple of Quetzalcóatl, as well as the macabre wall of skulls where the skulls of sacrificial victims were displayed by the Aztecs. Most of the Baroque southern façade and tiered columns were completed in 1681, while the asymmetrical twin towers and large central dome were added as late as 1813. This mixture of architectural styles houses an equally ornate interior, particularly the **Capilla de Los Reyes**►► and its gilded Baroque altar (1718–1725), although much of the cathedral's artwork was destroyed or damaged by fire in 1967. Serious structural problems caused by subsidence have not been helped by the 1985 earthquake: there is a noticeable 20-ft. difference in level between the entrance and the high altar—you can't miss the heavy metal supports. Next door stands the Churrigueresque-style **El Sagrario**►► (1760), its blindingly gilded interior originally designed to house the archbishop's archives.

►► Ex-Colegio de San Ildefonso *49E2*

Calle Ildefonso 43
Metro: Allende
This large college, one block north of the Templo Mayor, was built by the Jesuits in 1749, and boasts a rare display

The Catedral Metropolitana

of early murals by the three giants of this field: Rivera, Orozco, and Siqueiros. Between 1923 and 1933 they covered the central courtyard, main staircase and amphitheater with their dynamic works in a concerted effort to create a national muralist movement. The college now functions as a cultural center.

► Museo de la Ciudad de México (Mexico City Museum) *49E2*

Avenida Pino Suárez 30
Metro: Zócalo
Located three blocks south of the Zócalo, this museum is housed in a magnificent 1528 mansion, rebuilt in the late 18th century for the extravagant counts of Santiago de Calimaya and later redecorated in Art Deco style. Displays cover the geological and socio-political history of Mexico City, from volcanic eruptions to the first settlers (8000BC) and the inspired creators of Teotihuacán and Tenochtitlán. Dioramas and models of the city from Aztec days to the present give a strong visual idea of its changing fate.

►►► Palacio Nacional (National Palace) *49E2*

Metro: Zócalo
Flanking the eastern side of the Zócalo is Mexico's political powerhouse, home to the offices of the President, the National Archives, and the Federal Treasury. Hanging above the entrance is the highly symbolic "Freedom Bell," which announced Independence on September 15, 1810 in the town of Dolores, and which is now rung annually on the eve of Independence Day by the President. The building itself dates from the late 17th century and replaced two previous palaces, the second extensively damaged by the 1692 Indian revolt. Entrance to public areas is through a stately courtyard and up a staircase monopolized by Diego Rivera's celebrated mural depicting the history of Mexico. The walls of the second-floor gallery continue his prodigious and dramatic interpretation. On the third floor is a small museum dedicated to President Benito Juárez, leader of the Reform movement, who died here in 1872.

►►► Templo Mayor (Great Temple) *49E2*

Metro: Zócalo, Allende
The Aztecs' main temple, unearthed completely by accident as recently as 1978, was dedicated to their gods Huitzilopóchtli (war) and Tláloc (rain) before being razed to the ground by Cortés. Today visitors can explore the multiple layers of the site from a raised walkway: serpentine carvings, a giant conch shell, remains of pyramids, and a *chacmool* (a reclining statue on which sacrificial offerings were laid) are visible. More illuminating is the modern site museum based on the original temple layout where over 3,000 artifacts reflect the far-reaching significance of the Aztec empire. Pride of place is given to the huge votive stone disc of Coyolxauhqui, goddess of the moon—the first artifact to be discovered—while a scale model of the city of Tenochtitlán shows the urban sophistication of the Aztecs.

Shoe-shiners and scribes
Four blocks north of the Zócalo, in the lively Plaza Santo Domingo, a pervasive smell of shoe-polish masks the usual traffic fumes as shoe-shiners wait for customers, while under the arcades is a row of printing presses and *evangelistas* (scribes) who, using typewriters, which have replaced more antiquated methods, give words to the wishes of their illiterate clients, creating the ultimate love letter or plea for employment.

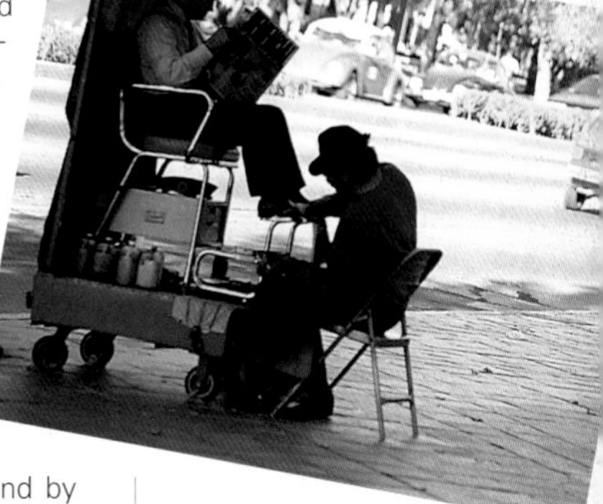

Shoe-shiners can be found on almost every street corner

Alameda

▶ Alameda Central (Central Park) *49D2*

Between Avenida Juárez and Avenida Hidalgo
Metro: Hidalgo, Bellas Artes

Street vendor

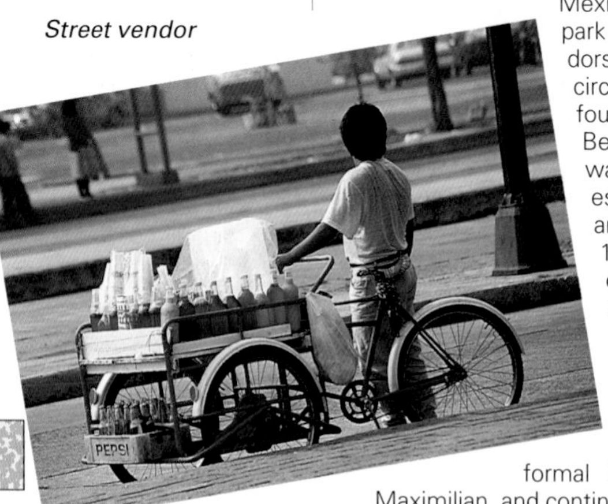

Mexico City's neatly tended central park is a focal point for street vendors, dog-walkers and children, all circulating along shady paths past fountains and a central bandstand. Before Independence, admission was restricted to the upper classes, a policy instigated when the area was developed in the late 16th century. The western side of the park has a particularly dark past as it was here, on the Plaza del Quemadero, that the Spanish Inquisition set up its stake for burning heretics. During the 19th century the park was re-landscaped in formal French style under Emperor Maximilian, and continued by Porfirio Díaz.

▶▶ Casa de los Azulejos (House of Tiles) *49D2*

Avenida Madero 4
Metro: Bellas Artes
This extraordinary example of Mexican colonial architecture, entirely faced in blue Talavera tiles (added in the 18th century), was built in 1596 for the Counts of the Valley of Orizaba, one of whom met his end on the main staircase at the knifepoint of his daughter's fiancé. The glassed-in courtyard displays an eclectic mix of Art Nouveau murals, stained glass, tilework, Mauresque carved stone and plaster, and a forceful staircase mural by Orozco. The mansion, now home to one of the Sanborn chain of restaurants and shops, can be visited daily till 10 p.m.

▶▶▶ Museo Franz Mayer (Franz Mayer Museum) *49D2*

Avenida Hidalgo 45
Metro: Hidalgo, Bellas Artes
If you only visit one art museum in Mexico City, this should be it. Opened in 1986 in a superbly restored 16th-century hospital, the museum contains an extraordinarily rich collection of 16th- to 19th-century European, Asian, and Mexican fine and applied arts collected over several decades by German immigrant and construction magnate, Franz Mayer. Carefully exhibited to highlight influences and contrasts, whether Chinese or Arab, the fine workmanship of Mexican artists is also brought to the fore. Inlaid furniture, tapestries, ceramics, carved wood sculptures, silver and gold objects, glass, chests, mirrors, and paintings (including works by Ribera, Zurbarán, and the school of Velázquez) fill rooms surrounding a delightful open-air courtyard. The Cafeteria del Claustro here makes a peaceful retreat from the frenetic streets outside and is also accessible to those not visiting the museum.

Aztec metro
Directly south of the Zócalo, at Pino Suárez, stands the city's most extraordinary metro entrance. While the metro was being built in the late 1960s, this important Aztec shrine, dedicated to Quetzalcóatl and dating from the late 14th century, was uncovered and subsequently integrated into the concourse.

►► Museo Mural Diego Rivera (Diego Rivera Mural Museum) *49D2*

Plaza Solidaridad
Metro: Hidalgo, Juárez

Devoted to one vast mural, Rivera's *Dream of a Sunday Afternoon in Alameda Central*, this small museum's existence is directly linked to the 1985 earthquake. Rivera's masterpiece had been displayed in the Hotel del Prado since it was painted between 1947 and 1948, but earthquake damage to the hotel was so great that a complex operation was undertaken to move it. Photographs show how the mural (51 ft. by 14 ft.) was elaborately mounted on to a 40-ton metal frame and transported across the road to its present site. The theme of this work is a lyrical and satirical fresco of Mexican history in the form of a promenade in Alameda Park at the turn of the century. Benito Juárez, Hernán Cortés, Emiliano Zapata, Emperor Maximilian and Carlota, and Porfirio Díaz all figure, while Rivera himself appears in boy and adult form, accompanied by Frida Kahlo. Considered highly controversial due to the inclusion of the words "*Dios no existe*" (God does not exist), Rivera finally agreed to backtrack in 1956 and substituted a more moderate statement. A side room is used for temporary exhibitions of photography and contemporary art.

►► Museo Nacional de Arte (National Art Museum) *49E2*

Calle Tacuba 8
Metro: Bellas Artes

The national art museum is housed in a Porfiriato extravaganza of great elegance and fronted by an equestrian statue of Carlos IV of Spain (*El Caballito*) which once stood on the Zócalo. Although its historical significance is, for the Mexicans, dubious, it somehow manages to survive. It displays Mexican painting and sculpture of the 19th and early 20th century. One of the highlights is a room devoted to the evocative works of José Maria Velasco, master of turn-of-the century landscapes of the Valley of Mexico. Similar in theme are the works of Saturnino Herrán and Gerardo Murillo, forefather of the muralists, while José Guadalupe Posada's biting political comments and Frida Kahlo's disturbing tortured self-portraits offer other radical visions. Nineteenth-century sculptures and drawings complete the collection on the third floor. Across Calle Tacuba stands the superb **Palacio de Minería►►**, which was built between 1797 and 1813 and is an outstanding example of neoclassical architecture.

► Museo Nacional de Artes e Industrias Populares (National Folk Art Museum) *49D2*

Avenida Juárez 44
Metro: Bellas Artes

Although the small museum is currently closed for rebuilding, a large craft shop, once the 18th-century Church of Corpus Christi, remains on the site, on the southern side of Alameda park. A varied display of folk art from all over the country includes hand-blown glass, embroidery, furniture, papier-mâché, and some finely woven basketware. Most of the pieces are of high quality but prices, though fixed, are equally elevated.

Jardín de Solidaridad
This small square at the western end of the Alameda was built in 1986 on the site of the Hotel Regis, one of the many buildings on the south side of the Alameda which collapsed in the 1985 earthquake, including a modern government health ministry and hospital on the north side. The Jardín de Solidaridad commemorates the tremendous interaction and solidarity among the capital's population, who organized relief and achieved far more success than any official organization.

The Palace of Fine Arts is also the home of the colorful Ballet Folklórico

Jai alai
Take a break from culture and watch a high-action game of jai alai. This old Basque sport is played at the Frontón México, Plaza de la República 17, from Tuesday to Saturday at 7 p.m. and on Sunday at 5 p.m. Professional players hurl fast-moving rubber balls with wicker rackets along a 266-ft. court. Betting is part of the fun, with odds changing as each game progresses. The Frontón México attracts a chic crowd who often combine an evening of jai alai with dinner at the adjoining Prendes restaurant.

Correo central
If you need to use a post office in Mexico City, try the one located at the back of the Bellas Artes on Tacuba. This grandiose edifice was designed by Adamo Boari of Bellas Artes fame. It was completed in 1908, and its interior, full of richly carved wood, resembles a Venetian palace more than your average post office.

PINACOTECA VIRREINAL
Dr. Mora No. 7
INBA
$ 7,000.00
Nº 6845

▶▶▶ Palacio de Bellas Artes (Palace of Fine Arts) *49D2*

Avenida Juárez
Metro: Bellas Artes
The extravagant forms of this massive theater and art gallery, built of Carrara marble, monopolize the eastern end of Alameda Central but are sinking fast into the capital's spongy soil. The Palacio was commissioned by Porfirio Díaz and designed by Italian architect Adamo Boari in 1900. Political upheavals—not least the Revolution—interrupted its construction, and it was not until 1934 that it was finally completed. It thus presents a curious and delightful blend of Neoclassical, Art Nouveau and Art Deco styles, the latter dominating the superbly proportioned interior. Some of Mexico's most outstanding murals by Rivera, Orozco, Siqueiros, and Tamayo can be seen on the third and fourth floors. The concert hall, which features a spectacular Tiffany stained-glass stage-curtain depicting the volcanoes of the Valley of Mexico, can be visited outside performance hours. Completing the offerings is the first-floor bookstore and café, a favorite haunt for the capital's *literati*.

▶ Palacio de Iturbide (Iturbide Palace) *49E2*

Avenida Madero 17
Metro: Bellas Artes
This superb Baroque mansion, bristling with coats of arms, gargoyles, and sculpted columns, was completed in 1785 for a marquis. Between 1821 and 1823 it was occupied by the notorious Independence leader Agustín de Iturbide whose Napoleonic illusions of grandeur led to him crowning himself Emperor after he had engineered Independence. Today, more prosaically, it houses the cultural foundation of Banamex, Mexico's national bank, and the peaceful courtyard is used for exhibitions of contemporary art.

▶ Pinacoteca Virreinal (Museum of Colonial Painting) *49D2*

Calle Doctor Mora 7
Metro: Hidalgo
This museum, in a former church and Dominican monastery dating from 1591, houses a collection of Mexican paintings dating from the colonial (vice-regal) period of the late 16th century to the early 19th century.

The highlights are works by Miguel Cabrera, a Oaxacan-born painter who, in the mid-18th century, produced some of Mexico's finest religious paintings.

▶ Templo de San Francisco de Asis (Church of St. Francis) *49E2*

Avenida Madero
Metro: Bellas Artes
The history of this church goes back to the early days of Cortés and the first Franciscan monks in 1524. Most of the structure, now sunk well below street-level, dates from the early 18th century when the stone portal and façade were elaborately fashioned in Churrigueresque style, but fragments of the early construction are visible.

The Church of St. Francis is a masterpiece of Churrigueresque (Spanish Baroque)

▶ Torre Latinoamericana (Latin American Tower) *49D2*

Corner Avenida Madero and Lázaro Cárdenas
Metro: Bellas Artes
This lofty downtown landmark, the capital's first skyscraper, was once the tallest building in the city at 595 ft., but today it is surpassed by the Pemex building. Views from the bar/restaurant on the 41st floor or the observation deck on the 42nd floor (open daily 10 a.m. to 11 p.m.) are most breathtaking at night when the lights of Mexico City blanket the horizons. Daytime views are often marred by a haze of pollution.

Blacklisted
A significant exhibit at the Palacio de Bellas Artes is Rivera's famous mural *Man at the Crossing of the Ways*, first commissioned for New York's Rockefeller Center in 1933 when it was entitled *Man in Control of his Universe.* The work was destroyed when Rivera refused to delete the face of Lenin. He painted this subsequent version depicting class struggles and the dehumanizing effects of industrialization with even more fire and venom. Nor did Siqueiros flinch in his work: his mural *Cain in the United States* clearly reveals his feelings about racism against blacks in the U.S., while *The Birth of Fascism* portrays the spread of Fascism and dictatorship

TORRE LATINOAMERICANA
Símbolo de la Ciudad de México

MIRADOR
2,422 M.
Sobre el nivel del mar

ACUARIO
Piso 38

MURALTO
Restaurante Bar
Piso 41

TELESCOPIOS
Piso 44

Serie Nº 42661 C

Torre Latino Américana
Propiedad de
"La Latino Américana Seguros, S. A."

Zona Rosa

Right: *a local artist exhibits his work in the Jardín del Arte*

El Ángel
Mexico City's celebrated gilded angel, symbol of liberty, has a checkered history. It was originally commissioned by Emperor Maximilian in 1864 to be placed in the Zócalo, but it remained unfinished for years, its pedestal forlornly empty—thus the word *zócalo* (meaning pedestal) came to denote the central plaza. Porfirio Díaz relaunched the project and in 1902 commissioned the architect Antonio Rivas Mercado to supervise its erection in the Paseo de la Reforma. On September 16, 1910 the majestic 118-ft. column was officially inaugurated to mark the centenary of Mexican Independence. Toppled by an earthquake in 1957, the statue gleams once more in restored splendor.

► Zona Rosa *48B1*

The triangular Zona Rosa is considered the city's most fashionable area for restaurants, clubs, boutiques, and movie theaters. It lies southeast of the wide Paseo de la Reforma, ending at the Avenida Chapultepec. The tree-lined streets are named after European cities—Berlin, Genoa, Marseilles. The area is undergoing a facelift: some streets are closed to traffic and building restrictions have been imposed to halt encroaching development.

►► Paseo de la Reforma *48B2*

This wide boulevard, laid out under Emperor Maximilian, slices through the city from Chapultepec Park, and northeast past the Alameda Central to the Plaza de las Tres Culturas. Buzzing with traffic and wandering vendors, dotted with statues and monuments, and lined with some of Mexico City's most daring contemporary architecture, it is often compared to Paris' Champs-Elysées. It is still *the* address for airline offices, banks, embassies, and the impressive buildings of the Lotería Nacional. Major statues at ringroads (*glorietas*) include the **Monumento a la Independencia**, more commonly known as El Ángel, the **Monumento a Cuauhtémoc**, Mexico's last Aztec Emperor, and the **Monumento a Cristóbal Colón**, by French sculptor Charles Cordier.

►► Museo de San Carlos (Museum of San Carlos) *49C2*

Puente de Alvarado 50
Metro: Revolución
A fine art collection is housed in this graceful early-19th-century mansion, designed in Neoclassical style, with hints of Baroque, for the Marqués de Buenavista. The origins of the collection date back to the founding of the Royal Academy of San Carlos in 1785, an art school and museum. Both Rivera and Orozco graduated from San Carlos. In 1968 the collection, though not the school, was moved to this site, offering an impressive panorama of 14th- to 19th-century religious painting which includes major works by Lucas Cranach the Elder, Tintoretto, Brueghel, Zurbarán, Rubens, Rembrandt, Goya, Titian, Ingres, and Reynolds.

Bosque de Chapultepec

Above: *Statue of Morelos, Chapultepec Castle*

▶▶▶ Bosque de Chapultepec (Chapultepec Park) *65A2*

Metro: Chapultepec, Auditorio, Constituyentes
The collapsing "lungs" of Mexico City are situated west of the center and incorporate small lakes and woods which are much enjoyed by the capital's inhabitants, particularly at weekends. The park (the word *chapultepec* means "grasshopper hill" in Náhuatl) was used as a summer residence under Moctezuma, and became public in 1530. Set in over 1.5 square miles of vegetation are several major museums, recreation areas, and a zoo.

▶ Castillo de Chapultepec (Chapultepec Castle) *48A1*

Metro: Chapultepec
On top of Chapultepec's hill looms a massive, austere construction built in 1785 as the viceroy's residence and converted into a military academy in 1843. It fell into the hands of American troops in 1847, was refurbished by Maximilian and Carlota and finally converted to the **Museo Nacional de Historia▶** in 1944. The museum's exhibits, although unimaginatively displayed, give a solid background to national history from Spanish rule to the Independence movement, the Republic, Maximilian and Carlota, Dictatorship, and the Revolution. Several important murals enliven the displays and offer incisive comments on Mexican history. Maximilian and Carlota's apartments can be visited through a separate garden entrance. To get there, follow the spiral path from the **Monumento a los Niños Héroes▶▶** (Monument to the Boy Heroes) up to the summit for spectacular views from the spacious terraces.

Boy heroes
A massive semicircular columned sculpture, the Monumento a los Niños Héroes, situated at the base of the hill, has great historic significance. This symbol of Mexican patriotism represents the six young military cadets (the oldest aged 16) who, during the American invasion in 1847, reputedly threw themselves from the castle ramparts rather than surrender. They wrapped themselves in the Mexican flag as they jumped rather than let it fall into American hands.

▶▶ Museo de Arte Moderno (Museum of Modern Art) *48A1*

Metro: Chapultepec
This large airy building, enclosing a circular marble atrium, offers temporary exhibitions of contemporary art alongside a permanent collection of modern and contemporary Mexican artists. Exhibits start from the 1920s with some Post-Impressionist-style works before moving into what was to become a very distinctive Mexican school. Included are Rivera's portrait of Lupe Marín (1938), a typical Zuñiga sculpture of a swathed Indian woman, Murillo's apocalyptic rendering of the eruption of the Paricutín volcano (1946), Frida Kahlo's painful autobiographical comment *Las Dos Fridas* (1939) showing her schizophrenic physical state, and numerous works by Siquieros, Orozco, Tamayo, Abraham Angel, Cuevas, Carrillo, Echeverría, Toledo, and Castro Leñero.

Tláloc or Chalchiuhtlicue? Greeting the visitor outside the Museum of Anthropology entrance is a massive pink stone sculpture, once thought to represent Tláloc, the god of rain. Unearthed in an area south of Texcoco in the Valley of Mexico, this 24½-ft., 167-ton stone monolith had to be transported on a specially designed 72-wheel trailer to its present site. Archaeologists now believe the subject of the statue to be Chalchiuhtlicue, the water goddess.

Carving of Chalchiuhtlicue—or is it Tláloc?

► Museo del Caracol (Snail Museum) *48A1*

The Caracol, also called the Galería de Historia, is located a short distance downhill from Chapultepec Castle, and is named after its snail-like shape. Of more interest for its innovative design which blends into the wooded slopes than for its exhibits, it was conceived by Pedro Ramírez Vázquez and opened in 1960. Diagrams, models, and reproductions aimed at instructing younger visitors illustrate Mexico's long fight for freedom, culminating with the 1917 Constitution. This is dramatically exhibited in the last room, a conically-shaped area of lava brick, skylit by a red dome.

►►► Museo Nacional de Antropología (National Museum of Anthropology) *48A1*

Metro: Auditorio, Chapultepec

The world-renowned Anthropological Museum, exemplary in its field, is one of the capital's musts. It was built in the early 1960s to a design by Pedro Ramirez Vázquez, and its lofty proportions and imaginative displays have hardly aged, paying a fitting homage to the sophistication and artistry of Mexico's pre-Hispanic cultures. Some criticism has nevertheless been made of the lack of updating with respect to new archaeological discoveries.

The focal point is a large semi-roofed courtyard with an inverted fountain around which are arranged two floors of exhibition halls, the first floor devoted to

Olmec head from San Lorenzo, now in the Museum of Anthropology

Mesoamerican history and artifacts, the upper floor to ethnographic exhibits illustrating Indian traditions today. The museum covers a vast field in great depth with an estimated 3 miles of exhibits, and merits at least two visits. In the foyer is an excellent bookstore and the Sala de Orientación, which gives an audio-visual preview of the museum's contents.

The galleries, followed counter-clockwise around the courtyard, start in the right wing with an introduction to world anthropology and ethnology, continuing with the origins of Mesoamerican man, before moving into pre-Classic civilization (1700–200BC). Then follow rooms devoted to Teotihuacán, Tula (the Toltecs), Méxica (the Aztecs), Oaxaca (Mixtec and Zapotec), the Gulf of Mexico (Olmecs, Huastecs, and Totonacs), Maya, northern cultures, and finally Occidente (western cultures in Nayarit, Jalisco, and Colima).

Particularly remarkable exhibits include a giant Toltec *Atlante* in the Sala de Tula, the Aztec Calendar Stone in the spectacularly laid-out Sala Méxica, and a huge Olmec head from San Lorenzo. Also worthy of note are the muscular *Luchador*, a well-preserved sculpture in the Sala Olmec, the Mayan mask of the God of the Sun, reproductions of Bonampak murals and a re-creation of King Pakal's tomb from Palenque outside the Sala Maya. Countless other equally precious and impressive pieces offer a wealth of discoveries—even more fascinating after visiting any of the archaeological sites in question.

▶▶ Museo Rufino Tamayo (Rufino Tamayo Museum) *48A1*

Metro: Chapultepec

Rufino Tamayo (1899–1991), one of Mexico's most revered 20th-century artists, left an impressive legacy to his adopted city (he originated from Oaxaca) in the form of this sleekly designed art museum. Located east of the Anthropology Museum and just across the road from the Museum of Modern Art is the low-lying, multi-planed granite structure, built in 1979 and much esteemed for its avant-garde contemporary art exhibitions, often covering international work. The permanent collection of 20th-century art includes many of Tamayo's contemporaries—Ernst, Masson, Lam, Matta, Léger, and Picasso, as well as George Segal, Francis Bacon, Warhol, and Botero. A small bookstore and conference facilities complete the scene.

Parque Zoológico (Zoological Park) *65A2*

Metro: Auditorio

This claims to be the world's first zoo (open: Wednesday to Sunday 9 a.m. to 4.30 p.m.), with a history going back to the Aztecs *ca.* 1500. The 2,000 species housed here are an obvious favorite with children. Chinese pandas, lions and tigers, together with pony-rides and a tram, all provide thrills for the young. Rowboats can be rented on the lake and there is an adjacent children's amusement park. The zoo is located along with the **Jardín Botanico▶** beside **Lago Chapultepec▶** on the south side of Paseo de la Reforma from the Anthropological Museum.

Charros

Sunday morning activities in Chapultepec Park include a *charreada,* a Mexican rodeo performed by *charros* (macho gentlemen cowboys) in a colorful spectacle which also features girl riders, singers and *mariachi* bands. Inspired by the *vaqueros* (cattlemen) who guarded vast herds of cattle in northern Mexico, they perform remarkable feats of horsemanship, galloping round the ring, lassooing runaway cattle and switching mounts in mid-flight. Performances are at 10am at the Rancho del Charro, off Avenida Constituyentes.

Another exquisite exhibit in the Museum of Anthropology

■ **Rivera and Kahlo were one of the world's most flamboyant "art couples." Centered on Mexico City's Coyoacán and San Ángel areas, surrounded by the intellectual and artistic élite of post-Revolutionary Mexico, their lives and works were fundamental to Mexico's cultural renaissance.....** ■

Cult figure
It is only recently that Frida Kahlo's works have found their place in the art market. An auction price of $1.5 million in 1991 became a record for a Latin-American artist's work. Adopted by feminists as a figurehead, Kahlo has achieved cult status. But it is hard to better the last great exhibition of her paintings in 1953. Organized by Lola Alvarez Bravo who, along with the painter and her entourage, saw the end approaching, it involved transporting the dying artist to the gallery to lie in state in her legendary four-poster. Dressed in her richest Zapotec costume and jewelry, she bravely received admirers and friends all evening in a conscious farewell to life.

Portrait of the flamboyant Rivera

When the couple first met, in 1923, Kahlo was a bright-eyed teenager and Rivera a 37-year-old man-of-the-world. Innocent versus womanizer, "dove" versus "elephant" (the words of Kahlo's father), beauty and the beast. Variously described as an ogre, a seducer, and a frog (Kahlo's description), Rivera was a provocative, violent character whose physical stamina, black humor, and egoism only served to attract more mistresses. By the time they met again, five years later, Kahlo had developed into a mature, arresting-looking but severely traumatized woman. A near fatal tramway accident in 1925 had shattered her spine, pelvis, and legs, but also inspired an exorcistic passion—painting. Convalescing in a four-poster bed at her family home in Coyoacán, she occupied the hours by transferring her image—reflected in a mirror on the canopy of the bed—onto paper and canvas, thus initiating a lifetime series of agonized self-portraits. "I've never painted a dream, I've always painted my reality," she once said.

The ogre Rivera, meanwhile, was at the peak of his career. After a 10-year stay in Paris where he had lived the life of a Montparnasse Bohemian, his return to Mexico in 1921 marked the beginning of 30 years as the uncontested leader of pictorial nationalism. Muralism was in its infancy, but by the time he and Kahlo married, in 1929, he had covered hundreds of square meters of government-owned walls with his powerful, stylized depictions of class-struggles and indigenous history. Inspired by the Revolution and a meeting with Stalin in 1927 in the U.S.S.R., he never lost the true socialist spirit, a characteristic which caused, in the case of New York's Rockefeller Center and Detroit's Art Institute, endless scandal and controversy, due to his overt glorification of Communism.

Magnetism Rivera and Kahlo's was a meeting of opposites, eased by a common dedication to Communism, shared by the post-revolutionary political climate and by exiles such as the great photographer, Tina Modotti. But their true mutual passion was painting—something which, in later blacker moments of Kahlo's life, saved her from suicide. The 25-year vagaries of their two marriages and one divorce were due as much to Rivera's uncontrollable need to seduce other women (his conquests included Kahlo's younger sister) as to Kahlo's deeply embedded psychological trauma, her obsession with bearing his child (two miscarriages left their profound marks) and her long periods of intense physical suffering following numerous operations. Rivera's career flourished; they spent long periods in the U.S. while he worked on commissions and she floundered in self-imposed linguistic and social isolation.

Truce Yet their confrontations and separations only served to stimulate an increasing flow of pictorial violence from Kahlo's brushes. Her former bitter-sweet world of flowers, birds, and animals gave way to increasingly tormented images of blood, laceration, self-mutilation, suicide and death. In the words of surrealist theoretician André Breton they were "bombs wrapped up in ribbon." Strong-willed and proud, she also indulged in sexual provocation, managing to seduce the aging Trotsky, as well as the sculptor Isamu Noguchi and the elegant American photographer Nickolas Muray. After divorce in 1939, their remarriage the following year announced a new basis to the relationship. Rivera lived in his San Ángel studio while Kahlo was entrenched in her newly repainted blue Coyoacán house; there were no sexual relations but instead the recognition of a profound emotional and spiritual bond. Rivera continued his overt socio-political provocation while Kahlo plunged more deeply into her inner struggle. Her death in 1954 ended years of deterioration and, although Rivera remarried the following year, the absence of her guiding spirit and inspiration contributed to his own death in 1957.

Mexican flamboyance
A mesmerizing woman, Frida Kahlo's striking features were part *mestizo* and part Austro-Hungarian, the latter inherited from her Jewish father. Her dark eyes and high forehead were accentuated by heavy, straight eyebrows which she exaggerated in her stiff, frontal self-portraits. Crowned by elaborate hairstyles and exuberant jewelry, her inimitable style of dress came from the liberated women of Tehuantepec and Juchitán in the Isthmus. Their brilliantly colored and embroidered costumes were the perfect foil for Kahlo as she retreated increasingly into her disdainful, high-priestess role.

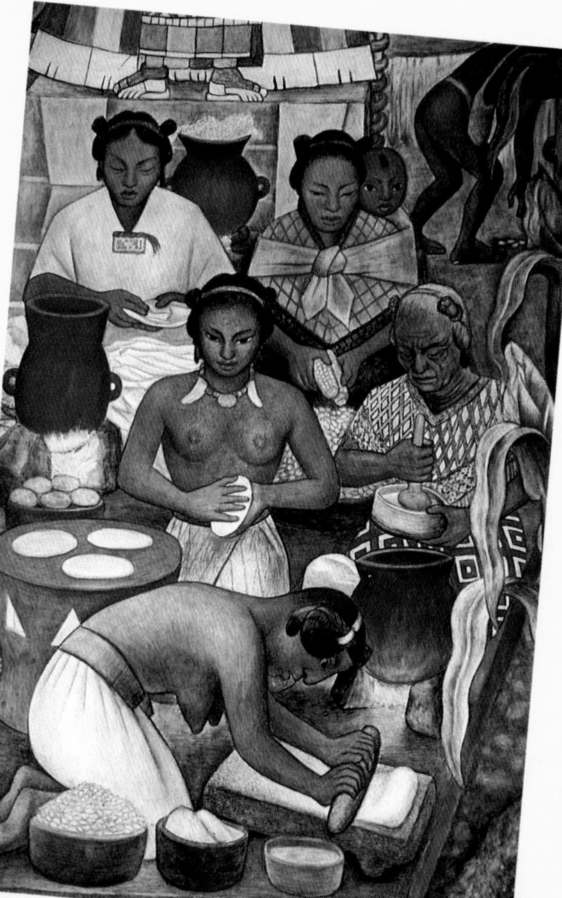

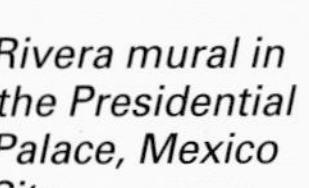

Rivera mural in the Presidential Palace, Mexico City

Frida Kahlo (1907–1954)

Children's band outside the basilica

Vision of the Virgin
On December 9, 1531 Juan Diego, a humble Indian, was walking to church in Tlatelolco over Tepeyac hill when he was stopped by a vision of the Virgin. Speaking in the Náhautl language, she ordered him to have a church built on the spot. Reporting back to the local bishop, Diego was treated with some skepticism, but on December 12 the Virgin reappeared, asking him to take roses to the Bishop as proof. This he did, but on opening his cloak before the Bishop to show them found in their place an image of the dark-skinned Virgin imprinted on the cloth. Named after the statue of the black-faced Nuestra Señora de Guadalupe found in 13th-century Spain, said to have been carved by St. Luke himself, her image has been adopted by thousands of churches all over Mexico, and December 12 remains a high point in the religious calendar. The shrine is the object of year-round pilgrimages.

Image of the Virgin of Guadalupe

►► Basilica de Nuestra Señora de Guadalupe (Church of Our Lady of Guadalupe) *65B3*

Metro: Basilica, La Villa

This should be a priority destination, if only to understand Mexico's obsession with her patron saint, the Virgen de Guadalupe. Two churches bear her name: the first, dating from 1533, though later completely remodeled, stands on Tepeyac hill and has now become the **Museo de la Basilica de Guadalupe►**; the second, built in 1976, is a gigantic, dramatic construction which now houses the much revered cloak imprinted with the Virgin's image. This is displayed over the main altar: closer views are aided by a mechanized walkway which spirits visitors under the altar. Set around the enormous stone plaza and up the hill are numerous other shrines and chapels, usually thronging with pilgrims and vendors of religious sou-

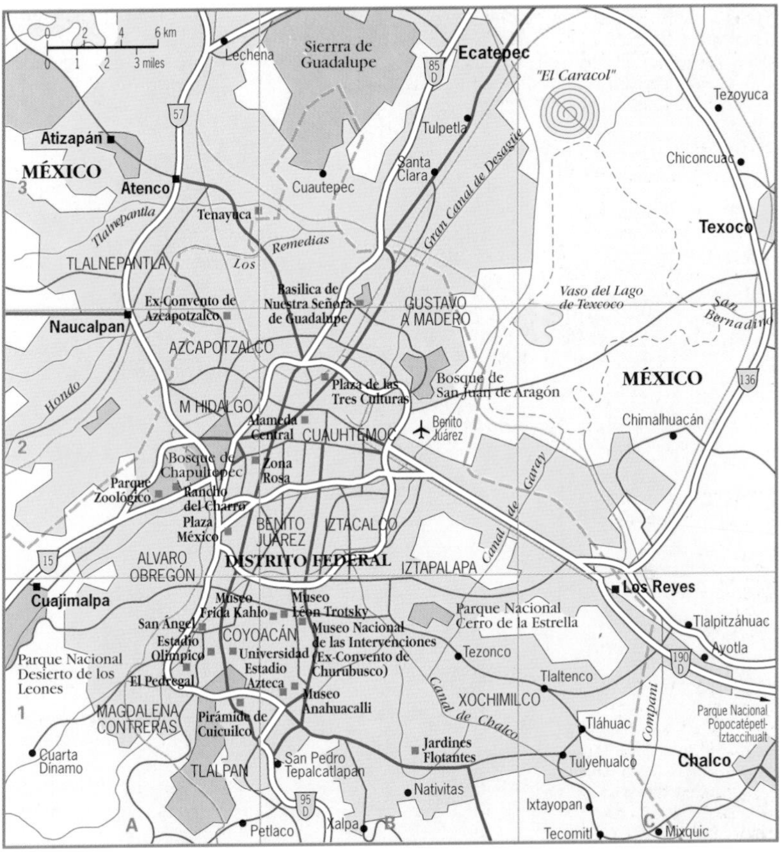

Mexico City environs

venirs. The spectacular basilica design is a creation of Pedro Ramírez Vázquez, also responsible for the Museum of Anthroplogy.

▶ Plaza de las Tres Culturas (Square of the Three Cultures) 65B2

Metro: Tlatelolco

This large square represents the meeting of three cultures—Aztec, Spanish, and modern Mexican. Located in Tlatelolco, it stands over what was once a gigantic Aztec market-place selling goods from all over Mexico. The ruins of Tlatelolco's main pyramid and other temple structures can be seen from a raised walkway, while in the center of the square a plaque recalls the Aztecs' last stand on August 13, 1521. Sensitive to Tlatetolco's significance, the Spanish built a church and Franciscan monastery before erecting San Diego in 1609. Unfortunately the Mexican aspect of this trio of cultures is less impressive. Modern buildings lining the plaza include the Ministry of Foreign Affairs, but are hardly the best exponents of contemporary Mexican architecture. Not to be forgotten in this context are the events of October 1968 (see page 47), when government troops fired on thousands of student demonstrators in the square, leaving an unknown number dead, including children.

Altarpiece, Cathedral of Guadalupe

Cortés and Cuauhtémoc
Inside the Casa de Cortés are two Rivera murals depicting the conquest, imprisonment, and torture of Emperor Cuauhtémoc, the last of the Aztec lineage. It was here that the 25-year-old emperor was held and tortured by Cortés to reveal the hiding-place of the great Aztec treasure, much coveted by the Spaniards. From here Cuauhtémoc was taken to Tabasco where he was killed.

Coyoacán

►►► Coyoacán 65A1

The pretty suburb of Coyoacán, a leafy retreat 5 miles south of Mexico City's roaring central hub, was under Aztec domination before Cortés moved in to watch Tenochtitlán's destruction. Many of Mexico's high society, former presidents and intellectuals live there today, following in the footsteps of Frida Kahlo, Diego Rivera, and León Trotsky, whose museums constitute three high points. The relaxed, student-like atmosphere (the university campus is not far) peaks on Sundays around the central **Plaza Hidalgo►►►** and adjoining **Jardín Centenario,** which throng with musicians, crafts-people and strolling Mexican families. On the northern side of the square stands the 18th-century **Casa de Cortés** opposite the **Parroquía de San Juan Bautista** which, with its adjoining former Dominican monastery, dates from 1582, but was heavily reconstructed in 1804. The main artery, **Avenida Francisco Sosa►►** runs west from here past the pink domes of the **Centro Cultural Coyoacán►►**, numerous beautiful colonial homes, lively local restaurants, and the charming **Plaza Santa Caterina►►**, to culminate at Avenida Universidad.

Casa de Cortés, Coyoacán

► Ex-Convento de Churubusco 65B1

Calle 20 de Agosto
Metro: General Anaya
The beautiful 17th-century monastery of Churubusco, scene of one of Mexico's most important military defeats at the hands of American forces in 1847, now houses a large museum (the Museo Nacional de las Intervenciones) covering not only foreign incursions into Mexico (U.S., Spain, France), but also more recent nation-alist expansionism worldwide. The U.S. stands strongly in the firing-line here.

►►► Museo Anahuacalli (House of Anáhuac) 65B1

Calle del Museo 150
Metro: Tasqueña, then taxi
This museum, dramatically situated on the southern edge of Coyoacán overlooking the volcanoes beyond, encapsu-

lates Rivera's imagination and identification with Mesoamerican cultures. He designed the labyrinthine lava-stone edifice to house his extensive collection of artifacts, as well as to incorporate an open studio where he briefly worked before his death in 1957, leaving some works in progress. Somewhere between a mausoleum and a fortress, the architecture combines dark corridors with onyx windows, staircases with open terraces and apertures, stone ceiling mosaics, arches, niches, and stepped altar-like displays. Within this extraordinary structure are some superb pieces representing most of Mexico's pre-Hispanic cultures, with the top floor devoted to the Aztecs. The name means "House of Anáhuac," Anáhuac being the Valley of Mexico, and it truly fits this description.

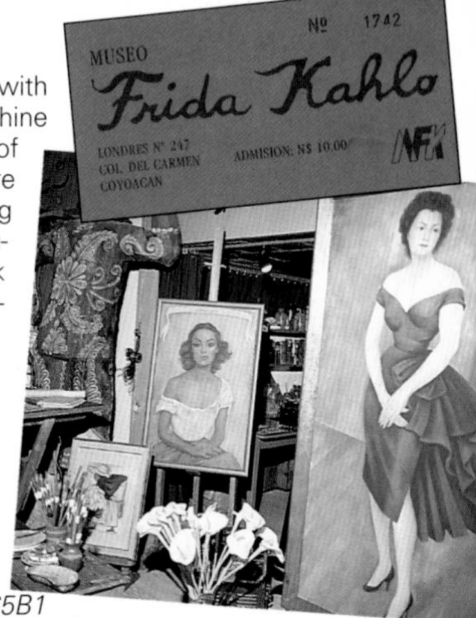

Diego Rivera's studio in San Ángel

►►► Museo Frida Kahlo (Frida Kahlo Museum) *65B1*

Calle Londres 247
Metro: Coyoacán
Deep indigo and terracotta walls picked out with green window-frames announce the former home and studio of eccentric, flamboyant, and talented Frida Kahlo, the most respected of Diego Rivera's wives (see pages 62–63). A lifetime of frenetic intellectual and artistic activity is reflected in the paintings and memorabilia of her birthplace and home, where brilliant color covers every wall and shelf, spilling into the deep green foliage of the luxuriant garden. Paintings by friends including Duchamp, Klee, and Tanguy hang beside showcases of her eclectic collections of masks, Teotihuacán sculptures, 19th-century ex-votos (votive offerings), glass, lacquerware, and ceramics. Her wheelchair and last unfinished painting (a portrait of Stalin), Rivera's famous hat and overalls and a neat accounts book all contribute to the atmosphere of this powerful personal museum.

Life on the run
A first assassination attempt on Léon Trotsky was made in May 1940 by an armed gang, presumed to have been led by the painter David Alfaro Siqueiros. Trotsky and his wife managed to survive this bloody attack by hiding under their beds. The second, this time successful, attempt was engineered by Ramon Mercader del Río, a Spanish Stalinist agent who gained the confidence of the Trotsky household and finally ended Trotsky's life with an ice-pick on August 20, 1940. Mercader was arrested and imprisoned. Trotsky's widow remained in the house until 1961, when she moved to Paris, dying a year later.

►► Museo Léon Trotsky (Léon Trotsky Museum) *65B1*

Calle Viena 45
Metro: Coyoacán
The fortress-home of Trotsky, from May 1939 until his assassination in August 1940, offers another fascinating psychological insight in the heart of residential Coyoacán. After fleeing Stalin, Trotsky was offered asylum by Mexico's President Lázaro Cárdenas and settled here with his wife Natalia, near their friends Rivera and Kahlo. This gloomy, delapidated edifice, much bricked up and fortified due to his justified paranoia about attempted assailants, nevertheless reflects his disciplined existence and interests, ranging from the poultry yard in the garden to his study and bedroom pockmarked with bullet-holes. His tomb, designed by Juan O'Gorman and topped by a red flag, hammer and sickle, stands in the garden.

Léon Trotsky's study—just as he left it

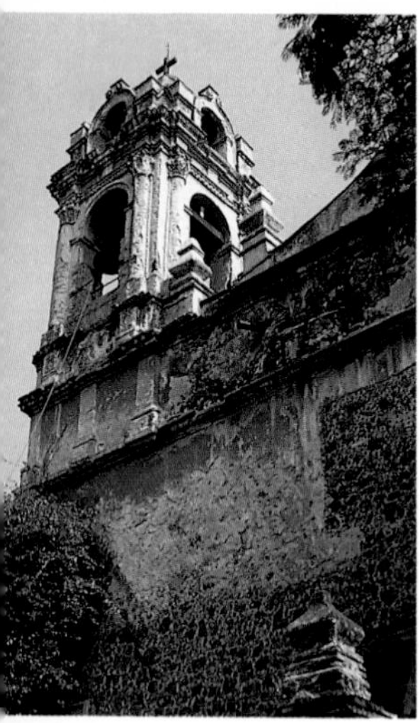

San Jacinto monastery

Desierto de los Leones
From the heart of San Ángel the Camino al Desierto de los Leones winds 15 miles west up into a national park of the same name. Pine-forest trails make it a favorite Sunday picnic destination for the capital's hordes in their desperate search for fresh air. Culture, in the form of concerts and exhibitions, is offered at a beautiful 17th-century Carmelite monastery, set in pretty gardens within the park.

Ruins of the 17th-century monastery of Desierto de los Leones

San Ángel

▶▶▶ San Ángel *65A1*

Bus: "San Ángel" *pesero* down Insurgentes

San Ángel is an exclusive residential area and a favorite tourist destination. Like neighboring Coyoacán, it makes a welcome, slow-paced change from the city center. It was originally an Aztec town named Chimalistac, later becoming a popular retreat for the city's wealthier classes. Packed with historical buildings, cafés, shops, and restaurants, its cobblestone streets and flowery patios wind around and outwards from the central hubs of Plaza de Carmen and Plaza San Jacinto.

▶▶ Museo de Arte Carillo Gil (Carillo Gil Art Museum) *69C2*

Avenida Revolución 1608

Metro: Viveros, then bus 43

Located on the northeastern edge of San Ángel, this pristine art museum and gallery displays an impressive private collection of contemporary Mexican and international art and Japanese prints, along with a video room, bookstore and a corner café. Mexico's big three (Rivera, Siqueiros, and Orozco) are well represented, including some unusual Cubist-inspired early works by Rivera, and Orozco's powerful *El Muerto* (1925–1928). Contemporary works move strongly into conceptual mode with one section devoted to computer-generated works.

▶▶▶ Museo del Carmen (Carmen Museum) *69C1*

Avenida Revolución

Bus: "San Ángel" *pesero* down Insurgentes

The tile-domed church and adjoining monks' quarters were built as a Carmelite monastery between 1615 and 1617, surrounding a pretty cloister garden which nurtures banana palms. Heavy studded wooden doors, delicate floral friezes on the embrasures, superb wood and gesso ceiling reliefs in the sacristy and Moorish tiles and frescos in the crypt contribute to the architectural feast. The important collection of religious art is particularly rich in 18th-century Baroque sculptures, but for many the highlight is down in the basement crypt where there is a room full of anonymous mummified bodies in glass-topped cases.

▶▶ Museo Estudio Diego Rivera (Diego Rivera Studio Museum) *69A2*

Calle Diego Rivera/Altavista

Metro: Viveros, then bus 43

Rivera and Kahlo's studio was designed by Juan O'Gorman in 1930, and this brightly colored functionalist structure preserves Rivera's jumbled studio and tiny bedroom upstairs, while lower areas are used for temporary exhibitions. The most interesting room is the artist's large studio. Pigments, clippings, photos, and masks are randomly exhibited beside his fleece-lined boots, ubiquitous denim jacket and a showcase of pre-Hispanic artifacts, reflecting the eclectic interests of this genius who died here on November 24, 1957.

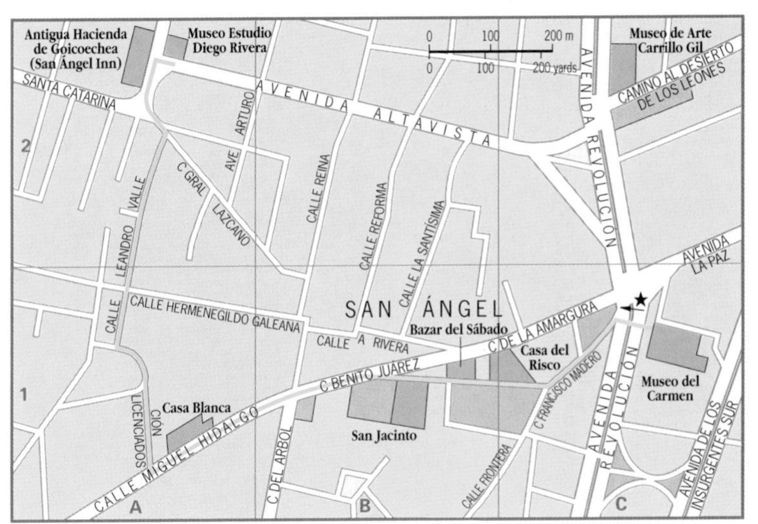

Walk San Ángel

This exploration of the elegant and historical suburb of San Ángel (see opposite), at its liveliest on a Saturday morning, finishes at the famous old San Ángel Inn. Allow 2 to 3 hours to visit monuments on the way.

Start from the domed church and museum of the **Museo del Carmen**, then walk past the Plaza del Carmen along Calle Francisco Madero to the central **Plaza de San Jacinto**, where a hive of Indian vendors and local painters exhibit their wares on Saturdays. On the right is the 18th-century **Casa del Risco** whose courtyard fountain is a riot of ceramic tiles, plates, and encrusted shells: upstairs rooms house a museum of colonial art. A little further is the **Bazar del Sábado**, an indoor crafts market open only on Saturdays and joined by an outdoor market at the northwest end of the plaza. Follow the cobbled Calle Benito Juárez west to the 16th-century church and former monastery of **San Jacinto**, unmistakable for its formal courtyard and bougainvillaea-draped walls. This colorful street lined with elegant town houses becomes the Calle Miguel Hidalgo as it leads into the heart of residential San Ángel. Walk past the 17th-century **Casa Blanca** on your right, a national monument but not open to the public, and take the next right. Brightly painted fortress-like walls surround many private properties in a patchwork of architectural styles as Calle Leandro Valle leads downhill to the junction with Avenida Altavista. Opposite stands the **Museo Estudio Diego Rivera**. At the superb 18th-century *hacienda* housing the **San Ángel Inn** you can have a drink or lunch.

San Ángel Inn

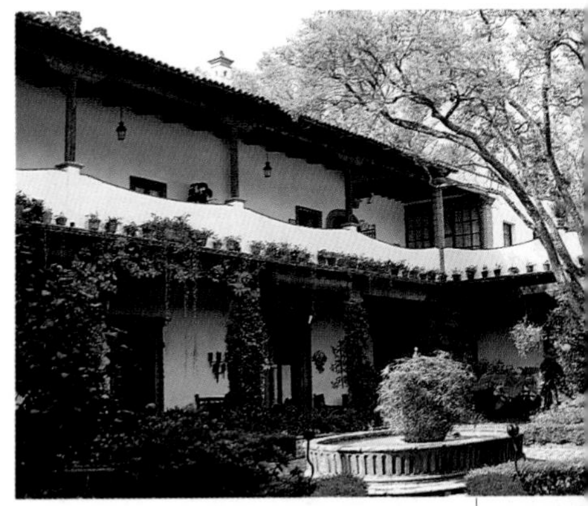

El Pedregal
Immediately south of San Ángel, and stretching through the University to Coyoacán, lies an area known as El Pedregal. It came into being about 2,000 years ago when the Xitle volcano erupted in great lava waves which eventually solidified into over 15 sq mi of craggy crevices and caverns. In 1945 the architect Luís Barragán developed a Utopian project to create a residential area which respected the existing lava formations and extraordinary natural vegetation. After creating three showcase gardens he laid out rigorous building restrictions, but these were not followed and although by 1960 El Pedregal contained more than 900 houses, few of them respected the founding vision.

Flower seller (above) and colorful punts on the canals at Xochimilco

▶ Pirámide de Cuicuilco *65A1*

Bus: from Ciudad Universitaria or San Ángel to "Cuicuilco"
Further south down Insurgentes, just beyond the intersection with the *periférico*, lie the remains of an important settlement, abandoned when Xitle erupted between 100BC and AD100. The main pyramid, tiered, circular and surmounted by an altar, is easily visible from the road, although now encircled by high-rise housing. Retrieved from beneath 32 ft. of lava, the pyramid is part of what is believed to have been a major residential and ceremonial site—other structures have been uncovered at the nearby Olympic Village. A small museum displays artifacts and information on the area.

▶ Universidad Nacional Autonoma de México (UNAM) *65A1*

Metro: Copilco
Latin America's oldest and largest university lies south of San Ángel and Coyoacán on the great lava field of El Pedregal. Although founded in the 1550s, the university campus (Ciudad Universitaria) dates from the early 1950s. Today over 300,000 students frequent what at the time was a particularly avant-garde complex, its landmark being the library designed by Juan O'Gorman. This 12-story block is entirely faced in a mural of natural stones, tile and glass illustrating Mexican history. Siqueiros, too, is represented by a vast mosaic frieze occupying the south wall of the Rectory, located near the university arts and science museum, while José Chávez Morado is responsible for the walls of the science building.

▶▶ Xochimilco *65B1*

Metro: Tasqueña then bus "Xochimilco"
Euphemistically described as "floating gardens," Xochimilco is in fact a network of polluted canals (now being cleaned up) running through fertile farmland lined with *chinampas* (firmly rooted rafts of reeds) used to grow flowers and vegetables. Xochimilco offers a clear vision of what Mexico City was like in Aztec times when Tenochtitlán was entirely built on a lake and transportation was by canoe. It is a favorite Sunday afternoon excursion for city-dwellers, offering tours on brightly painted boats, cruising *mariachis* (street bands) and Indian women selling *tortillas*, corn-on-the-cob, fruit and flowers from tiny canoes. Weekdays are quieter, but lack the high Mexican energy charge of the weekends.

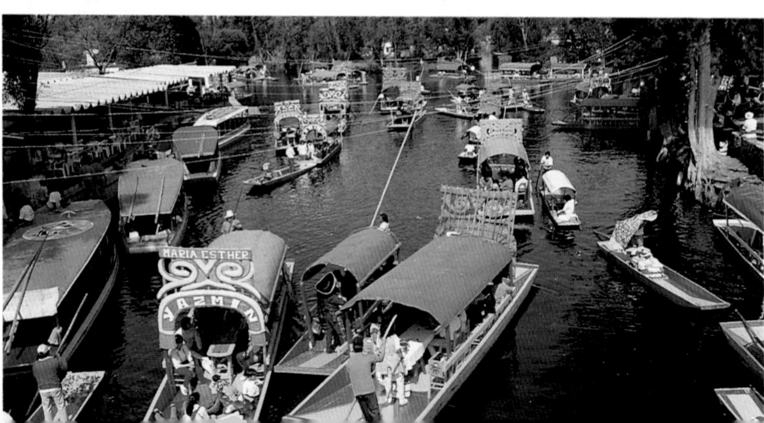

Accommodations

Visitors arriving in Mexico City will have no trouble finding accommodations, whatever the time of year and whatever their budget. Hotels range from the luxury giants and a few rare colonial beauties, to more basic establishments north, west, and south of the Zócalo. For details of hotels see page 270.

Luxury locations Mexico City's most luxurious hotels are clustered just north of Chapultepec Park in the residential area of Polanco. The dramatic 1960s architecture of the **Camino Real** is still a show-stopper, and its internal facilities include numerous restaurants, discos, pools, and tennis courts. The **Stouffer Presidente**'s well-appointed rooms also command panoramic views over the park. The latest addition is the towering Japanese **Hotel Nikko Mexico**. Closer to the historic center, on the Paseo de la Reforma, are a string of modern international hotels at more accessible prices. These include the **Holiday Inn Crowne Plaza**, the **María Isabel Sheraton** and the **Hotel Marquis Reforma**. Those looking for more personalized luxury should aim for the **Emporio**, recently upgraded to include Jacuzzis in every room. In the Zona Rosa, the **Galería Plaza** offers tranquility, good service and a popular nightclub, while the glass-fronted **Krystal Rosa**, popular with tour groups, maintains consistently high standards.

Middle range At the top of this category are two of Mexico City's best located hotels. The **Howard Johnson Gran Hotel** is a marvel of Art Nouveau design, with a soaring central lobby, open ironwork elevator and stained-glass roof. On the corner of Madero, the **Majestic** is housed in a former Spanish mansion, with a panoramic rooftop restaurant. A favorite with regular visitors is the **María Cristina**, just north of Reforma and the Zona Rosa. The delightful patio and garden of this pretty colonial-style hotel make it a welcome retreat from modern urban life. In a similar vein, though more imposing, the **Hotel de Cortés**, on the northern edge of Alameda park, was built as an 18th-century hospice for Augustinian monks. Their cells have been modernized, although rooms can be dark. The large **Hotel Casa Blanca**, just off Reforma, offers spacious rooms, a rooftop pool and good amenities.

Bottom range Hotels around the Zócalo are good for budget travelers. Those with a historical bent should make for the **Hotel Monte Carlo**, built as a monastery and once home to D. H. Lawrence. Just around the corner from the Templo Mayor is the clean, modern **Hotel Catedral**, while a few blocks north is the large, reasonably-priced **Hotel Antillas**. A cluster of budget hotels, dotted west of the Zócalo along Cinco de Mayo near metro Allende, include the **Hotel Canada** and the **Hotel New York**. Even the Zona Rosa has a charming old hotel, the **Vasco de Quiroga**, which, although at the top of the budget category, offers excellent value.

Cost factors
Upper-bracket hotel prices in Mexico City usually include a 15 percent tax, and in middle- to top-range hotels tipping is expected. By law, rates are posted either in the lobby or room, or both. In the off-season you may be able to negotiate a discount, or benefit from a special offer, but this is more common outside the capital. Remember to make use of the hotel's safe if it has one.

Hotel María Cristina

Comfort factors
One thing to bear in mind when booking a room is the decibel level. Mexico City's inner streets and boulevards can be very noisy, so always inspect a room before checking in. This goes for any other large town. In middle-range hotels televisions tend to take priority over phones, while showers, rather than bathtubs, are the rule everywhere except in top establishments. Even bottom-range hotels nearly always supply drinking-water (*agua purificada*) either in carafes in the room or in a corridor demijohn.

Bars and restaurants

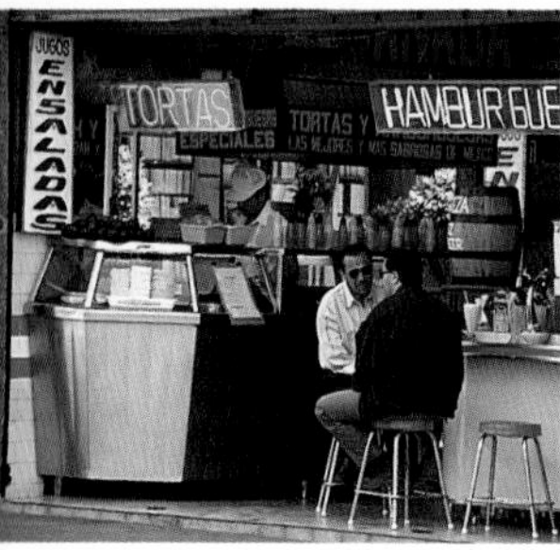

Taking a quick snack in a street café

Mexico City offers the widest range of international cuisine in the country, so profit from it before setting off on the *taco* and *tortilla* trail. It also has a diverse price range, from street-corner *taco*-stands to elegant establishments all over the city. Lunch is the main meal, starting around 2 p.m., and dragging on till dusk at weekends. This is the ideal time to witness Mexican family outings, whether in the southern suburbs of Coyoacán and San Ángel, or in some of the central historical settings. Many typical restaurants close early in the evening, so if you are intent on dinner phone beforehand (see pages 280–281 for details).

Historic hits Plunge into Mexico's *belle époque* past at the **Bar l'Opéra**, a Parisian-style bar and brasserie complete with carved mahogany and mirrored décor, just behind the Bellas Artes. Popular with the artsy crowd for after-theater drinks, it also offers meals, but these are slow to come and not the city's greatest. Similar in style is **Prendes**, dating back to 1892, whose walls are lined with images of former patrons—from Pancho Villa to Walt Disney—and which still dishes up mountains of paella and hearty Mexican fare. Another institution is the **Café Tacuba** which opened its doors in 1912 in a former monastery and has hardly changed since, leaving tiled walls and brass lamps intact, with a menu offering typical Mexican dishes. Close by is the more formal, but no less atmospheric, **Hostería de Santo Domingo**, a favorite family and *mariachi* destination at the weekend. Claiming to be the city's oldest restaurant—it dates from the 1860s—it offers excellent Mexican specialties and lots of atmosphere.

Café Tacuba is set in an old monastery with original fixtures and fittings still in place

For seafood served in colonial surroundings, head for the **Restaurant Centro Castellano**, southeast of the Alameda. This huge, three-floor establishment specializes in fresh red snapper and octopus, as well as kid (goat) and other meat dishes. Closer to Alameda, the unique **Casa de Azulejos** houses a branch of **Sanborns** in its spectacular Moorish patio: Mexican cuisine prevails at reasonable prices.

Zona Rosa International Vegetarian, Japanese, Italian, and Chinese cuisine jostles with more traditional fare in the Zona Rosa's haunts, not necessarily the city's most expensive. Pedestrian streets add to the attraction, allowing many restaurants to spill onto the sidewalk. The award-winning **Fonda El Refugio** offers Mexican specialties in a lively setting. Those bitten by the *mariachi* bug should head for **Carrousel International**, a relaxed bar/restaurant which serves drinks, snacks, and meals to familiar local sounds and is open till midnight. For diners missing *haute cuisine*, try the **Champs-Elysées**: it is *the* place to be seen in Mexico City, much frequented by politicians, and its food is on a par with top French restaurants. Similarly Gallic in style is the amusing though ostentatious **Les Moustaches**, located across Reforma. Apart from the fact that every waiter has a moustache, it offers a wide-ranging menu of international cuisine and high prices. More reasonable, but equally European, is **La Gondola,** which has a pleasant outdoor section and serves good, fresh Italian food.

This Mexico City institution is housed in an attractive restored 19th-century mansion

San Ángel and Coyoacán If you are not booked at the elegant **San Ángel Inn**, dine at the more relaxed and cheaper **Fonda San Ángel**, located right on the Plaza San Jacinto, popular throughout the day and evening. Just east of Insurgentes is another of the capital's exclusive establishments, **Los Irabiens**, which serves what could be classed as *nouvelle cuisine Mexicaine* in an up-market setting filled with contemporary art. Moving into Coyoacán, head straight for **Café El Parnaso** between the central squares, a long-standing intellectual café with a bookshop. For more substantial fare head back towards the Jardín Santa Caterina, where you can choose between the bustling **Hostería Santa Caterina** or the friendly **Las Lupitas**, both popular neighborhood restaurants serving good homey fare.

Restaurant with a view
Take in the pastoral delights of Chapultepec Park from a restaurant overlooking the fountain of the Lago Mayor in the western section of the park (beyond the wide Anillo Periférico which dissects the park north–south). The high-standard international menu of the Lago Chapultepec, completely remodeled in 1990, is backed up by good service and a pianist. Open till late at night, its delights unfortunately do not come cheap.

Cantinas* and *mariachis
Coyoacán's main square is the lively El Hijo del Cuervo, with its friendly atmosphere. In the historic city center aim for Plaza Garibaldi, which throbs to the tunes of local *mariachis* from nightfall until the early hours. Bars line the square, the most popular being the Tenampa, the ideal place for a shot of *tequila*. However uproarious the atmosphere, care should be taken with wallets, particularly later in the evening. *Tequila* also flows at Los Portales, a vast, tiled hall with dusty chandeliers on Calle Bolívar.

Shopping

Modern Mexico
The Galería Mexicana de Diseño (Calle Anatole France 13, metro: Reforma) is devoted to exhibitions of contemporary Mexican design. Equally 20th-century are the items and gadgets on sale at the Centro Cultural Contemporáneo (next to the Stouffer Presidente Hotel in Polanco), where the Mexican TV company Televisa sponsors major exhibitions of contemporary art. The gift shop here offers plenty of imaginative, often witty items.

Above: the Iron Palace department store
Right: Ciudadela market

Antique Mexico
Many of Mexico City's antique dealers trade in the Zona Rosa, in particular around the Plaza del Ángel. On weekends the interior plaza is filled with expensive antique stands, enticingly eclectic on Saturdays and more specialized on Sundays, particularly for antiquarian books and maps. Calle Estocolmo also harbors a number of antique shops, a good place to gaze at superb Talavera vases.

Often optimistically over-priced, Mexico City's markets are not always the best options. Better purchases can sometimes be found in specialist shops, where quality is also assured. The obvious buys are handicrafts, a diverse, living tradition that originates from every region of the country and is well represented in the capital.

City center Two good addresses are located within walking distance of each other near the Alameda Central. The large shop in the **Museo de Arte e Industrias Populares** (Avenida Juárez 44) displays a wide range of ceramics, glass, woodwork, weaving, embroidery, and countless other products from regional Mexico, while at No. 89, **Fonart** (Fondación Nacional de Artesanía) offers a similar, though slightly smaller selection. More reasonably priced and open to haggling is the sprawling **Mercado de la Ciudadela** on the corner of Calle Balderas and Plaza de la Ciudadela (metro: Balderas). This is the city's best treasure trove of *huipiles* (tunics), *rebozos* (shawls), Taxco silver, papier-mâché, glass, and guitars, and on the sidewalks lining the approach you can take your pick from second-hand books or cheap watches. In the Zona Rosa, the local **Mercado de Londrés** (Calle Londrés 154) mixes handicrafts with vegetable stalls and snack bars, but is overtly geared to well-heeled tourists.

Further afield Flea-market addicts should reserve Sunday for **La Lagunilla market** (corner of Comonfort and Rayón, metro: Guerrero), where craftwork and clothes are sold alongside anything remotely aging. This is also the day when young craftspeople sell their wares in Coyoacán's Plaza Hidalgo. Saturday is a favorite in San Ángel, when the **Bazar Sábado** throngs with visitors, Indian women set up their wares on the sidewalks, artists mount their easels in the square and the outdoor market springs into action. However, for real authenticity, go to the **Mercado de Sonora** on Fray Servando Teresa de Mier (metro: La Merced). Here pottery, toys, miniatures, and a weird and wonderful selection of medicinal plants and herbal fetishes set the tone.

Nightlife

To follow the capital's agenda of nocturnal activities, check the schedules in the weekly *Tiempo Libre* or the *Mexico City News*. Hardly the world's wildest city in terms of nightlife, the capital nevertheless has some firm favorites which add greatly to understanding the Mexicans and, quite simply, to having a good time.

Watching The scurrilous Saturday-night cabaret of **El Habito** in Coyoacán (tel: 524 2481 for reservations) only opened in 1990 but is already firmly entrenched in the city agenda. Visitors should have a good grasp of Spanish in order to follow its satirical twists. During the week the cabaret sometimes hosts blues or jazz singers, a rarity elsewhere in town. The **Ballet Folklórico** performs on Sunday mornings and on some weekday nights at the Bellas Artes between opera or concert performances. Colorful swirling skirts and stomping boots create a wonderful panorama of regional folk dances, supported by Mexico's much loved marimbas, guitars, trumpets, flutes, and drums. Costumes, choreography, lighting, and highly trained dancers make this a sophisticated taste of what you may come across in a more authentic form and setting traveling round the country. Tickets can be bought at the Bellas Artes or tel: 529 9320/7805 for information. The **Teatro de la Ciudad** (Donceles 36, tel: 510 2197) occasionally stages a rival folk dance company.

The ever-popular Ballet Folklórico

Participating The **Bar León** offers great sounds and a large dance-hall behind an uninspiring façade on Calle Brasil, thumping out a Latin-style beat till 3 a.m. An equally popular venue is the **Bar Veracruz** on Calle Veracruz behind the Bellas Artes. Flashier nightclubs can be found in any of the top hotels, notably the Camino Real's **Cero Cero** or the Presidente's **Club 84**. The Zona Rosa lures the capital's yuppy crowds, especially between Thursday and Saturday: **Valentino's** at Florencia 36 is a favorite for its non-stop dance music. Those with a penchant for the bizarre should make for **Catacumbas** (Calle Dolores 16), where a horror-movie theme inspires good salsa and reggae. Most of these clubs have low cover charges but high prices for drinks.

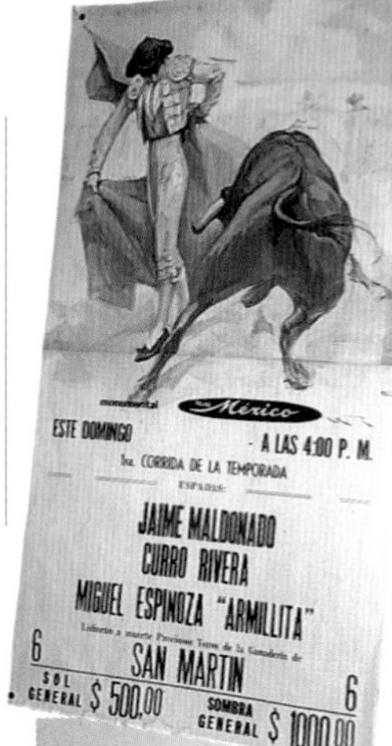

Bullfights
An alternative to dancing the night away is watching matadors dance with bulls. High season is December to March when top bullfighters perform, but the rest of the year novices display their growing talents in the face of smaller bulls. Bullfights are staged most Sundays from 4 p.m. at the immense Plaza México, just off Insurgentes, halfway to San Ángel—the bullring is the world's largest and holds up to 50,000 spectators! It's easiest to buy tickets in advance through your hotel or an agency.

Movies
The city's movie theaters show a reasonable range of international films, sometimes subtitled (marked VO—*version original*), but don't expect plush seating. At the Ciudad Universitaria there is a good movie-club which shows avant-garde films, although this is a bit of a trek from the center in the evening. More central theaters showing English-language films are the Cinéteca and the Filmoteca: check the weekly schedules.

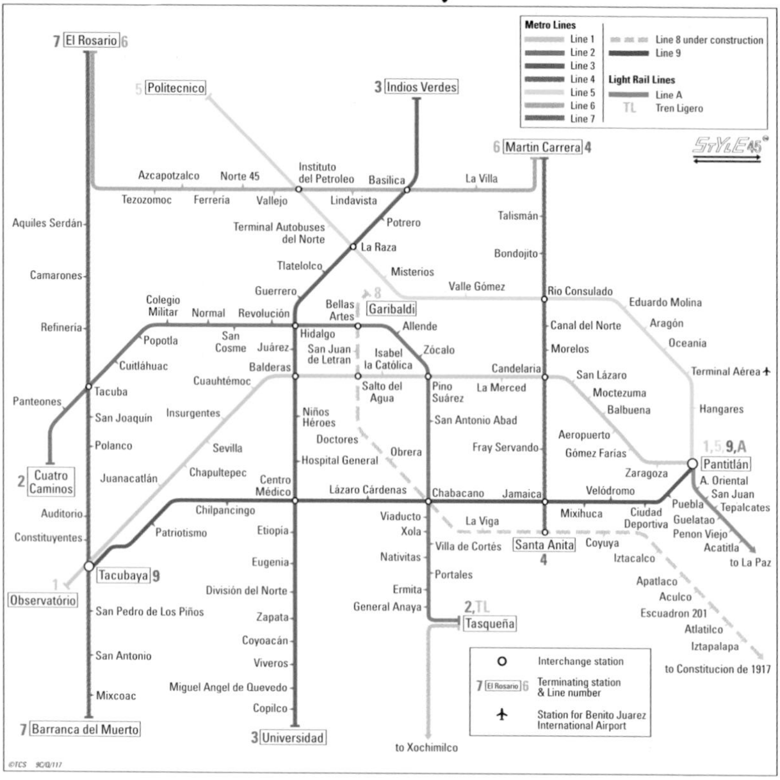

Metro Lines
Line 1
Line 2
Line 3
Line 4
Line 5
Line 6
Line 7
Line 8 under construction
Line 9
Light Rail Lines
Line A
TL Tren Ligero

STYLE 45

7 El Rosario 6
5 Politecnico
3 Indios Verdes
6 Martin Carrera 4
Azcapotzalco
Norte 45
Instituto del Petroleo
Basílica
La Villa
Tezozomoc
Ferreria
Vallejo
Lindavista
Aquiles Serdán
Talismán
Potrero
Terminal Autobuses del Norte
La Raza
Bondojito
Camarones
Tlatelolco
Misterios
Valle Gómez
Rio Consulado
Eduardo Molina
Guerrero
Colegio Militar
Normal
Revolución
Bellas Artes
8 Garibaldi
Refinería
Allende
Canal del Norte
Aragón
Oceania
Popotla
San Cosme
Juárez
Hidalgo
San Juan de Letran
Isabel la Católica
Zócalo
Morelos
Cuitláhuac
Balderas
Candelaria
San Lázaro
Terminal Aérea
Cuauhtémoc
Salto del Agua
Pino Suárez
La Merced
Moctezuma
Tacuba
Panteones
Balbuena
Hangares
San Joaquín
Insurgentes
Niños Héroes
San Antonio Abad
Aeropuerto
Doctores
Polanco
Sevilla
Obrera
Fray Servando
Gómez Farías
1,5,9,A Pantitlán
Hospital General
2 Cuatro Caminos
Juanacatlán
Chapultepec
Centro Médico
Lázaro Cárdenas
Chabacano
Jamaica
Velódromo
Zaragoza
A. Oriental
San Juan
Chilpancingo
Puebla
Tepalcates
Auditorio
Viaducto
La Viga
Mixihuca
Ciudad Deportiva
Guelatao
Patriotismo
Etiopía
Xola
Penon Viejo
Constituyentes
Villa de Cortés
Santa Anita 4
Coyuya
Acatitla
Nativitas
Iztacalco
to La Paz
Eugenia
1 Observatório
Tacubaya 9
Portales
Apatlaco
División del Norte
Ermita
Aculco
San Pedro de Los Piños
General Anaya
2,TL Tasqueña
Escuadron 201
Zapata
Atlatilco
Coyoacán
Iztapalapa
San Antonio
Viveros
to Constitucion de 1917
Miguel Angel de Quevedo
Mixcoac
Copilco
7 Barranca del Muerto
3 Universidad
to Xochimilco

Interchange station
7 El Rosario 6 Terminating station & Line number
Station for Benito Juarez International Airport

©TCS 90/Q/117

Mexico City—metro

76

Transportation Getting around the world's largest metropolis is actually a lot simpler than you might expect. Public transportation is excellent and easy to use, while taxis spring out of every *calle* or plaza. The metro is based on the Parisian system and is eminently user-friendly. Tickets are sold at every metro station: just insert the ticket at the entrance turnstile. Avoid rush-hours (roughly 8 to 9 a.m., 2 to 3 p.m. and 6 to 7 p.m.) as the crush facilitates the work of pickpockets.

White mini-buses (*peseros*), often blasting loud rock-music, tear along the main arteries, stopping at main street corners. Their routes are identified by destination plaques, usually metro stations, and the set flat fare is paid directly to the driver. Taxis, when not the pricey black limousines lying in wait outside big hotels, are predominantly V.W. Beetles with their front seats ripped out. The green ones are more ecologically correct since they run on *magna sin* (unleaded petrol). Make sure the meter is switched on and that

One of Mexico City's ubiquitous green taxis

Tourist help
The federal district tourist office is located in the Zona Rosa at Amberes 54 (metro: Insurgentes) and is open between 9 a.m. and 9 p.m. English-speaking staff can provide maps, brochures and general information, and you can also pick up the free *Daily Bulletin*, a useful events guide. A free phone service, Infotur, is theoretically available on 525 9380 for any queries about the city, but the line is often busy. A useful 24-hour emergency service (LO.CATEL) can be dialed on 658 1111, or go to their bright pink offices at Florencia 20, just off El Ángel in the Zona Rosa. Their bilingual staff will help with any problem, particularly stolen or lost property, as well as emo-

Tourist sightseeing tram—an easy option for getting around

you have change: this is often an excuse for rounding up the price. Tips are not essential. Remember, too, that the same street names crop up again and again all over the city, so make sure you know what *colonia* or *barrio* your destination is in and, even better, the nearest metro station or large intersections.

Money and security For changing travelers' checks or cash, the best rates are available at several Casas de Cambio on the Paseo de la Reforma around El Ángel, the Independence monument. Banks may offer marginally higher rates but their frustratingly protracted transactions cancel out any benefit. Cash dispensers at Banamex and Bancomer branches accept VISA cards. Avoid carrying large amounts of cash and be especially careful when using the metro, at bus stations, or wandering around markets.

Long-distance buses at Mexico City's largest bus station, Terminal Norte

TIJUANA
Tecate
2
Mexicali
Rosarito
4
Sierra de Juárez
5
San Luis
Río Colorado
Ensenada
Golfo de
Santa Clara
3
Sonoyta
Cabo
Colonet
San Vicente
Puerto
Peñasco
2
Sierra San Pedro Mártir
San Felipe
Nogales
San Quintín
Baja California
15
Cobarca
Agua Prieta
2
Ciudad
Juárez
Cananea
Janos
El Rosario
El Desemboque
Santa Ana
45
Nuevo
Casas
Grandes
Bravo del Norte
3
Ahumada
Desierto
de Cataviña
Nacozari
de García
Casas
Grandes
Bavispe
Ricardo
Flores
Magón
Bahía de
los Ángeles
Ures
Ojinaga
Punta Prieta
Isla del
Tiburón
Hermosillo
Sierra Madre
Sahuaripa
Madera
16
Bahía Kino
Sonora
Conchos
Cascada de
Basaseáchic
Bahía
Isla Cedros
San Sebastián
Vizcaíno
15
Yaqui
Aldama
Chihuahua
Golfo de California (Mar de Cortés)
San
Carlos
Empalme
Sierra
Tarahumara
Cuauhtémoc
Ciudad
Delicias
Punta Eugenia
Laguna Ojo
de Liebre
Guerrero Negro
Guaymas
Desierto
de Vizcaíno
Santa
Rosalía
Creel
Ciudad Obregón
Conchos
Ciudad Camargo
San Ignacio
Barranca
del Cobre
Urique
45
Navojoa
Hidalgo del
Parral
Mulegé
Álamos
2
Chihuahua
al Pacífico
Ciudad
Jiménez
Huatabampo
15
San Francisco
del Oro
Sierra de la Giganta
Fuerte
El Fuerte
Loreto
Sexin
Los Mochis
Guasave
Topolobampo
Guamúchil
Humaya
San Carlos
Villa
Constitución
Isla Magdalena
Santiago
Papasquiaro
Bahía
Magdalena
1
Navolato
Culiacán
45
Pichilingue
Isla
Santa
Margarita
La Paz
El Dorado
15
Durango
Presidio
Todos Santos
40
El Salto
1
9
1
Mezquital
San José del Cabo
Mazatlán
San Pedro
Cabo San Lucas
Rosario
Los Arcos
Cabo San Lucas
Escuinapa
de Hidalgo
Acaponeta
0 100 200 300 400 km
0 50 100 150 200 miles
Tecuala
Tuxpan
A
B
C
Santiago
Ixcuintla

BAJA CALIFORNIA AND THE NORTH

Sierra San Pedro Martír runs down the northern half of Baja California. Covered in pine and oak forests, its snowy peaks, which reach a height of nearly 2 miles, are the highest on the peninsula

Baja California and the North The coastline of northern Mexico is washed by the Pacific Ocean, the Gulf of California (Mar de Cortés), and the Gulf of Mexico. Between them lie interminable stretches of desert, plains, lofty mountains, and canyons, punctuated by huge sprawling industrial cities whose proximity to the U.S. ensures growing prosperity. From the still cave-dwelling Indians of the Sierra Tarahumara to colonies of American retirees residing on the coasts of Baja, the north matches its climatic extremes with an equally diverse population. But above all, an indelible impression has been left by the empty, eroded landscapes where millions of years of the earth's evolution seem to be still taking shape.

Indian cave paintings at San Francisco de la Sierra, estimated at over 1,000 years old, depict deer, wolves, and the Indians themselves

Hot, stony and dry ...
"The first stop is a town called Saltillo. It is the capital of one of those lonely vast territories stretching from the U.S. frontier roughly to the Tropic of Cancer: the States of Coahuila, Chihuahua, Baja California, Sonora and Durango, which are the limbo and ante-room to Mexico ... It is hot, stony, dry country, almost without rivers or rain, part desert, part mountain, part mining district. Innocent of art and architecture, yet innocent also of the amenities, these states are kind of natural poor relations to the Western American ones across the border, and a reminder that a very large portion of the earth's surface is, if not uninhabitable, unattractive to inhabit."
Sybille Bedford: *A Visit to Don Octavio*, 1953.

Historical circle
The nomadic hunters roaming the inhospitable north were called the Chichimecs (roughly translated as "descendants of dogs") although the more diplomatic term "Desert Culture" has since been coined. At the mercy of droughts, they sporadically forged south to the more fertile central highlands and many of the ruling dynasties during the post-Classic era were of Chichimec origin, including the Aztecs themselves. It took the Spaniards over 70 years and the added enticement of rich veins of silver even to begin to pacify the forbidding north. Mines and cattle ranches later prospered, but in 1848 the Mexican–American War sliced off today's California, Texas, Arizona, and part of New Mexico. The new frontier left Baja out on a limb and the vast *haciendas* of the northern states poised for the ferment of the Revolution, led by Pancho Villa in Chihuahua. With the demise of the silver mines and social and political turbulence the region foundered, but World War II's industrial needs provided a new economic boost. Since then, it has become the focal point for American investment. *Maquiladoras* (assembly plants for American products) flourish while thousands of workers head north to try and cross the border into the U.S.

Routes south Mexican border towns are notorious for their absence of character, seemingly absorbing the worst of both sides of *la frontera*, but for North American travelers there is no option: it's an unenviable toss-up between Tijuana, Nogales, Ciudad Juárez, Nuevo Laredo, Reynosa, or Matamoros. However, beyond the urban scars lie

Cabo San Lucas, the southernmost point of Baja California

some of Mexico's most spectacular landscapes, enticing coastlines, and rare colonial towns.

The northern coastline of the Gulf of Mexico, in the state of Tamaulipas, is an undeveloped, sparsely populated region of remote beaches and lagoons, known for its hunting and fishing potential, but offering little else. To the west, Monterrey and Saltillo respectively offer dynamism and relaxation, although both hold historical interest. The former now stands as a model of flourishing business and industrial concerns, matched by ambitious urban design. On the central route south, Chihuahua and Hidalgo del Parral have not forgotten Indian revolts and Revolution, and make interesting stops. And between here and the Gulf of California rises the mighty mountain range of the Sierra Madre Occidental, slashed by canyons and boasting the Chihuahua al Pacífico railroad.

Baja peninsula Across the Mar de Cortés lies the rugged sierra and desert of Baja, barely 4 percent of which is under cultivation. A third of its inhabitants live around Tijuana, although the Los Cabos area and La Paz are catching up fast. Between the two are vast tracts of cactus-strewn desert, shaped by an awesome moutainous spine, a merciless terrain that postponed Spanish settlement until 1697. Few Indians remain as most were wiped out by disease or mistreatment, and the land where Jesuits, whalers, copper miners and pirates once lived

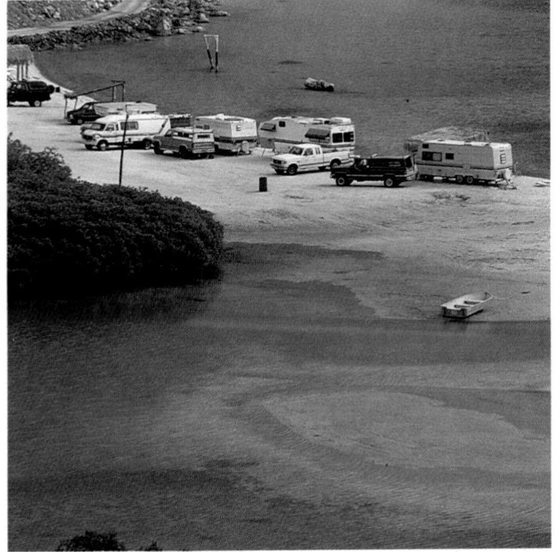

Bahía Concepción's beaches attract crowds of campers

has now been taken over by luxury marinas and trailer parks. Baja is set for the future as the land of nature tourism, its endless bays a prime target for sports fishermen, divers or whale-watchers, while its remote interior offers plenty of riding, hiking and camping opportunities. A necessity here is private transportation, preferably four-wheel drive, as bus routes miss the best places. More resorts and a four-lane highway from Ensenada down the west coast to Ciudad Constitución are planned, but most of Baja will long remain virgin territory.

The legends of Baja
Baja California was mentioned as early as the 11th century in the Anglo-Norman *Chanson de Roland* (*Song of Roland*) as Californe, a distant Eldorado. Legend grew over the centuries and it became the "fabulous island of California," home of Amazonian women ruled by Queen Calafia. From their base, by a lake filled with pearls, silver, gold, diamonds, and emeralds, these formidable women lured men to their destruction (allowing only a few to live for breeding purposes). The straits to the north of this so-called island were believed to be the route to the Moluccas (Spice Islands) and it was not until the 17th century that the peninsular theory was recognized.

The endless ebb and flow
"At that instant, in the old man's clear eyes were fused cities of gold, the expeditions that never returned, the lost priests, the nomadic and moribund tribes of Toboscos and Laguneros that had survived the epidemics of the Europeans and then fled the Spanish towns to master the horse, the bow, and later the rifle, in an endless ebb and flow of beginnings and dissolutions, mining bonanzas and depression, genocides as vast as the land itself and as forgotten as the accumulated bitterness of men ... Rebellion and suppression, plague and famine—the old man knew he was entering the restless lands of Chihuahua and the Río Grande, leaving behind the refuge of El Paso ..."
Carlos Fuentes: *El Gringo Viejo*, 1985.

Hacienda havens
Several of Álamos's old Spanish mansions have been converted into hotels, and these fine examples of colonial architecture should not be missed. Particularly noteworthy are the Hotel Los Portales on the main square and the Hotel Casa de los Tesoros, two blocks south on Calle Obregón, occupying an 18th-century monastery. Los Portales once belonged to Don José María Aldama, vice-governor of the state in newly independent Mexico, and has a typically Spanish stone-arched central courtyard.

▶▶ Álamos

78B2

A detour 33 miles inland from the Pacific highway, just south of Ciudad Obregón, leads up through rugged mountains to this small colonial town, once a thriving 18th-century mining town. By the 1920s this victim of chaotic 19th- and early 20th-century political upheavals had its mines closed, and *haciendas* abandoned, thus becoming a virtual ghost town. After World War II it was "discovered" by enterprising Americans, who soon made fortunes in real estate and restored the decrepit buildings to their former glory. Despite the artificial sprucing-up, Álamos has a beautiful central plaza dominated by **La Immaculada Concepción**, built in 1783 on the site of an earlier Jesuit mission. A small regional museum stands on the eastern side of the plaza but its coverage is limited.

▶▶ Bahía de los Ángeles

78A3

This magnificent bay on the Gulf side of Baja California Norte makes a welcome change from the dry central desert and lies 42 miles off the main highway along a well-surfaced road. A growing tourist settlement includes an airstrip, hotel, campsite, and trailer park. A recent addition is the excellent **Museo de Historia Natural.** Faced by the **Isla Ángel de la Guarda**, a large island nature reserve, the bay is alive with dolphins, finback whales and sea-lions, offering great snorkeling and diving as well as a sandy beach backed by dramatic craggy rocks. Some 15 miles south, and accessible only by boat, lies the camping and beauty spot of **La Unica**.

Bahía de los Ángeles' latest attraction is a museum of natural history, featuring such exhibits as this whale skeleton.

► Bahía Kino *78B3*

Virtually opposite Bahía de los Ángeles, but situated across the Gulf on the coast of Sonora, 67 miles west of Hermosillo, Kino is firmly divided into **Kino Viejo** and **Kino Nuevo**. The latter is geared to and mainly occupied by wintering Americans, its high-rise condominiums in marked contrast to the delapidated fishing village of Kino Viejo. The original inhabitants of the area, the Seri Indians, are known for their traditional hardwood carvings of wildlife, now sold all over town.

Bahía Kino, named after a famous Jesuit missionary, Eusabio Francisco Kino, is a popular resort, particularly with sports fishermen, swimmers, and campers

►►► Bahía Magdalena *78B1*

Bahía Magdalena, a seldom reached corner of Baja Sur, is accessible by a 35-mile surfaced road west from Villa Constitución which ends at the fishing village of **San Carlos**. The typically rocky Pacific coastline is protected by two elongated islands, **Isla Magdalena** and **Isla Santa Margarita**, which create a sheltered bay much favored by gray whales for breeding (see page 93). The warm waters are rich in aquatic life, wrecks of galleons (Sir Francis Drake sheltered here while searching for the North-West Passage), deserted beaches and mangrove inlets. Camping is, at present, the only option, but a mega-resort complex planned for the island will soon change the area's profile.

►►► Barranca del Cobre *78C2*

High in the Sierra Tarahumara, halfway between the Gulf of California and Chihuahua, stretches a landscape of spectacular canyons, known collectively as Barranca del Cobre (the Copper Canyon). Sliced out of the Sierra Madre Occidental, these sharply sculpted ravines have startling extremes in climate and vegetation. In winter the pine forests of their rims (which reach 9,200 ft.) are covered in snow, while their floors sprout tropical flora, a phenomenon that forces the area's impoverished Indian inhabitants, the Tarahumaras (see pages 100–101), to migrate twice-yearly. The Barranca del Cobre is five times wider and one and a half times deeper than the Grand Canyon, and has become a favorite destination for hikers and riders. Remote missions, ruined mining towns, wind-eroded rocks, waterfalls, lakes, and uncharted caves combine with a cool climate to attract visitors, who arrive by the famous and tortuous **Chihuahua al Pacífico** railroad (see page 87) or by road to **Creel** (see page 88). More difficult to reach, but in a superb canyon riverside setting, is the former silver-mining town of **Batopilas►►**, 88 miles south of Creel and approached by the Camino Real which snakes over 6,000 ft. down to the canyon floor.

Barranca gothic
In 1880 American politician Alexander Shepherd arrived from Washington with his family to preside over the prolific Batopilas silver mine. The only link with the outside world was by mule along five days of winding track, but Shepherd managed to bring pianos, pool tables and a railroad engine (in parts), as well as send back kilos of silver. Today his Gothic adobe mansion is shrouded in wild bougainvillaea and open to the winds, but you can still see the remains of the family swimming-pool.

Cabo San Lucas

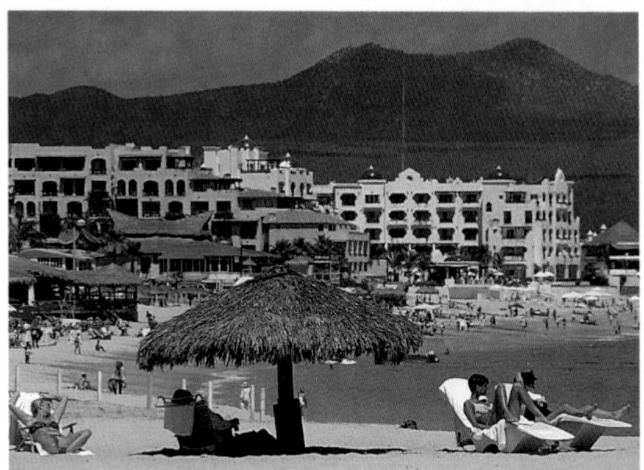

Cascade of sand
The presence of five underwater trenches, up to 10,000 ft. deep, which nurture a high level of plankton, has blessed Los Cabos with a wealth of underwater life. An estimated 800 species of reef fish glide through the waters and include several unique to the region. You might also spot the world's largest fish, the whale shark, or the giant manta ray with its span of up to 23 ft. However, it is a submarine canyon located in the bay of Cabo San Lucas that provides a unique spectacle, that of a sandfall. Discovered in 1960 and filmed by Jacques Cousteau, it is a weird and wonderful sight to watch the sand cascading from the canyon edge to the shadowy depths below.

▶ Cabo San Lucas *78B1*

Cabo San Lucas occupies the southernmost tip of the Baja peninsula. It is an expanding resort which, together with San José del Cabo, forms the much touted **Los Cabos** of official tourist literature. This harmoniously designed town, with low ocher-colored buildings fronting a small marina and bay, is a destination for serious anglers and divers, high on tourist facilities but low on authenticity. Its basic population of 10,000 fluctuates with the seasons, streets remain unfinished but nightclubs boom and hotels multiply. **Los Arcos▶▶**, a massive natural rock arch terminating the headland, has become the local emblem and is viewed from boats leaving from the western end of the marina. At low-tide boats stop off at the Playa de Amor, a fine white sandy beach. Other trips go to **Cabo Falso** where the Faro Viejo (old lighthouse) offers panoramic sea views which may include seals, sea-lions and whales on their way to Guerrero Negro or Bahía Magdalena.

The partially restored ruins of Casas Grandes indicate there was a high level of civilization in the area

▶▶ Casas Grandes *78C3*

Casas Grandes, situated about 180 miles by road south of the border town of Ciudad Juárez, is the most important archaeological site in northern Mexico. Presumed to date from AD1000, it was abandoned in the mid-14th century following attacks by Apaches. Structures include pyramids, ball-courts, platforms, underground chambers and the remains of three-story adobe houses. Excavations yielded Paquimé pottery (vessels decorated with natural pigments), necklaces of semi-precious stones, and carvings of Quetzalcóatl. Most of these can be seen in Mexico City's Anthropological Museum (see pages 60–61).

▶▶ Cascada de Basaseáchic *78C2*

Mexico's highest waterfall, whose torrents plunge over 980 ft. to the foot of the Candameña Canyon, is located in the Sierra Tarahumara, some 106 miles west of Cuauhtémoc and 88 miles north of Creel. Its scale and power are overwhelming, but access is notoriously difficult, requiring a bumpy car-ride followed by a short walk to the look-out point for the best view. A 1½-hour hike down to the bottom of the canyon brings you to the base of the waterfall.

■ One hundred and twenty species of cacti inhabit the Baja landscape, ranging from miniature cushions to the gigantic *cardons*. Whether stretching in endless forests, often standing as lone sentinels, they are not only visual symbols of the peninsula but also functional plants.....■

Due to the semi-isolation of the Baja California peninsula, many of its plants are endemic and of the 120 species of cacti no fewer than 70 are unique to the region. From north to south the varieties change according to terrain, and their appearance alters with the seasons, seemingly lifeless in the high and dry summer but bursting with vigor and wreathed in flowers and vines in the rainy season and spring. Their ridges and grooves expand to absorb water, which is retained by the waxy skin; they can hold water for up to five years.

Cardons and organ-pipes The tallest cacti on the horizon belong to the *cardon* family, a close relative of the *saguaro* of Arizona. These towering, fluted columns sometimes reach heights of over 65 ft. Thousands of them clothe the sierra as far north as San Felipe, and a dense forest grows inland from Bahía de Los Ángeles. In March and April the upper branches of cardons blossom with white flowers, followed by yellow fruits which split to reveal succulent red flesh. Pollination is carried out by bats, hawkmoths and humming-birds.

Branching towards the sky, the organ-pipe cactus of Baja, *pitahaya dulce*, is found in the southern half of the peninsula. Its nectar is much sought after by bats and was once favored by local Indians who would gather to gorge themselves on it. The stimulating effect was such that tribal conflicts and marital ties were soon forgotten, much to the dismay of local padres. Another functional cactus was the *biznaga* or bulky "barrel cactus" which grows in the central part of the peninsula and has served as an emergency source of water.

Whispered conversations
"The cacti stood in groups like people with feathered head-dresses leaning together and engaged in intimate whispered conversation... The cacti had no beauty—they were like some simple shorthand sign for such words as 'barrenness' and 'drought'; you felt they were less the product than the cause of this dryness, that they had absorbed all the water there was in the land and held it as camels do in their green, aged, tubular bellies."
Graham Greene: *The Lawless Roads*, 1939.

Boojum trees
Specific to the area between El Rosario and San Ignacio, as well as a small pocket of the state of Sonora, the hairy, undulating trunks of the boojum tree or cirio (related to the *ocotillo*) have also earned it the nickname of "elephant tree." In spring they burst forth with a mass of pink blossoms creating a roseate haze in the middle of the desert.

One of Baja California's numerous species of cactus

Dinosaur's egg
In 1993, the year "Jurassic Park" ephemera invaded Mexican markets, the state of Chihuahua witnessed the discovery of a dinosaur's egg. Found by a local farmer who thought he had stumbled upon a rather "curious stone," it was examined by paleontologists and found to be the egg of a *critosaurus*, some 73 million years old. The exact location of the discovery in the southern part of the state was not revealed through fear of dinosaur egg-plundering.

► Chihuahua *78C2*

The town of Chihuahua holds a few hidden secrets and makes an interesting stop-over. Situated on a high plateau, against the impressive backdrop of the Sierra Madre Occidental, this prosperous city, with a population approaching one million, is the capital of Mexico's largest state. Today's riches come from cattle, timber, mining, and industrial assembly plants whose chief customers lie across the border in the U.S. The little dog that bears the city's name did originate here but is nowhere to be seen.

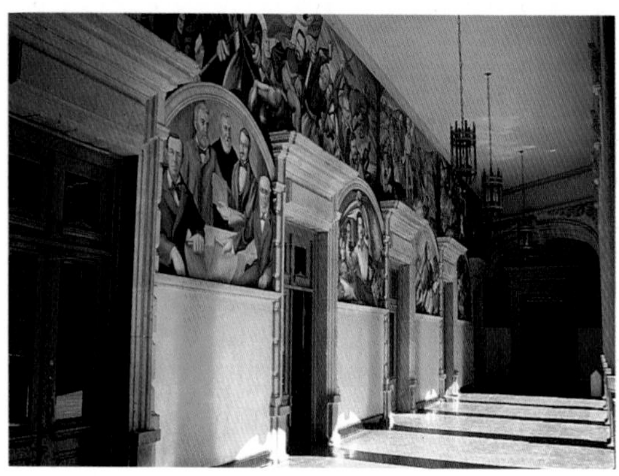

The courtyard walls of the 19th-century Government Palace are lined with murals portraying famous episodes in the history of Chihuahua

Hidalgo, Villa, and Co. Chihuahua was originally settled by silver-hungry miners in the early 18th century, but it suffered over the centuries from raids by Apaches from the north, as well as from uprisings by local tribes, goaded into action by the brutality of the Spanish overlords. During the War of Independence, Miguel Hidalgo fled here but was betrayed and subsequently executed, his head exhibited in Guanajuato as a warning to similarly inspired individuals. Benito Juárez also installed himself in Chihuahua, but it was during the turbulent period of the Revolution that the city hosted its greatest hero, Pancho Villa, who set up his headquarters here.

Around the zócalo All Chihuahua's institutional monuments are within easy walking distance east of the zócalo, the **Plaza de Armas**. Dominating the square is the Baroque **Catedral**►, begun in 1726 but only completed in 1826 due to the expulsion of the Jesuit founders and Apache attacks. In this central area Porfiriato mansions jostle with modern buildings, while pedestrian streets are lined with cowboy-boot shops and ice-cream parlors. Two blocks east on **Plaza Hidalgo** (Avenida Carranza and Calle Libertád) stands the Correos (post office) and the **Palacio Federal**►, an imposing building which saw Hidalgo's imprisonment in 1811. A small museum devoted to him opens on to the Calle Juárez side. Opposite stands the pale pink **Palacio del Gobierno**►►, originally a Jesuit college, faithfully rebuilt after a fire. Its courtyard walls incorporate a small altar on the site of Hidalgo's execution

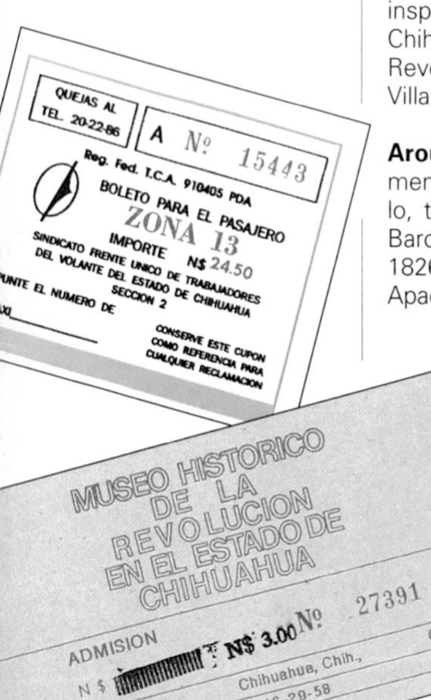

and have since been faced with murals by Aron Piña Mora depicting the history of Chihuahua.

South of the center On the elegant Paseo Bolívar, a road which surrounds the historic center, stands the extraordinary Quinta Gameros, a 1907 mansion which now houses the **Museo Regional▶▶**. This displays Art Nouveau at its very worst, a kitsch pastiche of the original. Angels, garlanded ladies, Little Red Riding Hood, gilded mirrors, stuccoed ceilings and stained glass exemplify the tasteless opulence of its pre-Revolution owners. The museum's only redeeming feature is a display of Paquimé pottery from Casas Grandes on the upper floor. Four blocks farther south is the eminently more tasteful Quinta Luz, now the **Museo de la Revolución▶▶▶**, where Pancho Villa lived with one of his 25 *compañeras*, Señora Luz Corral de Villa, later recognized as his official wife. Its Art Nouveau murals, tiled walls and patio are evidence that despite his egalitarian principles Villa appreciated the good life, but the black 1922 Dodge peppered with bullet holes recalls his bloody fate in 1923. Exhibits are displayed throughout the elegant home and include photos, original documents, equipment, arms (including a 1900 Hotchkiss machine-gun), clothes, and Villa's deathmask, making for a fascinating record of this key period in Mexican history and its chief protagonist.

▶▶▶ Chihuahua al Pacífico *78C2*

This celebrated railroad line, crawling through a deserted high-altitude wilderness, takes over 13 hours to wind through dramatic canyons, sierra and Alpine meadows before terminating on the Pacific coast at Los Mochis. The most spectacular section lies between Creel and Los Mochis, where it passes through 88 tunnels and 39 bridges, stops near the rim of the Copper Canyon at El Divisadero, then zigzags down past rock-faces and ravines to reach the tropical coastal plain. Two passenger trains cover the route—the first-class *Primera Especial* and the slower, cheaper and less comfortable *Tren Mixto*. Scenery is more stunning on the right if coming from Los Mochis: the *Primera* leaves at 6 a.m., the *Mixto* at 7 a.m. From Chihuahua departures are 7 a.m. and 7:20 a.m. respectively.

Chihuahua–Pacífico data
Started at the beginning of the century, this incredible feat of engineering was initiated by American mining companies under the name "Kansas City, Mexico and Orient Railroad." But, it was not until 1961 that the Mexican government finally completed the most complex section of the 420-mile railroad line, which involved blasting through solid rock (the longest tunnel measures over 3,000 ft.), building precipitous bridges (the highest stands at 360 ft. marking the border between the states of Sinaloa and Chihuahua) and creating breathtaking loops around mountains. Official and unofficial contributors to its construction include President Adolfo López Mateos, the magnate Enrique Creel, Ulysses Grant, President Porfirio Diáz, Pancho Villa, Benjamin Johnson, and the Tarahumara Indians.

Bottom left: Tarahumara Indians selling their crafts—one of the few ways they have to make a living
Below: the Copper Canyon is deeper than Colorado's Grand Canyon

The Mennonites
This austere, hard-working sect, founded by a Dutchman in the 16th century, adheres strictly to the words of the Bible. Refusal to bend to any other law led to persecution which drove them from Germany to Russia, Canada and finally, in the liberal, post-Revolutionary days of the 1920s, to Mexico. Mennonites only marry within their sect, thus they remain blonde-haired and blue-eyed, and speak an obscure ancient German dialect, in startling contrast to their host countrymen. Men dress in checked shirts and denim bib-overalls, women in long skirts, shawls and headscarves. Their diligence has transformed the desert into fertile farmland.

Ciudad Juárez *78C3*

This sprawling, unattractive city of over one million inhabitants is a major border town linking El Paso in Texas with Northern Mexico's central route south, but offers little to the visitor. Dusty, mercilessly hot in summer, confusingly laid out and overtly geared to cashing in on cheap services of all kinds, it is best passed straight through. If you have time to spare, however, the archaeological museum located in the Parque Chamizal, the **Museo Chamizal▶**, displays several interesting examples of pottery from Casas Grandes alongside numerous replicas. The Plaza Principal holds the **Catedral** and **Palacio Municipal**, and a new museum of history and art offers a general introduction to Mexican culture.

▶▶ Creel *78C2*

Creel lies 1.5 miles up in the Sierra Tarahumara. This popular stop-over on the Chihuahua al Pacífico railroad line is well suited for visitors, without losing its cowboy frontier-town soul. Consisting of one main street and one main square against a backdrop of rock-faces and pine forests, Creel has an easy-going atmosphere heightened by its isolation, the echoing whistles and shunting of trains and its colorful though impoverished Tarahumara inhabitants. Numerous day-trips are organized from here on horseback or by van into the surrounding canyons, to Lago Arareco, Cascada de Cusárare, the hot-springs of

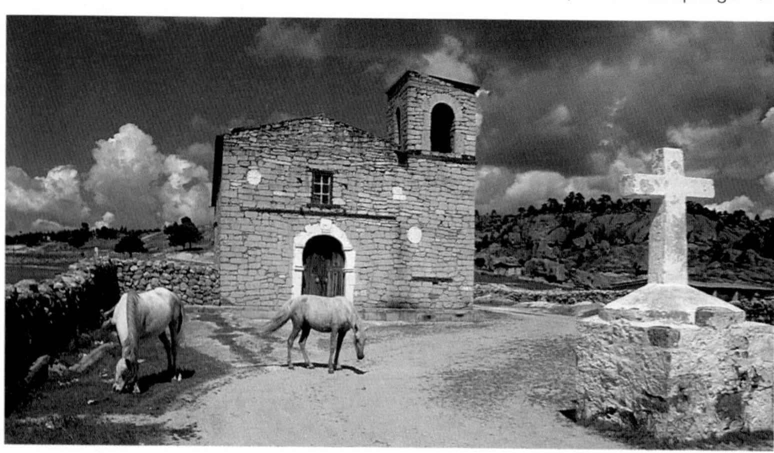

Isolated mission in the Sierra Tarahumara

Recohuata, or to Tarahumara cave dwellings and isolated missions. It is also an ideal base for hiking. Remember to make some purchases at the Jesuit mission shop, on the main square, which provides important assistance to the local Tarahumaras.

▶ Cuauhtémoc *78C2*

This central market town for the Tarahumara Indians, and Mexico's zealous Mennonite community who established themselves here back in the 1920s, lies in an undulating region of cattle farms and fruit orchards, 66 miles west of Chihuahua. The town's main monument is a statue of Cuauhtémoc, the last Aztec emperor, standing at the eastern end of the main street.

Durango's Baroque Catedral towers over the principal square with its massive structure and domed bell towers

►► Durango 78C1

Durango lies at the center of a rich mining area encircled by heavy industrial plants on a flat plateau 195 miles northeast of Mazatlán. Much of the its wealth comes from an iron ore deposit in one of the two hills looming over the town, the **Cerro del Mercado**. To the south the **Cerro de los Remedios** has been landscaped into a tranquil park with a chapel at the summit. Nine miles north of the town stand the reasons for Durango's more recent fame: a series of film sets constructed for Hollywood Westerns in the villages of **Villa del Oeste►** and **Chupaderos**. Tours are arranged by the tourist office (in the Palacio del Gobierno). The central Plaza de Armas is dominated by the domed bell-towers of the Baroque **Catedral**, begun in 1695 but not completed for several decades. Fronting another beautiful square, the handsome 18th-century **Palacio de Gobierno** was originally built for a Spanish mining baron. Murals around the arcaded patio relate the history of the state of Durango. Even more elaborate in style is the **Casa del Condes de Súchil►►**, the stunning 17th-century colonial-style home of Spanish governors, part of which now functions as a rather upscale shopping center.

► Ensenada 78A4

The former gold-mining boomtown of Ensenada, on Baja's Pacific coast, now pays the price for its proximity to the border. Only 68 miles south of Tijuana, it is a favorite weekend destination for Californians intent on a good time. During the week it returns to its sedate fishing and shipping activities, but the scars remain. The **Mercado de Pescas** (fish market) opposite the pier is a favorite destination for seafood addicts; numerous stalls dish out fresh oysters, fish *tacos*, or *ceviche* (raw fish marinated in lime or lemon), while the renowned *cantina* **Hussong's** attracts *tequila* and beer aficionados. Other interests here include sports fishing, particularly from May to October; winery tours, the largest of which, **Bodegas Santo Tomás**, organizes daily wine-tasting; and panoramic views of the coast from **El Mirador** on Chapultepec Hill. Good beaches for swimming lie 6 miles south at **Estero**, while surfers slice through the waves at San Miguel, Tres Marías, California, and La Joya.

La Bufadora (The Snorting One)
A strange marine phenomenon is visible, and audible, at Punta la Banda, 24 miles southwest of Ensenada and the southern headland of Bahía Todos Santos. Pounding surf periodically forces a jet of seawater up through a small blowhole in the roof of an underwater cavern, producing a geyser effect as it explodes with a thunderous roar some 50 ft. up into the air (best during high tide). Access to this sight is only posible by car or with a tour from Ensenada.

Street vendor, Ensenada

■ A constantly clear atmosphere, high-altitude light, spectacular desert scenery and relatively cheap Mexican technicians and extras once made northern Mexico a favorite location for Hollywood westerns. Not only that, its role as a convenient and exotic hideaway for outlaws (real or fictional) has provided some poignant character studies.....■

Filming in Mexico
"*The Exterminating Angel* was made in Mexico, although I regret that I was unable to shoot it in Paris or London with European actors and adequate costumes. Despite the beauty of the house where it was shot and my effort to select actors who didn't look particularly Mexican, there was a certain tawdriness in many of its aspects. We couldn't get any really fine table napkins, for instance, and the only one I could show on camera was borrowed from the make-up artist."
Luis Buñuel: *My Last Breath*, 1983.

Rancho La Joya, north of Durango, once John Wayne territory, is owned by Wayne's family and is part of a structure set in place by Hollywood over 35 years ago. In 1960 Wayne broke his bank making *The Alamo* (see picture above), a film about the Mexican–American War when 180 heroic Texans were eventually massacred by General Santa Ana's troops. Wayne's first film production put Mexico firmly on the Hollywood map: Burt Lancaster, Rock Hudson, Robert Ryan, Sydney Poitier and, more recently, Paul Newman, all passed through the sets during the heyday of westerns.

Hey *gringo*! For the average movie-goer these films produced a stereotypical vision of the Mexican which still clings today. All speak good English peppered with *señor* and *amigo*, wear sombreros, sport drooping black moustaches and are adept at dishonesty, cowardice, and double-crossing. The few Mexican heroes portrayed are played by American stars, thus Zapata assumes the features of Marlon Brando, and Juárez those of Paul Muni.

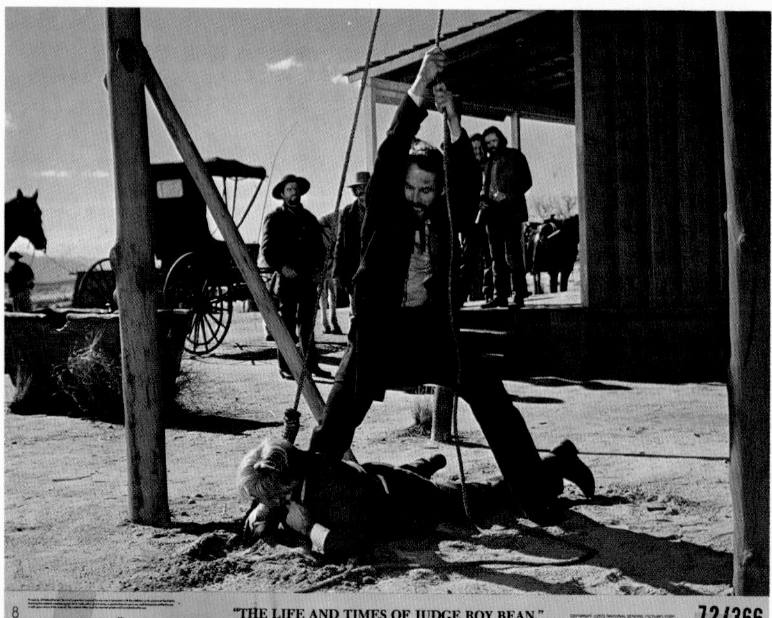

Mexico's Hollywood

Serie Balcón Nº 1259
EL PLAZA
Precio N$ 15.-

Through Hollywood's eyes, Mexico was a country in a chronic, albeit entertaining mess, without principles or pragmatism, and doomed to the rule of local interests, corruption and to the annoying habit of revolution. Mexican women, when not breast-feeding at the adobe-hut door or scuffing around the kitchen preparing *chilli con carne*, are flashing-eyed, dark-haired beauties who dance the night away, give the hero what he wants and nonchalantly fling a flower at the feet of his horse as he departs the next morning. These passive, flawless types are exemplified in Tony Richardson's *The Border* (1981), in which border cop Jack Nicholson falls for the noble simplicity of a Mexican girl in the towns of El Paso and dusty Ciudad Juárez.

Mexican escape Fateful, amoral and mysterious, Mexico also becomes a haven, a place to flee to, far from northern rigidity and justice. The outcasts of Sam Peckinpah's *The Wild Bunch* (1969) wander, raid, booze, and womanize, successfully entering an anarchistic, self-induced oblivion. Nostalgia for the good old days of the West can be successfully indulged in, perfected by Humphrey Bogart in John Huston's *The Treasure of the Sierra Madre* (1948), where the Mexico of *cantinas* and *banditos* is contrasted with that of a rural purity and utopian freshness.

Far more entrenched in the true Mexican spirit than any other Hollywood director, Huston produced two memorable existentialist portraits firmly rooted in Mexican soil: the glamorous figure of Ava Gardner in *The Night of the Iguana* (1964), regally ruling over the Pacific waves of tropical Puerto Vallarta in total abandon of social norms; and the British consul of *Under the Volcano* (1984) in which Albert Finney embodies Malcolm Lowrie's melancholic figure staggering from *tequila* to the Day of the Dead. Expanding the theme, Luis Puenzo's *The Old Gringo* (1989), based on Carlos Fuentes' novel, portrays an ageing American journalist (Gregory Peck) on the run from himself against a background of Pancho Villa's unruly Revolutionary forces. He eventually finds death, but not before meeting Jane Fonda. Ironically it is a young Mexican director, Roberto Rodríguez, who, in *El Mariachi* (1993), has managed to combine archetypal visions of local *banditos* with that of a wide-eyed innocent—a *mariachi* guitarist mistaken for a local killer. All the cast are Mexican—and so the tables turn.

Like Water for Chocolate
The greatest hit to have emerged from Mexico in recent years is undoubtedly *Como Agua para Chocolate*, a title which refers to Mexican hot chocolate made with boiling water; by extension someone who is (sexually) agitated is said to be "like water for chocolate." Directed by Alfonso Arau and released in 1992, it was based on the first novel of Mexican screenwriter Laura Esquivel, Arau's wife. With distinct surrealistic overtones, it recounts the frustrated love story of Tita and Pedro against a backdrop of revolution in the rugged northern state of Coahuila. As Pedro is forced to marry her elder sister, Tita transfers her sensuality into the realm of culinary seduction—what foodie can forget her lavishly and lovingly prepared quail in rose petal sauce?

Far left: The Life and Times of Judge Roy Bean*, starring Paul Newman*
Below: Villa del Oeste, near Durango—set for many Hollywood Westerns

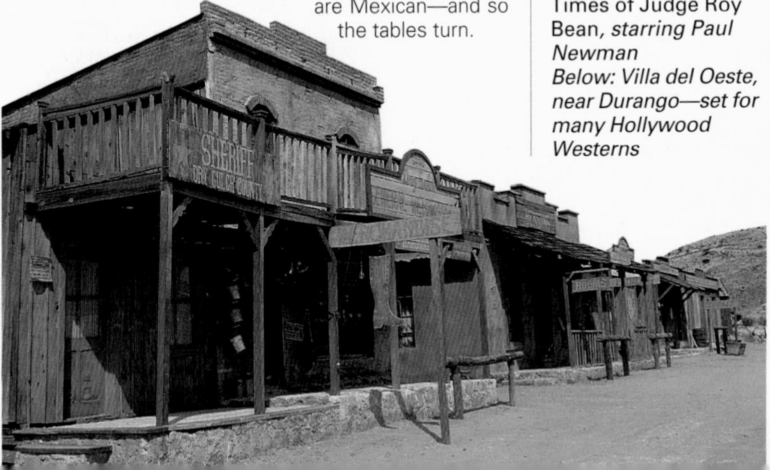

The 28th parallel
When crossing the 28th parallel from the north you leave the Pacific Time Zone and enter the Mountain Time Zone, one hour ahead. It was also the meeting-point of the builders of the Trans-peninsular Highway in 1973, one team working northwards, another southwards. A plaque commemorate the spot where they met. Elaborate plans were developed for an underground museum, and artifacts were actually installed. But then came Baja's notorious heavy rains, the museum was flooded and the artifacts were removed, mostly to Mexico City.

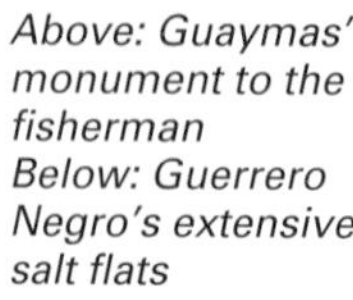

Above: Guaymas' monument to the fisherman
Below: Guerrero Negro's extensive salt flats

▶ Grutas de García *79D2*

These caves, lying some 28 miles northwest of Monterrey in the Sierra del Fraile, were formed over 50 million years ago and are said to be Mexico's largest and most beautiful cave network. They were discovered by a priest in 1843 and have become a popular local outing aided by direct buses from Monterrey on Sundays. A 1.5-mile tour leads through 16 vast cave chambers thick with dramatically illuminated stalactite and stalagmite formations. The entrance is reached by cable-car from the parking lot.

▶ Guaymas *78B2*

The main port of the state of Sonora on the Mar de Cortés has a spectacular mountain-backed harbor, but its revenue lies firmly in trade and commerce, not tourism. Founded in 1701 by missionaries (the original **Mision de San José** lies 6 miles north of town), over the years it inspired the covetous ambitions of Americans, British and French invaders, most notably the French Comte Gaston Raousset de Bourbon, who twice attempted to establish a personal empire here but whose days were ended with a bullet in 1854. More interesting than the town itself are its surroundings. The nature reserve of **El Sahuaro▶▶** has a wonderful variety of cacti and other indigenous plants, the bays north of town towards San Carlos (see page 99) offer good fishing, swimming and snorkeling, and offshore islands attract sea-lions and aquatic birds.

▶ Guerrero Negro *78A2*

This dull town of salt-flats, vats and warehouses announces the end (or the beginning) of the monotonous Desierto de Vizcaíno, on Baja's 28th parallel. Basic services include an incongruous luxury hotel, but Guerrero Negro is mainly concerned with the production of salt, which is transported to the Isla Cedros before being exported, mainly to the U.S. and Japan. The main attraction here is nearby Laguna Ojo de Liebre, also known as **Scammon's Lagoon**, now a protected national park where gray whales come to breed (December to March only). Access to observe these giant mammals is severely restricted: there are look-out posts along the shore, reached from a turn-off about 15 miles from Highway 1.

■ **Every fall thousands of gray whales leave their summer grounds in the Bering Sea off Alaska and migrate 5,000 miles south through the Pacific to the sheltered bays and coastal lagoons of Baja California to court, mate and give birth—one of Mexico's greatest wildlife spectacles.....■**

From the 1840s to the 1940s waves of whalers preyed upon the "devilfish" (so-called because of the mothers' ferocious protection of their threatened calves) and the Californian gray whales were reduced from an estimated 24,000 to a mere few thousand. On the verge of extinction, the species finally received full protection from commercial whaling 26 years later. In 1972 Mexico declared Laguna Ojo de Liebre (Scammon's Lagoon) and Laguna Guerrero Negro refuges for gray whales—the first such sanctuaries in the world. With the addition of Laguna San Ignacio in 1979 and the naturally protected Bahía Magdalena, these gentle giants, weighing between 20 and 40 tons, have made a dramatic recovery and their numbers are now estimated at 20,000.

The next generation Courting and mating generally take place at the entrance to the lagoons where as many as 500 whales cruise in and out daily. The amorous giants lunge through the water, spouting vapor from their blowholes like geysers, in a promiscuous free-for-all copulation. With calving mothers outside the courting action in the shallower parts of the inner lagoon, the number of available females is greatly reduced, a factor which sometimes leads to indiscriminate mating of up to 20 whales at once. Meanwhile, the mothers-to-be (impregnated the previous season) produce their young after a nine-month period of gestation. The calves grow quickly on their mother's milk, which, at 53 percent fat, is one of the richest in the world, and by winter's end have added over 3 ft. to their length and doubled their weight. In March and April the whales begin the long haul north, followed by the mothers and calves, once the latter have accomplished a "training session" in the mouth of the lagoon, consisting of an intensive workout to build up their strength.

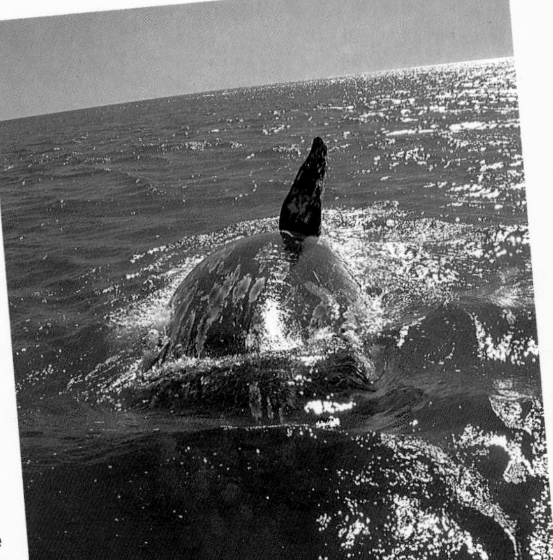

Whale behavior
Heaving up and down, crashing through the waves, spouting water like a geyser, the gray whale displays still unfathomed behavioral traits that continue to intrigue whale watchers. Swimming against the tide with its mouth wide open enables the whale to sieve huge amounts of water and trap rich plankton that blooms in the warm lagoon shallows. "Bottom-grubbing" or stripping the lagoon floor with vacuum-cleaner suction techniques also provides food (mostly crustaceans).

Hermosillo's Plaza de los Tres Pueblos marks the site of the original Seri Indian settlement

The end of Villa
At 8:30 a.m. on July 20, 1923, General Francisco "Pancho" Villa, accompanied by six bodyguards, cruised unsuspectingly along Calle Gabino Barreda in Hidalgo del Parral. For the previous 103 days, nine conspirators had been lying in wait to ambush him ... the moment had come. Opening fire on Villa's black Dodge, they sprayed it with bullets and mortally wounded his bodyguards. Irrepressible until the bitter end, the dying hero of Mexico's revolution managed to fire a last, successful shot, killing one of the conspirators, before dying shortly after. The leader of the ambush, Jesus Salas Barraza, had no qualms about surrendering himself to the authorities, accusing Villa of dictatorial ambitions, and although sentenced to 20 years' imprisonment was mysteriously released a few months later.

► Hermosillo *78B3*

The oven-like summer temperatures and industrialization of Hermosillo, capital of the state of Sonora, mean that it is often bypassed by travelers or used only as a lunch stop. However, it is strategically placed on Highway 15, 142 miles south of the border town of Nogales and 85 miles from Guaymas. Although prosperous and modernized, it still has a certain charm. Founded in 1700, Hermosillo's colonial center revolves around the shady **Plaza de Zaragoza►►**, flanked to the west by the **Catedral de la Ascensión** (1779) and to the east by the **Palacio del Gobierno**, where colorful murals depict Sonoran history, rich in locally-born Revolutionary protagonists, including General Alvaro Obregón. South of the center lies the interesting **Centro Ecológico de Sonora**, a zoo and beautiful botanical gardens full of indigenous and desert specimens. The **Museo de Sonora, set** on the slopes of the Cerro de la Campana, a hill dominating the town to the east, covers local history and anthropology.

►► Hidalgo del Parral *78C2*

The old mining center of Hidalgo del Parral (or just Parral) lies 188 miles south of Chihuahua. The town is still dependent on the prolific mines of the surrounding hills which inspired its settlement in 1629. Its early history, however, is blackened by the slavery of local Indians. Rebellions ensued and the **Templo de San Nicolás** was actually the site of a mass hanging of Indian leaders in 1676. There are several elaborate 18th-century silver-miners' mansions, most striking being the **Palacio Pedro Alvarado►►**. The **Templo de Nuestra Señora del Rayo**, completed in 1728, was reputed to have been financed by a Tarahumara Indian who struck gold. Parral is famous, too, as the site of Pancho Villa's assassination in 1923; the town commemorates this event with photos and memorabilia in the small **Museo de Pancho Villa.**

►► Isla del Tiburón *78B3*

"Shark Island," Mexico's largest island, lies off Sonora's coast opposite Bahía Kino. It has been transformed into a biosphere reserve, although few of its indigenous species (the desert turtle, mule deer, and Cimarron sheep) remain. The only inhabitants are Seri Indians, known for their ironwood carvings of birds and fish. Access to the island requires a special permit, obtainable from licensed boatmen in Kino.

►► La Paz *78B1*

Great plans await La Paz, state capital of Baja California Sur, an expanding town with a life of its own outside tourism, unlike nearby Los Cabos. Located in a magnificent bay studded with outlying islands and backed by dramatic sierra, it has a pleasantly low-key atmosphere. Its dark and difficult past was set in motion by Hernán Cortés in 1535 and involved vicious conflicts with local Indians, further exacerbated by droughts, famines, smallpox, pirates, American troops during the Texan War and, in 1853, the infamous William Walker, intent on installing a state of slavery. Rumors of the black pearls adorning local Indians had also spread and led to massive exploitation of

the nearby oyster beds, finally wiped out by a mysterious disease in 1940. However, La Paz (meaning "peace") was reborn when American sports fishermen discovered its waters, and today its population of 250,000 has the highest per capita income in Mexico.

Although modernized, La Paz has preserved elements of its past, best reflected in the Mediterranean feel of the palm-fringed *malecón* (sea promenade). Stunning sunsets over the bay, superb beaches lining the Pichilingue peninsula to the north, island boat trips, good snorkeling and fishing, duty-free shopping, excellent seafood and reasonably priced hotels: these are its attractions. Buildings of note are limited to the 19th-century **Catedral de Nuestra Señora de la Paz**, built on the site of a 1720 mission in the central Plaza Constitución and faced by the **Palacio del Gobierno**. For informative displays about the early Pericue, Cochimí, and Guaicura Indians, as well as Baja's numerous cave paintings, go to the **Museo Antropológico**▶▶ (three blocks inland from Plaza Constitución on Calle Altamirano).

La Paz's pleasant palm-shaded malecón *is perfect for strolling*

Boating from La Paz
La Paz has daily car-ferry services to Mazatlán and thrice-weekly boats to Topolobampo, the port of Los Mochis. The Mazatlán service normally leaves at 3 p.m., arriving at about 7 a.m. the next day. The Topolobampo service departs at 8 p.m., arriving at 6 a.m. (too late to catch the Chihuahua al Pacífico train). Timetables do, however, vary considerably with bad weather, the seasons and less definable factors. Tickets can be bought at the ferry terminal, about 14 miles north of town in Pichilingue, or more easily at any travel agent in the center. For more information the tourist office at Paseo Alvaro Obregón 2130 will help.

Lining up for a shoeshine in La Paz

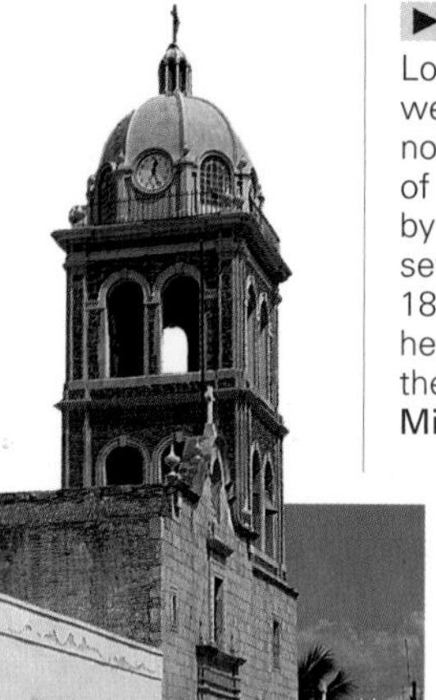

Loreto's Misión de Nuestra Señora has been restored after suffering great damage from earthquakes

▶▶ Loreto *78B2*

Loreto, another southern Baja favorite with fishermen, as well as with hunters, lies on the Mar de Cortés 225 miles north of La Paz, beyond the magnificent purple contours of the **Sierra de la Giganta**▶▶▶. It was founded in 1697 by an Italian Jesuit, and is the region's oldest permanent settlement; it remained the capital of the peninsula until 1829 when it was virtually wiped out by a hurricane. From here Father Junipero Serra set out in 1769 to evangelize the Californias. The cloisters of the beautifully restored **Misión de Nuestra Señora de Loreto** incorporate the charming **Museo de los Misiónes**▶▶ (closed at weekends), an informative introduction to local Jesuit, Franciscan, and Dominican activities. Around the church is an area of pedestrian streets leading down to the harbor and beach where Loreto's few hotels are situated. Slow paced, with superb offshore islands and great sierra hiking, Loreto is a development that never got off the ground, and as such is worth visiting. Although things may change with a "mega-project" planned 15 miles south at Puerto Loreto, nearly 60,000 acres are being conserved as a nature reserve.

Los Mochis *78B2*

Los Mochis is unavoidable for anyone embarking on or disembarking from the Chihuahua al Pacífico train. This unexceptional town, with its over-priced hotels, rip-off taxis and giant mosquitoes (which spend the day at the airport and migrate to town in the evenings) is, along with nearby Culiacán, the center of Mexican drug-trafficking, so gunfights are a common occurrence. If you have to spend the night in the area try the little fishing port of **Topolobampo,** where basic accommodation is available.

▶ Matamoros *79E2*

This typical border town, lying on the estuary of the Río Grande across from Brownsville, Texas, offers the usual semi-planned vision of Mexico, although it is generally cleaner and less Tex-Mex than its counterparts. The town museum, the **Museo del Maíz,** is entirely dedicated to the subject of corn (an important crop in the history and development of Mexico) with an underlying theme on the eternal struggle between private and communal land ownership. The old fort of **Casa Mata** symbolizes confrontations during the Mexican–American war and contains items of military history and Indian artifacts. The main beach of **Playa General Lauro Villar,** 23 miles east of town, is fronted by some reasonable seafood restaurants.

▶▶ Monterrey *79D2*

This gleaming modern city (Mexico's third largest), capital of the state of Nuevo León and industrial capital of the nation, has a fast-paced lifestyle in keeping with its key location, 145 miles south of the Texan border on the Panamerican Highway. Its factories flourish and it is now concentrating on a cultural life to match its renowned business, commercial, and educational facilities.

Monterrey's 1908 Government Palace

Monterrey nestles in the valley of the Sierra Madre Oriental, dominated by the mighty, saddle-shaped **Cerro de la Silla** (Saddle Mountain). Spectacular contemporary architecture, a sleek new metro and imaginative city planning have made it an urban showcase. The main downtown area is concentrated around the **Gran Plaza** (popularly called the Macroplaza because of its size) and the adjoining **Plaza Zaragoza**. Beyond the new, elevated **Palacio Municipal** and a monumental sculpture by Rufino Tamayo, lies a blend of government buildings, fountains, the Baroque **Catedral** and Monterrey's symbol of modernity, the orange tower of Luís Barragán's **Faro del Commercio** (Lighthouse of Business) whose green lasers are beamed across the city at night. A block farther north stands the **Teatro de la Ciudad**, the **Esplanada de los Héroes**, (with statues of Mexico's heroes) and a sunken garden, the **Bosque Hundido** (Hidden Forest). Immediately west of these plazas lies the busy **Zona Rosa**, a partly pedestrian area full of upscale hotels, shops and restaurants with a typical Monterrey buzz.

However, Monterrey's latest and brightest jewel is the **Museo de Arte Contemporáneo▶▶▶** (MARCO), an architectural masterpiece by Ricardo Legorreta which opened in 1991 next to the cathedral. Laid out around a central patio, the 14 luminous exhibition rooms are exemplary in their design, and home to outstanding temporary shows.

Art, baseball and beer
In the gardens of the Cervecería Cuauhtémoc, a short bus trip north of the center of Monterrey, is an incongruous amalgam of attractions sponsored by Mexico's largest brewery, manufacturer of Tecate, Bohemia, Carta Blanca and Superior. Naturally enough, free beer is all part of the visit. The old 19th-century brewery houses the Museo de Monterrey which holds good temporary exhibitions alongside its permanent collection of contemporary Mexican artists. Next door is the Salón de la Fama (Hall of Fame) with a collection of photos and memorabilia of Mexican baseball players and a Museo Deportivo (sports museum). Brewery tours take place three times a day (closed Mondays) but are not obligatory.

Out and about in Monterrey
Eight blocks west of Monterrey's Zona Rosa along Hidalgo is the 1946 Church of La Purísima. Designed by Enrique de la Mora, it was the first example of modern ecclesiastical design in Mexico. Half a mile farther, the more historical El Obispado stands on a small hill. Built in 1786 it served as a bishop's palace and military headquarters, but now houses the Museo Regional de Nuevo León as well as offering fine views over the city and mountains. For information on trips farther afield go to the tourist office located in the State Congress under the Gran Plaza.

Monterrey's Fountain of Life

►► Mulegé 78B2

This sleepy tropical town, backed by the Sierra de Santa Lucia, occupies a prime site on the magnificent **Bahía Concepción►►►**, halfway down the Baja peninsula. It was founded beside Baja's only navigable river, which is lined with date palms and olive trees and dominated by the 1705 Jesuit **Misión de Santa Rosalía**. Also overlooking the town is an old *hacienda*, once an open prison, now converted to the **Museo de Mulegé**. Eclectic exhibits range from the desk of Earle Stanley Gardener (creator of the *Perry Mason* sagas, who often withdrew to Mulegé, as did John Wayne) to old diving and mining gear. The beach below saw the disembarkation of American troops during the Mexican–American war which left the invaders victorious. Mulegé has since been rediscovered by American retirees and sports fishermen, yet retains a lot of charm and offers numerous activities: scuba-diving, kayaking upriver or to outlying islands, trips inland on horseback or by jeep to see spectacular cave paintings in the **Cuevas de San Borjita** or exploring the ruggedly beautiful sierra. Hotels and restaurants remain, for the moment, low-key.

Nature's living laboratory
Eight miles northwest of the beaches of San Carlos and San Pedro lies the unusual island of San Pedro Nolasco. Despite its small size (1.15 sq mi) and proximity to the coast, it is one of the Gulf's most important islands for its rare but prolific flora and fauna. Seven types of native cacti and four species of reptiles are joined by frigate birds, pelicans, cormorants, penguins, kingfishers, herons, falcons and sea gulls. The rocky, craggy coastline, typical of the Gulf islands, also makes it a popular habitat for sea-lions, 25,000 of whom are estimated to inhabit this northern part of the Mar de Cortés. Boat trips are made from San Carlos.

Mulegé is a delightful little oasis on the banks of the Mulegé River

Nogales 78B3

Nogales (named after the Spanish for walnut tree) is the unavoidable border town for visitors heading south from Tucson, Arizona, and the starting point for Mexico's Highway 15 which runs down the Pacific coast. Located in the vast Sonora–Arizona desert, a region of spectacular scenery and remarkable flora and fauna, it is also a major transit center for travelers connecting with Greyhound buses or the Ferrocarril del Pacífico, so there is no shortage of accommodation.

►►► Real de Catorce 79D1

The extraordinary town of Real de Catorce lies high in the Sierra Madre Oriental, roughly halfway between Saltillo and San Luis Potosí, with access through a 2-mile mining tunnel. This once-thriving silver-mine town, with a population of 40,000, is now a mere ghost of itself, echoing with the footsteps of only 800 or so survivors. It was founded in the mid-18th century, and reached its zenith in the late 19th century when its silver veins were considered second only to Guanajuato (see pages 134–137), but from the 1920s sank into a rapid decline. Today its mansions have either crumbled or are shuttered up, although once a year life is re-injected into the town when thousands of pilgrims flood in for the festival of San Francisco (October 4). The Baroque **Parroquía de San Francisco**,with its image of St. Francis of Assisi and hundreds of naïve ex-votos and offerings, is proof of an undying faith. Three other relics of the town's heyday remain: a recently restored **Plaza de Toros** (bullring), the **Palenque de Gallos** (cockfighting arena), designed in Roman amphitheater style and today a cultural center, and the **Casa de Moneda** (mint).

► Saltillo 79D2

Saltillo, capital of the state of Coahuila, is well known for its walnut trees, vineyards, pleasant high-altitude climate and old colonial buildings, and makes a relaxed and interesting stop-over. This former cattle-farming center is a much smaller and less frenetic place than Monterrey, 53 miles northeast, although it is now attracting new industry and modernizing fast. Downtown activity and sights are concentrated around the **Plaza de Armas** and, two blocks northwest, the **Plaza Acuña**. Flanking the former is the impressive Churrigueresque **Catedral de Santiago►►**, built between 1746 and 1801, its ornate façade crowned by two towers (which can be climbed). Facing it is the elegant **Palacio del Gobierno** (1808). Saltillo is famous for its colorful handwoven *serapes* (blankets), much in evidence at the lively **Mercado Juárez** on Plaza Acuña.

► San Carlos 78B2

San Carlos, 10 miles north of Guaymas on the Sonoran coast of the Mar de Cortés, is rapidly turning into a nightmare resort. Two of Mexico's largest marinas, a string of trailer parks and motor homes, a golf course and over-priced services all combine to blot out the attraction of its magnificent bay setting. However, good beaches do remain, and fishermen and divers revel in the prolific waters around the outlying islands.

Bathing in the Bahía
Pelicans, gulls, sea-lions and dolphins are all part of the marine paradise of Bahía Concepción, a deeply indented bay which starts from Punto Chivato and curls past Mulegé and El Coyote to end in a peninsula. Studded with islands and lined with beaches renowned for their wealth of sea shells and marine life, it has become a favorite destination for campers. To the south of Mulegé, Playa Punta Arena, Playa Santispác, and El Requesón are all stunning beaches, while to the north Punto Chivato offers a luxury hotel as well as more stretches of blissful white sand strewn with shells.

Finely woven shawl, Saltillo

Tarahumara indians

■ The Tarahumara, scattered over the magnificent but harsh gorges of the Sierra Madre Occidental, manage to live outside the confines of civilization, preferring a life close to the earth of the bleak, rocky ravines. North Mexico's largest Indian group, they have preserved a unique, albeit impoverished lifestyle.....■

The Sierra Tarahumara is incomparable, with its wild, rugged mountains, canyons and gorges covered by cacti, forests, and lush vegetation

Nature's strange signatures
"Tarahumara country is full of signs, of shapes, of natural effigies which do not seem to exist by chance, as if the gods, who are omnipresent here, had wanted to signify their powers in these strange signatures ... Of course this is not the only place on earth where Nature, moved by a sort of capricious intelligence, sculpted human forms. But this is a different case, because it is over the entire geographic expanse that Nature decided to speak."
Antonin Artaud: *Un Voyage au Pays des Tarahumaras,* 1945.

Some 50,000 Tarahumara live in the region surrounding the Barranca del Cobre and the Barranca de Urique in the southwestern corner of the state of Chihuahua. Their rugged homeland covers about 13,500 square miles of mountains, gouged by the rushing torrents of the Río Fuerte and the Río Conchos. It is in the arable land along the tributaries of these rivers that most Tarahumara choose to live, often in caves, farming the canyon tops (at over 10,000 ft.) for most of the year, descending with their sheep and goats to the semi-tropical floors during winter.

The running people Related to the Apaches, the Tarahumara call themselves the Rarámuri, the "running people," a result of their legendary ability to sprint barefoot up rocky mountainsides or even outrun deer—often spurred on by copious consumption of *tesquino*, a potent corn-beer. Respect for the individual is their greatest

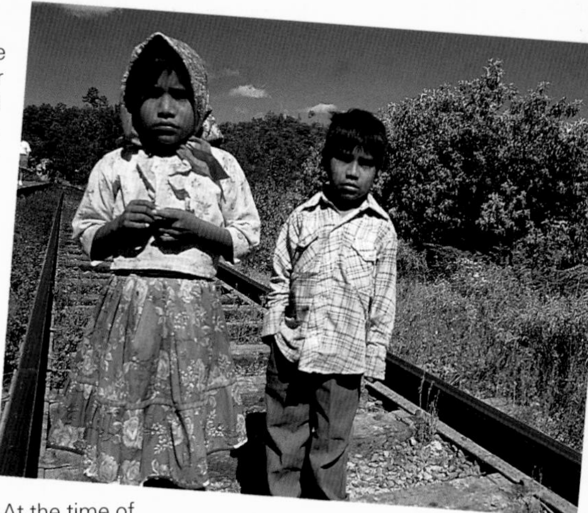

belief, to which is linked a unique certainty in their control over time, an intense spirituality and conviction of life after death. Long isolated, reserved, disdainful of "civilization," and in close touch with the land, they have developed strong telepathic powers. This innate mystical bent incorporates *peyote* (see page 149) into rituals which have fascinated many a Westerner, not least the French writer and actor, Antonin Artaud, who spent several weeks observing the Tarahumara in 1936.

Transformation and resistance At the time of the Spanish Conquest the Tarahumara occupied over 17,000 square miles. Change soon came in the guise of the Jesuits who, despite strong local resistance, had established numerous missions by the mid-17th century. Christianity was absorbed into the Tarahumara calendar, providing the social focus of Sunday church, but for everyday problems they still clung to their traditional belief in the spiritual world as the exact reverse of the physical one: while the body sleeps the soul is at work. More transformation came with the opening of silver mines which brought in foreign blood, from *mestizos* to Africans and Indians from Central Mexico, and by the early 19th century mixed-race individuals outnumbered the indigenous Indians (in 1980 the proportion had risen to 6 to 1). By the late 19th century this new state of affairs triggered violent revolts and forced many Tarahumaras to retreat to less accessible and less fertile areas. The same period saw large-scale exploitation of Chihuahua's pine forests by American lumber interests, leading to the construction of logging roads and the Chihuahua railroad. Only the disruption of the Mexican Revolution stopped the wholesale destruction of the Sierra Tarahumara forests, but it also saw widespread losses of Tarahumara cattle and crops to Pancho Villa's indiscriminate forces.

Today's status Although the 1950s saw the return of parts of the sierra to the Indians under the *ejido* (communal holding) system, many supplement their income working in sawmills for a minimal wage in a rotational system aimed at ensuring work for everyone. Subsistence farming remains their main activity but this meager existence has led to the death of thousands through malnutrition, parasites, and problems related to the lack of food and clean water. Although their population remains stable, in the 1960s 80 percent of Tarahumara children died before the age of five. Today this has been reduced to 40 percent largely thanks to humanitarian Jesuit intervention. Yet, however entrenched the Catholic missionaries may be in the Sierra, they have not managed to eradicate the Tarahumara gods Raiénari (the sun and protector of men) and Mechá (the moon and protector of women).

Easter *fiesta*
The Easter procession most dramatically displays the Tarahumara synthesis of Christianity and ancient rites. Men with painted bodies and mud-caked hair, dressed in headbands and loin-cloths divide into two groups: the Pharisees (with turkey-feather headdresses) and the soldiers (with wooden swords). Processions and dances to drums and flutes lead up to Good Friday when effigies of Judas appear and dances peak around the church altars. By the next day Judas has been ritually stabbed in an orgy of *tesquino* consumption and the Tarahumara go home.

Misión de San Ignacio, one of Baja California's most beautiful mission churches

Cataviña Desert
This spectacular region of sculptural rocks lies in Baja's Parque Natural del Desierto Central, roughly halfway between San Quintín and Bahía de los Ángeles. In among the other-worldly boulders scattered across the desert is a unique display of desert vegetation. Cardons, cirios, ocotillos, and hairy boojum trees create a weird and wonderful landscape, although many of the boulders beside the highway have become victims of the graffiti bug. Camping is the only way to truly savor these unique surroundings.

Shaded avenue in the pleasant, sleepy little town of San José del Cabo

► San Felipe *78A3*

Nearly 320 miles south of the Baja border town of Mexicali lies San Felipe, at the end of Highway 5. Sports fishermen discovered a giant sea bass in the waters off San Felipe in the 1950s, and since then this fishing village has mushroomed into a modestly scaled fishing and boating resort. Big tides make the main beach south of town a popular target for dune-buggying, and it is lined with an increasing number of upscale hotels, trailer parks, beach camps, bars and restaurants. The road south is unpaved and not always easily negotiable.

►► San Ignacio *78A2*

Set beside a lagoon and palm groves, San Ignacio is the second of central Baja's oasis towns after Mulegé, and marks the point where the Transpeninsular Highway veers from the west to the east coast. Its shady central plaza has a true Mexican village feel to it, with small stores and old colonial buildings clustered around the **mission church**. Originally built by the Jesuits in 1728 in adobe, it was replaced by the present stone Dominican structure in 1786. In the surrounding sierra, excellent for hiking, are caves with **Indian paintings►►**, but they can only be reached with the help of a local guide by horse or mule.

►► San José del Cabo *78B1*

San José, the more traditionally picturesque town of the Los Cabos partnership, dates back to 1730 when its Jesuit **mission** was founded. Evangelization was not a smooth business, as depicted by a ceramic frieze over the church entrance which shows Brother Tamaral being "martyred" by Pericué Indians in 1734. However, the stone and stucco 19th-century houses that line Paseo Mijares, San José's broad, main street, prove that perseverance paid off and today the town presents a clean, prosperous face to its mainly American visitors. From the small, shady plaza by the church the avenue passes the stately **Palacio Municipal**, real-estate agencies, trendy boutiques, restaurants and a few lively bars before descending to the hotel-lined coast.

Although condominium and hotel development is happening fast, San José's 40,000 inhabitants are also employed with cattle and agriculture: mango, avocado,

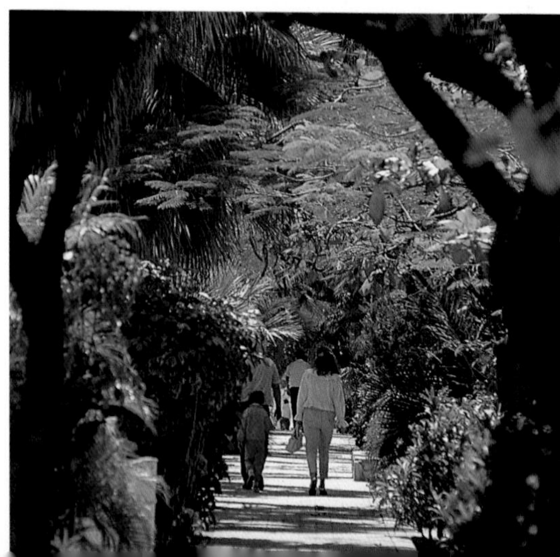

and orange trees grow in abundance in this semi-tropical region. There are horseback excursions to a bird sanctuary located by **La Playa** (a popular surfing beach 1 mile east of town) or the primeval swamp-style lagoon of **Estero de San José**, habitat for 200 bird species, right behind the luxury Stouffer Presidente hotel. This jungle-like stretch has recently been declared an ecological reserve.

▶ San Quintín *78A3*

The bay and town of San Quintín lie 120 miles south of Ensenada, reputedly the windiest spot in Baja where, at certain times of the year, chilly sea mists roll inland towards the dry, brown desert. The beautiful beaches are, however, popular for fishing, diving, surfing, and their fertile clam-beds. The present basic infrastructure of trailer park, hotels and motels will no doubt develop farther.

▶ Santa Rosalía *78B2*

Santa Rosalía owes its existence to a 19th-century French mining company, El Boleo Copper. Built in the 1880s, it remained an entirely company-owned town for nearly 70 years and, although El Boleo closed in 1953, a Mexican company kept operations going until 1985 when it shut down apparently for good. Copper and manganese were shipped from a man-made harbor, now expanded to include floating docks with ocean-cruiser capacity, regularly used by the Guaymas ferry. The town's main monument is the prefabricated iron-plated **Iglesia de Santa Barbara▶▶**, designed by Gustave Eiffel and exhibited in Paris in 1889 before being shipped here in 1895. Adjacent streets are lined with unusually elegant clapboard houses, some with wrought-iron verandahs, the most impressive being the graceful **Palacio Municipal**, and a French-style bakery, **El Boleo**.

Cave paintings
In the sierras of San Francisco and Santa Lucía, to the north and south of San Ignacio respectively, lie the greatest concentration of Baja's cave paintings, unfortunately all difficult to reach. Executed by Paleo Indians, probably to invoke the favors of the gods for successful hunting, they mostly depict hunters standing with their prey of horned animals, pierced with arrows. Panels are larger and more numerous than the celebrated paintings of France's Lascaux Caves—those at Cueva Pintada reach 6 ft. Trips can be arranged from hotels in San Ignacio or Mulegé, or more lengthy riding and camping tours through "Off the Gringo Trail," Apartido Postal 1, Todos Santos 23300, BCS tel: (682) 40218.

The "corridor" beaches
Linking Cabo San Lucas and San José del Cabo is a 19-mile highway known as "the corridor." Foothills covered with scrub and cacti front a blissful stretch of cobalt blue ocean and the best beaches of Los Cabos. Developments leap out of this otherwise harmonious landscape and include five golf courses. In 30 years Los Cabos may have changed radically, but the waves haven't—they can still be dangerous. Areas that are safe to swim from are, working west to east, the city beach of El Medano, Playa Cementerio (2.5 mi); Playa de las Viudas (7 mi); Bahía Chileno (8.5 mi) and Playa Palmilla (17 mi).

Santa Rosalía's buildings have a distinctively French character

Damiana
Todos Santos is the place to sample a drink of the real *Damiana*, a regional specialty which is brewed from the twigs and leaves of the *damiana* plant. Reputed to have great curative powers against flu, chills and general lethargy, it is also imbued with aphrodisiac qualities. In its most kitsch Los Cabos form, *Damiana* is marketed as a yellow liqueur in a bottle shaped like a woman's body, but in Todos Santos you are more likely to find it brewed as tea.

Tijuana *78A4*

Before heading for Tijuana, remember that more American tourists visit this town than any other in the world. Catering solely for those across the border and above all from San Diego, just a few miles north, Tijuana offers a range of services and attractions from cheap marriages, souvenirs, divorce, prostitution, car repairs, drugs, liquor and dentists to betting on horses, greyhounds and jai alai ... the list is endless. Perversely, these very services lend the town a certain fascination of its own, and 2 million inhabitants live off the proceeds. The result is a developing modern city bristling with skyscrapers and shopping malls.

Historical sights are nonexistent, but Tijuana's city authorities have invented alternatives. **Mexitlán**, a cultural theme park, provides an instant overview of Mexico's centuries of civilization, covering an entire city block with 150 scale-models of pre-Hispanic and colonial sites, folk-dance performances, restaurants and "craft" shops. The **Centro Cultural▶▶**, a spectacular building designed by Pedro Ramírez Vázquez, houses a history museum, theater, handicraft stores, restaurants, and the Omnimax Theater where spectators are propelled into the landscapes and sites of Mexico projected onto a 180-degree screen.

Town beaches are crowded and not particularly clean, so it is best to head for **Rosarito**, half-an-hour south by road. This once-small seaside village mushroomed during the 1980s and is now a modern resort with condos branching out in all directions. It, nevertheless, has a slower-paced atmosphere than Tijuana and a wider, more enticing beach.

▶ Todos Santos *78B1*

This expanding tropical town, founded in 1724, lies 40 miles north of the Cabo San Lucas and just beyond the Tropic of Cancer. Indian inhabitants were wiped out three times by diverse epidemics and the town was resettled by *mestizos* (mixed Spanish and Mexican blood) who set up a sugar industry. Mango groves compete with date palms for supremacy, but it is the long, deserted beaches that are the chief attraction here, in particular **Punta Lobos** which lies at the foot of a dramatic rocky bluff.

Tijuana's impressive Centro Cultural is a fine example of contemporary architecture

Drive Baja California

This drive takes you away from the developments of Los Cabos along rough unsurfaced roads to a stretch of coast which few visitors reach. Allow a full day for negotiating the terrain and for swimming stops.

From **San José del Cabo** drive 5 miles north on Highway 1 (in the direction of La Paz) and after the village of Santa Rosa turn right towards **Palo Escopeta**. Depending on the time of year this normally dry, scrub landscape can look lush, with thousands of cacti draped in exuberant wild flowers or vines, and the occasional palm tree in the valleys. While driving watch out for cattle that stray into the road—penalties are high for injuring them. The bumpy track leads through the occasional village where ambiguous-looking turnings can be clarified by consulting the friendly inhabitants. Stark, cacti-studded hills predominate, while roadrunners, hares, and zebu cattle are the most conspicuous fauna. Certain stretches of the road have been much improved and speed can be picked up. When glimpses of cobalt blue appear on the horizon (1½ to 2 hours later), the hardest stretch of the drive is nearly over.

Along the coast take your pick of the endless beaches and warm waters of the **Mar de Cortés**. For a good lunch and proximity to the coral reef of **Los Pulpos**, drive through Punta Lobera to a high rocky outcrop at **Los Frailes**, Baja's most easterly point. Here a discreet, though pricey hotel overlooks a sheltered beach, making an excellent swimming stop. The reef surrounds most of Cabo Pulmo, immediately to the north, where the road regains a viable tarmac surface. Pass Punta Arena's small **lighthouse** and at La Rivera turn left to cut across to the village of **Las Cuevas** on Highway 1. Driving south back to **Los Cabos** the magnificent **Sierra de la Laguna** looms to the west all the way.

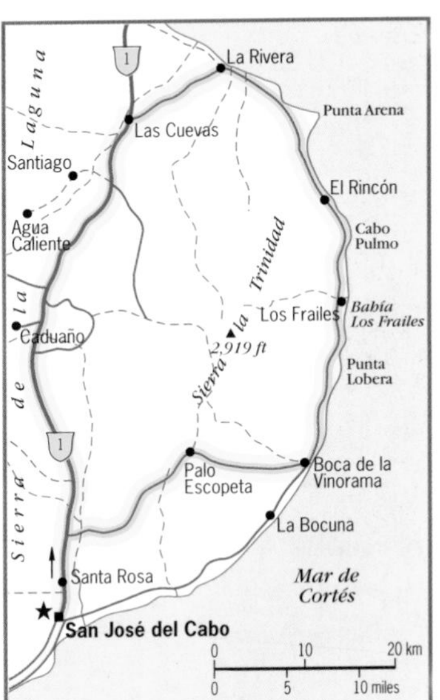

The pace of life slows down considerably in the afternoon

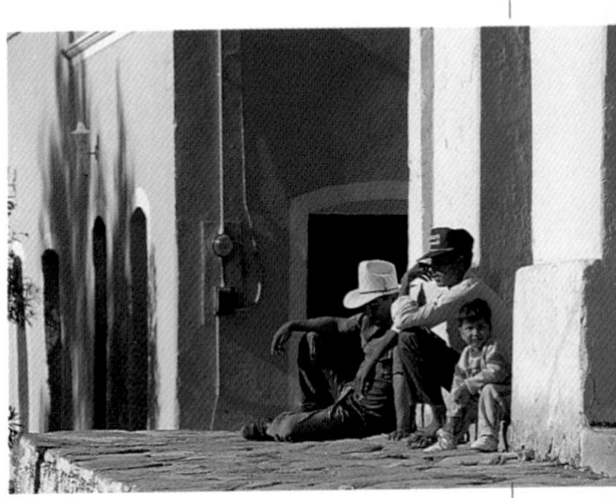

Westin Regina Resort, Los Cabos

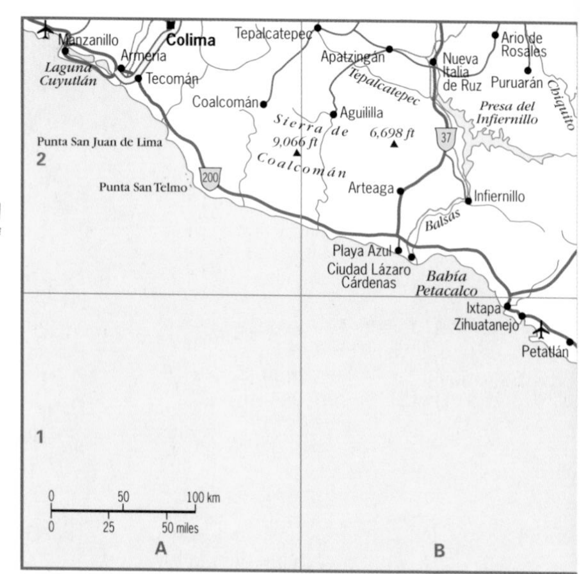

Right: Pacific Coast (south)

THE PACIFIC COAST

Visitors to the state of Guerrero can enjoy vast expanses of beautiful deserted Pacific beach, if the glitz and glamor of places like Acapulco palls

The Pacific Coast From Mazatlán to Acapulco, the Pacific coast cuts southeast through the states of Sinaloa, Nayarit, Jalisco, Colima, Michoacán, and Guerrero before moving into Oaxaca (see **The South**, page 188). This is Mexico's most spectacularly beautiful coastline, backed by the craggy mountain ranges of the Sierra Madre Occidental and the Sierra Madre del Sur. Not surprisingly it has been a long-standing target for sun worshippers, jet-setters, sports fishermen, and surfers, who home in annually to its thundering waves, elevated temperatures, tropical blooms, and technicolor sunsets. Mega-resorts continue to expand, but there are still long tracts of coast that remain undeveloped and industrial pollution is limited. Short forays can be made inland to mountain villages where history has not been completely erased, while out in the deep blue of the Pacific every possible watersport can be indulged. Bus routes cover most inhabited destinations, but to reach unpopulated areas and beaches a car is essential.

Background Before the Spanish descended to the Pacific coast the area was inhabited by local tribes now loosely described as "Culturas del Occidente." Nayarit, Jalisco, and Colima together formed the epicenter of this civilization, thought to date from between 300BC and AD150. As their artifacts were all probably looted from underground tombs, the term "tomb culture" is often used. Only one important site remains from this era, at Ixtlán del Río. Although maritime trade already existed before the arrival of Cortés, it was in the 1560s that a direct link with the riches of the Orient was created from the ports of Acapulco, Barra de Navidad, and Manzanillo. San Blas saw the first missionaries set sail for Baja California in 1768,

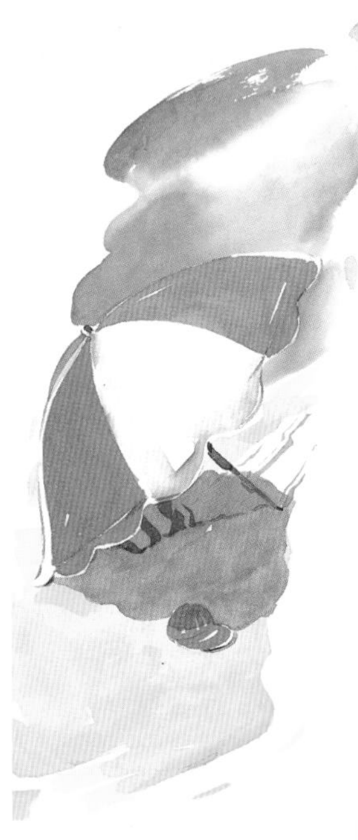

1950s Acapulco
"We discovered what one knew but had not realised, that at daytime in the tropics, unless one has to earn a living, there is nothing for one to do ... One could be rowed by Mulattos looking like Chinese under an awning of mats across an even bay, bathe with a straw hat in waters of topaz and pellucid green, alas warm; sit in a sweltering grove drinking the milk of freshly opened coconuts wishing that it were water and that it were cold. One could be drawn across the town by mules, and up the cliff, sit in a transparent frigidaire above the sea, order from a list of forty-six rum cocktails, watch boys dive off a ninety-foot crag for coins, listen to Riviera voices dropping names ...." Sybille Bedford: *A Visit to Don Octavio*, 1953.

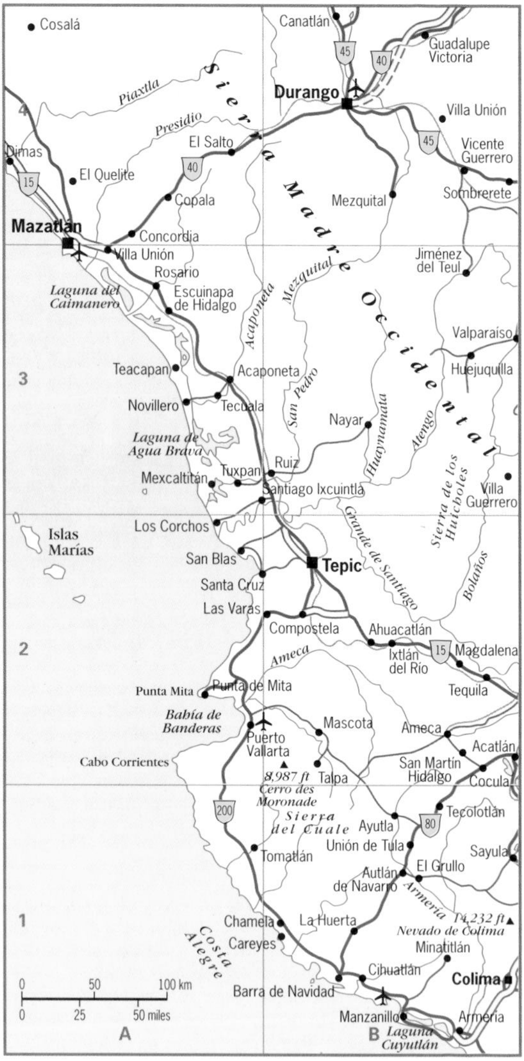

Right: Pacific Coast (north)

Coconuts drying in the sun to make copra

while Mazatlán thrived as an important fishing port. Along with this external input came a new ingredient to the population, African slaves, brought in to do the work the native Mexicans were not considered capable of. Their genetic influence is particularly visible in the villages of Guerrero and in Acapulco itself. After Independence the area lost its colonial trading importance and lapsed into a long period of decline. Then came the 1950s, the first commerical airlines and Acapulco's phoenix-like rise from the ashes, soon followed by Puerto Vallarta and, more recently, Mazatlán, Manzanillo, and Ixtapa-Zihuatanejo, one of the latest of Mexico's artificial mega-resorts.

Today's high profile... The Huichols and Coras, some of Mexico's most undeveloped Indian groups, still inhabit the sierras of Nayarit and Jalisco, but their remoteness

makes little imprint on the coastal towns. Above all, the Pacific is geared towards the great outdoors: fishing, diving, surfing, parasailing, and sun worshipping. Early celebrities such as Elizabeth Taylor and Richard Burton drew the wealthy to the area. As a result, today's reality lies somewhere between Jacuzzi-infested hotels, happy-hour bars and time-share condos, while the luxury villas retreat over the horizon. Little can stop the tidal wave of visitors who flood into the international airports for a two weeks' binge of sea and sun, and their needs are well catered for.

Colorful hammocks for sale—the coolest way to spend a night on the beach or to have a siesta

...and low profile Commercialism may plague the large resorts, but explore the coastline between them and you enter an ecological paradise of lagoons, secluded coves and steep slopes thick with tropical vegetation. Careyes may now cater for a more exclusive clientele, but a few miles away lie the still low-key resorts of Barra de Navidad and Chamela. Between San Blas and Mazatlán is a long stretch of undeveloped, scenic land, part tropical jungle, part open lagoon, perfect for those wishing to escape sophistication. Other last frontiers are dotted along Michoacán's coast, east and west of Playa Azul. The only problem is the ferocity of the Pacific waves, ideal for surfers, attractive for sports fishermen and divers, but often dangerous for swimmers.

Local women wash clothes in the time-honored way

Enticing plunder
Plying the Acapulco–Manila route were sturdy new trading galleons, *naos de China*, constructed of Filipino teak by Malays and Chinese and laden with the riches of Nueva España and the Orient. Cargoes of silver, spices, ivory, porcelain and silks soon became prime targets for covetous Dutch and English buccaneers who included Sir Francis Drake and Thomas Cavendish. Pichilingues (Dutch pirates), buccaneers, corsairs, filibusters and pirates added new color to the high seas and to local vocabulary, but the amount they plundered was a mere drop in the ocean compared to the immense wealth the Spaniards were amassing. From Acapulco their colonial plunder was loaded on to mules and trekked across country to Veracruz, from where it was shipped home to the courts of Spain.

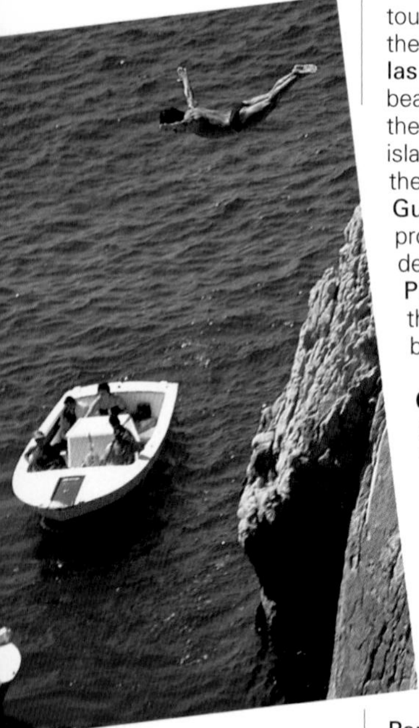

High diver, La Quebrada, Acapulco

► Acapulco *107C1*

However much the myth has been shattered, nothing can alter Acapulco's breathtaking site commanding two bays and backed by the dramatic Sierra Madre del Sur. About 240 miles south of Mexico City by a fast new toll-road, it attracts plane-loads of package tourists geared up for its resort offerings. A tacky concrete nightmare for some, a steamy playground for others, Acapulco specializes in extremes. Beachlife or nightlife, these are the alternatives, yet this fun-loving settlement approaching 2 million inhabitants lies on the coast of one of Mexico's poorest states, an oasis in the wilderness.

Before the crowds Acapulco's early development was due, quite simply, to its status as the nearest Pacific port to Mexico City. The "place where the big reeds grow" was reached by Cortés and others around 1530, and port and shipbuilding facilities were soon established in the generous natural harbor. In 1565 the first Spanish galleon set sail from Manila to Acapulco, marking the beginning of a trade route that saw the wealth of the Orient exchanged with that of Nueva España. With Independence the Spanish ships sailed away forever, Acapulco went into decline and by the early 20th century had all but ceased to exist. However, in 1927 a paved road from Mexico City and, finally, an international airport in the 1950s brought it back to life.

Layout The 7-mile horseshoe-shaped bay of Acapulco starts in the east at the headland of Punta Bruja, crowned by a giant illuminated crucifix, with the watersports bay of **Puerto Marqués** at its feet. Sweeping past the main tourist developments and beaches along La Costera to the old town it ends at Punta Grifo on the **Peninsula de las Playas**. Here **Caleta** and **Caletilla**, two adjacent beaches, attract visitors with their calm waters and are the embarkation point for **Isla de la Roqueta**►►, an island popular for more gentle waves, lush vegetation and the submerged bronze statue of the **Virgin of Guadalupe** in her polluted grave. To the west of the promontory is the celebrated **La Quebrada**, where daredevil divers plunge 130 ft. into the waters below, and **Playa La Angosta**, another sheltered cove. From here the road follows the coast to **Pie de la Cuesta**►►, the beginning of a vast and beautiful lagoon.

Central sights and beaches Fronting the main harbor is the old town, a surprising breath of Mexican air in what is otherwise an anonymous international resort. Narrow, lively streets lead off the shady central plaza and uphill to the **Fuerte de San Diego**►►, built between 1615 and 1617 to protect the port from pirate attacks and now converted into an interesting history and anthropology museum, with panoramic views over the bay and mountains. A few streets north is the sprawling **Mercado de Artesanías** offering good deals on handicrafts and clothes. Farther east, children will enjoy the **Parque Papagayo**, an amusement park which lies right behind **Playa Hornos**, where fishermen unload their catch. In the middle of the bay is **Playa Condesa**, the hottest beach in

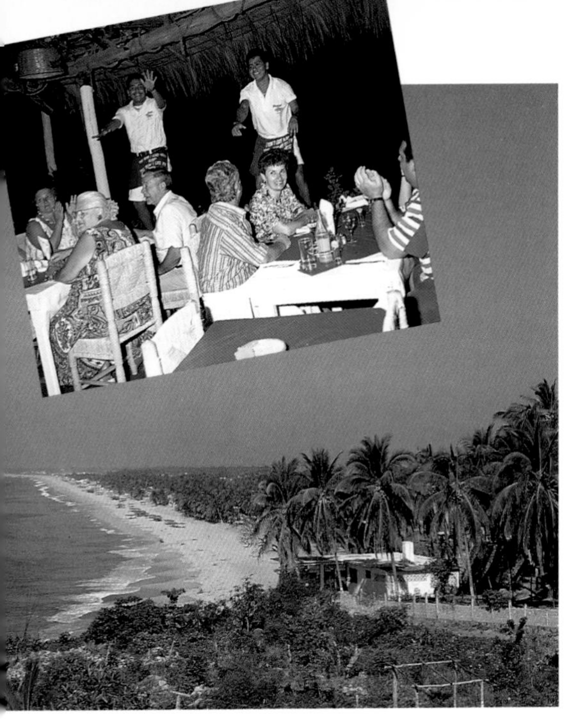

The curving sweep of Pie de la Cuesta, famous for its sunsets
Inset: Paradise restaurant

Pie de la Cuesta
Six miles northwest of Acapulco, a long narrow spit of land separates the thundering Pacific ocean from the mangrove- and palm-fringed Laguna Coyuca. Once a birdwatchers' paradise, and now a favorite with water-skiers, the lagoon extends 6 miles west and is dotted with tropical islands. Horseback riders and sunset fanatics home in on the beach of Pie de la Cuesta, almost impossible to swim off due to its pounding surf and strong undertow, although daredevil locals show off their fearlessness in the towering waves. Modest hotels and seafood restaurants line the shore, making a pleasant alternative to Acapulco.

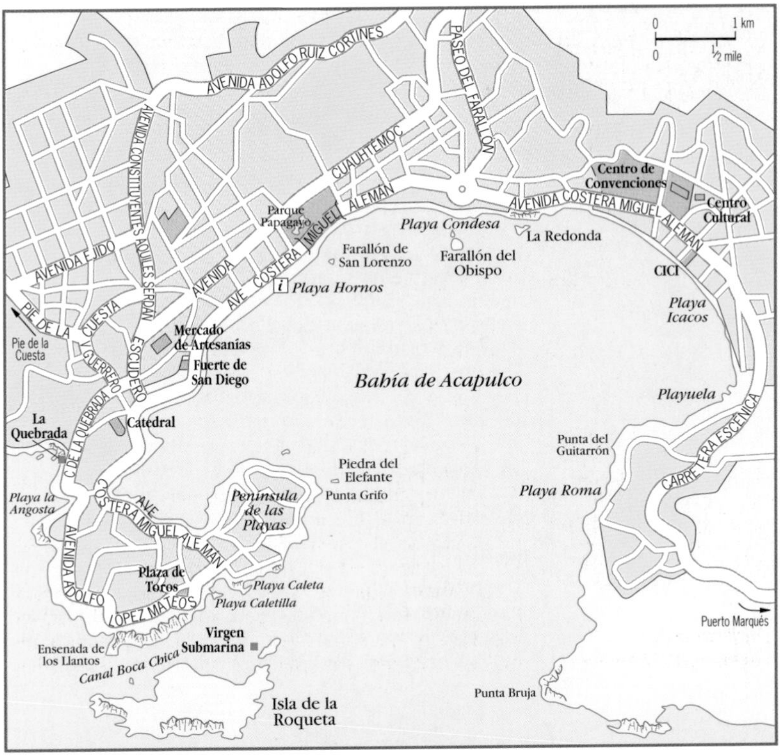

town, where being seen wins out over swimming. Another hive of entertainment clusters around the Centro Internacional Acapulco, farther along La Costera, and includes the aquariums, dolphins, and water-rides of the **CICI** children's park.

►► Barra de Navidad *108B1*

This tiny, picturesque fishing village and relaxed resort marks the southern point of Jalisco's majestically mountainous and indented coastline and lies at the eastern end of the wide sweep of Bahía de Navidad. The main street is named after Miguel López de Legazpi, the Spanish captain who set sail from here for the Philippines in 1564. Well supplied with modest hotels and seafood restaurants, the village culminates in a sandbar recently extended with a seawall promenade built by the villagers themselves. To the west is a sandy beach, good for surfing in the winter months, and to the east lies a vast lagoon, sheltered by the peninsula of **La Culevra**. A public boat serves its pretty waterfront village of **Colimilla►** lined with low-priced seafood restaurants and *palapa*-thatched houses nestling in tropical vegetation. Resort developments and a golf course are, however, already taking shape, and Barra's sleepy atmosphere may change fast.

Preparing oysters at a beachside restaurant

►► Careyes *108B1*

Careyes occupies a prime stretch of Jalisco's tropical coast where palm-strewn hills roll into the Pacific, small sandy coves offer sheltered waters, and turtles are a common underwater sight. Unfortunately reserved for the very well-heeled, the area has been monopolized by a 3,700-acre resort owned by an Italian millionaire, Gianfranco Brignone, and includes the incongruity of a polo club in the jungle and a wildlife reserve and exclusive hotel run by Isabel Goldsmith, daughter of Jimmy, the international business magnate.

►► Colima *108B1*

Barely 38 miles inland from the Pacific coast, in the foothills of the Sierra Madre del Sur, the placid capital of the tiny state of Colima (which covers exactly 0.27 percent of the Mexican Republic) is rarely visited by tourists. Yet a warm, year-round climate, numerous tropical parks and gardens, stately buildings and a good archeological museum make it a refreshing climatic and cultural change from the Pacific trail. It was the third city established by the Spaniards in Mexico, in 1523, but most of its monuments date from the 19th century. Exceptions are the **Convento de Almoloyan,** a former 16th-century convent, and the Plateresque **Iglesia de San Felipe de Jesús,** inhabited in 1772 by the priest and subsequent instigator of Independence, Miguel Hidalgo. A few blocks northeast of the Plaza Principal stands the **Casa de la Cultura,** a modern cultural complex which combines galleries, libraries, workshops and a theater with the **Museo de Las Culturas de Occidente►►** (Museum of the Western Cultures), Colima's main attraction. Its many pre-Hispanic artifacts include the famous stylized pot-bellied Colima dogs, modeled in every conceivable pose, as well as other, often humorous, clay figurines of note.

Volcanoes
Still occasionally emitting blasts of sulphurous smoke, El Fuego (Volcán de Fuego) rises 13,000 ft. into the skies of Colima just north of the state capital. A national park has been created around it, and dirt roads run high enough up the slopes to enable the summit to be reached on foot. Farther north looms El Nevado (Nevado de Colima), which peaks at nearly 14,000 ft. Also known by its Náhautl name of Zapotépetl, it is Mexico's sixth highest volcano, now extinct. This whole region is a dramatic spectacle of hills, valleys and deep gulleys crossed by bridges—well worth exploring on the highway to Guadalajara.

►► Concordia *108A4*

This pretty town, set in lush tropical vegetation, is located on the spectacular Highway 40 winding north and distinctly uphill from Mazatlán to Durango, and is well known for its fine hand-carved furniture and pottery. On the tiny

Three Rivers Project
Two broad rivers, the Humaya and the Tamazula, cross the state of Sinaloa and on reaching the state capital of Culiacán join to create a third, the Río Culiacán, which eventually flows into the Pacific. Trees and vegetation line these watercourses and the surrounding fertile valleys are considered to be Mexico's bread and butter (and unofficial drug center). A massive development project already under construction will create 10 bridges, 30 miles of riverside promenades and 20 miles of new highway, as well as harness the waters of an unruly *arroyo* (stream) into El Bledal reservoir.

Concordia's Iglesia San Sebastián dominates the main square

main square the imposing 18th-century **Iglesia San Sebastián** has a fine Baroque façade, its pink stone contrasting with the modestly scaled, whitewashed houses. The surrounding hills are much visited by locals for their abundant mineral and hot-water springs and this lush, fresh region, only 30 miles from Mazatlán, makes a welcome change from the heat of the coast.

▶▶ Copala *108A4*

About 15 miles farther north of Concordia, the picture-postcard village of Copala, founded in 1565 and once noted for its silver mining, clings to the Sinaloan mountainside. Two-story houses with decorative ironwork balconies line cobblestone streets which wind precariously around the verdant slopes. The late-18th-century **Iglesia de San Joseph** incorporates a 16th-century bell-tower and atrium.

▶▶ Cosalá *108A4*

Another of Sinaloa's treasures, the former mining town of Cosalá lies lost in the inland sierra between Culiacán and Mazatlán, about two hours' drive from the latter. Red-tiled roofs of whitewashed houses retreat into the shade of cedar trees, and the main square offers an interesting **Museo de Minería e Historia** housed in a colonial mansion. The main church, the 18th-century **Templo de Santa Ursula,** has an unusual sundial, but more unusual is the Palacio Municipal clock, which functions by means of a 24-hour pulley weighted by a rock.

The charming town of Copala is surrounded by gently rolling slopes that form the foothills of the Sierra Madre Occidental

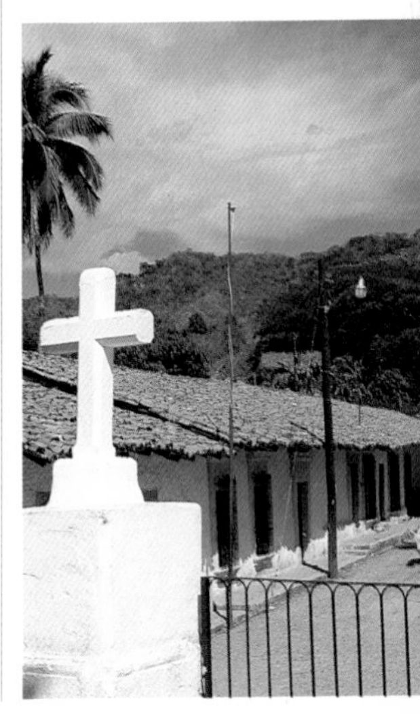

Las Hadas
This completely self-contained, Moorish-style fantasy of domes, towers and arches offers every imaginable luxury in a high-class Disneyworld setting. The product of the imagination of Bolivian tin magnate and multi-millionaire, Antenor Patiño, it was initially conceived as an ultra-deluxe resort where he and his friends could gather at any time of the year for the temperate weather and suitably exclusive atmosphere. Bo Derek and Dudley Moore tested the pool here while shooting the film *10*, and since then the 220 rooms, 18-hole golf course, private marina and beach have been ranked among the world's top 10 hotels.

▶▶▶ Costa Alegre *108A1*

This newly-coined name refers to Jalisco's spectacular and still relatively undeveloped coastline which curves northwest from the Bahía de Navidad and ends at the Bahía de Chamela, a distance of about 65 miles. It is truly tropical, with superb beaches fronted by rocky islands, while amenities range from the luxury developments of Careyes to more affordable options in Melaque, Chamela, or Tenacatita. **Melaque▶**, also known as San Patricio, lies at the western end of the lovely Bahía de Navidad facing Barra (see page 112) and is popular with Mexican families. To the north, the growing coastal settlement of **Chamela▶▶** sits on a 7-mile stretch of beach facing numerous outlying islands and is the nearest to Puerto Vallarta (95 miles northwest).

▶ Ixtapa *106B1*

Now twinned with nearby Zihuatanejo (see page 122) as a major government-sponsored resort, Ixtapa, lying 150 miles west of Acapulco, was, until the mid-1970s, nothing more than a coconut plantation. Development has brought the coastal highway and an international airport, but the lush tropical valley still remains, ending on the white sands of the lovely **Playa del Palmar**. The town lacks the majestic scale and history of Acapulco, and has become a sterilized agglomeration of over-priced high-rise hotels, restaurants, bars, discos, shopping centers, mandatory golf course, and marina. The soul of Mexico retreats behind the Sierra Madre del Sur, but a taste of unadulterated nature can be found on **Isla Ixtapa▶▶**, an island wildlife sanctuary where armadillos, deer and raccoons vie with *palapa*-style seafood restaurants for attention. Beaches here are more sheltered for swimming than Playa del Palmar, and snorkeling and diving more rewarding.

Ixtapa's wide sandy beaches set against a tropical background have become a firm favorite with Mexican families

▶ Ixtlán del Río *108B2*

Nayarit's only archeological site, which flourished during the 2nd century AD, lies 50 miles east of Tepic on the highway to Guadalajara. Several low structures are dominated by the circular **Temple of Quetzalcóatl** mounted via four staircases, and with walls perforated by cruciform openings. The cross shapes could have referred to a pre-Hispanic concept of the universe. Other ruins date from a later period, probably AD400, and the site is thought to have remained occupied by local tribes until the Spanish conquest. Located in agricultural land on the outskirts of the village, it is worth seeing for those whose route misses more elaborate structures elsewhere.

▶ Manzanillo *108B1*

Manzanillo was founded in the early 16th century as a major shipyard and port for the trade route to Asia, and is said to have hosted junks from the Orient long before the Spaniards arrived. Today it is a sprawling, unattractive town curling around an immense, mountain-backed bay. Ocean liners, cargo boats, fishing boats and yachts dot the harbor and the main town is situated on an isthmus separating the Pacific from the Laguna Cuyutlán. Resort hotels, condominiums and the better beaches lie across the bay on the road west to Playa de Oro airport. Most famous of all the hotels is **Las Hadas** (The Fairies), a surrealistic Arabian Nights-style development which climbs up a hill overlooking the bay. Named after the camomile tree (*manzanilla*), this tropical port, known as the "Sailfish Capital of the World," is renowned as a base for deep-sea fishing expeditions. Manzanillo sprouts an abundance of vegetation, but the general atmosphere is rundown, and harbor installations are less than picturesque. It ranks as Mexico's most important west coast shipping center, with a railroad link inland to Guadalajara, and is strategically placed for local produce (coconuts, limes, bananas, mangoes, avocados, and sugar-cane). For visitors the main interest lies in the white or black volcanic beaches lining the Bahía de Santiago at the chic western end of the main bay: **La Audiencia, Santiago, Olas Altas**, and **Miramar**. The last two have good surfing waves while the cove of La Audencia is ideal for swimming and water-skiing. From October to May, it is the turn of sports fishermen tracking down abundant red snapper, marlin, sea bass, and giant tuna.

Olas Verdes
The Pacific waves around Manzanillo are known for a spectacular nocturnal phenomenon, that of an emerald-green phosphorescent microscopic organism (Olas Verdes) which sporadically invades the water. This naturally illuminated plankton creates a most remarkable effect, and if you plunge into the waves at the right time you will emerge covered in sparkling pinpoints of light.

Manzanillo is a good base for fishing expeditions

Valentino's Disco Club, a Moorish-style palace by the sea at Punta Camaron, is a long-time favorite in Mazatlán

▶▶ Mazatlán *108A4*

This unashamedly booming resort town, approaching half a million inhabitants, is rapidly expanding northwest along the coast of Sinaloa. As a major commercial and fishing port it also boasts Mexico's largest shrimp fleet. Less sophisticated than its chief resort rivals, Puerto Vallarta and Acapulco, Mazatlán still has a life of its own outside tourism with an atmospheric old town sitting on a headland which firmly separates harbor and tourist activities. Its situation due east of the southern tip of Baja California, at the confluence of the Mar de Cortés and the Pacific, endows it with warm water and abundant year-round shoals of marlin and sailfish, as well as Mexico's longest *malecón* (sea boulevard) which stretches 13 miles along the beach-lined bay.

Mazatlán was founded in 1531, but did not develop properly until the mid-19th century. Relics from this era can be found in the relaxed old town which revolves around the Plaza Principal with its Moorish-style **cathedral** and, two blocks south, the impressive 1860s **Teatro Ángela Peralta▶▶**. Other sights are the **Mercado Central**, brimming with crafts and food-stalls, and the small **Museo de Arqueología** (Sixto Osuna 76). Towering over this downtown area is the **Cerro de la Nevería** (Icebox Hill) with panoramic sea views, while a short hike to the end of the peninsula ends at **El Faro▶▶**, a lighthouse open to the public, which claims to be the world's second highest—after Gibraltar's. A helpful tourist office is also located in this area at Paseo Olas Altas 13000 in the Banco de México building.

From the surfing beach of **Playa Olas Altas** at the base of Cerro de la Nevería (where high-divers plunge from a tall rock called El Mirador), the celebrated *malecón* runs past the **Playa del Norte** and into the **Zona Dorada** (Golden Zone). Here condominiums, large hotels, discos, and restaurants look out across Mazatlán's best beaches and

Laying bricks out to dry in the sun

surf to outlying islands. Every imaginable watersport is indulged in, island boat trips are part of the action, while time-share sharks abound. However, with tracts of prime real estate still empty, Mazatlán keeps an attractively imperfect air and, despite visitors pouring into its international airport and a giant tourist complex taking shape at its western end, strikes a good balance between old and new.

▶▶ Mexcaltitán *108A3*

Once thought to be the legendary island of Aztlán, the original home of the Aztecs, Mexcaltitán lies 44 miles northwest of San Blas along Nayarit's lagoon-indented coast, and is reached by ferry from the town of **Santiago Ixcuintla**. Local transportation is by canoe through a network of narrow canals criss-crossed by causeways, hence its nickname the "Venice of Mexico." No tourist facilities exist, but Mexcaltitán has not been not forgotten: Mexican presidents periodically visit the island village in a symbolic gesture to its ultimate Mexican character.

▶▶ Playa Azul *106B2*

Squeezed between the states of Guerrero and Jalisco is the remote, undeveloped coastline of Michoacán, with an immense, polluted black-spot at the industrial port of Lázaro Cárdenas, but otherwise offering several low-key destinations. Playa Azul is popular with Mexican tourists who flood down from inland Michoacán, but it remains a pleasant resort with a beautiful beach and good surfing—its waves compare with those in Hawaii. Dangers lie in stingrays and strong currents, but these are outweighed by the dramatic setting of mountains descending sharply into the sea, cheap accommodation and a string of open-air seafood restaurants lining the waterfront.

▶ Punta Maldonado *107D1*

This last outpost of Guerrero's Pacific resorts lies roughly halfway between Acapulco and Oaxaca's burgeoning Puerto Escondido (see page 207). The road along this 250-mile-long stretch runs inland, passing through flat grazing country and small towns, many of whose inhabitants are descended from African slaves. Rivers and lagoons alternate with some superb beaches. Punta Maldonado is visited above all, for its fabulously clear water and good snorkeling, but facilities remain limited.

Carnaval
Every year since 1898, during the week before Ash Wednesday, Mazatlán bursts into life with its Mardi Gras, one of Mexico's liveliest fiestas. Activities take place all over town but the main festivities concentrate along Playa Olas Altas. Wandering *mariachis* keep the background sounds going till late, fireworks shoot over the bay, mock sea-battles take place and fancy-dress balls propel inhabitants and visitors into a fantasy world. Considered the world's third best carnival after Río de Janeiro and New Orleans, it also means that Mazatlán's many hotels are booked solid. If you want to take part in the fun, make reservations several months ahead.

Mazatlán's islands
Of the outlying islands, the Isla de la Piedra (Stone Island) is the most ecologically appealing for its saltwater canals, thick, lush mangrove swamps, numerous seabirds and superb uncrowded beaches. Boats leave from Mazatlán's *embarcadero* (landing place) in the docks behind the old town, situated right beside a huge tuna-, sardine- and shrimp-packing plant. Three islands lie a short distance out from the Zona Dorada: Lobos, Venados and Pájaros. Venados (Deer Island) is particularly good for snorkeling and diving and also boasts some interesting old cave paintings. Boats leave from the Muelle Pier, just east of the lighthouse, and from larger hotels.

Modern architecture

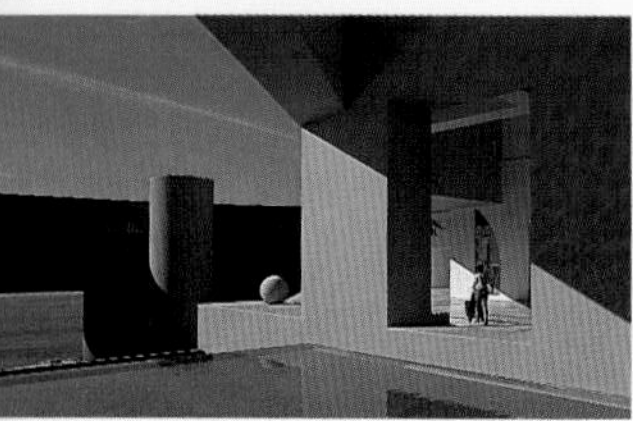

■ No other nation can claim such a profound 20th-century architectural imprint as that of Luís Barragán on Mexico. Inspired by Juan O'Gorman, Barragán's vivid, geometric lines have spawned hundreds of copies all over the country and created a typically Mexican school of contemporary architecture.....■

Omnipresent architecture
"Mexico has always been a country of architects, from pre-Columbian times to the present. Nearly all our towns and the majority of our villages possess remarkable edifices and monuments, and some of them are really grandiose. The number of these buildings and urban complexes that have miraculously survived the ravages of time is surprising."
Octavio Paz: *Labyrinth of Solitude*, 1950.

In every city of Mexico, from Monterrey to Acapulco, Mexico City to Puerto Vallarta, modern architecture is a high-profile element in the urban picture. Sleek office buildings, innovative museums, sophisticated villas, luxury hotels, and even bus stations all bear the signatures of Mexico's new generation of architects, following a spirit that started with the great Maya and Aztec temples, was nurtured by the Spanish, and peaked in grandiose excess under Porfirio Díaz. Post-revolutionary Mexico saw a new democratic accent on integrating art, architecture and the applied arts, stimulated by the flourishing muralist movement and much influenced by the theories and designs of Juan O'Gorman.

Precursors Behind the post-revolutionary thrust of new forms was the figure of José Villagram García, who propounded the theory of "contemporary Mexican architecture as the result of the historical development of our art ... and of a form of expression suited to our culture." His rejection of the copying of European forms which had monopolized the Porfiriato style was adopted by his students, who included Juan O'Gorman, Enrique del Moral, and Enrique Yañez. O'Gorman, the son of Irish immigrants, advocated the Bauhaus principles of functionalism, but combined this with the burgeoning new spirit of Mexican–Indian identity. His private houses, built in the early 1930s in San Ángel, are among the country's first modern buildings, a major landmark being the indigo-and-red studio he designed for Diego Rivera and Frida Kahlo, which regenerated the brilliant color that once coated pre-Hispanic façades. Ultimate symbol of this cultural renaissance was Mexico City's Ciudad Universitaria (1951–1955), an astonishing collaboration between nearly 100 architects and engineers which remains a showcase for decorative passion and generous use of space.

Modern architecture at the New Stock Exchange, Mexico City

Barragán O'Gorman's emphasis on utilitarian rationalist forms and color was taken one step farther by Luís Barragán who, inspired by a visit to Spain's Moorish palace, the Alhambra, sought to inject beauty, emotion and spirituality into modernist forms. Together with Enrique del Morral and Mathías Goeritz, Barragán embarked upon a style of architecture where bold wall color, scale and angle defined a space in which, when possible, nature was fully integrated.

Their own private homes, built in the 1940s in the Calle Francisco Ramírez in Tacubaya, Mexico City, became the controversial models for a style which left its signature on countless commissions over the following decades. Massive constructions, thick walls and small openings laid out in geometric purity juxtapose planes of pink, ocher, violet and peach, while water is channeled along pathways or gushes from overhead aqueducts. An exhibition of his work at New York's MoMA (Museum of Modern Art) in 1976 confirmed Barragán's satellite status, crowned in 1980 by the Pritzker Prize (architecture's equivalent of the Nobel). In 1988 Barragán died at the ripe old age of 86, leaving a legacy of 20th-century monuments and an enduring Mexican style.

Zealous disciples Parallel to Barragán's trail-blazing are the structures of Antonio Attolini (see his majestic Iglesia Santa Cruz in Mexico City) and Ricardo Legorreta, the latter now considered the doyen of contemporary architecture. Legorreta's first major project was Mexico City's Hotel Camino Real (1968), an exercise in using color to emphasize the harmony of architectural relations which he has mastered more strikingly in the last decade for the same chain at Cancún and at the luxury resort of Ixtapa. His *pièce de résistance* is Monterrey's spectacular new art museum, MARCO, which Legorreta describes as "a traditional Mexican building (where) movement is achieved through a central patio." The 1990s see no abatement in Mexico's talent for architectural innovation, and dramatic, vividly colored façades combined with monumental scale continue to represent the Mexican identity.

The Westin Regina Resort, Los Cabos

Magic
"Architectural publications no longer contain the words: beauty, inspiration, bewitchment, magic, spell and also serenity, silence, intimacy, astonishment. All these words have been warmly received in my heart."
Luís Barragán.

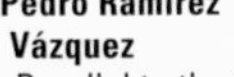

Pedro Ramírez Vázquez
Parallel to the integration of color into form, Mexico's architects were clearly influenced by the concepts of the Bauhaus and Adolf Loos. Pedro Ramírez Vázquez, best known for his museum architecture at Mexico City's Museum of Anthropology and the Caracol, is master of a synthesis of their functionalism with imaginative form and subdued decoration.

Gilardi's Satellite Towers, Satellite City, Mexico State

A breath of history
Originally called Las Peñas, Vallarta's history goes back to 1851 when a certain Guadalupe Sánchez built the first house on the banks of the Río Cuale. He developed a successful mule operation, hauling minerals from inland mines to the small port for shipment and bringing salt from the outlying Islas Marías. As word of the area's great beauty spread, other settlers arrived and in 1886 the small town was officially recognized. When Las Peñas changed its name to Puerto Vallarta in 1918 to honor Jalisco's governor, its population stood at 200. In 1954 an airport was built and Puerto Vallarta began to be touted as a Pacific paradise. Then 10 years later along came John Huston...

Statue on Puerto Vallarta's malecón

▶ Puerto Vallarta *108A2*

Beach-buggies, Chevrolets, fuming buses, *taco* stands, "2 for 1" happy-hour bars—Puerto Vallarta is blatantly aimed at the tastes and wallets of *gringos* (foreigners) who flood through the international airport to invade the high-rise hotels lining the world's second largest bay. Now legendary, its early development was kickstarted in 1964 by the filming of John Huston's *Night of the Iguana* starring Ava Gardner and Richard Burton. Elizabeth Taylor came too, and the famous couple set up home in the winding cobblestone streets of what is now termed Old Vallarta. The rest, as they say, is history.

South of Río Cuale The main downtown area is divided by the Río Cuale with an elongated island at its mouth, which has become home to a tiny, uninspired museum, stores, and various bars and restaurants. To the south lies the downscale side of Vallarta, although restaurants now find it perversely chic to open up here near the town's noisy bus stations. Longer established expatriates are also moving over here in an attempt to escape the circus across the river. Modest hotels and restaurants make it the best place for budget travelers and those looking for the flavor of Mexico. The waterfront here claims the town's "in" beach, **Playa de los Muertos**, and a string of towering hotels and condos. At the back, the main road leads south out of the center to wind around the spectacular cliff, past more luxury hotels, villas, and beaches before reaching the end of the bay at **La Mismaloya**, the cove of *Iguana* fame, now graced by a monstrous hotel.

Town center This is the focus of the town's main action, sandwiched between a steep hill and the sea. Red-tiled houses along the central streets are now chic galleries, clothes or craft stores, and the palm-lined *malecón* (seafront) is lined with the liveliest bars and discos. The much modernized main square, **Plaza de Armas**, is flanked by the strangely crown-topped **Nuestra Señora de Guadalupe** and the **Palacio Municipal**, which also houses a helpful tourist office. Walk a few streets inland from here up the steep and picturesque streets and you touch the pulse of Vallarta's fishing-village origins.

Beyond the old town center the highway crosses a completely soulless hotel zone, passes the port (packed with cruise ships, battleships and trawlers) and ends at **Marina Vallarta**. This self-contained commercial and residential area, which includes a golf course and an American school, lies just before the bold pink forms of the airport. Yet Vallarta and the Bahía de Banderas do not end here. More coastal developments are mushrooming in an area to the north named **Nuevo Vallarta** and, finally, at the northern headland of this mighty bay, **Punta Mita**, are the bay's best surfing beaches.

Out and about in Vallarta There is no shortage of excursion opportunities in Vallarta, and you hardly need to search them out as tour agents promote their services liberally. Snorkelers and divers should head for **Mismaloya** where an underwater park lies around the outlying rocks of **Los Arcos▶▶**, or take a speedboat to the **Islas Marietas▶▶**, about an hour away, where reefs and

underwater caverns teem with marine life. **Punta Mita▶▶**, the northern headland of the bay, is also a worthwhile destination. Deep-sea fishing is particularly profitable from November to May, but throughout the year there are plenty of smaller, eminently edible fish. Vallarta's best swimming beaches can only be reached by boat and lie at the southern end of the bay. The most visited is **Yelapa**, but **Quimixto▶** and **Playa de las Animas** remain relatively uncrowded. Jungle-hunting, horseback riding, and a wide range of watersports are also available, but most telling is perhaps the high profile of Alcoholics Anonymous, the result of one-too-many happy hours.

Dangers
Vallarta is knowingly on the make, so there are some factors to bear in mind for a more peaceful and less costly holiday. Visitors are the easy victims of well-practiced tricks. A taxi-driver may insist that your desired restaurant is closed or that he knows a better one. This is where his commission lies. Avoid it. Worse still are the oily tones of those who offer "tourist information" or unbeatably cheap jeep-rental. Some are even attached to hotel developments and spring a "complimentary" breakfast on guests at check-in. Beware!

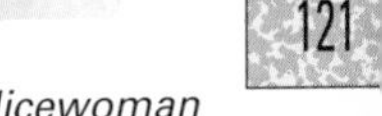

Tourist policewoman

Puerto Vallarta has retained some of its former charm in its narrow streets and red-tiled houses

More ecological delights
Around the border of Nayarit and Sinaloa, roughly halfway between San Blas and Rosario, stretches a region of cattle ranches, undulating hills clothed in tropical vegetation, *palapa*-roofed villages and wetlands punctuated by the occasional rocky outcrop. Lagoons and islands fringed by vast coconut plantations are havens for diverse birdlife as well as abundant marine species. At Escuinapa, 14 miles southeast of Rosario, follow the road to Teacapán, past lagoons, to reach the pristine and still undeveloped beaches of La Tambora, Las Cabras and Los Angeles where great seafood can be savored while watching the sun set over the Pacific.

Tepic's 18th-century cathedral is noted for its two fine Gothic towers

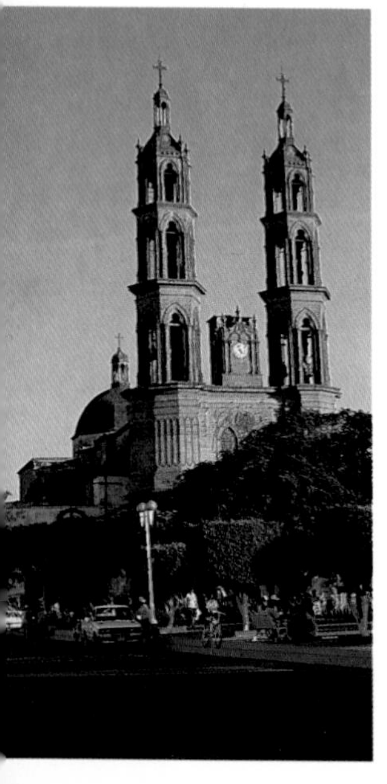

►► Rosario — *108A3*

Forty-seven miles southeast of Mazatlán, Rosario is a relic of the region's former mineral riches, now a center for the less illustrious cultivation of mangoes. Founded in 1655, by the late 18th century it had become the richest town in the northeast. Over 40 miles of underground tunnels were dug in a frenetic search for its prolific gold and silver, and mining continued until 1945. The **Misión de Nuestra Señora del Rosario**, finished in 1759, contains the ultimate symbol of this former glory, a massive and elaborate gold altarpiece. The church, now located on the main square, had to be moved stone by stone from its former site where the tunnels below had led to its collapse.

►►► San Blas — *108A2*

Gnats, birds and surf are the outstanding features of San Blas, a sleepy fishing town and resort which lies 81 miles northwest of Puerto Vallarta. Surrounded by lush mangrove-fringed lagoons and estuaries, palm groves and 19 miles of beaches, it would be a tropical paradise were it not for the clouds of voracious insects which descend at dusk. However, with a correctly screened hotel and plenty of insect repellent, San Blas becomes an atmospheric destination offering good facilities, historic sites, ecological interest and, reputedly, the longest (as opposed to highest) waves along the Pacific coast, perfect for surfers. The **Bahía de Matanchén** was an important 16th- to 18th-century departure point for Spanish expeditions including that of Fra Junipero Serra, who set off in 1768 with 14 missionaries to "conquer" the Californias. Ruins from this period include the old **Aduana** (Customs House) by the port and, on a hill overlooking the town and estuaries, the **Fuerte de Basilio►►** and a 1769 **church**, the subject of Longfellow's poem *The Bells of San Blas*.

Jungle boat trips go to the lagoons of **La Tovara►►** and **Camalota**, inhabited by turtles, iguanas, alligators, herons, egrets, and cormorants, while from November to March ornithologists come to see 200 or so species of migrating birds join 150 native species. The entire area is considered one of the most important natural bird refuges in the Western hemisphere.

► Tepic — *108B2*

The modest capital of Nayarit is a crossroad town for train, bus and car travelers, departure point for the coastal destinations of San Blas and Mexcaltitán, the inland road to Guadalajara and the coast route to Puerto Vallarta. It also serves as a weekend market town for the Cora and Huichol Indians who live in remote villages of the sierra to the northeast, beyond the rolling fields of sugar-cane plantations. The **Museo Regional de Antropología e Historia►** gives a good background to their unique *peyote*-inspired crafts (see page 149) and also displays "tomb culture" archeological finds from the region.

►► Zihuatanejo — *106B1*

Zihuatanejo is the "fishing-village" partner in the much promoted Ixtapa-Zihuatanejo resort project (see page 114), a distinctly jazzed-up version of the real thing. However, its fabulous bay setting and fine swimming beaches more than compensate. Dirt streets are replaced by cobble-

stones, pedestrian malls invade the old town and hotels front the beaches, but Zihuatanejo still has only 35,000 inhabitants, a far cry from the Pacific's mega-resorts. The **Playa Principal** bordering the old town is the least attractive beach, but moving southwest across a canal and around the bay are far better propositions. **Playa Madera**, lying beyond a headland, offers cheap accommodation and restaurants and is a popular family beach. Better still is **Playa la Ropa** backed by cliffs (with good views) and fringed with palm trees, not surprisingly the target for the town's better hotels. At the end of the bay lies **Playa las Gatas**►►, a lovely sheltered beach flanked by palms, naturally protected by an underwater reef and easily reached by boat from the town pier or by a rocky path from Playa la Ropa. Open-air *palapa*-roofed restaurants dish up fresh lobster, and scuba and snorkeling gear can be rented here—the only drawback is the fly invasion, so take insect repellent.

The fishing village of Zihuatanejo offers a total contrast to its more famous neighbor

The Bells of San Blas

What say the bells of San Blas
To the ships that southward pass
From the harbor of Mazatlán?
To them it is nothing more
Than the sound of surf on the shore,
Nothing more to master or man.

But to me, a dreamer of dreams,
To whom what is and what seems
Are often one and the same,—
The Bells of San Blas to me
Have a strange, wild melody
And are something more than a name.

Henry Wadsworth Longfellow's last poem, 1882.

La Sirena Gorda restaurant, Zihuatanejo

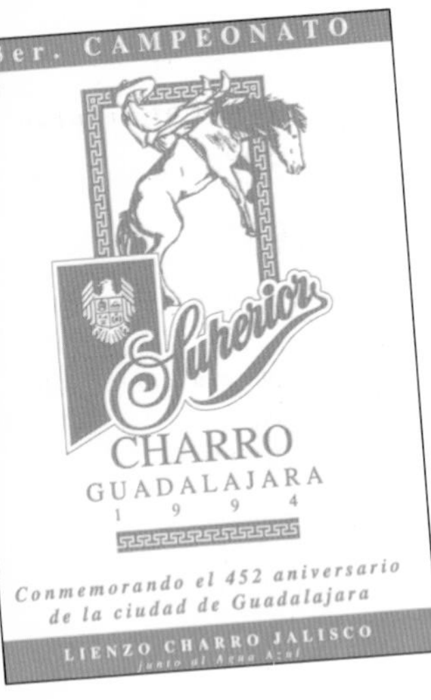

3er. CAMPEONATO
Superior
CHARRO
GUADALAJARA
1 9 9 4
Conmemorando el 452 aniversario
de la ciudad de Guadalajara
LIENZO CHARRO JALISCO
Junto al Agua Azul

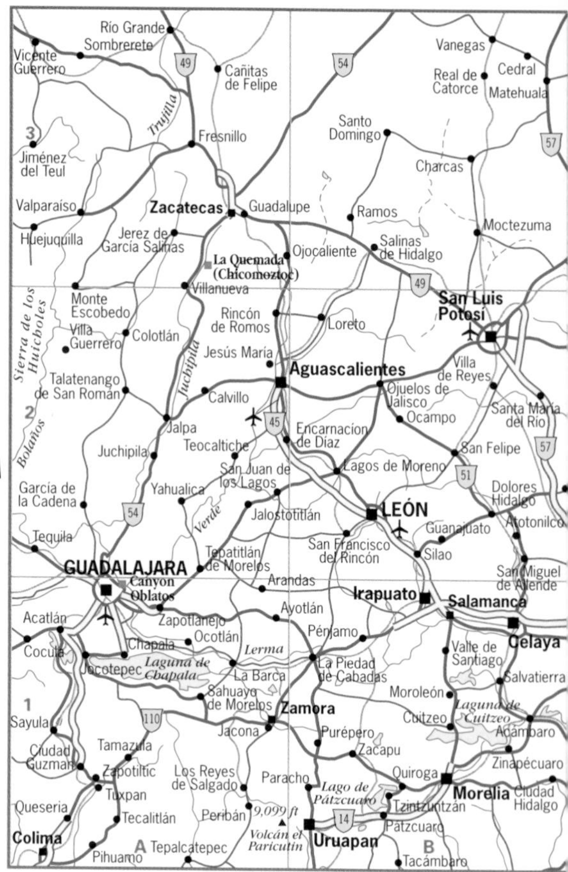

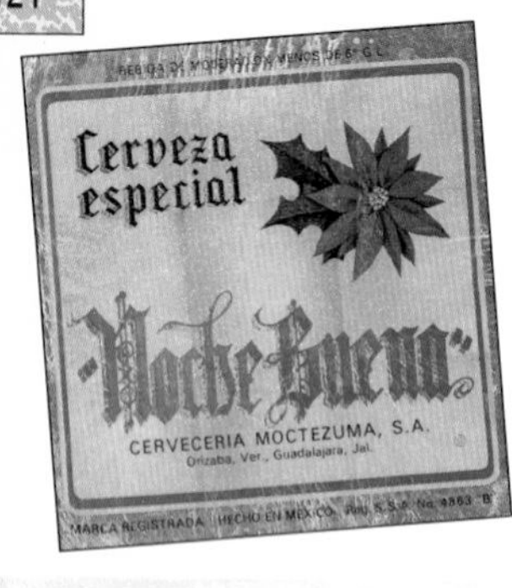

Cerveza
especial
Noche Buena
CERVECERIA MOCTEZUMA, S.A.
Orizaba, Ver., Guadalajara, Jal.
MARCA REGISTRADA HECHO EN MEXICO

Río Grande
Sombrerete
Vicente Guerrero
Cañitas de Felipe
Vanegas
Real de Catorce
Cedral
Matehuala
Santo Domingo
Trujillo
Fresnillo
Jiménez del Teul
Charcas
Valparaíso
Zacatecas
Guadalupe
Ramos
Moctezuma
Huejuquilla
Jerez de García Salinas
La Quemada (Chicomoztoc)
Ojocaliente
Salinas de Hidalgo
Villanueva
San Luis Potosí
Sierra de los Huicholes
Monte Escobedo
Rincón de Romos
Loreto
Villa Guerrero
Colotlán
Jesús María
Juchipila
Talatenango de San Román
Aguascalientes
Villa de Reyes
Ojuelos de Jalisco
Calvillo
Ocampo
Santa María del Río
Bolaños
Jalpa
Encarnación de Díaz
Teocaltiche
San Felipe
Juchipila
San Juan de los Lagos
Lagos de Moreno
García de la Cadena
Yahualica
Dolores Hidalgo
Verde
Jalostotitlán
LEÓN
Atotonilco
Tequila
Guanajuato
San Francisco del Rincón
Silao
Tepatitlán de Morelos
GUADALAJARA
San Miguel de Allende
Canyon Oblatos
Arandas
Irapuato
Salamanca
Ayotlán
Acatlán
Zapotlanejo
Celaya
Pénjamo
Ocotlán
Cocula
Chapala
Lerma
Valle de Santiago
Jocotepec
Laguna de Chapala
La Barca
La Piedad de Cabadas
Salvatierra
Moroleón
Sahuayo de Morelos
Zamora
Sayula
Cuitzeo
Laguna de Cuitzeo
Jacona
Purépero
Acámbaro
Tamazula
Zacapu
Ciudad Guzmán
Zinapécuaro
Zapotiltic
Los Reyes de Salgado
Paracho
Quiroga
Lago de Pátzcuaro
Morelia
Ciudad Hidalgo
Tuxpan
Queseria
Tzintzuntzán
Tecalitlán
Peribán
9,099 ft
Pátzcuaro
Colima
Volcán el Paricutín
Uruapan
Pihuamo
Tepalcatepec
Tacámbaro
49
54
57
45
51
110
14
1
2
3
A
B

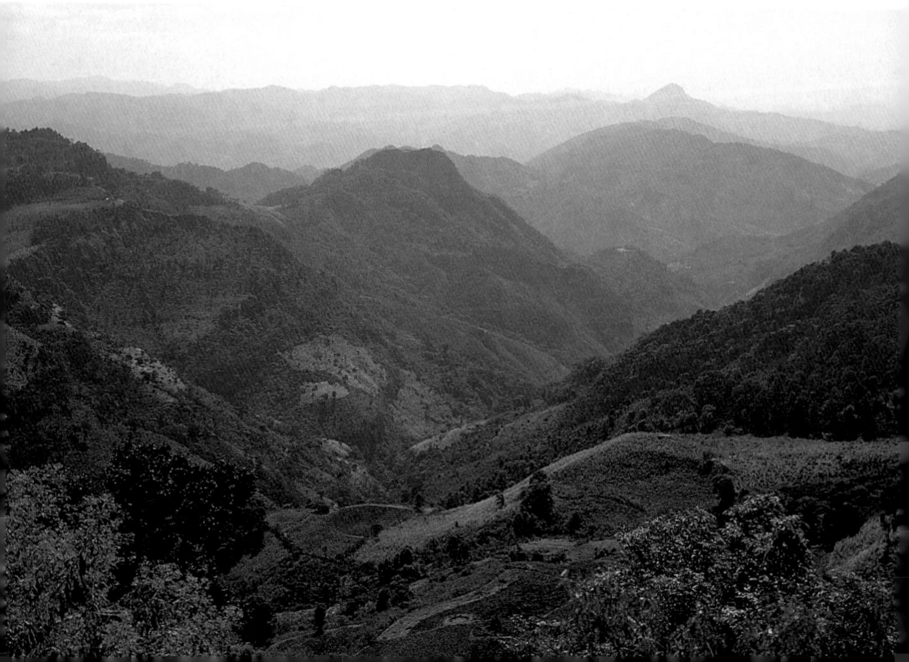

THE CENTRAL HIGHLANDS

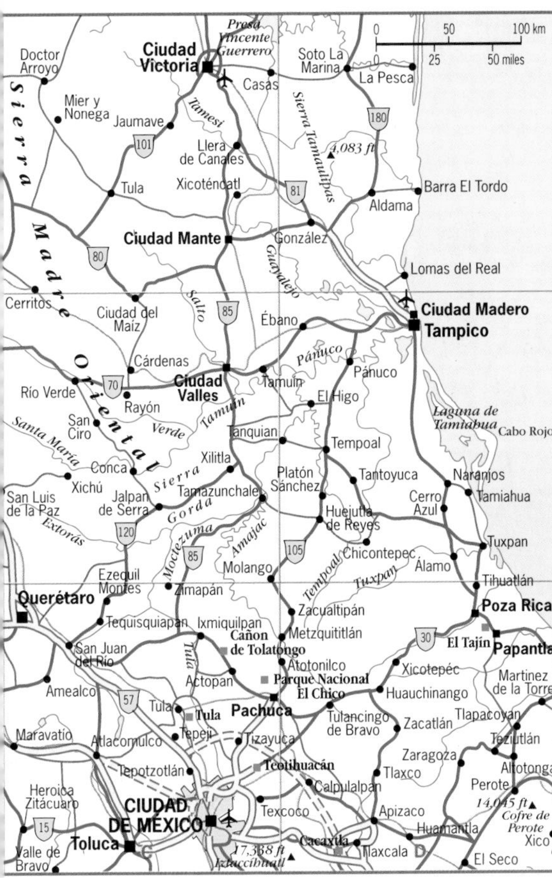

The aptly named Mil Cumbres (which means "A Thousand Peaks" in Spanish) in the Sierra Madre Occidental National Park. The views over this thickly wooded mountain range, which seems to go on for ever, are immense

The Central Highlands Northwest of Mexico City extends a network of colonial cities, spectacular embodiments of the nation's former wealth. From the high plateau of Zacatecas the northern plains break up into a series of low ranges sandwiched between the two mountainous spines of Mexico: the Sierra Madre Occidental and the Sierra Madre Oriental, which run down the west and east of the region respectively. In the triangle formed by the historic old towns of San Luis Potosí, Querétaro, and Aguascalientes lies the region known as the Bajío, where fertile valleys alternate with arid sierra, source of much of the nation's mineral wealth. South of this area lie the lush hills of the state of Michoacán, where abundant water creates yet another geographical face, while to the west it culminates at Guadalajara, Mexico's second largest city and gateway to the Pacific.

Real de Catorce, now almost a ghost town

Getting around
Public transportation in this region is perhaps the most efficient in Mexico. Buses between cities are frequent, and many luxury lines ply the routes, making colonial city-hopping an easy and relatively inexpensive occupation. Bus stations are increasingly being moved to the outskirts of larger cities—in the extreme case of Guadalajara its modern terminals are located more than 3 miles from the city center. But as always, a car is necessary to penetrate the heart of the country, whether the picturesque villages of Michoacán or the old mission towns of the Sierra Gorda.

History The Central Highlands were originally inhabited by diverse Indian peoples who were allied by agricultural needs and trade. No major sites remain that can compare with those found farther south, although the Purépechas (later christened the Tarascans by the Spanish) are known to have rivaled the Aztecs in power and culture. From their base around Michoacán's Lago de Pátzcuaro they withstood Chichimec attacks from the north and Aztec attempts at domination from the east. Their advanced craft techniques were subsequently nurtured by the enlightened first Spanish bishop of Michoacán, Don Vasco de Quiroga. Most of the other sites in this central region were left by the bellicose Toltecs who, between the 10th and 13th centuries, forged north beyond the state of Zacatecas from their base at Tula. The site of La Quemada reflects their influence and the importance of the turquoise trade. Otomís and Huastecs, the latter a mysterious Mayan-linked culture based around the Gulf coast, occupied much of the area when the Spanish arrived in the 16th century.

Precious metals Lusting after the gold, silver and gemstones buried in the dry hills, the Spanish wasted little time in establishing a silver route from Zacatecas through Aguascalientes, Guanajuato, San Miguel de Allende, Querétaro, and San Juan del Río south to Mexico City. Another branch of the route came from San Luis Potosí, farther east. Every one of these towns flourished with the riches pouring out of the deposits, and by the late 18th century reached a dubiously glorious peak of production, exploitation of Indian labor and world renown. However, posterity has inherited the benefits in the magnificent structures erected as proof of the cities' prosperity. Hand in hand with Spanish colonialism went catholicism, inspiring ambitious cathedrals, convents, monasteries, and gilded chapels.

The area was also the source of the early 19th-century Independence movement. The movement was begun in Dolores by the recalcitrant priest Hidalgo, aided by Allende, and soon the towns of San Miguel, Guanajuato, San Luis Potosí, Zacatecas and Morelia were drawn into their net. After the leaders' capture, the battle was taken up by José María Morelos, a native of Morelia (then called Valladolid).

New faces Today these colonial cities are encircled by 20th-century industrial concerns. Textiles, shoes and other light industries have left their urban mark, and visitors must fervently believe in the attractions of each city to want to penetrate beyond the barrier of ugly, anarchistic constructions. An exception is Guadalajara, the region's most Americanized city and Mexico's high-tech capital, whose voracious tentacles spread from a much modernized center.

Agriculture remains an important economic factor, particularly in the more fertile states of Michoacán, Querétaro and Aguascalientes, while Zacatecas and Guanajuato continue to lead the nation in mineral production. Yet at the heart of these towns lies an awesome choice of monuments, always conveniently laid out around an animated central square, typically called the Plaza de Armas. Some towns are now remarkably preserved with strict conservation regulations, notably Morelia, Guanajuato, San Miguel, and Pátzcuaro, and many museums are housed in beautifully restored convents or 18th-century mansions.

Purchases
Tarascan traditions have left a wealth of crafts (woodwork, ceramics, embroidery, weaving, papier mâché) still practiced in the villages near Pátzcuaro, at Uruapan, famed for its lacquerware, and at Santa Clara del Cobre, where gleaming copper pots and vases monopolize the village. High-quality glass, furniture, pottery and Huichol beadwork and yarn paintings are made in and around Guadalajara, and there is the superbly crafted "cowboy" leatherwork of Zacatecas. Silver, too, is a favorite purchase although Taxco, south of Mexico City, is the acknowledged capital. The state of Querétaro continues its craft traditions, embodied in wickerwork, but more ostentaciously in jewelry studded with precious and semi-precious stones.

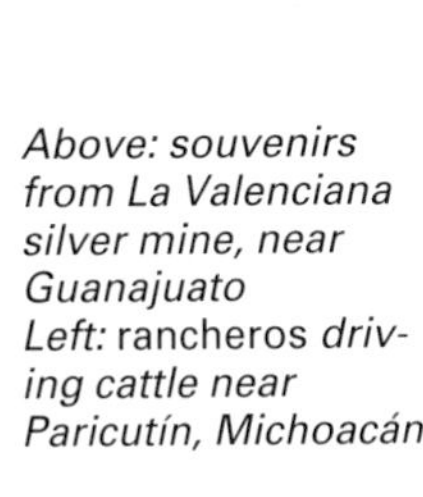

Above: souvenirs from La Valenciana silver mine, near Guanajuato
Left: rancheros *driving cattle near Paricutín, Michoacán*

Relief of Venustiano Carranza, in Aguascalientes

Local specialties
Aguascalientes means "hot springs," and here visitors can sweat it out in the local mineral pools. The best known and most convenient is the Balneario Ojo Caliente. Farther afield is the Balneario Valladolid, about 12 miles north of town. Both are set in recreational parks. The town is also known for its clothing and textile industry: numerous outlets offer factory-priced goods, while *aguítas*, open-work embroidery, can be purchased at the Centro Comercial Plaza Vestir. Bull-breeding ranches can be toured, and local brandy or guava wine makes a perfect end to the day.

► Aguascalientes 124A2

"Clear waters, blue skies, good land and good people" is the motto of the city of Aguascalientes, capital of one of Mexico's smallest states and generally considered the geographical center of Mexico. Constant attacks by hostile Chichimecs delayed Spanish settlement until 1565, when Aguascalientes became a strategic garrison on the silver route from Zacatecas to Mexico City. Discovery of local silver-veins in the 18th century generated a new wealth, and independent statehood was granted in 1857. With a population approaching half a million, it is a booming industrial city, although its prosperity also derives from agriculture, vineyards and cattle ranches in the fertile surrounding plain. The old colonial center livens up considerably in late April when Mexico's oldest and longest fair, the Fería de San Marcos, draws thousands of visitors—reserve a hotel room well in advance if you plan to visit at this time.

Monumental splendor lies in the **Palacio del Gobierno►►**, located on the south side of the Plaza Principal, which was begun in 1665 but has been much remodeled since. Built of volcanic rock and pink quarry stone, its elegant courtyard made a fitting residence for the wealthy Rincon Gallardo family. Today its walls are faced with murals by Oswaldo Barra relating local history. Opposite stands the 18th-century **Catedral de Nuestra Señora de la Asunción►** whose religious paintings include major works by Miguel Cabrera. Alongside is the ornate Porfiriato **Teatro Morelos** where the Convention of Aguascalientes failed to reconcile Revolutionary leaders in 1914 and, half a block down Carranza, is the **Casa de Cultura.** This 17th-century former mansion and convent now hosts numerous cultural activities. Farther culture is offered by four museums, the **Museo Regional** (local history), the **Museo de Aguascalientes►►** (mainly devoted to the works of native artist Saturnino Herrán), the **Museo de Arte Contemporáneo** and the **Museo José Guadalupe Posada**.

►► Cuitzeo 124B1

The pretty, rural town of Cuitzeo lies on the shores of a large lake, 21 miles north of Morelia. Access from the south is across the lake causeway to a promontory where colonial Cuitzeo was founded in 1550 by Augustinian monks. Their beautiful **Monastery of Santa María Magdalena**, profusely decorated by Tarascan Indians, is the town's main monument. Apart from this and the 18th-century Franciscan hospital, Cuitzeo presents a harmony of 19th-century architecture. Unfortunately the shallow water of the lake has become severely polluted by waste from Morelia and, like Chapala, is suffering from an invasion of water lilies.

► Dolores Hidalgo 124B2

Thirty-four miles northeast of Guanajuato lies the town which witnessed the start of the Independence movement, and its interest is directly linked to this event. On the Plaza Principal, the **Parroquía►►**, a protracted 18th-century building with an impressive Churrigueresque façade, was where the priest Miguel Hidalgo uttered his famous *grito* (cry), inciting the population to rise up

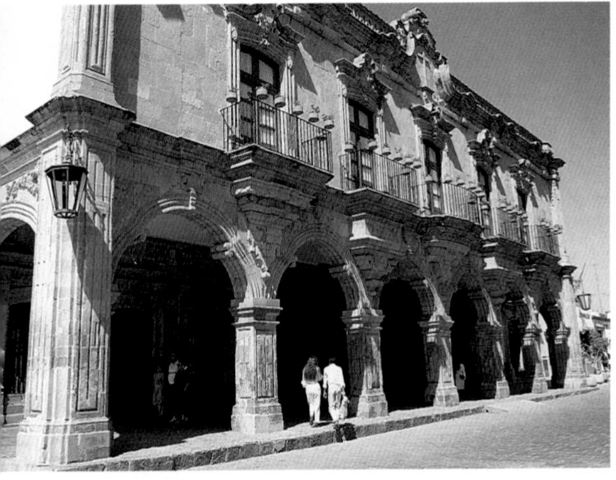

Dolores Hidalgo, where the church bells rang out for revolution in 1810

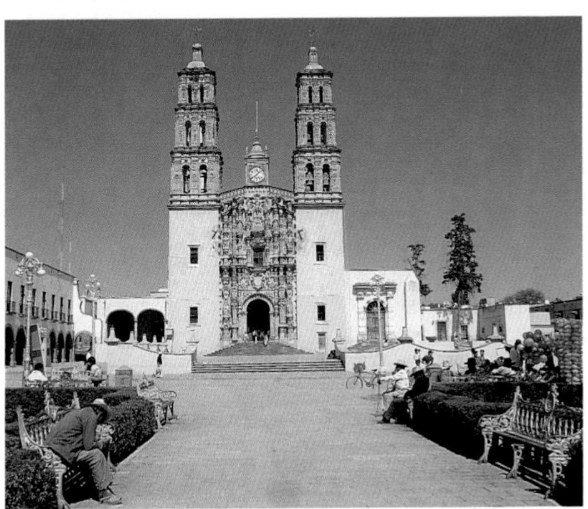

The parish church of Our Lady of Sorrows in Dolores Hidalgo is a magnificent example of 18th-century Mexican Baroque architecture

against their Spanish rulers. Two museums offer a background to the movement: the **Museo de la Independencia Nacional** gives statistical and documentary information about the conditions, decline and sporadic rebellions of the Indian population; the **Museo Casa de Hidalgo**, former home of the national hero, displays personal items and documents.

▶▶ Guadalupe *124A3*

In a little village 4 miles east of Zacatecas stands one of Mexico's most remarkable religious museums, the **Convento de Guadalupe▶▶▶**. It was founded in 1707 as a Franciscan seminary and now functions as a museum and church. The ornately gilded pink interior of the church is best viewed from the elevated choir, reached through the labyrinthine museum. Paintings and furniture collected from churches throughout the state of Zacatecas form a treasure-trove of 17th- to 19th-century religious images and artifacts, superbly displayed within the monasterial stone structure. In an adjoining building, the **Museo Regional** displays an extraordinary collection of early transportation, from old stage-coaches and carts to a 1930 Cadillac convertible.

Hidalgo's *Grito*

Miguel Hidalgo's *grito* ("call to arms") was uttered on the evening of September 15, 1810 and inspired the momentous national struggle to throw off Spanish oppression. Ten months later he was captured and executed in Chihuahua, thus ending a life of unorthodoxy —which included questioning the authority of the Pope, and having a mistress. Much influenced by the legacy of Don Vasco de Quiroga, Michoacán's 16th-century bishop, Hidalgo's sympathies lay firmly with the *mestizo* and Indian population, and his physical leadership of the angry mob of insurgents again set him apart from conformity within the Church.

José Clemente Orozco
Orozco, Guadalajara's most famous 20th-century artist (1883–1949), along with Rivera and Siqueiros, was one of Mexico's *Tres Grandes*, the three pioneers of muralism. He was the most tragic and dramatic, revealing in his monumental works a humane spirit and fierce sense of identification with his times. In the early 1930s he left for the U.S. to escape public criticism of his work, and there his great talent was recognized. On his return to Guadalajara he was given major public commissions. Less overtly political, but more emotive than his fellow muralists, Orozco's masterpieces are among the city's greatest sights. His former home at Avenida Aceves 27 has been converted into a museum.

Below: Independence Day parade
Far right: graced with elegant buildings, lovely churches, flower-filled squares, and fountains, Guadalajara retains its colonial character

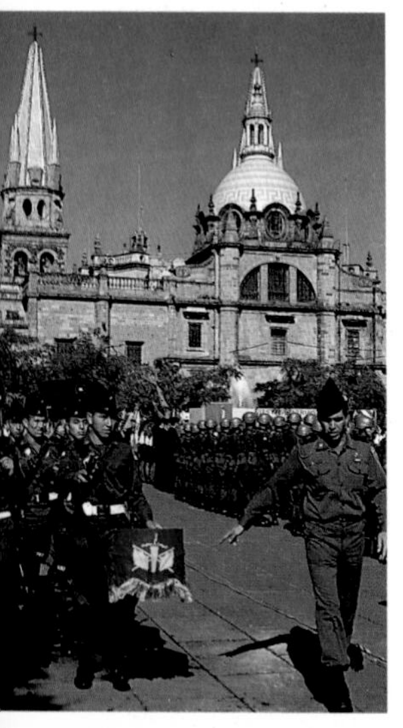

►► Guadalajara *124A1*

Guadalajara is often unjustly dismissed as an overbearingly large, industrialized city (Mexico's second largest), but in fact it offers a compact center laid out on an easy grid pattern, a refreshing climate, relaxed pace and helpful, though conservative inhabitants. Now promoted as Mexico's Silicon Valley, it is one of the world's leading producers of high-tech electronic goods. With over three million inhabitants (of whom 40,000 are resident Americans), this overtly prosperous, much modernized city is also the source of numerous Mexican traditions—from *mariachis* to the Mexican Hat Dance and *tequila*.

History The city was founded in 1542 on the site of today's historic center. For centuries it vegetated, although its role as a halfway point between the central colonial cities and the Pacific port of Manzanillo brought commerce and the whole fertile region became an agricultural hub. It was only in 1920, with the extension of the Southern Pacific Railroad from California to Jalisco, that Guadalajara's fate was sealed. When the railroad was sold off to the Mexican government 30 years later, the city was still a quiet provincial town of cobbled streets, but since then it has boomed, integrating its forward-looking industries into a new urban façade. Much of today's wealth stems from its traditionally close links with the U.S.

Central monuments Guadalajara's historic sites all stand conveniently around the central plazas, four of which surround the cathedral, while the fifth, the Plaza Tapatía, stretches nine blocks east from the Teatro Degollado along a revamped pedestrian esplanade. Immediately visible are the yellow-tiled spires of the **Catedral►►**, a massive edifice begun in 1561 but not completed for over 50 years. Toppled by an earthquake in 1818, the spires were rebuilt in Byzantine style, while other architectural influences create a strange amalgam of Gothic, Moorish, Tuscan, and Corinthian styles in a Baroque wrapper. On the south side is the animated Plaza de Armas centered around a Parisian kiosk and flanked by the **Palacio de Gobierno►►**, dating from 1643, but considerably altered in the 18th century. Here, in 1810, Hidalgo declared an end to slavery, an event captured by Orozco's powerful staircase murals which continue in the Sala Jalisco, the legislative chamber on the third floor devoted to portraits of Mexican statesmen and revolutionaries.

To the north of the cathedral, overlooking a rotunda memorial, is the excellent **Museo Regional►►►**, housed in a magnificent seminary dating from 1701. The collection, arranged round a series of patios, covers prehistory and pre-Hispanic eras, while upstairs 17th- and 18th-century paintings include works by Miguel Cabrera and José de Ibarra. Caricatures by Rafael Ponce de León and numerous elements of Jalisco's history and ethnography (Huichol and Cora Indians) complete this wide-ranging museum. Behind the cathedral lies the Plaza de la Liberación, lined with government buildings and ending at the neoclassical **Teatro Degollado►►**, Guadalajara's cultural pride and joy. The theater is home to the state symphonic orchestra, and also the Grupo Folklórico of the University. The gilded, five-tiered interior was inaugurated

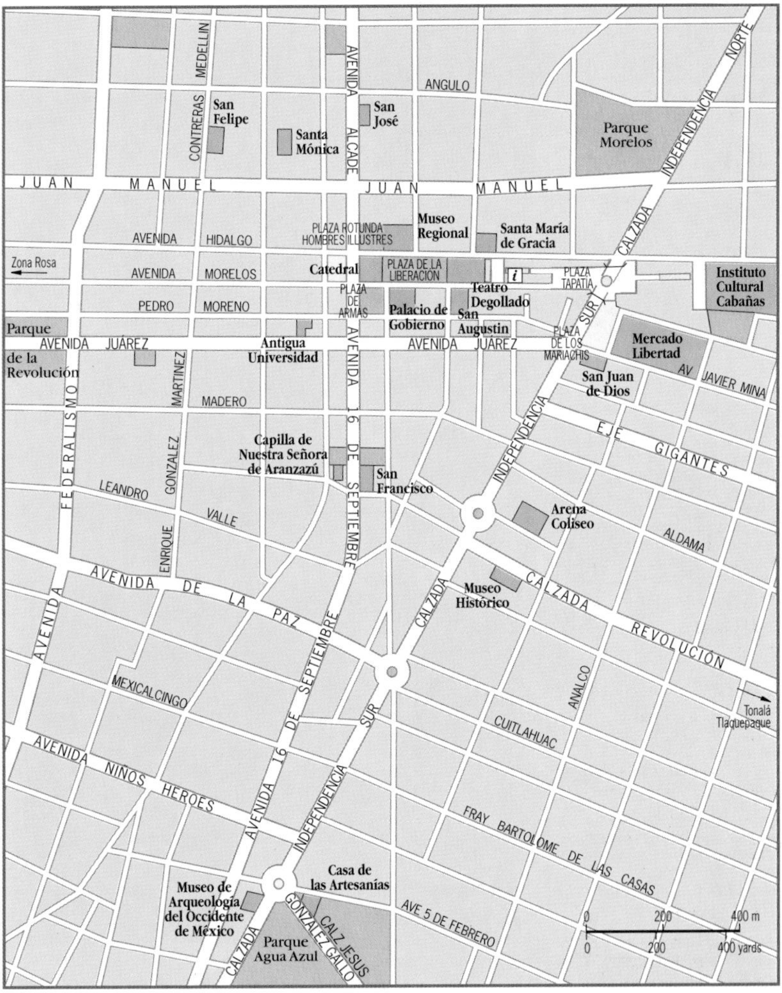

MEDELLIN
AVENIDA ALCADE
ANGULO
NORTE
San Felipe
CONTRERAS
San José
Santa Mónica
Parque Morelos
INDEPENDENCIA
JUAN MANUEL
JUAN MANUEL
PLAZA ROTUNDA HOMBRES ILLUSTRES
Museo Regional
Santa María de Gracia
CALZADA
AVENIDA HIDALGO
Zona Rosa
AVENIDA MORELOS
Catedral
PLAZA DE LA LIBERACIÓN
PLAZA TAPATIA
Instituto Cultural Cabañas
PEDRO MORENO
PLAZA DE ARMAS
Palacio de Gobierno
Teatro Degollado
San Augustin
SUR
Parque de la Revolución
AVENIDA JUÁREZ
Antigua Universidad
AVENIDA JUÁREZ
PLAZA DE LOS MARIACHIS
Mercado Libertad
AV JAVIER MINA
San Juan de Dios
MARTINEZ
MADERO
FEDERALISMO
INDEPENDENCIA
EJE GIGANTES
GONZALEZ
Capilla de Nuestra Señora de Aranzazú
San Francisco
AVENIDA 16 DE SEPTIEMBRE
LEANDRO VALLE
ENRIQUE
Arena Coliseo
ALDAMA
AVENIDA DE LA PAZ
CALZADA
Museo Histórico
CALZADA REVOLUCIÓN
AVENIDA
MEXICALCINGO
SUR
ANALCO
Tonalá Tlaquepaque
CUITLAHUAC
AVENIDA NIÑOS HEROES
AVENIDA 16 DE SEPTIEMBRE
INDEPENDENCIA
FRAY BARTOLOME DE LAS CASAS
Casa de las Artesanías
Museo de Arqueología del Occidente de México
CALZADA
GONZALEZ GALLO
CALZ JESUS
Parque Agua Azul
AVE 5 DE FEBRERO
0 200 400 m
0 200 400 yards

Restaurant at Tlaquepaque's El Parián

in 1866 by the celebrated soprano Angela Peralta, watched over by a mural of Dante's *Inferno* from the domed ceiling.

From here the Plaza Tapatía stretches west past fountains, sculptures, trees and benches down to the impressive **Instituto Cultural Cabañas▶▶▶**, designed by Manuel Tolsa in 1805 as an orphanage. It is now the focal point of the city's cultural activities. Over 20 interconnecting patios planted with grapefruit trees and enclosed by a low-lying arched structure create a sober and harmonious backdrop to the *pièce de résistance*, Orozco's 1930s mural *Man of Fire*, painted on the chapel's central dome. Symbolic representations of air, water and earth surround a central figure of fire and damnation, while other panels depict the agonies arising from the Spanish Conquest. The museum here exhibits a collection of over 100 works by Orozco, a native of the city, as well as temporary exhibitions of contemporary art.

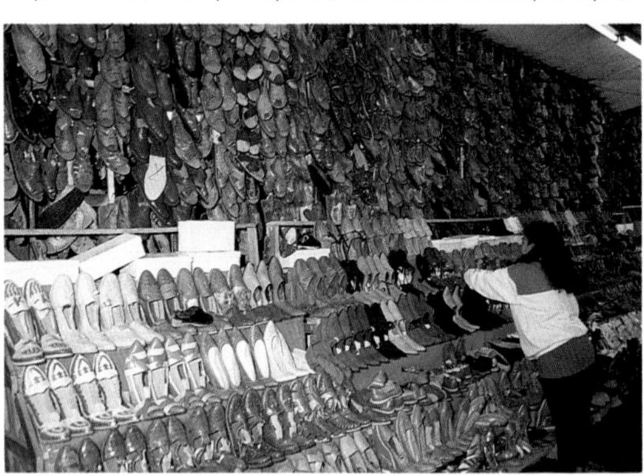

Shoes for sale at the huge Mercado Libertad

Tequila
Thirty-one miles west of Guadalajara, on Highway 15, lies the small town of Tequila, Mexico's main *tequila*-producing area (see page 217), an industry which has functioned since the 18th century. Fields of *agave tequilana*, a spiky-leafed succulent of the maguey family, surround the town where many familiar brands are distilled. The two largest distilleries, Sauza and Cuervo, offer tours and sampling: the Sauza plant contains a striking mural by Gabriel Flores illustrating early production methods.

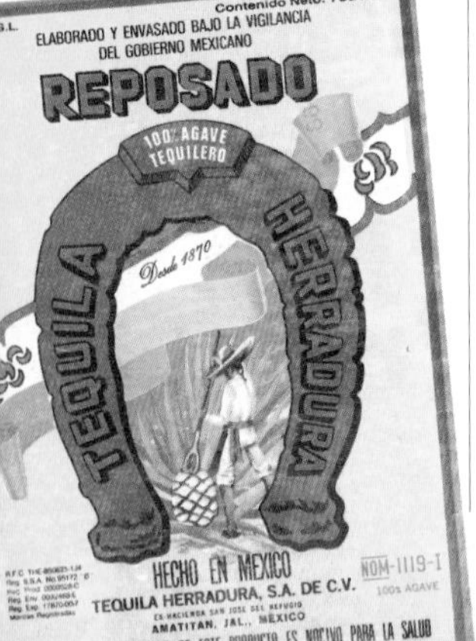

South of the center Immediately south of the Instituto Cultural Cabañas lie two monuments to Guadalajara's deeply-rooted traditions: the **Mercado Libertad▶▶** and the **Plaza de los Mariachis▶▶**. The former, a gigantic market, dominates four city blocks and claims to be the largest in the Western hemisphere. Shoes, belts, guitars, chairs, hats, pottery, and onyx as well as fruit, fish, meat, and vegetables are hawked in this multi-storied edifice, but vendors are aggressive, so be warned. One street south, beside a small church, is the pedestrian alleyway of the *mariachis* (see page 138) where cafés and restaurants overflow onto the sidewalk and the city's musicians gather late into the evening.

Several blocks south of the cathedral, down Avenida 16 de Septiembre, stand two churches, relics of a Franciscan monastery destroyed during the Reform period. To the east the **Templo de San Francisco▶** has a wonderful Plateresque façade, but its interior is of little interest. Across the street, the more severe mid-18th-century **Capilla de Nuestra Señora de Aranzazú▶▶▶** surprises with its two magnificent Churrigueresque altars and impressive ceiling and wall paintings.

Farther south on the same street, at the junction with Calzada Independencia, is the city park, **Parque Agua Azul**▶, fronted by a stark modern entrance and offering plenty of recreational escape for children. The **Museo de Arqueología del Occidente de México**▶ located opposite the entrance, contains a limited but interesting display of pre-Hispanic artifacts from the western states, while on the northern side the upscale **Casa de las Artesanías**▶ offers a wide selection of high-quality local craftwork for sale.

Tlaquepaque and Tonalá Guadalajara's urban sprawl has now engulfed the villages of Tlaquepaque and Tonalá, both easily reached by bus from the center. Although obviously geared to foreign purses, **Tlaquepaque**▶▶ makes a colorful and picturesque outing, its elegant 19th-century mansions which were once summer retreats for wealthy *tapatios* (Guadalajarans) now converted into craft boutiques or restaurants. The village atmosphere centers around the **Jardín Hidalgo** and adjoining **El Parián**▶▶▶, an arcaded structure dating from 1878 but remodeled in 1978. Its shady courtyard is where Guadalajarans and visitors gather for protracted weekend lunches to the tunes of the ubiquitous *mariachis*. Meanwhile, the surrounding pedestrian streets offer an endless and eclectic display of jewelry, glass, leatherwork, ceramics and antique furniture, the best that you will see in Mexico. The **Museo Regional de Cerámica y los Artes Populares**▶▶ (at Independencia 237) displays fine Huichol embroidery, ceramics by contemporary potters, and Jaliscan folk art in a pretty, old building.

A few miles to the southeast lies **Tonalá**▶, a less pretentious village where many of the craft workshops are to be found, particularly for those interested in stoneware pottery and glass. The **Museo Nacional de la Cerámica**▶ is located here at Constitución 110, but Tonalá is best visited on Thursday or Sunday when a huge market invades the streets. Superb views over the city and plains of Jalisco can be seen from the 8,200-ft. **Cerro de la Reina**, the site of a historic battle between Tonaltecan rebels and the pernicious conquistador Nuño de Guzmán.

Zona Rosa
Modern and prosperous Guadalajara is best experienced in the area west of the center which starts at Avenida Chapultepec, often known as the Zona Rosa. Wide, tree-lined streets harbor chic shops and restaurants, and the overall feel is more American than Mexican. The Plaza del Sol is the largest of the city's many shopping centers and is crowned by a giant Hyatt hotel, its latest addition being a glass pyramid for special events.

Canyon
Escape the 20th century by going 6 miles north of the city, up Calzada Independencia, to the Cañon Oblatos, a 1,970-ft. gorge cut by the Santiago and Verde rivers. Panoramic views from the edge stretch endlessly over the surrounding landscape. Nearby is Parque Natural Huentitán, where an open zoo houses monkeys, elephants and giraffes alongside the colorful animal sculptures of local artist Sergio Bustamante. Other offerings include a planetarium, a science and technology center, an aviary, and a snake-house.

Government Palace

Guanajuato, once the richest city in the land

Hidden plazas
The town's first public park, the Jardín de la Unión, was laid out in 1861 and is the focus of evening action, but there are countless other pretty plazas tucked away in the maze. The Plazuela de San Fernando, just north of Juárez, has a spirit typical of the town and is lined with bookstores, small restaurants, and the occasional craft shop. A winding alley to the west leads to the Plaza de San Roque, dominated by a 17th-century church. Both plazas are used during the October Festival Cervantino for outdoor performances. More formal is the nearby Jardín de la Reforma, with its neoclassical columns and arched stairs opening on to Juárez.

386128
TRANSPORTES URBANOS DE GUANAJUATO
AVALOS
BUENO POR UN PASAJE
CENTRO
EL PASAJERO VIAJA ASEGURADO
EXIJA EL BOLETO
AL NDUCTOR

▶▶▶ Guanajuato *124B2*

The charm and beauty of Guanajuato lie as much in individual monuments as in the overall harmony and liveliness of the city. A mosaic of brightly colored houses, sprawling over a narrow valley, is encircled by ever-present mountains—its Tarascan name means "mountainous place of frogs." Frogs are now rare, but Guanajuato is firmly placed on the national calendar for its October arts festival, the **Festival Cervantino**. This lively university town, packed with underground tunnels, overground *callejónes* (alleys) and countless pretty plazas, is central Mexico's most seductive and stimulating destination.

Background Sparsely settled by Chichimecs in the early 16th century, by 1554 the area's rich silver veins had been discovered and Real Minas de Guanajuato was founded. Riches poured out of the mines, barons flourished and the Indians suffered. However, in 1810 Miguel Hidalgo's call for Independence at nearby Dolores led to the famous battle in Guanajuato when the Alhóndiga (granary) was captured by Hidalgo's forces, greatly aided by local citizens. Retaliation by the Spanish was ferocious: after reconquering the town they held a gratuitous lottery, randomly choosing citizens to be tortured and hanged. Redistribution of wealth after Independence led to the erection of many of Guanajuato's elegant mansions, but violence reappeared during the Revolution and in religious conflicts between 1927 and 1946. Since the official founding of the University, in 1945, the town has regained peace and prosperity, further stimulated by the Festival Cervantino which began in 1972. In 1988, Guanajuato was declared part of UNESCO's world cultural heritage.

Layout The tunnels that carry heavy traffic beneath the center are confusing to some, but an essential element in Guanajuato's uniqueness. Although their stone arches, vaulted ceilings and winding steps appear straight out of the Middle Ages, they actually date from 1905 when the town was flooded, and have been sporadically extended up until 1982. Above ground, two main arteries—Pocitos and Juárez—preserve visitors from this subterranean purgatory, and their slopes, twists, plazas and branches add to the urban quaintness. Most of the main sights lie along these roads, while to the north and south the town takes off into a maze of steep, picturesque *callejónes* (alleys): the narrowest was romantically named the **Callejón del Beso** (Alley of the Kiss), as courting couples could actually kiss from their opposing balconies.

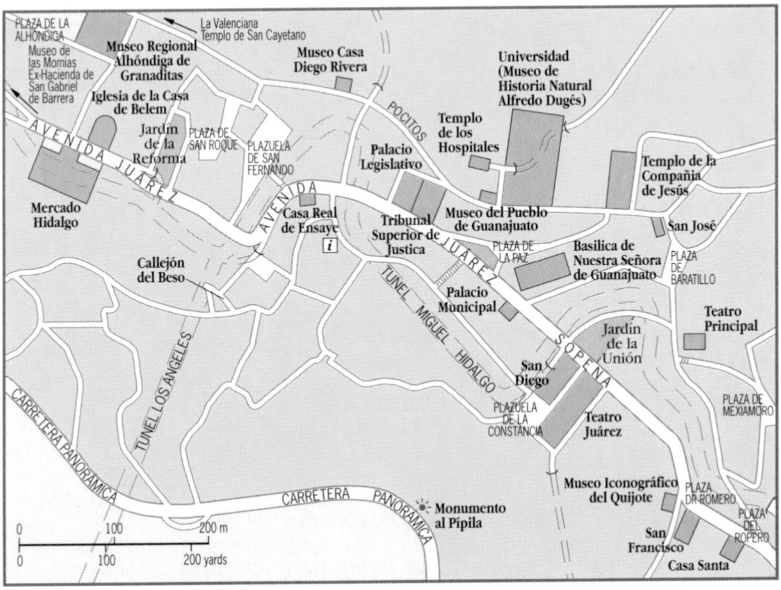

Sights Between Juárez and Pocitos stands the forbidding **Museo Regional Alhóndiga de Granaditas▶▶**, built as a grain warehouse in the late 18th century, used as a fortress in 1810 and subsequently the macabre show-

The striking Baroque Basilica of our Lady of Guanajuato

Al Pípila
Standing high on a hilltop south of town on the Carretera Panoramica is a monument dedicated to José de los Reyes Martínez, "Al Pípila," the miner who burned the doors of the Alhóndiga for Hidalgo's forces but died in the process. The pink-stone statue can be climbed and offers fabulous views over the city. The easiest means of access is by bus (marked "Pípila") running west along Juárez, but don't miss the twisting downhill walk back.

case for the heads of the captured rebels. The hooks from which they were suspended can still be seen, but the fortress has since been converted from a prison into a museum of Guanajuato's archaeology, ethnography, mines, and history, and displays Chávez Morado's mural of the struggle for Independence.

Just over a mile west of here, on a hilltop, stands another of Guanajuato's specialties, the **Museo de las Momias▶▶**. This decidedly gruesome museum exhibits 117 mummified bodies of local citizens excavated from the mineral-rich soil of the local cemetery which preserved them so well. Propped up in glass cases which line the tunnels beneath the cemetery, some still wear their boots, others their ragged suits, while child mummies are dressed up like dolls and a mummified foetus is proudly displayed as "the world's smallest."

To the south of the Alhóndiga, along Juárez, stands the enormous cast-iron 1910 **Mercado Hidalgo,** displaying crafts upstairs and produce downstairs. The main road continues east past the 17th-century **Basilica▶**, a sober construction whose main interest lies in a jewel-encrusted Spanish statue of the Virgin, said to date from the 7th century. Far more impressive is the **Templo de la Compañia de Jesus▶▶▶** which lies behind and uphill from the Basilica, next to the University. Built in 1746, its pink stone façade is one of Mexico's outstanding examples of Churrigueresque architecture and is surmounted

Below: statue of Peace, Plaza de la Paz
Right: the pink stone Templo de la Compañía (Jesuit church) is a jewel of Churrigueresque architecture

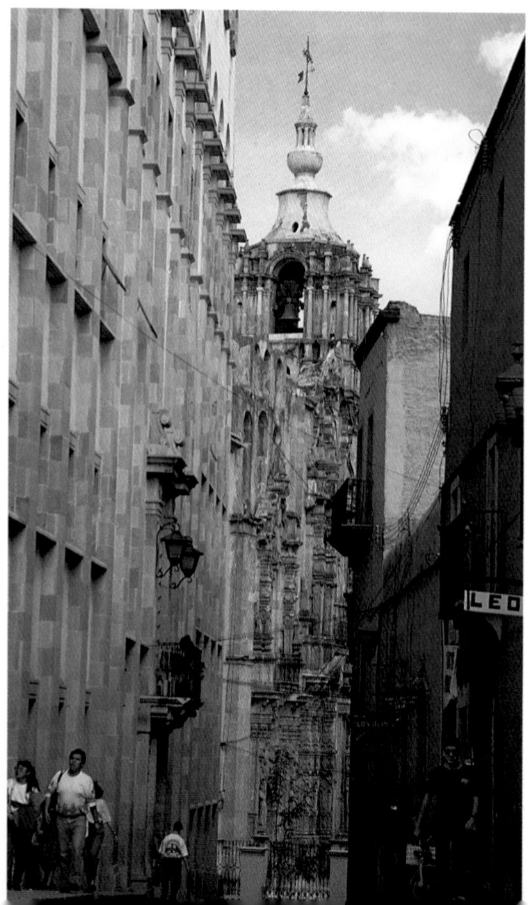

by a 19th-century neoclassical cupola. The interior, currently under restoration, displays paintings by Miguel Cabrera, the prodigious 18th-century artist.

To the west looms the grandiose, crenelated façade of the **University**, completely remodeled in 1955 from a 16th-century Jesuit college. On the top floor is the **Museo de Historia Natural Alfredo Dugés▶** (open weekdays only), while tucked away to the left of the main entrance is Guanajuato's first parish church, the **Templo de los Hospitales** (1560–1565), home to the image of the Virgin before it was transferred to the Basilica in 1696. Opposite the University, at Pocitos 7, the **Museo del Pueblo de Guanajuato▶▶** is housed in a lovely 17th-century mansion where mainly colonial paintings are displayed. Farther west along Pocitos, at No. 46, is the **Museo Casa Diego Rivera▶**, where the painter was born in 1886, and which now displays his family's belongings alongside a collection of his paintings and sketches.

Guanajuato's soul lies in the **Jardín de la Unión▶▶▶**, a small, shady plaza lined with hotels, bars and restaurants and fronted by the magnificent San Diego and the Teatro Juárez. The original **Templo de San Diego▶▶** was damaged by a flood in the late 18th century and rebuilt in ornate Baroque style, in contrast to the adjacent **Teatro Juárez▶▶▶** which dominates the square in Doric splendor. Begun in 1873 and inaugurated by President Porfirio Díaz in 1903, its superbly crafted, Moorish-inspired interior, interwoven with elaborate Art Nouveau touches, makes a fitting memorial to the excesses of that epoch. Streets leading off the Jardín meander past countless other interesting churches, alleys and plazas, well worth exploring on foot.

Out of town An integral part of Guanajuato's history and beauty lies 3 miles north along the winding panoramic highway at **La Valenciana**. By the time this mine was registered in 1770, it was producing 25 percent of the world's silver. After several closings it reopened in 1968 as a cooperative. Visitors can walk around the site, but the mine-shaft is strictly off-limits. On the main road stands the exquisite **Templo de San Cayetano▶▶▶**, erected in 1775 by the Count of Valenciana and another outstanding showcase of Churrigueresque design and detail. The high-relief gold altar is a masterpiece of this style, while the sacristy, completed in 1788, contains some fine original furnishings.

The immense private wealth generated by Guanajuato's mines is exemplified in the **Ex-Hacienda de San Gabriel de Barrera▶▶▶**, a museum and park which lies a few miles west of the town on the main road. This late 17th-century hacienda belonged to Captain Gabriel de Barrera, and the extensive grounds were once used for processing the precious ores. It is now completely re-landscaped into a delightful patchwork of garden styles (Roman, English, Oriental, Arab, Italian, and French), which leads away from the hacienda itself. The beautifully restored mansion displays 17th- to 19th-century furniture and *objets d'art* from France, Spain, and England.

Las Callejóneadas
Take a seat in the Jardín de la Unión at nightfall for a free show of Guanajuato's typically provincial vibrancy. By 8 p.m. flower-sellers, *mariachis* and children are replaced by high-spirited students perpetuating a tradition which dates from 1963. Following the rediscovery of student songs of Spanish origin, a vociferous procession (*callejóneada*) now takes place daily, led by the younger generation. The route winds through narrow *callejónes* (passageways) south of the Jardín, pausing in the Callejón del Beso, and finally culminates in the Plazuela de los Angeles two hours later; songs and wine accompany students and visitors all the way.

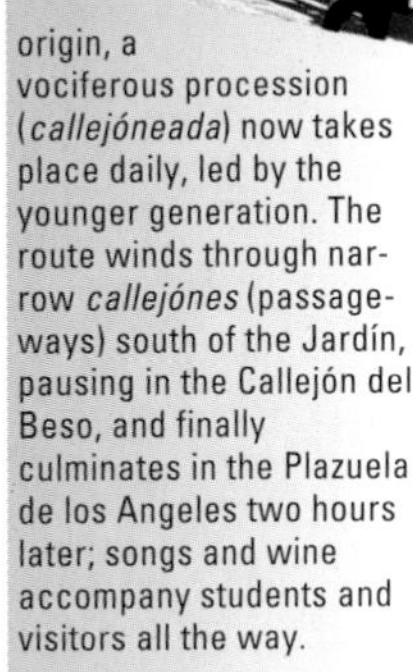

■ Sit in any self-respecting Mexican restaurant and you will be assailed by the brass and string sounds of a sombrero-hatted *mariachi* band. Hard to ignore, these musicians are part of a well-entrenched and much-loved tradition that expresses the Mexican soul in melodramatic odes to love and death for the sake of honor.....■

***Mariachi* haunts**
Apart from Mexico City's Plaza Garibaldi, Guadalajara is the best place to experience top-quality interpretations by these traditional musicians. From the classic rendezvous of the Plaza de los Mariachis to the chic restaurants west of the city center, you may encounter local figures such as Machete, Bigotes (moustache) or Pato (duck) plucking, blowing and vocalizing Jaliscan emotions. However, this once male bastion is now being encroached upon by women: keep an eye out for Las Perlitas Tapatías (Guadalajara's Little Pearls) or, in Mexico City, track down the pastiche cabaret act of Astrid Hadad, Mexico's answer to Madonna.

The state of Jalisco is the birthplace of the *mariachi* tradition. Accepted legend has it that these troubadour bands first became popular during the brief reign of Emperor Maximilian in the mid-19th century, who had them play at marriage feasts in Mexico City's Chapultepec Castle. The name *mariachi* is thus said to derive from the French word *mariage*. However, another, more convincing theory is that the tradition existed well before then and that the word derives from a Cocula Indian word for "tree" which described the platform the musicians played on.

Whatever its origins, the roving minstrel practice has successfuly taken root all over the country: double-basses disappear over the brow of a sierra, guitars are packed into buses and trumpets flash at a lakeside jetty as the *mariachi* groups travel from one gig to the next. As the sun sets, town zócalos (main squares) are monopolized by figures in uniformed finery inspired by *charros* (Mexican cowboys): felt hat, high-waisted jacket, white shirt, embroidered belt, gilt or silver chains and trims—a distant cousin of Spain's flamenco costume. When café or restaurant customers finally rise to the occasion and demand their favorite lament, these slick musicians embark on a rousing repertoire of *ranchera* music in which love, death and destruction, suffering, alcohol and defeat assume unique proportions.

The basic instruments are the *guitarrón* (a domed bass guitar), the *vihuela* (small treble guitar), violins and trumpets with regional variations, which in Veracruz include the *marimba* (wooden xylophone). The sign of a truly inspiring *mariachi* band is when the participating customers end the evening in melodic tears ...

Mariachi *music originated in the state of Jalisco and is now common all over Mexico*

▶ Lagos de Moreno *124B2*

This rarely visited, peaceful colonial town lies 50 miles southeast of Aguascalientes on a major highway intersection. Built beside a river, its pretty streets climb up the hillside, culminating at the summit with a monastery and superb views over the green hills of Jalisco. A few small hotels and restaurants are inevitably clustered around the zócalo, as are the historical sights which include the Baroque **Iglesia de Santa María de los Lagos**, the turn-of-the-century **Teatro Rosas Moreno**, and the **Convento de Capuchinas**, now converted into a museum.

▶▶ Laguna de Chapala *124A1*

At certain points over 18 miles wide and almost 65 miles long, Laguna de Chapala is Mexico's largest lake, situated 30 miles southeast of Guadalajara. The temperate climate (it lies at an altitude of 5,000 ft.) and beautiful, mountain-circled setting lured many a wealthy Mexican earlier this century—including Porfirio Díaz, who built his summer residence there, and it has since been discovered by a growing community of North American artists, writers and retirees. Another recent invasion is that of water lilies, along with consequent silt build-up and toxic waste, all of which bodes ill for the aquatic life. Three main towns lie along its northern shore: **Chapala**, an expatriate focal point which still boasts some grandiose turn-of-the century mansions; **Ajijic,** with its emphasis on arts and crafts, and **Jocotepec**, home to the 1529 Church of Señor del Monte and famous for its handwoven *serapes* (blankets). Boat trips visit the two islands of **Los Alacranes** and **Mexcala**, the former thick with willows, *tabachines* (orange-flowered trees), and the lake's best and most scenic fish restaurants.

Literary Chapala
Two celebrated authors inspire today's Chapalan pen-pushers: D. H. Lawrence and Sybille Bedford. It was in Chapala in the early 1920s that Lawrence wrote the first draft of his novel *The Plumed Serpent*, while comfortably housed in a villa on Calle Zaragoza. This has now been converted into a pricey hotel, the Quetzlcóatl Inn. Much of Sybille Bedford's inspired travelog, *A Visit to Don Octavio*, is set on the shores of Lake Chapala where she stayed in the early 1950s. Her descriptions of the area, and its expatriate and local personalities make a colorful, insightful and amusing read.

▶ La Quemada *124A3*

The ruins of La Quemada, also called Chicomoztoc (Place of the Seven Caves), lie 25 miles south of Zacatecas. This impressive hilltop fortification rising out of the cacti-strewn sierra was probably erected to guard against Chichimec invasions, and was one of the most northern outposts of civilization during Toltec times (roughly 10th to 13th century). Platform pyramids and walled courts occupy the summit, while outside the walls, on the lower slopes, the ceremonial center contains a small pyramid and remains of a colonnaded hall.

Boats for rent (above) and fine copperware for sale, Lake Chapala

The aqueduct and Tarascan specialities
Over a mile of arched stone aqueduct runs from the eastern end of Avenida Morelos beyond the Bosque Cuauhtémoc, the city park. Built between 1785 and 1789 to supply water to the expanding city, its 253 arches are now superbly illuminated at night. Marking the beginning of the aqueduct is the Fuente Tarasca, a not-so-splendid 1960s fountain with sculptures of bare-breasted Tarascan maidens holding a platter of Michoacán fruits. Crystalized versions of these fruits (*cubitos de ate*) can be sampled at the Mercado de Dulces (Candy Market), an elevated market area which flanks the western side of the Palacio Clavijero. Made from guava, coconut, or quince and cooked with milk, these *dulces* (sweets) are an integral part of Morelia's fame.

 Morelia *124B1*

Aristocratic Morelia, capital of the undulating and fertile state of Michoacán, lies 195 miles west of Mexico City. It was founded in 1541 under the name of Valladolid, and attracted many families of the Spanish nobility; at Independence its name was changed to Morelia in honor of Morelos, a native son and key figure in the movement. This dynamic, yet compact, university town of half a million inhabitants was declared a historical monument by UNESCO, and it takes this dual role very seriously, restoring and maintaining the homogenous center while keeping cultural activities alive and visitors happy.

In and around the zócalo Pride of the central Plaza de Armas is the massive pink-stone **Catedral▶▶▶**, begun in 1640 but not completed till 1744. Said to be the third largest in Latin America, its Baroque twin towers and tiled dome surmount a neoclassical interior whose main features are a monumental German organ consisting of 4,600 pipes, an ornate silver altarpiece, and a much revered corn-paste Christ. Eighteenth-century arcades and imposing colonial buildings surround the buzzing plaza, the north side being a favorite for outdoor cafés. The **Palacio de Gobierno▶▶** is worth entering for its grandiose courtyard and gallery murals, while farther east along Avenida Madero stands the Baroque masterpiece of the **Templo de las Monjas▶▶** (1729–1737). In the southwestern corner of the plaza is the **Museo Regional Michoacano▶▶▶**, founded in 1886 and housed in a magnificent mansion. The extensive collection covers geology, archaeology, Tarascan ethnography and colonial history, and contains some rare finds: look for the Mayan *chacmool* (a reclining statue on which sacrificial offerings were laid) found at Ihuatzio on Lake Pátzcuaro. Flanking the western end of the zócalo is another Baroque mansion with two later stories, now converted into the **Hotel Virrey de Mendoza▶**.

Northwest of the Plaza de Armas lie more rich historical finds. First along Madero is Mexico's oldest college, the **Colegio de San Nicolás▶**, founded in 1540 in Pátzcuaro but later transferred to Morelia. Former students include Morelos and Hidalgo, whose statue dominates the patio, while the heart of another Mexican hero, Melchor Ocampo, is preserved in a memorial room upstairs. On the corner of Nigromante, the **Palacio Clavijero▶▶▶** is a sober, superbly proportioned construction with a large, elegant patio. Dating from 1660, when it functioned as a Jesuit school, it has been converted into municipal offices which include the tourist office and a library, strangely housed in the former chapel.

Converted convents One block down Nigromante lies Morelia's oldest building, the **Templo de las Rosas▶▶** (1590) which adjoins a former convent, now a music academy. Northwest of here stands another ecclesiastical conversion, the **Ex-Convento del Carmen▶▶**, built in 1596 but extended in the 17th and 18th centuries. It now functions as the **Casa de la Cultura**, a lively center for arts workshops and performances, and also houses the **Museo de la Máscara**,

Morelia's pink-stone cathedral overlooks the main square

with a small but choice display of regional masks. Even Morelia's bus station once echoed with the footsteps of Carmelite nuns, but a more inspiring conversion is the former convent of San Francisco, now the **Casa de las Artesanías**▶▶. Situated due east of the zócalo on its own spacious plaza, the cloisters, cells and arcades are now invaded by traders of Michoacán's richly diverse handicrafts. Demonstrations of craft techniques can be seen in the upstairs rooms.

Left: fine exhibit of Michoacán craftsmanship

José María Morelos
Like Hidalgo, Morelos was an enlightened, active priest and rapidly assumed leadership of the Independence movement after Hidalgo's execution in 1811. Born in a house on the street of Corregidora in 1765, Morelos later bought a residence one block east where he lived from 1801. He too succumbed to government forces and in 1815 was executed. Both houses have been converted into museums of memorabilia devoted to this priestly freedom fighter.

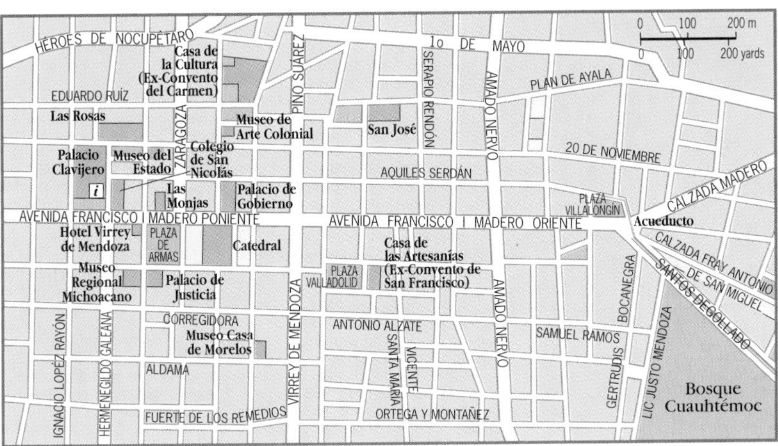

The island of Janitzío rises sharply from the middle of Lake Pátzcuaro

▶▶▶ Pátzcuaro *124B1*

The town of Pátzcuaro lies at an altitude of 6,988 ft. just over 37 miles west of Morelia in the heart of Michoacán. It is situated in a pastoral region of lakes and pine forests where wood-smoke fills the air and quaint cobbled streets wind uphill from the scenic lake lying at its feet. Local Indians, the Purépechas (later called Tarascans), appeared in the area in the early 14th century and still flourish, thanks in part to the enlightened policies of Michoacán's first bishop, Don Vasco de Quiroga, who established the state capital in Pátzcuaro in 1540. Faithful to traditional costumes and crafts, their presence in and around the town gives it a unique atmosphere which, combined with its architectural harmony, makes Pátzcuaro a fascinating living meeting-place of two cultures.

Quiroga and Utopia
Quiroga, the most visionary of all the first Spanish settlers, was sent by the colonial government to straighten out the havoc wrought in the area by the merciless conquistador, Nuño de Guzmán, whose massacres and slavery had shattered the Purépechan kingdom. From his first base in Tzintzuntzán, Quiroga moved to Pátzcuaro in 1540, from whence he worked incessantly to establish models of egalitarian communities, directly based upon the philosophy of his English contemporary, Thomas More, in his book *Utopia* (1516). He built hospitals and schools and traveled from village to village inspiring trades and crafts, converting rapidly as he went. Today, the devout descendants of the Tarascans are among Mexico's most talented crafts people.

Around Plaza Vasco de Quiroga Two plazas constitute the core of the town. The grander of the two, the arcaded **Plaza Vasco de Quiroga,** is flanked by stately 18th-century mansions, many of which have been converted into hotels, restaurants and craft shops. The streets east of here wind uphill to the heart of Pátzcuaro, located along Calle Enseñanza. On the corner of Alcantarilla is the delightful **Museo de Artes Populares▶▶▶** (Museum of Popular Art), housed in the former Colegio de San Nicolás, founded by Don Vasco in 1540. Local pottery, masks, textiles, straw figures, lacquerware, copper and ex-votos (votive offerings) are beautifully displayed in this ecclesiastical setting, surrounding a verdant patio. Towering across the street is the once-Jesuit **Templo de la Compañia▶** (1540), Pátzcuaro's first Basilica which, although modified with Baroque elements, retains a simple, barrel-vaulted ceiling. The massive adjoining hospital is currently being converted into a cultural center. Buried under the church foundations is a Tarascan pyramid similar to that of Tzintzuntzán, while immediately opposite

Weaving in the House of Eleven Patios

The pace of life is slow in Pátzcuaro

stands the walled church of **El Sagrario**. A livelier destination tucked away down a nameless side street is the **Casa de los Once Patios▶** (House of the Eleven Patios), a former Dominican convent (1745) which is now home to a plethora of small craft shops. One block north on Enseñanza stands the **Basilica de Nuestra Señora de la Salud▶▶**, started in 1554 but rebuilt in 1883 after countless catastrophes. It contains Don Vasco's mausoleum and the more celebrated corn-paste image of the **Virgen de la Salud** (Virgin of Health), made for their bishop by local Tarascans and a miraculous survivor of the Basilica's fires. The church plaza comes alive on the eighth day of every month when pilgrims flock to the church to make healing requests, although any service here is striking for the fervor of the Indian worshippers.

Around Plaza Gertrudis Bocanegra The smaller but livelier **Plaza Gertrudis Bocanegra** (named for a heroine and martyr of the Independence movement) lies one block north of the main square and is where the town's shoeshiners, *colectivo* buses, street vendors and cheaper hotels are clustered. Dominating the northern end is the **Biblioteca Bocanegra▶** which occupies the former church of San Agustín. Next door stands the **Teatro Emperador Caltzontzín**, a former convent, while immediately to the west a lively market area full of *serape* (blanket), hat and food stalls ends at the **Santuario de Guadalupe** (1833). In the evening the plaza end of the market is transformed by gaslit food stands, where local specialties are dished up to a colorful crowd.

Down to the lake From Plaza Gertrudis Bocanegra streets of whitewashed houses with red-tiled roofs run downhill to the main highway, railroad and Lago de Pátzcuaro beyond. Boats leave the main *embarcadero* (landing place) for **Janitzío ▶▶**, a picturesque, though commercialized, pilgrimage island crowned by a giant statue of Morelos, which commands fabulous views over the lake. Fishermen with their famous butterfly nets trawl the tranquil waters, and their freshwater catch can be sampled at countless restaurants along the jetty or on Janitzío itself. Boats to smaller, less visited islands leave from the Embarcadero San Pedro, located to the west of the main jetty down a side road.

Corn-paste sculptures
Even before the Spanish arrived, the Tarascans were making figures of their idols out of a special paste, *pasta de caña*. This modeling paste was made from the ground kernels of corn mixed with gum derived from a type of orchid. With Franciscan approval of the substance and technique, it was used to create images of Christ and the Virgin which are found in several Michoacán churches. Most famous and revered is that of the Virgin of Health in Pátzcuaro's Basilica: her miraculous powers have even been attributed to the figure's expansion, though this is due, more prosaically, to temperature changes.

Day of the Dead

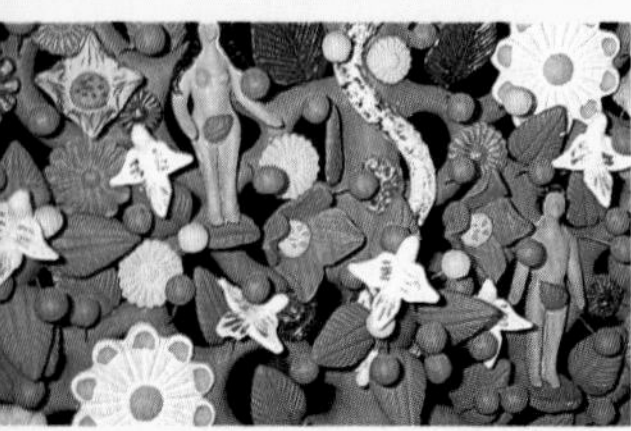

■ **Of the countless religious festivals that punctuate the Mexican calendar, the *Día de los Muertos* (Day of the Dead) is the most spectacular and closest to the indigenous spirit. Celebrated throughout the country on November 1 and 2, it is the focus for extremes of artisan imagination as well as nocturnal spectacles of moving ritual.....** ■

Aztec poem
We only come to dream,
We only come to sleep;
It is not true, it is not true
That we come to live on
Earth.

Where are we to go from
here?
We came here only to be
born,
As our home is beyond,
Where the fleshless abide.

Does anyone really live on
Earth?
The Earth is not forever,
But just to remain for a
short while.

Symbols of the Day of the Dead adorning a street lamp

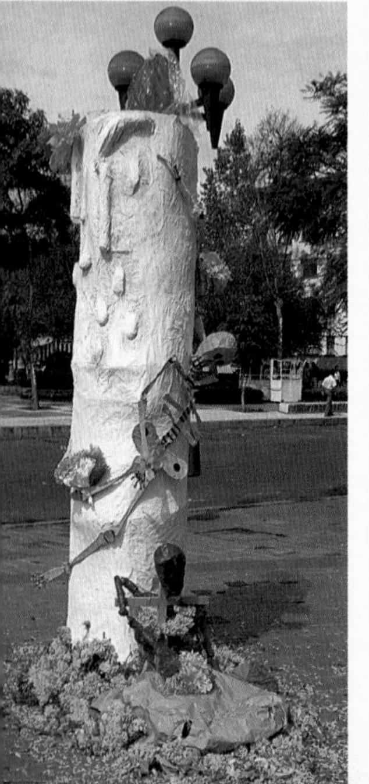

All Saints' Day is the moment when the whole of Mexico plunges into a unique celebration of death, the culmination of weeks of preparation in order to communicate with departed family members. Not only does it tighten the family nucleus but it also strengthens community relationships, while the placing of offerings on family altars continues a tradition that dates from pre-Hispanic times. Whether at Mixquic or Milpa Alta (Valley of Mexico), Iguala (Guerrero), Lago de Pátzcuaro or the mountains of Oaxaca, the Day of the Dead is a highly charged moment which reveals the depths of the Mexicans' spirituality and their ambivalent relationship with death.

Death During their rule, the Aztecs were known as the "people of death," believing that after a fleeting encounter with life, man entered the realm of nine underworlds in the infinite cycle of the cosmic process. Two months of the year were dedicated to worshipping the dead—one for departed children and the other for adults; the latter included massive human sacrifices associated with the god Huitzilopochtli. Five centuries later this tradition has fused with Catholic teachings about death to produce symbolic sugar skulls (relics of pre-Hispanic *tzompantli* or skull-racks), bread-rolls shaped like human bones (*pan de los muertos*), and grotesque papier-mâché skeletons.

Preparations In the preceding weeks craftsmen achieve heights of fantasy making elaborate altars destined for private homes, while bakers and confectioners surpass themselves creating miniature candy coffins and animals. Market-places spill over with inventive goods and food (particularly in the Valley of Mexico and adjoining states), from decorative candles of all sizes and shapes and wreaths of fresh and plastic flowers to candlesticks, incense-burners, pots and sugar *calaveras* (skulls). Households are spring-cleaned and women prepare traditional dishes to be placed on the altar: *mole* (the celebrated Pueblan sauce), desserts, *tamales* and, of course, *calaveras*. Personalized offerings can include cigarettes, a glass of *tequila*, clothes, hats or anything related to the occupation of the departed—from an ear of corn to a plow or machete. It all depends on regional customs as much as the tastes of the dead person.

Celebrations To ensure that the departed find their way from the cemetery, flower petals are strewn along the path leading to the family altar where the souls of the dead will feed on the aromas from the offerings and enjoy

their favorite music. Church bells start tolling on the evening of October 31 to announce the visit of child spirits, and continue throughout the next day to herald the arrival of the adult souls for whom the altar is rearranged. In some areas *calaverear* (door-to-door chanting and praying for the souls that nobody remembers) is carried out in the evening. The family's offerings are then collected up and consumed in the church itself. However, American Hallowe'en traditions are fast replacing this old custom.

November 1 and 2 see nocturnal family pilgrimages to local cemeteries where hundreds of candles are lit, food offerings made, pictures of saints installed and wreaths laid. This is also an excuse for picnicking, heightened by the ritual consumption of *pulque* (maguey beer). The Day of the Dead culminates with visits to relatives to distribute offerings, interspersed with welcome glasses of *mezcal* or *tequila*.

Special of the day
The famous Day of the Dead celebrations around Lago de Pátzcuaro now draw hundreds of visitors. From sunset on November 1, Tarascan Indians from lakeside villages canoe across the dark waters to the island of Janitzío where candlelit processions, accompanied by chanting and dancing, lead to the cemetery. The all-night cemetery vigil is now out of bounds to tourists to preserve a necessary intimacy, but other ceremonies can be observed at the nearby pyramid site of Tzintzuntzán. At the village of Mixquic (some 31 miles from Mexico City), rituals involve costume parties and processions to the cemetery: the skeleton assumes a high profile here.

Some of Mexico's greatest art celebrates death. Papier-mâché skeletons like this one are produced by the thousand

La Corregidora
Querétaro's indisputable heroine, Doña Josefa Ortíz de Domínguez (*La Corregidora*), wife of the royal governor (*el corregidor*), is widely commemorated in the city. Her statue crowns a semicircular square bearing her name at the northern corner of the pedestrian zone, and the Palacio de Gobierno is often referred to as the Casa de la Corregidora. She saved the lives of the insurgent plotters who often met secretly at her home. When her husband learned of her involvement, he locked her in a room of their house but she managed to get a message out through a keyhole, saving the revolutionaries from imminent discovery. Immediately after, Miguel Hidalgo's *grito* sparked the Independence movement.

▶▶ Querétaro *125C1*

The sprawling, dusty city of Querétaro, whose hard-edged atmosphere and commercialism reflects its proximity to Mexico City, 138 miles away, is considered the crossroads of the nation, yet within the untidy outskirts lies a renovated historic center breathing memories of key events in Mexican history and with enough monuments to occupy a full day's visit. Querétaro was originally an Otomí settlement, later conquered by the Aztecs, and was taken over by the Spanish in 1531. By the late 17th century it had become the third city of the kingdom, but it was the following century that saw the building of most of Querétaro's surviving monuments. The Independence movement began here in 1810, and in 1848 the notorious Treaty of Guadalupe Hidalgo was signed which handed over half of Mexico to the U.S. Twenty years later Querétaro witnessed Emperor Maximilian's last stand and execution and finally, in 1917, saw the birth of the new constitution.

Pedestrian zone An extensive and lively pedestrian area of flowery, cobbled streets winds uphill to the east of the central Jardín Zenea (formerly Jardín Obregón), culminating at the stately Plaza de Armas. Dominating the Jardín is the striking church of **San Francisco▶▶** (1540–50), whose interior is faced in *trompe l'oeil* murals. The adjoining monastery has been converted into an excellent **Museo Regional▶▶▶**. Aspects of local archaeology and history are displayed along with a collection of religious paintings and objects—particularly remarkable is the Galería de San Ignacio de Loyola, a corridor of oil paintings by Miguel Cabrera. Military history figures prominently, as does the 1917 Constitution. On the shady Plaza de Armas, several superb 18th-century mansions now function as government buildings: at the northern end is the **Palacio de Gobierno**, from where the governor's wife secretly sent a warning to the conspirators in the plot for Independence. On the eastern flank is the **Méson de Santa Rosa**, now converted into an elegant hotel and adjoined by the local tourist office.

Directly east and uphill from this square stands the

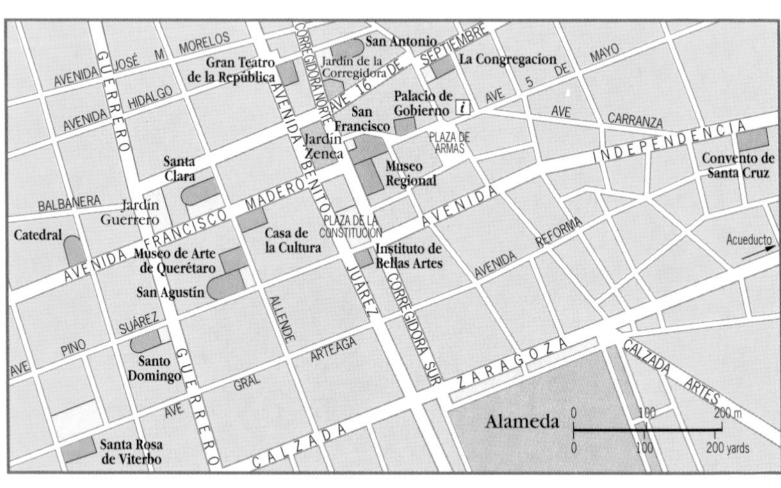

impressive Franciscan monastery, the **Convento de Santa Cruz▶▶** (1683), built on the site of the Otomí defeat in 1531, and once prison to Emperor Maximilian. Its religious function continues today and visits are by guided tour only, although it is well worth stopping off for a number of bizarre features, including a tree sprouting cross-shaped thorns. Beyond the monastery is the start of Querétaro's **aqueduct** (1726–38), its 74 stone arches rising 75 ft. over the town.

West of the center On the Jardín Guerrero, a square which is thick with laurel trees and graced by a 1797 fountain of Neptune, stands one of Querétaro's Baroque masterpieces, the **Templo de Santa Clara▶▶▶** (1633). The austere exterior of this former convent belies its interior, an overwhelming gilded riot of high-relief altar-pieces which cover practically every wall. Two blocks south is the equally magnificent **Templo de Santa Rosa de Viterbo▶▶▶** (1752), its flying buttresses carved with masks and an interior boasting a Churrigueresque altarpiece, an ornately carved choir, and a unique inlaid marble pulpit. Between these two masterpieces stands another former convent, San Agustín, now revitalized by the **Museo de Arte de Querétaro▶▶** whose collection of 16th- to 20th-century paintings is overpowered by the scale and mastery of the stone carving in its 18th-century cloister.

The Church of Santa Rosa

Theatricality
The Gran Teatro de la República, one block north of the Jardín Zenea, was the setting for several momentous historic events. Inaugurated in 1852 with the name Gran Teatro Iturbide, in 1867 it was the meeting place for the Council of War, which condemned the unlucky Emperor Maximilian to death. In 1917 it witnessed the formal signing of the Mexican Constitution: the stage backdrop still lists the names of the delegates. Finally, in 1929, it saw the beginning of over 60 years of one-party rule when the PRI (Partido Revolucionario Institucional) was founded there.

Queretaro, renowned for its opals and other gems, is a quiet, elegant city despite undergoing rapid industrialization

Masks
One of Mexico's most compelling displays of ceremonial masks is found at the Museo de la Máscara, opposite the Teatro de la Paz on the Plaza del Carmen in San Luis Potosí. Over 700 examples reveal the fertile imagination of pre-Hispanic and post-Hispanic Mexican communities, and are displayed to reflect the nation's social, political and religious history. Traditional costumes and descriptions of dances contribute further to understanding the incredible rituals which still play a fundamental role in Mexican life.

► San Juan del Río *125C1*

The market town of San Juan del Río is set in vineyards 32 miles southwest of Querétaro. It is famous for its lapidary business, which originated with the mining of local opals, but now extends to the polishing of gemstones from all over Mexico. The old colonial center is notable for the **Templo de Santo Domingo**, a 17th-century Baroque church and former convent, the multi-domed **Templo de Sagrado Corazón** and adjoining **Parroquía**, both dating from the 18th century and overlooking the Plaza de la Independencia, and the hilltop ex-convent of **Santa Veracruz►►** which houses a small history museum. A large **crafts market►** is located on the main intersection of Juárez and Hidalgo, with a gemstone market opposite.

► San Luis Potosí *124B2*

San Luis Potosí, capital of the vast state of the same name, was founded in 1592 when silver and gold were discovered in the area. With a particularly bad record for mistreatment of Indians, it redeemed itself somewhat when it became the site for Juárez' government-in-exile and later nurtured revolutionaries, particularly Francisco Madero, whose 1910 Plan de San Luis Potosí got the political ball rolling. Since then industry has left its mark on the crowded city, although the majestic center still offers a wonderful array of colonial architecture.

On the Plaza de Armas the twin-towered **Catedral►►**, completed at the turn of the 18th century, faces the **Palacio de Gobierno** where a small museum is dedicated to Juárez. One block northeast on the Plaza de Fundadores stands the main university building, once a Jesuit college (1653), flanked by its exquisite Baroque chapel, the **Capilla de Loreto►►** (1700). To the south, the quieter Plaza de San Francisco is dominated by a former Franciscan convent and church with a lovely Baroque sacristy. The convent now houses the rather dusty **Museo Regional**, whose outstanding feature is the Churrigueresque **Capilla de Aranzazú►►**. However, the jewel in Potosí's crown is the 1764 **Templo del Carmen►►►**, two blocks east of the cathedral. A richly carved exterior leads to an even more elaborate interior which culminates in the Chapel of the Virgin, covered entirely in gilded cherubim and decorative carvings.

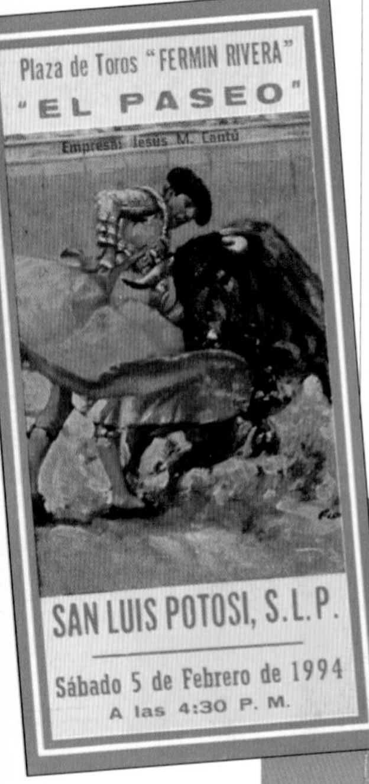

San Luis Potosí's attractive zócalo

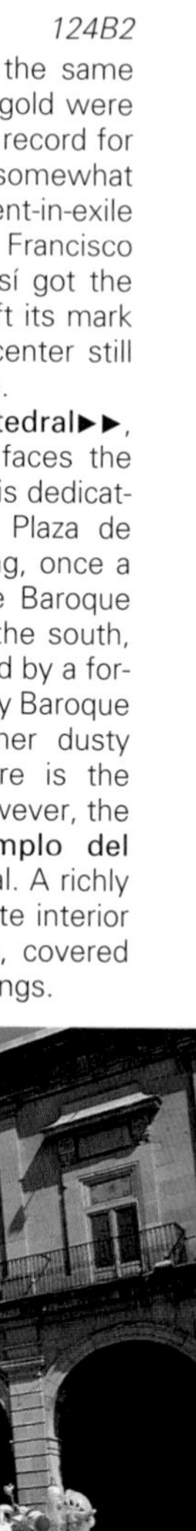

Huichol peyote pilgrims

■ Year in, year out the Huichol Indians of Nayarit and Jalisco struggle hundreds of miles across the central highlands to the northern region of San Luis Potosí in search of the precious *peyote* plant, their drug, their god and their *raison d'être*.....■

Thought to have been based originally in the sierra of San Luis Potosí before they fled from the Spaniards, today's 52,000 Huichols have become one of Mexico's purest and most isolated Indian groups. Scattered in farms throughout the inaccessible mountains and canyons of Nayarit and Jalisco, they have systematically rejected outside influences and maintained their own mythology, which sees everything as divine, or possessing a soul (*kupuri*). As a result the rugged landscape is dotted with natural shrines where they leave offerings and make requests. Their celebrations blend complex healing traditions passed down through generations of shamans with Huichol legends and gods, namely the sun, fire, water, corn, deer, and *peyote*. Considered the fount of life, the sacred *peyote* "button" is chewed in mystical rituals to stimulate predictions of the future, and diagnosis and healing of sickness. It is to gather the year's provisions of this hallucinogenic cactus that the Huichols trek 43 days across the Sierra Madre to Wirikuta, following a highly ritualized route.

***Peyote* creations** The role of the Huichol shaman (*maarakame*) is primordial. Only he can communicate directly with the gods, interpret the divine will and translate the hallucinations brought about by *peyote*. As a result, other Huichols channel their visions into art and offerings, above all *nierika* (yarn paintings), which are psychedelic expressions of their mythology. Brilliantly colored and contrasting yarn is pressed into a wax base (a form of *peyote* juice) in a similar process to that used for their votive beaded gourds and carved wooden objects. These are coated with beeswax before glass beads are individually placed with a cactus thorn in magical, symbolic designs. The glass beads represent another change in tradition: brought by the Spaniards, they gradually replaced the traditional decoration of seeds, nuts, pebbles, and corn kernels.

***Peyote* effects**
The unassuming appearance of the small tufted cactus known as *peyote* belies the radical effect created by its alkaloid ingredient, mescalin. By no means a monopoly of the Huichols, its use by the Aztecs (their relatives) was described with disgust by Spanish chroniclers, and under colonial rule it was soon banned. Despite the frightening hallucinations which can last three days, *peyote* is reputed to build up physical strength, give an illusory sense of invulnerability and reduce appetite and thirst, all of which help the Huichols accomplish their annual jaunt. The drug is strictly banned in Mexico for everyone except Indians.

Huichol Indian

The elegant Parroquía is one of Mexico's colonial gems

AUTOTRANSPORTES TRES ESTRELLAS DE ORO, S. A. DE C.V.
TRANSPORTES NORTE DE SONORA, S. A. DE C.V.
AUTOTRANSPORTES TRES ESTRELLAS DEL NORTE, S. A. DE C.V.
AUTOTRANSPORTES CORSARIOS DEL BAJIO, S. A. DE C.V.
SERVICIO DE PRIMERA CLASE
SEGURIDAD COMODIDAD CORTESIA
BOLETO DEL PASAJERO
149973
12 SEP 1993
S.M.DE ALLENDE, GTO.
A: GTO
HORA 12:30
ASIENTO
$ N$ 11.00
SUPLICAMOS RECTIFICAR SI ESTAN CORRECTOS LOS DATOS ANOTADOS
ESTE BOLETO NO TIENE VALIDEZ DESPRENDIDO DE SU TALON

Crafts and markets

Behind San Felipe Neri is a market area with a very traditional Mexican feel. Indian women chop cactus leaves and men sit in front of mountains of eggs, backed by rows of *huachi-piles* (leather sandals). Descend some steps and you come to the "crafts market" where vendors aim their wares at tour groups and in the process often attain rare heights of kitsch. Far more attractive goods can be found in the town's craft shops which line the streets leading off the Plaza Allende.

▶▶ San Miguel de Allende *124B2*

San Miguel was founded in 1542 by a Franciscan monk. During the colonial period it was a busy crossroads for the great mining towns of the Bajío region, Guanajuato and Zacatecas. Climbing up a steep hillside, in a region of arid sierra dotted with ranches and goatherds, San Miguel is now home to a community of expatriate artists and writers from the U.S. Upscale restaurants, hotels, galleries and craft shops have followed in their wake, reactivating the elegant old mansions of the center and lending the town a unique, albeit *gringo*, flavor.

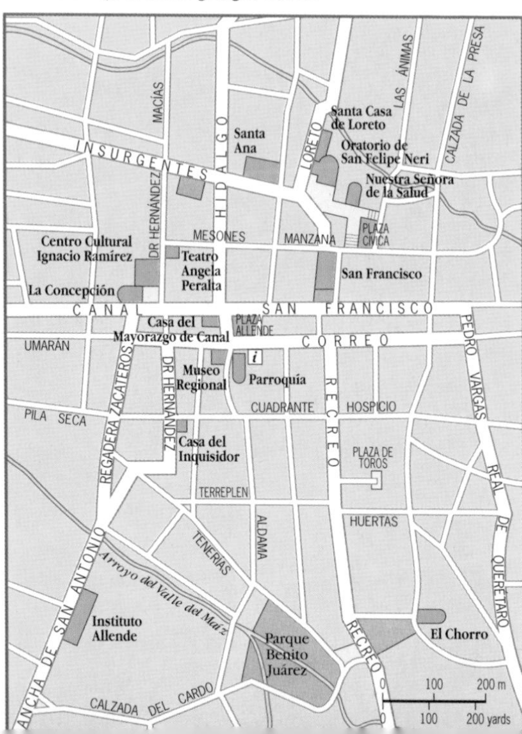

In and around the Plaza Allende One of the few towns in Mexico to be designated a national monument, San Miguel's chief attraction is the harmony of its narrow cobblestone streets, low-lying red-roofed houses, tree-lined patios and elegant mansions on the Plaza Allende. There are no major monuments, although the lofty, fluted spires of the extraordinary neo-Gothic **Parroquía▶▶** are a wonder in themselves. The church was designed in 1880 by Indian mason Zeferino Gutiérrez. Across the side-street stands the 17th-century **Casa Allende**, birthplace of Ignacio Allende, who engineered Mexico's independence movement along with Miguel Hidalgo. Now the **Museo Regional▶▶**, it displays the city's archaeology and history, with strong emphasis on Independence and the life of Allende. On the northwest corner stands the **Casa del Mayorazgo de Canal**, once home to the Count of Canal and now used for temporary art exhibitions. The **Casa de los Conspiradores** is where Allende and fellow conspirators plotted in the basement as the bourgeoisie danced the night away on the first floor.

Churches Along Canal's uphill route stands the **Iglesia de San Francisco**, begun in 1779 in Churrigueresque style. Two blocks north, flanking a terraced plaza, stand three 18th-century churches. To the east, the **Iglesia de Nuestra Señora de la Salud** has a pretty scalloped stone entrance, but it is the **Oratorio de San Felipe Neri▶▶** (1712) that is of more interest, with its Indian-influenced vegetal motifs on the façade and paintings of the life of San Felipe. To the west is the beautiful gilded chapel of **Santa Casa de Loreto▶▶** (often closed).

Cultural centers San Miguel's finest building is the **Bellas Artes▶▶▶**, housed in the 18th-century **Convento de la Concepción**, whose church boasts one of Mexico's largest domes. The spacious cloister now serves as San Miguel's lively **Centro Cultural Ignacio Ramírez**. Art exhibitions and murals line the arcades and one room is devoted to an unfinished work by Siqueiros. Several blocks south of here, at San Antonio 20, is the celebrated **Instituto Allende▶**, an arts-and-language school founded in 1938 that drew the first Americans to San Miguel. Housed in the imposing 1735 mansion of the Conde de Canal and set in a lovely park, it is still a focal point for North American students.

Atotonilco
Nine miles north of San Miguel, on the road to Dolores Hidalgo, is the tiny Indian hamlet of Atotonilco, an important pilgrimage site closely linked to the struggle for independence. It is dominated by a 1740 church, scene of Miguel Allende's wedding in 1802 and, eight years later, the first destination for the insurgent forces on their march from Dolores to San Miguel. The object of their visit was a banner depicting the Virgin of Guadalupe, which was seized and held aloft by Hidalgo and Allende's followers as they triumphantly entered San Miguel. The banner now hangs in San Miguel's Museo Regional.

Detail on church façade

San Miguel de Allende has been designated a national monument

Volcán Paricutín
Uruapan's lush, rolling hills may be famous for their avocados, but it is the volcano of Paricutín which draws the visitors. It looms 9,101 ft. over the horizon, 9 miles west of town, and is accessible from the village of Angahuán where horseback tours can be organized. A vast, furrowed, black field of lava covers the slopes and it is here that you can see the church spire of the village of San Juan Parangaricútiro, buried for eternity when the volcano erupted in 1943 in a cornfield, much to the horror of the local farmer. It spewed fire and lava more or less continuously for nine years, engulfing two villages and petrifying the region in the process, but now stands inactive.

Franciscan missions
The Franciscans were an official and integral part of the Spanish Conquest, particularly active in the state of Querétaro from where they sent missionary expeditions to the north and into the U.S. It was not until 1750, however, that the celebrated Franciscan Junipero Serra managed to set up churches in five mission towns of the inaccessible Sierra Gorda. Each one is a work of art, its fine, descriptive Baroque carvings reflecting a synthesis of Spanish and indigenous art. Jalpan, Tancoyol, Concá, Tilaco, and Landa are all dominated by these magnificent structures, the most ornate being that of Landa, where the façade is alive with figures of saints.

►► Sierra Gorda *125C2*

In the northeast of the state of Querétaro, crossing into the states of Hidalgo and San Luis Potosí, lies a mountainous, semi-desert region, the Sierra Gorda, where roads climb through pine forests to over 8,000 ft. before descending rapidly to tropical valleys. Indian resistance to Franciscan missionaries led to war in 1600, but by the 1750s five missions had been established here in a unique, highly ornate style. **Jalpan de Serra►►**, the region's crossroads, lies 100 miles north of San Juan del Río on Highway 120, and offers the best facilities for visitors. A further 30 miles northwest lies **Concá►►**, site of another beautiful church, while to the east are **Landa►►**, and **Tancoyol**, accessible only by dirt road.

► Tampico *125D2*

Although it lies on the Gulf Coast, Tampico only merits a visit from those touring the Central Highlands who are in need of a sea breeze. It is easily reached from San Luis Potosí. This sprawling industrial city, the southernmost and largest in the state of Tamaulipas, is completely monopolized by the oil industry. It was first inhabited by the Huastecs, and later came under Aztec rule before being settled by the Spanish in 1534. The port was completely sacked by pirates in the 17th century, and rebuilt in the 19th century, but it was the discovery of oil in 1901 that led to its heyday. Transformation came along with British and American oil men, and its waters soon became an environmental disaster. Things are cleaner now and the **Playa de Miramar** and **Playa Altamira**, just north of town, are suitable for swimming. The **Museo de la Cultura Huasteca**, in the satellite town of Ciudad Madero, is well worth a visit for its fine collection of ceramics and sculptures, but Tampico itself remains a rundown, seedy port.

►► Tequisquiapan *125C1*

Tequisquiapan is the last major town before Highway 120 climbs into the Sierra Gorda, and is popular for its temperate climate, thermal springs, wines, cheese, and crafts. Located 112 miles from Mexico City, the numerous spas in the area draw crowds from the capital at weekends but it remains a picturesque, sleepy place which depends economically on its basketware, wickerwork, jewelry, and ceramics. About 10 miles to the north is the archaeological zone of **Ranas**, inhabited between the 7th and 11th centuries and, 10 miles east of this, the ruins of the ceremonial center of **Toluquilla**.

►►► Tzintzuntzán *124B1*

On the eastern shores of the Lago de Pátzcuaro (see pages 142–143 and 156–157) is the village of Tzintzuntzán (Place of the Hummingbirds), one of the three cities which once formed the 14th-century Tarascan League and the first base for the enlightened bishop of Michoacán, Vasco de Quiroga, in 1538. Today the village has become a crafts center for handpainted ceramics, straw figures, and wood-carvings, and also attracts a growing number of affluent lakeside residents. The Tarascan site of **Las Yácatas** is located up an access road to the south of the village. A row of five stepped, circular

The village of Tzintzuntzán was dedicated to Curicaveri, the god of fire

pyramids (*yácatas*) offers lake views, and a small museum gives the background to this once flourishing kingdom. The 16th-century **Templo de San Francisco** is now partly in ruins, but its peeling interior and atmospheric, rambling garden of pine and olive trees (reputedly planted by Quiroga himself in defiance of an edict forbidding their cultivation) are well worth the visit.

► Uruapan *124B1*

Although lacking the magic of Pátzcuaro or the majesty of Morelia, Uruapan, famous for its fine lacquerware, makes an interesting stopover on Michoacán's main road south to the Pacific. It lies in a beautiful, lush sub-tropical region, one of Mexico's chief fruit-growing areas, with avocados figuring prominently. Urupuan's main attraction is the **Parque Nacional Eduardo Ruíz►►** which envelops the source of the Río Cupatitzio at the northern end of town and is thick with mossy trees, tropical vegetation and artificial waterfalls. On the Plaza Principal stands the **Museo Regional Huatapera►**, housed in one of Bishop Quiroga's first hospitals (1533), which exhibits Michoacán crafts with a special emphasis on lacquerware. Between the zócalo (main square) and the park, craftshops and workshops line Calle Independencia, finishing at the Mercado de Artesanías opposite the park entrance.

Fine church detail, Uruapan

Uruapan's attractive cathedral

A short trip by cable-car takes you up the Cerro de la Bufa to the Patrocinio Chapel

Cerro de la Bufa
The easiest way to the top of this hill is via cable-car from the slopes of the Cerro del Bosque, also accessible from the northern exit of the El Edén mine. Views across the city are spectacular, particularly at sunset, and the hill can be descended by a path which leads directly back to the center. At the summit an 18th-century chapel contains a much-revered portrait of the Virgin; pilgrims sometimes spend the night in the courtyard. Behind stands the Museo de la Toma de Zacateca with memorabilia concentrating on Villa's victory over the Federales.

Beside the craggy summit stand three monumental statues of the Revolutionary leaders, and at the top is an observatory.

►► Xilitla *125C2*

In the remote mountains of southern San Luis Potosí, roughly 150 miles southwest of Tampico, the village of Xilitla holds an unusual attraction, the fantasy home of English eccentric, Edward James (1907–84). On his arrival in 1954 he invested in an area of steamy jungle where he set about building a palace of Daliesque inspiration. His local mentor, a Yacqui Indian, meanwhile constructed a village home in a parallel anarchistic spirit. Neither is an official monument but James' increasingly overgrown jungle home is worth exploring before it disappears.

►►► Zacatecas *124A3*

The industrious mining city of Zacatecas, gateway to the north, blankets a magnificent plateau at an altitude of 8,200 ft., rimmed with arid hills. With few visitors and even fewer Indians, it epitomizes the prosperity of colonial Spain. Baroque monuments pepper the pink-stone center at the base of the Cerro de la Bufa (8,750 ft.), but it also has a lively market area which contributes to the friendly atmosphere. A panoramic cable-car, silver crafts, semi-precious stones, leatherwork, and a robust local wine add to the attractions of Zacatecas.

Silver town The founding of Zacatecas in 1546 was directly linked to its silver deposits, already exploited by the Zacateco Indians, and within a few years operations were already sending wagon-loads of the precious ore south to Mexico City. Fortunes were rapidly made, but the political upheavals of the 19th and early 20th centuries, including Pancho Villa's capture of the city in 1914, announced the end of the boom. However, silver is once again the city's main resource and it now mines 34 percent of the nation's production. One of the major sights is **La Mina del Edén►**, located northwest of the center at the base of Cerro del Bosque. Guided tours start with a ride on a small train which drives straight into the heart of the 16th-century mine and continues on foot past garishly illuminated shafts, multi-leveled galleries, chasms, pools, and even a shrine. Guides reveal horrifying statistics which describe mining conditions of the past and their Indian victims.

Central sights Two parallel streets cut through the center: Avenida Hidalgo (becoming Avenida González Ortega) and Calle Tacuba. Monopolizing this junction is the **Catedral►►►**, completed in 1752 and one of Mexico's outstanding expressions of Baroque. Its northern side is flanked by the Plaza Hidalgo and the **Palacio de Gobierno**, a fomer silver baron's mansion, as is the imposing **Palacio de Mala Noche** opposite. South of the cathedral the city's upscale shopping center, **El Mercado**, is housed in a cast-iron market building, while across Avenida Hidalgo stands the elegant 19th-century **Teatro Calderón**.

Uphill to the west, in a street of old silver barons' mansions, lies the pretty **Templo de Santo Domingo►►►** (1746), the richest in Zacatecas, filled with Baroque gold-leaf altar-pieces. It was built on massive foundations that compensate for the uneven terrain. Its former monastery now houses the **Museo Pedro Coronel►►►**, a remark-

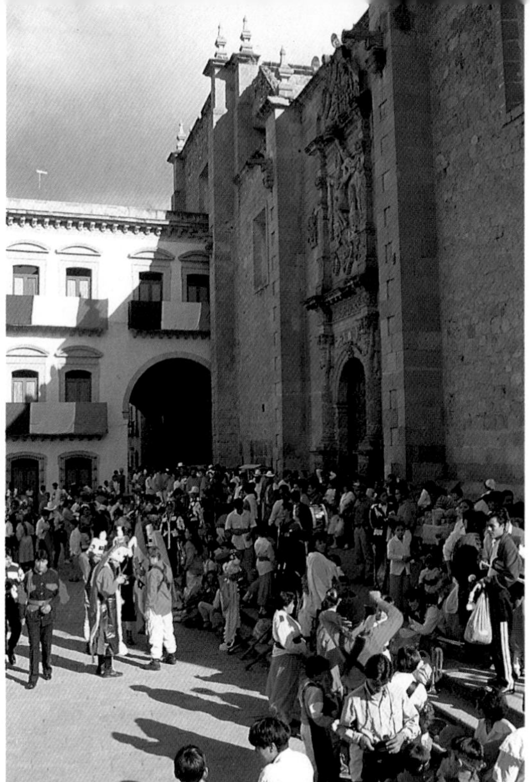

Celebrating Independence Day in Zacatecas' zócalo

able collection of exhibits covering every civilization from Ancient Greece to Asia and Africa. Another private collection of the Coronel family is the **Museo Rafael Coronel▶▶**, housed in the Baroque monastery of San Francisco, still partly ruined by Villa's bombardment. This large complex is located at the northern end of town (take bus No. 5 or 8), and the museum includes a collection of Mexican masks and sketches by Diego Rivera.

South of the center Avenida Hidalgo runs south past imposing 19th-century buildings to Avenida Juárez, which marks the end of the old center. To the west it becomes the **Alameda**, for centuries the fashionable Zacatecan promenade. South lies the **Parque Enrique Estrada**, flanked to the west by the **Museo Francisco Goitia**, a memorial to this famous Zacatecan painter, and to the east by the remains of an 18th-century aqueduct. Just behind this is the luxury, colonial-style **Quinta Real▶▶** hotel, constructed around a 17th-century bullring in 1849. A few streets northwest the **Jardín Independencia** becomes the shoeshiners' domain, and beyond this start Zacatecas' rambling market streets.

A destiny of eccentricity
Edward James spent much of his time and fortune patronizing artists of the Surrealist movement. During World War II he fled to the safer delights of Beverly Hills where he wined and dined the likes of Humphrey Bogart and Orson Welles. But the fascination of this dissolute existence soon palled and thus began his Mexican episode in the village of Xilitla. With the help of his Yaqui friend he started putting his marijuana and *peyote*-inspired dreams into practice, directing a team of local builders to create his personal delirium of Oriental temples, Greek columns, arches and bridges, which was never finished.

Pancho Villa looks out over Zacatecas, the city he liberated from General Huerta during the Revolution

Drive Lagos de Pátzcuaro and Zirahuén

This pastoral round-trip drive between Lago de Pátzcuaro and Lago de Zirahuén takes you through the small lakeside villages of Michoacán. Pyramids, early Franciscan churches, Utopia and, above all, thriving local crafts are the reasons for visiting this area. Allow a full day.

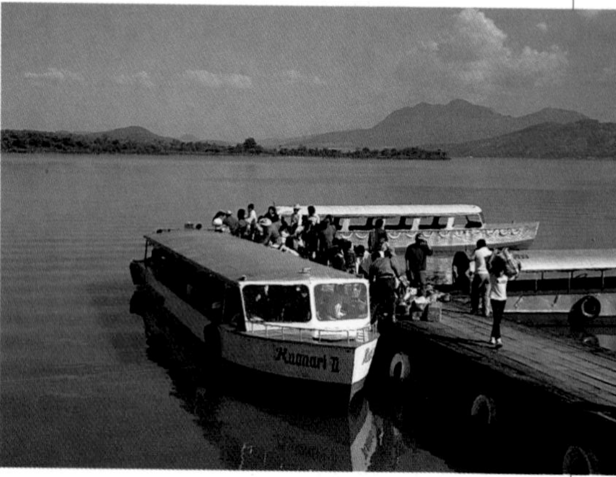

Boarding the ferry for Janitzio Island

From **Pátzcuaro** (see pages 142–143) follow the road down to the lake and turn right on to the road to Tzintzuntzán, which leaves the main highway at Tzurumutaro. Skirting the lake through lush green farmlands you can make a short detour left to **Ihuatzío** (signposted) to see the unexcavated lakeside ruins of an old Tarascan town. The main road continues away from the lake through gentle hills of eucalyptus trees, and after 4 miles descends to **Tzintzuntzán** (see page 152). On your right before entering the village is a turn-off winding uphill to an important Tarascan archaeological site where five circular pyramids (*yácatas*) overlook the lake. The village itself is known for its elaborate wood-carving displayed along the main street, woven straw figures, and for a particular style of hand-painted pottery. Visit the 16th-century **Franciscan church** and its atmospheric gardens just behind the main square.

From here the road continues past old and new lakeside houses, flat pastures and roadside crafts vendors to the main junction at **Quiroga**, the busiest and largest commercial town of the lake. Turn left at the arcaded main square and drive a few miles on to **Santa Fé de la Laguna**, the first of more than a dozen Indian villages hugging the lake. It was here in Santa Fé that Don Vasco de Quiroga, Michoacán's first bishop in the 1540s, tried to set up a model of Thomas More's *Utopia*. The 16th-century hospital and chapel still stand, and the village square has recently been completely renovated.

Continuing on MEX 14 you pass pine woods and several local restaurants serving freshwater fish straight from the lake. Just beyond

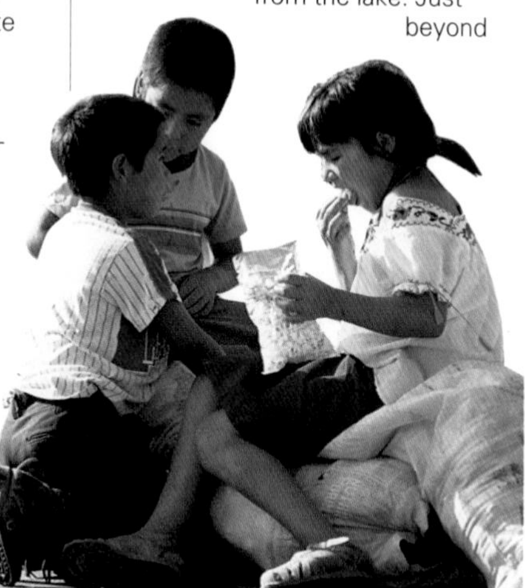

Young Tarascans enjoying a bag of popcorn

Chupícuaro the road branches: turn left to **San Jerónimo**, a sprawling village of dirt roads, red roofs and spires on a lakeside promontory. The main activities here are carving wood and boat-building. A few miles farther through verdant countryside the road goes south through San Andrés to the villages of **Puácuaro** and **Napízaro**, a mere mile apart. The inhabitants of these villages are pure Indian and they specialize in basket-making. A short distance on is the large fishing village of **Erongaricuaro**, whose name means "lookout tower on the lake" in Purépecha. Visit the 16th-century **Franciscan church** and **seminary** for good lake views and to admire the old Spanish-style architecture. Crafts include fine inlaid furniture, weaving, and embroidery.

Just over a mile south lies **San Francisco Uricho**, a tiny village whose 16th-century church boasts a superb altar. **Arocutin**, the next stop, is known for its fine embroidery, and from here you can reach the island of **Jarácuaro**, which specializes in hat-making. Another mile or so farther is **Tocuaro**, the main village on Lago de Pátzcuaro for making masks, and as you round the southern shores of the lake you come to the *pulque*-(maguey beer) distilling village of **San Pedro**. The lake road finally rejoins MEX 14 back at Pátzcuaro. From here follow signs to Uruapan until the road branches off to the left to the small Lago de Zirahuén, a peaceful and scenic spot to relax.

Lake Zirahuén is noted for its deep, blue waters

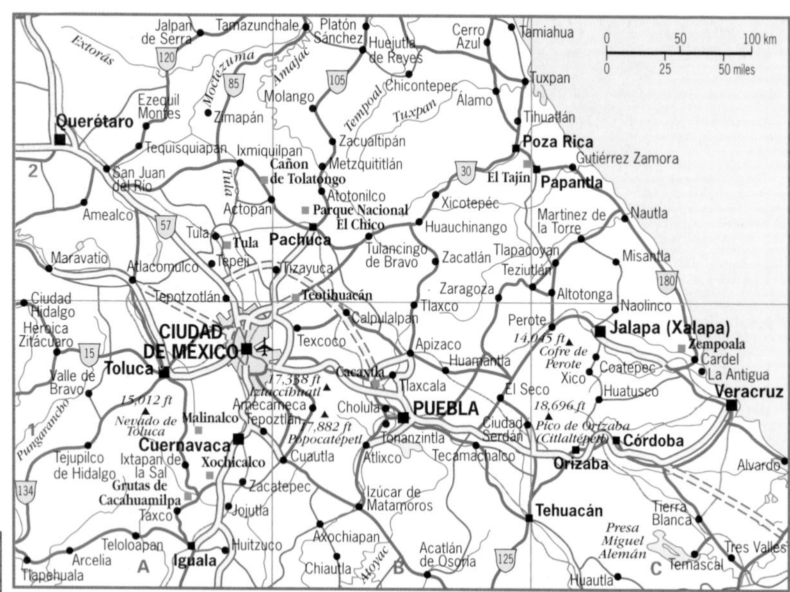
Jalpan de Serra
Tamazunchale
Platón Sánchez
Huejutla de Reyes
Cerro Azul
Tamiahua
0 50 100 km
0 25 50 miles
Extorás
120
Moctezuma
Amajac
85
105
Tempoal
Chicontepec
Tuxpan
Álamo
Ezequil Montes
Zimapán
Molango
Tihuatlán
Querétaro
Tequisquiapan
Ixmiquilpan
Zacualtipán
Poza Rica
2
San Juan del Río
Tula
Cañon de Tolatongo
Metzquititlán
30
El Tajín
Papantla
Gutiérrez Zamora
Atotonilco
Amealco
Actopan
Parque Nacional El Chico
Xicotepéc
Martinez de la Torre
Nautla
57
Tula
Tula
Pachuca
Huauchinango
Tulancingo de Bravo
Zacatlán
Tlapacoyan
Teziutlán
Misantla
Maravatío
Atlacomulco
Tepeji
Tizayuca
Zaragoza
180
Ciudad Hidalgo
Tepotzotlán
Teotihuacán
Tlaxco
Altotonga
Naolinco
Heroica Zitácuaro
Calpulalpan
Perote
Jalapa (Xalapa)
CIUDAD DE MÉXICO
Texcoco
14,045 ft
Cofre de Perote
Zempoala
15
Apizaco
Cardel
Toluca
Huamantla
Xico
Coatepec
La Antigua
Valle de Bravo
17,338 ft
Iztaccíhuatl
Cacaxtla
Tlaxcala
El Seco
Huatusco
Veracruz
15,012 ft
Nevado de Toluca
Amecameca
Cholula
18,696 ft
Pungarancho
Malinalco
Tepoztlán
17,882 ft
Popocatépetl
PUEBLA
Ciudad Serdán
Pico de Orizaba (Citlaltépetl)
Córdoba
1
Cuernavaca
Tonanzintla
Tejupilco de Hidalgo
Ixtapan de la Sal
Xochicalco
Cuautla
Atlixco
Tecamachalco
Orizaba
Alvarado
134
Grutas de Cacahuamilpa
Zacatepec
Taxco
Jojutla
Izúcar de Matamoros
Tehuacán
Tierra Blanca
Presa Miguel Alemán
Teloloapan
Huitzuco
Axochiapan
Acatlán de Osoria
125
Tres Valles
Arcelia
A
Iguala
Chiautla
Atoyac
B
C
Temascal
Tlapehuala
Huautla

THE CENTRAL VALLEYS AND THE GULF

The Central Valleys and the Gulf From Toluca in the west to Veracruz in the east, the central valleys of Mexico dance across high plateaux and even higher, snowcapped peaks, sweeping across fields of corn or maguey and up into pine forests before sloping down to the coastal plain of the Gulf. Some of the country's richest and poorest inhabitants live in this region, from wealthy refugees from the big city who reside in the hills of Morelos to farmers scraping a living on the arid slopes of Hidalgo. Between these two extremes are the industrialized cities of Puebla and Cuernavaca, the artisan villages of the vast state of Puebla, and the picturesque tropical garden of the state of Veracruz. It was not for nothing that so many of Mesoamerica's dynasties graduated to these fertile valleys, and the relics of their civilizations add infinitely to the region's seduction.

From the beginning to Baroque One of Mesoamerica's most astounding sites is Teotihuacán, its sheer scale and symmetry sufficient evidence of this civilization's sophis-

The magnificent Nevado de Toluca volcano, Mexico's fourth highest summit at 15,355 ft. The two lakes in its crater are named after the sun and the moon

Beyond Cuernavaca
"How continually, how startlingly, the landscape changed! ... a strange planet where, if you looked a little further, beyond the Tres Marías, you would find every sort of landcsape at once, the Costwolds, Windermere, New Hampshire, the meadows of the Eure-et-Loire, even the grey dunes of Cheshire, even the Sahara, a planet upon which, in the twinkling of an eye, you could change climates and, if you cared to think so, in the crossing of a highway, three civilisations; but beautiful, there was no denying its beauty, fatal or cleansing as it happened to be, the beauty of the Earthly Paradise itself."
Malcolm Lowry: *Under the Volcano*, 1947.

tication. It can be visited in a day from the capital or absorbed into a wider exploration of the rural state of Hidalgo. Less spectacular is what remains of Tula, home to the militaristic Toltecs. To the south of Mexico City lies scenic Xochicalco and, to the east, the exquisite murals of Cacaxtla, the massive pyramid of Cholula and spectacular El Tajín. You can follow the trail of the conquistadors who struggled over mountain passes from Veracruz to Tlaxcala and Cholula before besieging the Aztec capital. Some of their earliest buildings can be seen, as well as sublime heights of Baroque design, from the extraordinary church at Tepotzotlán and the encapsulation of Indian imagination at Tonanzintla to Puebla's Santo Domingo and Taxco's Santa Prisca. The whole region is a minefield of historical events. The state of Morelos is named after the radical priest José María Morelos, who was instrumental in bringing about Mexico's independence, basing himself for a time at Cuautla. French intervention in 1862 and 1863 centered upon Puebla, while Cuernavaca echoes with the doomed footsteps of Emperor Maximilian and Carlota. Revolutionary machinations reverberate in Veracruz, scene of Venustiano Carranza's U.S.-backed government in 1915 and, closer to the soil, in Morelos, where Indian guerilla forces were mobilized by Emiliano Zapata's cry of *tierra y libertad* ("land and liberty").

Unadulterated nature No fewer than nine national parks cover the slopes of the mountain ranges ringing Mexico City. Closest to the capital and most symbolic is the

The Atlantes of Tula

Parque Nacional Popocatépetl–Iztaccíhuatl, but the Pico de Orizaba (Mexico's highest peak), La Malinche (near Puebla), the Nevado de Toluca (southwest of Toluca), the Cofre de Perote (west of Jalapa) and El Chico (near Pachuca) all offer stunning landscapes.

The central Gulf Coast, although not equaling the splendor of Pacific beaches or the turquoise waters of the Yucatán, makes a pleasant low-key destination. Costa Esmeralda, the narrow coastal strip below Jalapa, is lined with lagoons, fishing villages and lush vegetation, as well as a few hotels, but also plays host to Mexico's only nuclear energy plant, Laguna Verde, at the southern end. You can test the water in one of the many spa towns of Morelos, although in some cases a theme-park atmosphere has been over-developed. Man has left his agricultural mark too, with coffee, vanilla, tobacco, sugar-cane, grain, fruit, vegetables, and flowers widely cultivated throughout the valleys.

Urban visits The most popular destinations in the region are Puebla, Cuernavaca, and Taxco, along with Veracruz. The first two, although both offering unique cultural interest, have developed into polluted cities, stimulated by fast highway connections to Mexico City. Taxco, the "world silver capital," offers a slower pace and scale, while less visited and therefore often more rewarding in atmosphere are towns such as Pachuca and Jalapa. Jalapa's landmark Museum of Anthropology should be a priority for anyone interested in the cultures of the Gulf, and it can be combined with a visit to the nearby sites of El Tajín and Zempoala.

Colorful bark painting, Taxco

The Tree of Life
The region surrounding Mexico City is rich in craft traditions—embroidery, weaving, and onyx work from the villages of Puebla, Talavera tiles from Puebla itself. The handicraft which is perhaps most associated with Mexico, however, is the *arol de la vieda* "tree of life." The center of manufacture is the village of Metepec, just south of Toluca. These elaborate, colorful clay constructions develop a theme which originated in the Middle East and was brought, via a tortuous route first to Spain and then to Mexico. Commemorating the story of Adam and Eve in the Garden of Eden, they depict flowers, foliage, the couple and their imminent fall, symbolized by a snake or a skeleton.

Spas
The state of Morelos is renowned for its thermal springs, many of which have been transformed into large recreational centers aimed at pollution-fleeing inhabitants from the capital and Cuernavaca. The region's largest spa is found 6 miles north of Cuautla at the Centro Vacacional Oaxtepec: 25 pools, an artificial lake, sports facilities, cable-car, hotels and cabins make this a favorite weekend playground, sponsored by the Mexican Social Security. El Recreo and El Bosque offer similar amenities, though on a smaller scale. Another cluster of spas is found due south of Cuernavaca around the towns of Zacatepec, Jojutla, and Tehuixtla, the latter boasting five sulfurous baths.

► Actopan *158A2*

The town of Actopan, located 23 miles northwest of Pachuca in the lush foothills of the Sierra Madre Oriental, is known, above all, for the superbly preserved **Convento de San Nicolás►►►**. Constructed in 1548 by Augustinian monks, it was one of a series of imposing, fortified monasteries founded throughout the state of Hidalgo. Behind the Plateresque façade its cloisters and stairwell contain beautiful frescos which continue on the walls of the vaulted *capilla abierta* (outdoor chapel). A similar structure is found at **Ixmiquilpan**, 25 miles farther north on Highway 85.

►► Cacaxtla *158B1*

On a hilltop 16 miles southwest of Tlaxcala are the ruins of an Olmeca-Xicallanca site, unearthed in the mid-1970s. This Mayan-speaking culture flourished in the 8th to 10th centuries and bequeathed Mexico's most descriptive ancient frescos. Technically very advanced, these warmly toned figurative paintings depict elaborately costumed warriors and priests, ceremonies, battles, plants and animals, offering a unique record of the epoch. The main battle-scene mural is located on the northern wall of an open space called the **Plaza Norte**, and others cover the walls of a structure immediately to the northeast. Despite being protected, the destructive effect of the sun means that the site is only open between 10 a.m. and 1 p.m.

Discovered as recently as 1975 by tomb-robbers, these well-preserved Mayan murals at Cacaxtla have retained their vibrant colors after hundreds of years

► Cañon de Tolatongo *158A2*

On Highway 85, roughly halfway between Actopan and Ixmiquilpan, is a dirt-road turn-off which winds precipitously upwards beside a spectacular canyon. Tumbling down its walls, a waterfall marks the entrance to a network of caves, the **Grutas Xoxoti**, which shelter a series of hot springs. The further you penetrate the caves, the hotter the waters become, thus providing nature's own version of a *hammam* (Turkish bath).

►► Cholula *158B1*

Cholula was famed as a ceremonial town dedicated to Quetzalcóatl. The "place from which the water flows" was the object of plundering and a massacre by Cortés' army and his Tlaxcalan allies on their march to Mexico City. After destroying many temples the invaders replaced

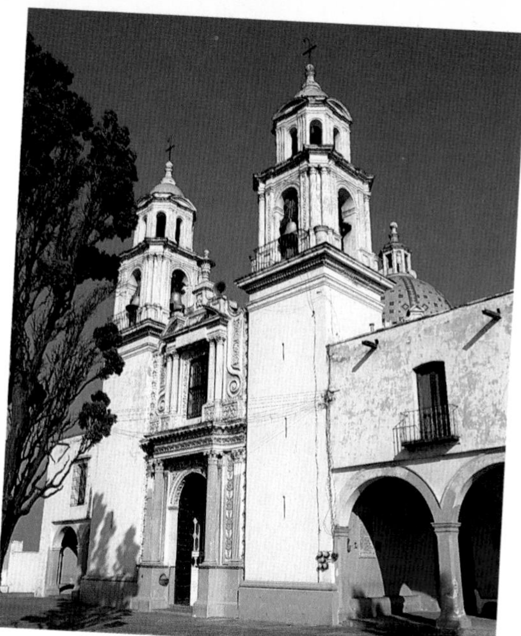

The Spaniards built churches over many pagan temples in the ancient ceremonial center of Cholula. The Templo de Nuestra Señora de los Remedios stands on top of the Gran Pirámide

them with shrines and churches, many of which still pierce the skyline, including the **Convento Franciscano▶▶** (1549) and the 49 domes of the **Capilla Real**. However, it is the **Gran Pirámide▶▶**, the largest in the Americas, which dominates the otherwise uninspiring town, situated 7.5 miles northwest of Puebla. Built in several stages, its massive scale reflects Cholula's role as Mesoamerica's spiritual Mecca, although the partly overgrown slopes now diminish the impact. The colonial **Templo de Nuestra Señor de los Remedios** (1594) symbolically crowns the summit, while beneath the pyramid 5 miles of passages have been dug to reveal the remains of murals. At the base of its main staircase restored platforms surround the 2nd-century **Patio de los Altares** which contains three large stone stelae inscribed with motifs reminiscent of El Tajín. A small museum provides background and displays a reproduction of a mural depicting a *pulque*-drinking session.

▶ Cuautla *158B1*

Cuautla's temperate climate makes it a popular retreat for the capital's jet set. Just over 25 miles east of Cuernavaca, and little more than an hour's drive from Mexico City, its main *raison d'être* is its spas: even Moctezuma is said to have reveled in them. In 1812 the town played a major role in the Independence struggle when Morelos set up base here in an attempt to attack Mexico City. Although a three-month siege resulted in his defeat, Morelos is honored by a small museum in the **Ex-Convento de San Diego▶▶**, which also houses the tourist office. More history is found at the 16th-century **Convento de Santo Domingo**, but visitors will probably be more interested in heading for the spas. **Agua Hedionda**, situated on the east side of the river, is famed for its curative waters which fill two large pools. Smaller private pools can also be rented by the hour—Agua Linda, El Almeal, and Los Limones are the other three *balnearios* in town.

In the eyes of a conquistador

"Cholula is situated on a plain with many other towns around it ... It is a land rich in maize and other vegetables, and in peppers, and in the maguey from which they brew their wine. They make very good pottery of red and black and white clay painted in various designs, and they supply Mexico and all the neighbouring provinces with it ... At that time the city had many lofty towers, which were the temples and shrines in which they kept their idols, in particular the great *cue* which was higher than that of Mexico, although the *cue* at Mexico was very grand and tall."
Bernal Díaz: *The Conquest of Mexico*, 1568.

Cuernavaca's Palace of Cortés, built by the conquistador in 1529

Expatriate legacies
Cuernavaca's expatriate residents have firmly left their mark. The town first achieved world fame through Malcolm Lowry's novel of human despair, *Under the Volcano* (1965), later made into a film. The former Japanese-style residence of Barbara Hutton, the Woolworths millionairess, which includes contemplation pools with stones placed by a priest flown in from Kyoto, now functions as a Japanese restaurant (Restaurant Sumiya). Behind the cathedral in the former Franciscan convent, is the Museo Brady which displays valuable paintings and antiques from all over the world, collected by Robert Brady who lived in the building until his death in 1986 (by appointment only tel. 188554 or 142931).

SERVICIOS COORDINADOS Nº 368275
BOLETO DEL PASAJERO
BUENO POR UN VIAJE SENCILLO
DE
A
CUERNAVACA
TAXCO
HORA
SEGURO DEL VIAJERO
ASIENTO
IMPORTE
FECHA DE VIAJE
$ 9.00

▶▶ Cuernavaca *158A1*

Cuernavaca is said to have the greatest number of swimming pools per capita of any city in the world. This overtly prosperous, increasingly polluted town with a population of over one million is only 48 miles south of Mexico City and has long been a popular weekend and retirement spot—the Aztec nobility, Hernán Cortés, and Emperor Maximilian all vacationed here. Many Mexicans from the capital and American retirees now live here in splendid isolation behind high-walled properties, and expatriate renown has drawn droves of visitors, imparting a lively cosmopolitan air and generating countless bars and chic restaurants.

Unable to pronounce its Náhautl name, the Spaniards substituted their word for "cow horn," hardly a promising start. In 1522 Cortés set about building a massive fortress-palace, followed by an equally bulky cathedral, placing these two edifices among Mexico's oldest colonial monuments. The **Palacio de Cortés** switched roles over the centuries and now houses the **Museo Cuauhnáhuac▶▶▶**, an extensive collection covering regional archaeology, colonial history, and the Revolution, with strong emphasis on the role of Zapata, who was born and assassinated in the state of Morelos. A second-floor loggia displays a masterful mural by Diego Rivera depicting the brutality of the Spaniards and subjugation of the Indians, factors which are further symbolized by the ruins of a pyramid visible beneath the fortress. Below its towering façade are Cuernavaca's lively main squares, focal point for nightly promenades, street peddlers and people-watching.

Two blocks west up Calle Hidalgo is the **Catedral▶▶▶**, built by the Franciscans in 1530. Standing at the back of a walled garden, flanked by the 16th-century Capilla Abierta and the Capilla de la Tercer Orden, it is the uniquely renovated interior that is of interest. Contemporary design elements and color create an airy, purist style which highlights another curiosity, delicate 17th-century murals painted by a Japanese convert, depicting the martyrdom of 25 Franciscan missionaries in Japan.

Opposite the cathedral precinct, on the other side of Avenida Morelos, is the **Jardín Borda►►**, a formal landscaped garden surrounding a magnificent mansion financed by the French silver magnate José de la Borda in 1783, and once a favorite retreat for Emperor Maximilian and Carlota. The house displays historical documents, a large section dedicated to Benito Juárez, and temporary art shows. One of the artificial lakes is the site of an open-air theater, with boating and ducks. Maximilian's country residence, the **Casa del Olvido** or **Casa de Maximiliano►** includes the cottage of his Indian mistress and now houses a museum of herbal medicine and a botanic garden. It is located south of the center at Calle Matamoros 200.

►►► El Tajín *158B2*

Fifteen miles southeast of the industrial town of Poza Rica, in the state of Veracruz, lie the magnificent ruins of the Totonac civilization (4th- to 12th-century), ringed by hills. This vast site, 90 percent of which is still engulfed by lush vegetation, is rarely visited yet it is the most impressive north of Teotihuacán. Dominating the central excavated area is the **Pirámide de los Nichos**, a modestly scaled, tiered edifice perforated with 365 niches (representing the solar year) which looms over numerous other buildings and at least 10 ball-courts. The walls of the main ball-court are carved with fine bas-reliefs depicting warriors, ballplayers, human sacrifices, and a *pulque*-drinking bout. Uphill, behind the main pyramid, lies another center, **El Tajín Chico**, a network of buildings dominated by the **Edificio de las Columnas.** Many of the massive columns here display geometric stone mosaics similar in motif and technique to those at Mitlá, Oaxaca (see page 195).

At the entrance to the site an immaculately designed modern museum displays artifacts from the site, with explanatory panels. The 66-ft. pole in the forecourt outside is used by the celebrated *voladores* (flying dancers): their dangerous ritual is enacted daily around noon and should not be missed (see page 170).

Mexican legacies
David Alfaro Siqueiros, one of Mexico's three great muralists along with Rivera and Orozco, had his workshop and home in Cuernavaca, where he worked from 1964 until his death in 1974. Located at Calle Venus 7, the Taller y Museo Alfaro Siqueiros displays four unfinished murals, photos and assorted memorabilia. About 3 miles from town, at Atlacomulco, is the Hacienda de Cortés, a 17th-century construction which belonged to Martin Cortés who succeeded his father, Hernán, as Marquis of the Valley of Oaxaca. During the Revolution it served as Zapata's military base before being abandoned. Now completely restored, it functions as a luxury hotel and restaurant.

Totonac voladores preparing to "fly" in El Tajín. This ritual dates back to pre-Hispanic times

Cacahuamilpa's spectacularly lit cave system contains graffiti by such famous people as the Empress Carlota

More caves
Farther south in the mountainous wilds of the state of Guerrero are the caves of Juxtlahuaca and Oxtotitlán, the former situated 32 miles east of Chilpancingo and the latter farther north, 7 miles from Chilapa. The Grutas de Juxtlahuaca contain a spectacular underground pool overhung by stalactites, and one cave chamber where rock paintings dating back 3,000 years show a human couple, a snake and a jaguar. At the Grutas de Oxtotitlán strong Olmec influences have been found in cave paintings, one of which depicts a richly costumed figure on the back of a jaguar. It is thought to be a personification of the god of fertility and rain.

Ixtapan de la Sal is an oasis of cascading fountains, green lawns, and flowers

▶ Grutas de Cacahuamilpa 158A1

Between Cuernavaca and Taxco, about 20 miles from the latter, lies the national park of Cacahuamilpa which shelters a network of extraordinary underground caves riddled with 10 miles of man-made tunnels. Although no cave paintings have been discovered here, these caverns are impressive for their outstanding rock formations, stalagmites and stalactites, many named according to the shapes they create. Hourly guided tours lead visitors through illuminated passages and into 16 vast chambers, where there is a spectacular sound and light show.

▶ Ixtapan de la Sal 158A1

The popular spa resort of Ixtapan de la Sal, in a lush mountainous region 50 miles south of Toluca on Highway 55, has rich mineral waters whose curative properties have long been associated with relief from muscular and circulatory problems. The largest and smartest establishment is the Balneario Nuevo Ixtapan, which has been developed into a recreational area of artificial lakes and waterfalls surrounding the thermal pools.

►►► Jalapa 158C1

High in the *tierras templadas*, 85 miles inland from Veracruz, Jalapa is a lively university town of 400,000 inhabitants which has preserved its colonial heart of steep winding streets. Jalapa's altitude and sub-tropical surroundings, overlooked by the Cofre de Perote volcano, endow it with a micro-climate of clear sunny mornings and cooler, misty afternoons. Gardens and parks proliferate, the most celebrated being the **Parque Juárez►**, a small, formal terraced garden created during Porfirio's regime which acts as the town zócalo. It is flanked to the north by the arcaded **Palacio Municipal** and to the west by the **Palacio de Gobierno**, seat of the Veracruz state government and home to a 1962 mural by Mario Orozco Rivera. Opposite stands the 18th-century **Catedral**, whose main features are a steeply sloping floor and an antique English clock in the bell-tower. From here the main street of Enriquez continues east into a lively zone of stores and cafés while, one block downhill, Calle Zaragoza is the focus for colonial hotels and budget restaurants. At the foot of the hill lies the **Paseo de los Lagos►**, a pretty lakeside park with its **Casa de Artesanías** and, at its southern end, the university campus. East of the center on the main road to the bus station is the **Galería del Estado►►**, a beautifully renovated colonial building which houses temporary art exhibitions.

Jalapa's main interest, the superlative **Museo de Antropología►►►**, lies at the northern end of town on Avenida Xalapa. This remarkably designed museum (1986), second only to Mexico City's in scale and quality, slopes gently down a landscaped hillside, its terraced marble halls opening on to sunlit patios. The vast collection concentrates on the three great cultures of the Gulf Coast: Olmec, Totonac, and Huastec. Unmistakable are the Olmecs' extraordinary giant carved basalt heads from San Lorenzo, reflecting the sophistication of Mexico's oldest civilization (1200BC to 400BC), equally apparent in their tiny clay sculptures of baby heads and jade masks. The later Totonac culture, based at El Tajín and Zempoala, is exemplified by their wonderful "smiling" sculptures, expressive finely modeled clay figures, their votive *hachas*, and the astounding life-size Cihuateco sculptures of women. The Huastecs, believed to be distantly related to the Mayas, are represented by volcanic rock sculptures of gods, shell carvings, and superb pottery.

From coffee to waterfalls
Jalapa is the center of an extensive region of coffee and tobacco plantations, both of which have contributed to the fame of the state of Veracruz. Just south of Jalapa, the lushly situated town of Coatepec is an orchid-growing center and major coffee producer: cafés in Jalapa serve the real, freshly ground brew. A few miles farther south lies Xico, a picturesque town of brightly colored houses surrounded by exuberant tropical vegetation and plantations. Just outside the center is the spectacular waterfall of Texolo, equaled by the 262-ft. Naolinco waterfall which lies 20 miles to the north of Jalapa among hills, valleys, and ravines.

Exhibit in Jalapa's Museum of Anthropology

► Malinalco 158A1

The hilltop ceremonial center of Malinalco, reached from a turn-off on Highway 55, 31 miles south of Toluca, displays some rare, well-preserved examples of Aztec stone sculptures. Built after its annexation to the Aztec kingdom in 1476 the principal structure, the **Templo de los Guerreros Aguila y los Tigres** (Temple of the Eagles and Jaguars) is a circular pyramid carved out of the mountain. The summit temple, surmounted by a reconstructed *palapa* roof, displays two seated jaguars flanking the central stairway, while through the entrance, shaped in the form of an open-mouthed snake, stand eagles and a recumbent jaguar. **Building IV** was once the Templo del Sol, focus for major Aztec festivities every 260 days.

Ball games and human sacrifice

■ No other ancient civilization in the world had such a profound taste for blood as the Aztecs. Possessed, obsessed, they sent thousands of young men up the temple steps to the sacrificial altar in regular attempts to pander to their gods. Even the favorite pre-Hispanic sport of the ball-game had more sinister undertones.....■

Peppers and tomatoes
"... we saw our comrades who had been captured in Cortés' defeat being dragged up the steps to be sacrificed ... they made them dance in front of Huichilobos. Then after they had danced the *papas* laid them down on their backs on some narrow stones of sacrifice and, cutting open their chests, drew out their palpitating hearts which they offered to the idols. Then they kicked the bodies down the steps and the Indian butchers who were waiting below cut off their arms and legs and flayed their faces which they afterwards prepared like glove leather and kept for drunken festivals. Then they ate their flesh with a sauce of peppers and tomatoes."
Bernal Díaz: *The Conquest of New Spain*, 1568.

The ball game is thought to have originated with the Olmecs (see pages 30–31) but it took many centuries for it to assume the strictly defined shape of the courts at El Tajín, Monte Albán, Tula, Xochicalco, and Chichén Itzá. Using a rubber ball which was propelled by the players from their hips and knees, the game had deep religious significance and its outcome was literally a matter of life and death. Players would wear protective belts and knee-pads but this did not prevent their fate: the losers (or winners— this remains uncertain) were sacrificed. The court also became the macabre stage for the sacrifice of captives whose blood was smeared over the ground afterwards. The most graphic depictions of these ceremonies are in the bas-reliefs surrounding the south ball court of El Tajín, in which the skeletal and ever-ravenous Death God figures prominently.

Divine nutrition With the Aztec concept of death as a means of approaching the gods, sacrifice was considered an honor. The souls of victims of war or sacrifice went directly to the paradise of the Sun God where they were incarnated as humming birds, while their blood assured the equilibrium of the cosmos and the daily return of the sun. Priests, painted or dressed in black and their hair matted with blood, were the purveyors of this divine nutrition in an emotive ceremony that would last all night, conch shells blasting, drums beating and copal burning. Victims would be led to the sacrificial altar crowning the pyramid, where their hearts were removed and burned for the gods' consumption. They were finally decapitated and flayed and their skin donned by the priest in recognition of their passage into the realm of the divine.

Monte Albán's famous ball court

►► Pachuca 158B2

Pachuca, capital of Hidalgo, one of Mexico's poorest but most beautiful states, has a history of silver mining which dates from 1534, although it never attained the same importance as the great mining centers to the northwest. The mines on the edge of town and at Real del Monte still function and also bring with them a Pachucan curiosity, the local meat pie specialty (*paste*), directly imported by miners from Cornwall in England in the 19th century. These immigrant workers also inspired Mexico's national passion—soccer.

Sandwiched between two mountain ranges at an altitude of over 7,800 ft., Pachuca is a minor version of Guanajuato, with the same winding streets, plazas and wealth of colonial buildings. At its center is the **Plaza de la Independencia**, crowned by a symbolic clock-tower erected in 1910 and decorated with sculptures representing independence, liberty, the constitution, and the reform. A few blocks southeast is Pachuca's oldest building, the **Iglesia de la Asunción►►** (1533) and the adjoining **Convento de San Francisco** (1596). The church contains the mummified body of Santa Columba, brought from Sens in France where she was martyred in the 3rd century, and the monastery has now become the **Centro Cultural de Hidalgo►►**. Permanent structures here include the **Museo Nacional de la Fotografía** and the **Museo Regional.** The photography collection exhibits early apparatus, with selected prints from its archives of over 1.5 million photos, dating back to 1873. This fascinating record of national history dwells in particular on the revolutionary period, with Pancho Villa and Emiliano Zapata figuring prominently. The Museo Regional covers Hidalgo's history, archaeology (the Toltecs) and ethnography. Other sights include the **University**, housed in a former hospital (1758) and on the north side of the market square (Plaza de la Constitución), the **Cajas Reales** (1675) which was used for storing the infamous Quinta Real, the "King's Fifth" (a fifth of all precious metals was sent directly to the Spanish king).

Mineral Real del Monte
Vast fields filled with rows of maguey plants, from which *pulque* is produced, cover the high slopes surrounding Pachuca, but 6 miles east lies the source of much of the state's former prosperity, Real del Monte. Silver, gold, lead, and precious stones were mined here during its peak in the 18th century, but notoriously evil conditions led to a historic strike in 1766. No longer able to tolerate their exploitation, miners rose up and killed the mayor. The mine later passed into the hands of an English company.

The neoclassical clock tower rises above Pachuca's main square. Its carillon imitates London's Big Ben

Descendants of the ancient capital of the Totonac kingdom still live in Papantla today

Voladores
For centuries man has attempted to fly, not least the *voladores* of Papantla. Re-enacting an ancient pre-Hispanic ritual, five men dressed in traditional costume climb a 100-ft. pole crowned by a tiny platform where a short ceremony takes place. The chief starts a giddy dance to the tune of his pipe and drum, turning to each of the four cardinal points in honor of the Sun god. Meanwhile the four *voladores* wrap themselves in rope, fastened to a suspended frame. Launching themselves headfirst into space they plunge to the ground, spinning exactly 13 times each, their arms outstretched to greet the sun, while the rope slowly unwinds.

►► Papantla *158C2*

The small town of Papantla, 132 miles northwest of Veracruz, and 25 miles inland from the coast, is situated in a veritable garden of Eden. Citrus orchards, vanilla plantations, and cattle ranches cover the lush slopes of a region still strongly steeped in Totonac traditions. It is visited mainly for its proximity to the site of El Tajín, but it has a sleepy, picturesque charm of its own. Sprawling up a hillside it culminates in the central plaza, the Parque Téllez, dominated by a rather unspectacular church. In its turn this is towered over by a rather immense hilltop statue of a pipe-playing *volador* (flying dancer), symbol of Totonac tradition. The lofty pole in front of the church was once used by *voladores* every Sunday but is now reserved for major festivals. At one corner of the square is a busy daily market which sells vanilla "sculptures" (made from vanilla bean pods), embroidery, jewelry and the costumes worn by many of the local men: loose baggy white pants and tunics.

► Parque Nacional El Chico *158B2*

Nature reserves are a recent development in Mexico, with 2 percent of land now protected by government regulations. El Chico National Park is situated high in the Sierra Madre Oriental just over 18 twisting miles north of Pachuca. It offers great hiking terrain through pine forests, past lakes, spectacular rock formations, and into caves. The mining town of **Real El Chico** lies on its western side and to the north, on Highway 105, is the 16th-century Augustinian monastery of **Atotonilco**.

►► Parque Nacional Popocatépetl–Iztaccíhuatl *158B1*

Along Mexico's central plateau stands a series of volcanoes that forms the transvolcanic region. Towering over a region between Mexico City and Puebla are the second and third highest peaks, Popocatépetl (17,887 ft.) and Iztaccíhuatl (17,343 ft.). Climbing the snowcapped peak of Popocatépetl ("smoking mountain") has become a popular pastime for the capital's more energetic inhabitants and is quite feasible for beginners. From a turn-off at Amecameca on Highway 115 the road winds up between the two peaks, passing a rare monument to Cortés (who supposedly first saw the lake city of Tenochtitlán from

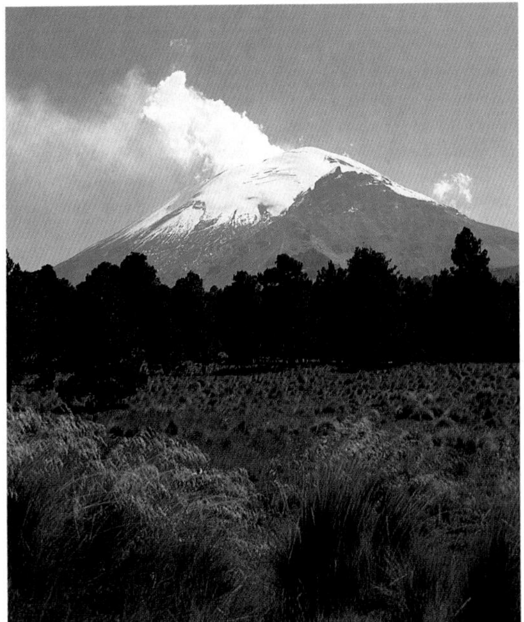

Popocatépetl as seen from the national park that surrounds it. You can climb "Popo" in six to eight hours

Legend
The towering forms of Mexico's twin peaks inspired a Náhautl legend. A warrior (Popocatépetl) fell desperately in love with a beautiful princess (Iztaccíhuatl), but her father would only grant their marriage if Popocatépetl conquered a neighboring tribe. This he did, but on his return found that the princess, fearing him dead, had died of a broken heart. Carrying her body to the site of two hills he laid it on one and watched over her in eternal sorrow from the other. The shape of Iztaccíhuatl is said to resemble the profile of the recumbent princess, while that of Popocatépetl, the kneeling warrior.

this vantage point) before curling up to the village of **Tlamacas.** Here, on the edge of a pine forest which already lies at 12,960 ft., a large hostel caters for climbers' needs. Most set off before dawn to reach the summit before it becomes swathed in clouds around noon. The seven-hour climb is strenuous but is rewarded by an unparalleled view of Mexico City on the left, the peak of Iztaccíhuatl ("white lady") in the middle and Puebla to the right. Although both volcanoes are dormant, Popocatépetl occasionally puffs steam, and in 1921 a new cone was formed in its crater. Iztaccíhuatl is reserved for more experienced climbers as the long routes to the summit involve serious rock-climbing. Base-camp is at **La Joya**, reached via a dirt road north from the Cortés monument crossroads.

▶▶ Parque Nacional Pico de Orizaba *158C1*

Pico de Orizaba, also called Citlaltépetl ("mountain of the star"), lies 93 miles east of Puebla on Highway 150. Although its slopes are gentler than either Popocatépetl or Iztaccíhuatl, its superior height (over 18,700 ft.) makes it a serious climbing challenge, and the lack of infrastructure necessitates more preparation. Departure points are from the villages of **Ciudad Serdán** or **Tlachichuca**, reached by a turn-off running west from Highway 140. Transportation can be arranged here to reach a base-camp where limited lodging and camping is available. An exhausting 10-hour hike is necessary to reach the peak but the pine-clad lower slopes are criss-crossed with easier trails. This spectacular mountainous region marks the point where the tropical airstreams from Veracruz and the Gulf meet the cooler air of the central plateau: the result is often a permanent misty drizzle (particularly in October and November) which considerably reduces visibility.

Baroque architecture

■ The Baroque, born in early 17th-century Italy, soon spread to Spain and by the 18th century dominated Mexican architecture. Exuberant decoration and expansive, curvaceous forms blossomed above all in the *nouveau riche* colonial cities of central Mexico where they characterized heights of ecclesiastical extravagance.....■

Eighteenth-century Mexican Baroque embodied a socio-economic confidence that in 1783 was replaced with Neo-classicism by order of the Spanish Crown. Early examples were limited to surface decoration in a development of the Plateresque, a Renaissance style characterized by finely carved ornamental motifs and named after the word *platero* (silversmith), which had held sway since the Spanish Conquest. However, by the 1730s Mexican Baroque had become an elaborate, highly charged ornamentation known as Churrigueresque, after the Spanish architect Churriguera (1665–1725), who specialized in lavishly carved retables. Masterpieces of this exceptionally rich decoration and architecture pepper the mineral-rich cities of central Mexico, as well as Oaxaca and San Cristóbal, and are as visible a part of the national heritage as pre-Hispanic pyramids.

Eighth wonder of the world
The inauguration of Puebla's Capilla del Rosario inspired a book entitled *The Eighth Wonder of the World at the Great Chapel of the Rosary* which details the decoration and transcribes every sermon pronounced during the nine days of opening ceremonies.

Relative sobriety The birth of early Baroque can be seen in Oaxaca's San Felipe Neri and the later Basilica de la

The interior of Puebla's Chapel of the Rosary is richly decorated with gold leaf, tiles, sculptures, and carvings

Soledad (1682), both of which display intricately carved green-stone façades. In Querétaro the restrained stone entrance of the Ex-Convento de San Agustín (started in 1731) develops into a harmoniously proportioned cloister dominated by superbly carved stone pillars. Moorish influence, brought by the Spaniards from Andalucia, is particularly evident in the tiled *mudejar* domes which crowned many churches of central Mexico from the 17th century on, the most astonishing precursor being the 49 domes of Cholula's Capilla Real (1540). However, one exception in the early Baroque period soon pointed the way to the Churrigueresque: the Capilla del Rosario in Puebla's Santo Domigo. Completed in 1690, the profuse and lavishly carved chapel was described by contemporaries as the eighth wonder of the world.

Churrigueresque By the mid-18th century the ultra-Baroque style had swept the country, producing delirious peaks of craftsmanship in carved, gilded altars, polychrome stucco-work and lace-like stone façades. Ignoring the classical rules of design, Churrigueresque architects often worked without plans, and concentrated on drama as opposed to harmonious proportions. Paintings and sculptures were integrated into massive, high-relief altarpieces, and classical order became inverted by placing more delicate elements at the base. Extensive use of the *estípite*, a type of pilaster tapering towards the base and often elaborately carved at the top, helped give Churrigueresque its characteristic top-heavy impact. Floral motifs, sashes, scallops, bows and scrolls were inextricably entwined with countless cherubs and organically-shaped abstract motifs in a distinctive style which swept through the country's ecclesiastical buildings.

The ultimate expressions of this labor-intensive and costly offering to the glories of Christianity can be seen at Taxco's Santa Prisca (created in the 1750s by Spanish students of Churriguera and financed by the mining baron José de la Borda), Mexico City's El Sagrario, and Guanajuato's Templo de la Compañia (1746) and La Valenciana (1775). Other prominent examples are Tepotzotlán's Camarín de la Virgen in San Francisco, Zacatecas' Santo Domingo (1746) and Catedral (1752), San Luis Potosí's San Francisco and Querétaro's Santa Clara and Santa Rosa (1752). The pulpit of Santa Rosa is entirely encrusted with an intricate marquetry of marble, tortoise-shell, ivory, and mother-of-pearl.

Indian input However Spanish the origins of the Baroque were, it was also an expression of indigenous creativity by Indian artists in their own whimsical interpretations of the Bible. Outstanding in this field is the church of Santa María, near Tonanzintla, the façade of which is covered in sculpted Indian figures paying homage to the Virgin Mary, surrounded by an abundance of naïve angels, fruits and flowers. In Oaxaca the magnificent church of Santo Domingo was also decorated by Indian artisans, as were several churches in the valley, notably San Jerónimo at Tlacochahuaya.

Twenty-five years of hard labor
The astonishing Sanctuario de Octotlán, which overlooks Tlaxcala, is a typical example of Churrigueresque top-heaviness. Above the delicately carved white stucco façade rise twin towers which widen towards the top. Inside, in the Camarin del Virgen, and in front of the main altar, the riotous gilded and painted decoration is the result of a quarter of a century of concentrated work by Francisco Miguel. The octagonal shrine to the Virgin is taken for a yearly outing to other Tlaxcalan churches on the third Monday in May.

Carved with consummate skill, countless figures of saints and angels adorn the façade of Tepotzotlán's church

Mole and _chiles en nogada_
Whether or not *mole* originated in the nuns' kitchen at Santa Rosa is questionable, but it is dished up in restaurants all over town, traditionally accompanying turkey or chicken. The list of ingredients in this spicy brown sauce includes fresh and dried chilli, pepper, peanuts, cloves, almonds, cinnamon, aniseed, tomato, onion, garlic and chocolate, as well as virtually any other available herb or spice. Another visually more inspiring specialty is *chiles en nogada*, a delicious combination of stuffed chillies in a creamy walnut sauce topped with pomegranate seeds, traditionally available only in August and September but now served all year round.

▶▶ Puebla 158B1

Puebla sits in the foothills of the Sierra Madre, ringed by four volcanoes—Popocatépetl, Iztaccíhuatl, Pico de Orizaba, and La Malinche. Mexico's fourth largest city is famed for its Spanish character and hand-made Talavera ceramics, and was already an important manufacturer of pottery when Spanish settlers founded the strategic stronghold in 1531. Its historical highpoint came on May 5, 1862 when the superior forces of French invaders suffered a rare defeat at the hands of General Ignacio de Zaragoza's troops: the event is commemorated in Cinco de Mayo street names all over Mexico and inspires major annual festivities. No celebration is made, however, of the French army's subsequent victorious siege which left Puebla an occupied town for four years.

Ecclesiastical monuments At the heart of this sprawling, industrialized city lies the enormous Plaza Principal. The much-vaunted **Catedral▶▶** is a vast, stylistic hodgepodge crowned by a tiled dome, whose construction dragged on from 1575 until 1649. Inside are a beautifully carved choir, no fewer than 14 chapels and some notable Baroque paintings in the sacristy. Immediately behind is the **Palacio Episcopal** which houses the tourist office, a prestigious library, and the Casa de la Cultura. The city's crowning glory, however, is two blocks north of the square up Avenida 5 de Mayo at the **Templo de Santo**

Buildings in Puebla make lavish use of Talavera tiles

Domingo▶▶▶ where the Capilla del Rosario (1690) constitutes the most sumptuous Dominican construction in the world. A profusion of gilded and carved stucco blankets the dome and walls, framing polychrome statues, huge paintings, tiles and the bejeweled Virgin, resplendent in her freestanding altar.

More religious history comes to the fore at the 17th-century Ex-Convento de Santa Rosa▶, five blocks farther north. Converted into the Museo de las Artesanías, every nook and cranny is filled with an extensive collection of craftwork from the state of Puebla, making the obligatory guided tour a lengthy process. Pride and joy is the last stop, the nuns' kitchen where, against a background of superlative Talavera tiles, it is said that Puebla's famous *mole* sauce was invented. Two blocks north is the Ex-Convento de Santa Mónica▶, another 17th-century convent whose interest arises from its 80 years of clandestine activities following the closing of monasteries and convents in 1857. It now functions as a museum of religious art, and is a masterpiece of disguised doorways and secret passageways.

Domestic architecture and museums Puebla's originality lies in its feast of highly original, decorative and colorful mansions dotted around the central streets, usually incorporating Talavera tiles and often dripping with ornate stuccowork. The Casa del Alfeñique▶▶ now houses the Museo Regional, located opposite a local crafts market, El Parián, and on the edge of a pretty though much commercialized "artists" quarter. Here, too, stands the Teatro Principal (1759), said to be Mexico's oldest theater. On the main boulevard of 3 Poniente, two blocks west of the zócalo, the Museo Bello▶▶ displays an eclectic private collection of European, Asian, and Mexican antiques. Two blocks southeast of the zócalo the Museo Amparo▶▶▶ exhibits Puebla's archeological and vice-regal collections in a state-of-the-art setting, successfully incorporating high-tech into what was originally a 16th-century hospital.

Problems
Despite its high cultural profile, Puebla is under serious attack from environmental lobbyists. The daily dumping of 1,800 tons of solid waste allows toxic sludge to seep into underground aquifers, and outmoded industrial plants lack basic anti-pollution safeguards. In 1993 Governor Díaz unveiled the controversial Angelopolis program, offering a radical solution mainly aimed at multiplying profits. It includes the creation of an industrial corridor, a low-cost housing area and a downtown riverwalk. The latter will become the Río San Francisco commerical and tourist zone, bulldozing what are deemed to be "unprofitable" colonial buildings and evicting Puebla's traditional potters, who have worked there with open-air kilns since 1653.

Puebla's 1796 El Parián market

Mr. Spratling
William Spratling was a professor of architecture in New Orleans before he came to Taxco in 1929. His passion for pre-Hispanic art extended to silver design, and in 1931 he set up a workshop with a silversmith from nearby Iguana. He soon had 400 workers under him and, as the years went by, his apprentices set up on their own workshops. By the time he was made a "son of Taxco," in 1953, the town had achieved international recognition as the silver capital of Mexico. After surviving financial ruin brought on by a disastrous business partner, his life ended tragically in a car accident in 1967.

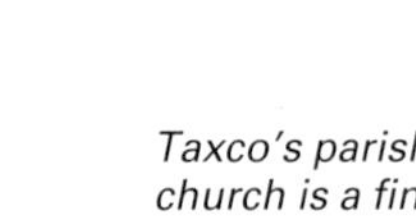

Taxco's parish church is a fine example of Churrigueresque architecture, a florid extension of Baroque

▶▶▶ Taxco 158A1

Taxco has long been established as a destination for silver-hungry tourists, but its spectacular natural site manages to redeem the negative side-effects, notably the *pase pase* ("come in") refrain of the shopkeepers. Spilling down the slopes of Monte Atache, high in the forested mountains of Guerrero, it has grown considerably from its early days as a staging post on the royal road south to Acapulco, yet still maintains the quality of an Andalusian village. Silver was already flowing in the 1530s but it took two more centuries for Taxco really to blossom, hand in hand with the fortunes of José de la Borda, an enterprising Frenchman who left his mining-magnate's mark here and in Cuernavaca. Another protagonist in Taxco's destiny was William Spratling, who was responsible for regenerating the dormant silver industry in 1932.

Exploring the maze Red-roofed, whitewashed houses pile on top of each other in the jumble of Taxco's crooked cobblestone streets which zigzag uphill from the main road. At the center of the web lies the small Plaza Borda, a social focal point and site of the **Iglesia de Santa Prisca y San Sebastián▶▶▶** (1758), built in seven years, and entirely financed by Borda. The church is one of Mexico's most harmonious and complete expressions of the Churrigueresque style, its interior crafted by students of the Spanish architect Churriguera. No expense was spared, as can be seen from the exquisitely carved façade, the luminous high-relief of the 12 gilded altarpieces, the many paintings by Cabrera, and the German organ, brought in pieces by mule from Veracruz.

On a tiny plaza behind the church the **Museo Guillermo Spratling▶▶** exhibits pre-Hispanic artifacts mostly from Spratling's private collection, alongside some replicas. An explanatory panel states that the collection was assem-

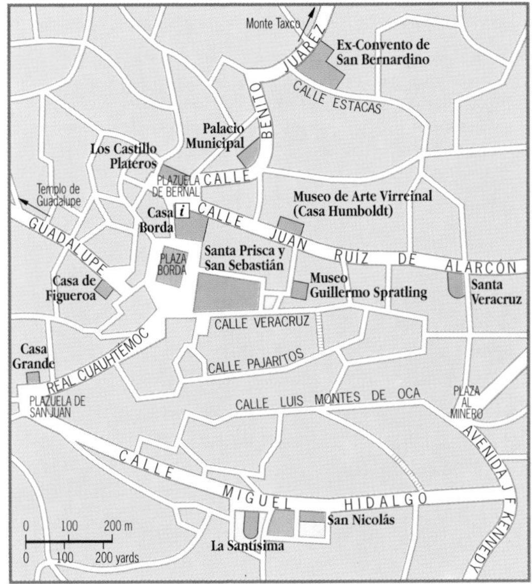

Mr Borda
"God gives to Borda, so Borda gives to God" were apparently José de la Borda's words when he decided to finance the extravagant construction of Santa Prisca and import artisans from France and Spain. Legend goes that he had been lured to Taxco by stories of untold riches lying below its surface. His search proved fruitless until one day his horse slipped on a steep slope, dislodged a stone and in doing so revealed a motherlode of silver!

The town is known principally for its exquisite locally crafted silverware

bled according to esthetic criteria only, thus authenticity is not assured. A few twisting steps down from here, on Calle Juan Ruíz de Alarcón, stands a museum honoring another of Taxco's illustrious foreign residents, the German explorer Baron von Humboldt, who lived here in 1803. The **Casa Humboldt** now houses the **Museo de Arte Virreinal▶▶**, a beautifully presented collection of colonial art assembled from Taxco's many mansions and churches. Curiosities include a rare 18th-century *catafalque*, a tiered funerary altar found in Santa Prisca during restoration in 1988. Other fine mansions and churches (notably the **Casa de Figueroa**, the **Casa Grande**, the **Ex-Convento de San Bernardino**, and the hilltop **Templo de Guadalupe**) nestle in Taxco's maze, while a lively market area sprinkled with silver shops occupies the narrow streets below Santa Prisca.

Above the labyrinth The winding main road from Mexico City passes under **Los Arcos**, the last remaining arches of a 16th-century aqueduct which once continued past the Hacienda del Chorrillo, situated up an access road. The main tourist office is located beside the arches and the gardens of the hacienda, now an applied arts school, harbor the *teleférico* terminus, the quickest and most scenic means of getting to the summit of **Monte Taxco▶▶** (7:30 a.m. to 7 p.m.). Views from the cable-car and the hotel at the top take in pine forests, waterfalls, ramshackle hillside houses and, if you are lucky, the distant peaks of Popocatépetl and Iztaccíhuatl.

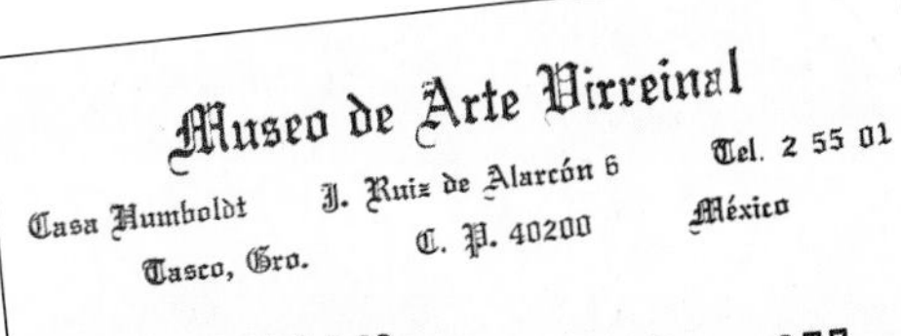
Museo de Arte Virreinal
Casa Humboldt J. Ruiz de Alarcón 6 Tel. 2 55 01
Tasco, Gro. C. P. 40200 México
Cooperación N $ 5.00 Nº 977

The Avenue of the Dead runs the length of Teotihuacán. At a time when most European cities were little more than villages, Teotihuacán was probably the biggest city in the world

New theories, new questions
Until recently it was thought that Teotihuacán was governed by pacifist priests dedicated to advancing the arts and sciences. However, recent discoveries made in the citadel and the Temple of Quetzalcóatl point to the practice of human sacrifice and have modified Teotihuacán's purist image. A sacred city which attracted pilgrims from afar, it was also a thriving and aggressive center of trade with specialized quarters for potters, jewelers and other artisans. The end came between 650 and 700 when the city was abandoned, but several question marks remain. Archaeological finds indicate that it was set on fire, but by whom and why is not known. Time may yet tell ....

▶▶▶ Teotihuacán *158B2*

Monumental Teotihuacán, site of the most urbanized civilization in Mesoamerica, was designed to be seen from the heavens. It once covered an area of 8 square miles and had a population estimated at between 100,000 and 120,000. Today, over 1,200 years after the fall of its sophisticated and influential civilization, the ruins of this ceremonial city remain Mexico's most awesome archaeological vision. Distances here are vast, so visitors should be well prepared for the adversities of the Valley of Mexico climate: intense sun and/or afternoon storms in the summer months. Numerous paths branching off the main, well-trodden avenue lead to smaller and less-visited ruins which still impart a sense of the greatness of the sacred city. Psychological preparation is also necessary to confront the hordes of diverse hawkers and visitors.

Layout Some 30 miles north of Mexico City, Teotihuacán can be entered from the south, location of a museum and restaurant or, further north, at the Pirámide del Sol. Despite its incredible symmetry Teotihuacán is aligned slightly off the north–south axis, a factor believed to be inspired by astronomical calculations. Crossing the city east–west is the modified course of the Río San Juan and bisecting it south–north is the 2.5-mile-long Calle de los Muertos (Avenue of the Dead) which culminates in the shadow of the volcano, Cerro Gordo. Lining this broad avenue are Teotihuacán's major monuments: opposite the southern entrance lie the fortified walls of the vast Ciudadela (citadel) which enclose the tiered pyramid of the Templo de Quetzalcóatl; a mile or so farther north, past ruins of palaces, looms the Pirámide del Sol, behind which lies the Palacio de Tepantitla. The next monument along the Avenue of the Dead is the Palacio de Quetzalpapálotl (Palace of the Quetzal Butterfly), located on the left before the *grande finale*—the Pirámide de la Luna (Pyramid of the Moon).

Main monuments Like the main pyramids, the **Temple of Quetzalcóatl** belongs to Teotihuacán's earliest period (*ca.* AD200), although it was later built over. Stone carvings (366 in number) depict the plumed serpent (Quetzalcóatl), the rain god (Tláloc) and the fire serpent; these were once brightly colored, as were all Teotihuacán's structures. The **Pyramid of the Sun**, 230 ft. high and with base walls measuring 728 ft., follows Egypt's Cheops pyramid and

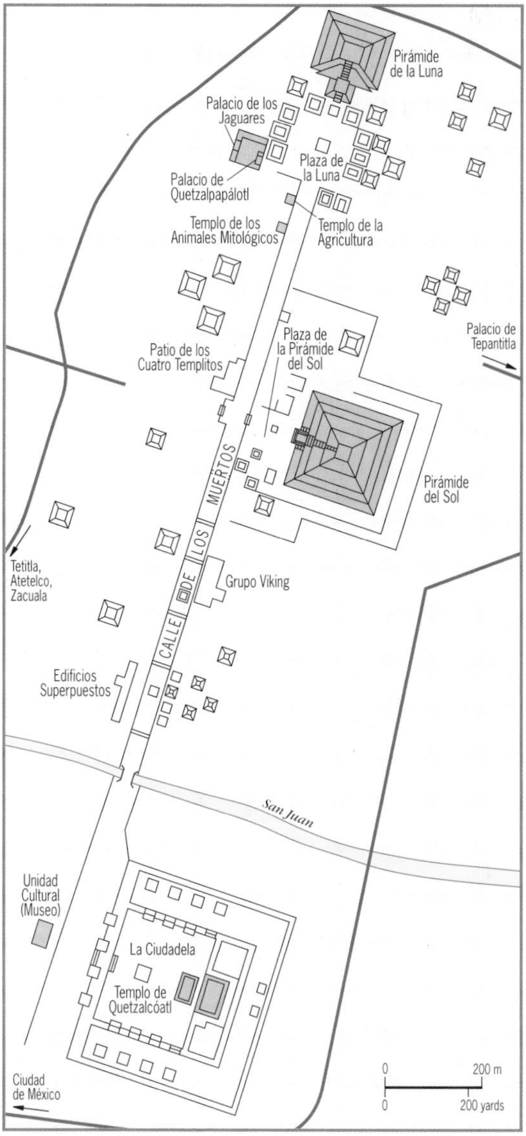

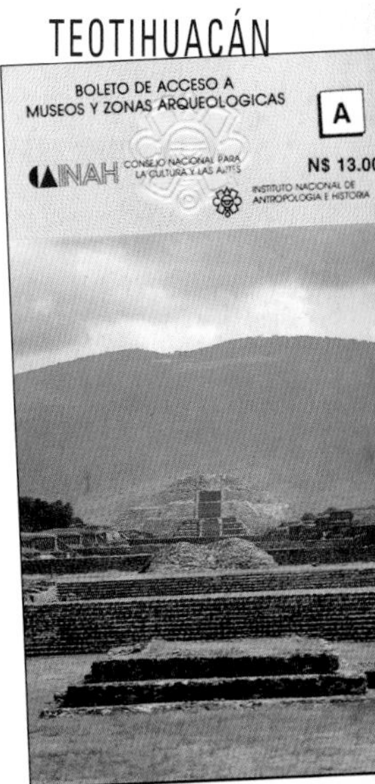

Pirámide de la Luna
Palacio de los Jaguares
Plaza de la Luna
Palacio de Quetzalpapálotl
Templo de los Animales Mitológicos
Templo de la Agricultura
Palacio de Tepantitla
Patio de los Cuatro Templitos
Plaza de la Pirámide del Sol
Pirámide del Sol
CALLE DE LOS MUERTOS
Tetitla, Atetelco, Zacuala
Grupo Viking
Edificios Superpuestos
San Juan
Unidad Cultural (Museo)
La Ciudadela
Templo de Quetzalcóatl
Ciudad de México
0 200 m
0 200 yards

that of Cholula in scale. Although substantially altered by misguided excavations and reconstruction between 1905 and 1910, its ceremonial significance was confirmed in 1971 by the discovery of an underground tunnel filled with religious artifacts. The **Palacio de Quetzalpapálotl** lies in a restored, elevated patio of square columns carved with bird and butterfly designs, its walls covered by a mural. At the back of this palace lie more patios with murals and carvings depicting the jaguar god, decorated conch shells (a recurring Teotihuacán motif) and birds. Dominating a large plaza lined with 12 temple platforms, the **Pyramid of the Moon** offers the final sweeping view of Teotihuacán from its summit.

Murals
Practically every wall of Teotihuacán was once painted with gods, mythical creatures, plants, shells, animals (real and imaginary), and priests in allegorical and eloquent expressions of the population's complex culture. The most visited murals are those in the Palacio de Quetzalpapálotl and its sub-structures, but 500 yards east of the Pyramid of the Sun stands a priest's residence (Tepantitla) filled with murals dedicated to Tláloc. A more legible full-scale copy of this is displayed at the Museo de Antropología in Mexico City. In the far west lie the palaces of Atetelco, Tetitla, and Zacuala, where jaguars, coyotes, snakes and eagles are easily discernible.

Wall painting in the local museum

FOCUS ON *Gods*

■ For the Mesoamericans the gods were omnipresent. Their identities and importance differed from one Indian culture to the next, but a recurring figure was that of Quetzalcóatl, the plumed serpent, who figured from Teotihuacán to Chichén Itzá. Even today some Indian worship combines traditional gods with the concepts of Christianity.....■

Aztec legend
During the final flood of ancient times, the sky fell to earth. Quetzalcóatl and Tezcatlipoca changed themselves into two trees that grew and grew, pushing the sky back to its original position. Finally, leaving the trees in place, one at each end of the earth, the two deities climbed over the rim of the sky and met at the center of the Milky Way. Thus they became the "lords of heaven and of the stars."

Mayan genesis
"In the beginning there were no people, no animals, no trees, no stones, there was nothing, all was desolation and emptiness ... In the silence of the mists lived the gods called Tepeu, Gucumatz and Hurakan, names that guard the secrets of creation, of life, death, of the earth and of the beings that inhabit it ... The gods conferred and agreed on what was to be done ... and light was created in the void."

From the *Popoh Vul*, the sacred book of the Quiché Maya, discovered at the beginning of the 18th century.

Passion, fervor and an obsession with the supernatural dominated Indian civilization when the Spaniards arrived. Every gesture, thought and act was governed by divine personalities to the extent that faith was even stronger than the basic instinct to survive. Intricately linked with, and visible in the sun and stars, Mesoamerican gods also entered nature as animals, plants or the land itself, and nearly every Indian civilization had—and, in some cases, still has—their god of corn.

Primal pairs For the Aztecs, violence was a way of life. Their belief that the world had passed through four cataclysmic cosmic ages before entering the final Fifth Sun featured titanic fights between Quetzalcóatl and Tezcatlipoca to dominate each cycle. God of sorcery, creator of sky and earth and considered the supreme Aztec power, the invisible Tezcatlipoca ("smoking mirror") was only manifest as a shadow or as the wind, but his antics constantly opposed Quetzalcóatl, the benign creator of mankind from his own blood. Duality was thus firmly established, echoed in the origins of the terrible Huitzilopochtli, the Aztec god of war who started life in conflict. According to legend, his widowed mother Coatlicue (an earth goddess) was made pregnant by a ball of feathers, much to the horror of her 400 sons (the stars) and daughter (the moon). To avenge her disgrace they decided to kill her, managing her decapitation but not preventing the birth of the fully armed Huitzilopochtli. Thus born in anger, he proceeded to slay his sister, defeat his brothers and develop an insatiable thirst for warrior blood.

This "pairing" of gods is also found amongst the Lacandon Indians (Hachakyom and Kisin) and the

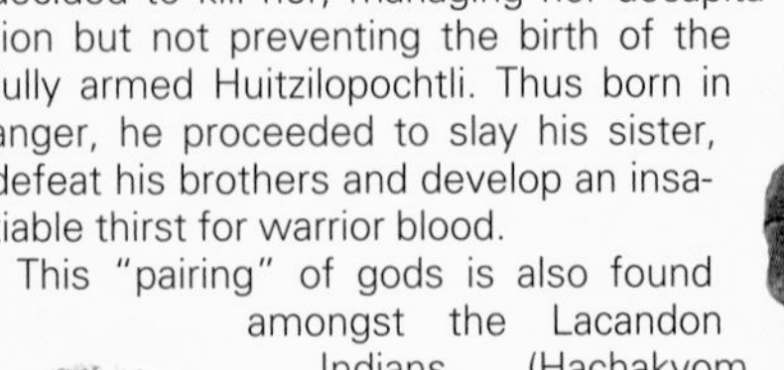

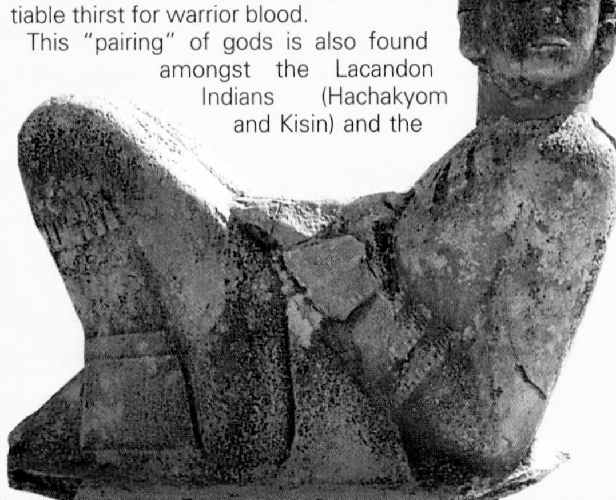

To appease the gods, the hearts of sacrificed victims were removed and placed on a chacmool altar such as this one at Chichén Itzá

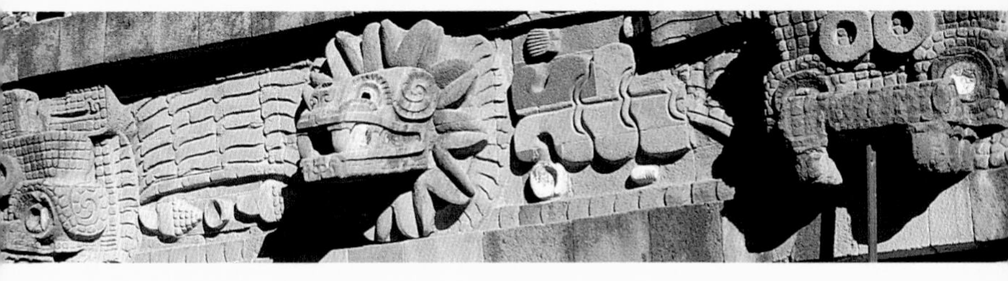

Tarahumara (Elder Brother and Younger Brother). Amongst contemporary Indians, the primal mother and father have been absorbed into the Christian God and the Virgin, in turn identified with the sun and moon.

Gods of nature For such an agriculturally-dependent race, rain assumed primordial importance. At Teotihuacán an entire mural in the palace of Tepantitla depicted the paradise of Tláloc, the rain god who was central to Aztec agricultural rites. At the end of the dry season mass sacrifices of young children took place on mountains to appease him, but his paradise also offered peaceful retirement for anyone who died by water-related means such as drowning. More terrifying still was Xipe Totec, the god of spring and rebirth of vegetation, represented by priests wearing the flayed skin of sacrificial victims. Nature also reincarnated the dead: the Aztecs believed that the souls of warriors could return as birds or butterflies.

In the Yucatán, the Maya corn god Yam Kax governed all agricultural rites while Chac, the rain god, would not suffer any delay in sowing (the date was announced by the first seasonal appearance of the winged ant), a factor which actually halted the Indian attack on Mérida during the bloody 1840s War of the Castes. Maya fidelity to their ancient beliefs is still reflected in their view of heaven: seven levels are pierced by the sacred *ceiba* (cohune palm), and it is by climbing this tree that dead souls progress to the divine summit, home to the God of Christianity.

Animal magic
Belief in the magic function of animals was widespread. The main deity depicted by the Olmecs, Mexico's mother race, combined a snarling jaguar with a fat baby, often squalling and gesticulating, a concept that spread as far as the cave paintings of Guerrero. For the Maya the jaguar's spotted coat represented the night sky (he was a god of the underworld), while the macaw with its brilliant plumage was an agent of the sun god. The dog, although not a deity, had a major role in leading souls across the river to the Aztec underworld, a belief that recurs amongst Tarascans, Mixtecs, and Tzotzils.

Images of Chac, the god of rain, adorn the temples at Chichén Itzá

Natural spring at Tehuacán

► Tehuacán 158B1

Tehuacán's fame stems from its mineral water which is bottled and sold all over Mexico. Just over 69 miles southeast of Puebla on the mountainous main road south to Oaxaca, the chief interest of this pleasant, small town lies around the central **Parque Juárez** and, two blocks northwest, at the **Ex-Convento del Carmen**. The former monastery now houses the **Museo del Valle de Tehuacán** which exhibits significant archaeological finds from the region, considered one of the first to be cultivated around 7000 to 5000BC, as well as an astounding collection of over 6,000 mineralogical specimens. Mineral baths which date from pre-Hispanic times still function on the outskirts of town.

►►► Tepotzotlán 158A2

Barely 19 miles northwest of Mexico on the way to Tula, this small colonial town is famed for one thing: its fabulously ornate **Templo de San Francisco Javier►►►** and the adjoining monastery, now home to the **Museo Nacional del Virreinato►►►** (Viceroyal Museum). This Jesuit church was built in the 1670s but most of its rich ornamentation, both inside and out, dates from the mid-18th century. The museum displays superlative religious paintings, statues, reliquaries and chalices, as well as furniture, *objets d'art*, arms and costumes from the 16th to 19th centuries (the vice-regal or colonial period), some of which originated in Asia. Off the pretty cloister is the **Capilla Doméstica**, another Baroque flight of fantasy, while a well-tended walled garden offers nature's respite from these astonishing creations.

Tepotzotlán's church

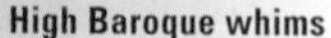

High Baroque whims
The zenith of Tepotzotlán's Church of San Francisco, considered the ultimate expression of Churrigueresque detail, is reached in the Camarín de la Virgen, an eight-sided chapel with mirrors, cherubs, flowers, fruit and geometric motifs in a delirium of gold-leaf and color. The spectacle of the main church nave and chapels is equally dazzling: floor-to-ceiling gilded altarpieces incorporate paintings and statues of saints, all glowing in the soft light of alabaster windows.

►► Tepoztlán 158A1

Tepoztlán's setting, long isolated in a beautiful valley edged by towering cliffs, has a rare quality which made it a favorite destination for mystical escapists of the 1960s and '70s. Just 15 miles northeast of Cuernavaca and easily reached from Mexico City, it has become a favorite Sunday outing for its crafts market and draws an annual pilgrimage for its riotous *pulque* festival on September 7. Dominating the town center is a 16th-century fortified Dominican monastery and church, the **Ex-Convento Domínico de la Natividad** (open Wednesday to Sunday). In a street just behind is the **Museo Arqueológico►►** which displays a small but fine selection of pre-Hispanic animal and human figures collected by the poet Carlos Pellicer. Tepoztlán's setting can best be appreciated from the **Pirámide de Tepoztec►►**, high on a hilltop north of town. A good hour's climb up a steep path leads to this ruined Tlahuican temple dedicated to Tepoztécatl, the Aztec god of *pulque*, which commands spectacular views over Tepoztlán's famed rock formations and valley.

▶▶ Tlaxcala *158B1*

The town of Tlaxcala was instrumental in Cortés' victory over the Aztecs, and was immediately granted special privileges by the Spanish Emperor, but its population was decimated by a plague between 1544 and 1546. Today it remains a small, quiet town, capital of Mexico's tiniest state (of the same name) and only 19 miles north of sprawling Puebla. The lovely main square, the **Plaza de la Constitución**, is enclosed by fine 16th-century government buildings incorporating Moorish architectural elements, while to the southeast stands the austere **Ex-Convento de San Francisco**. The 1520s monastery contains the **Museo Regional▶▶**, with historical and archaeological exhibits arranged around its cloisters. In the neighboring church a beautifully decorated wood ceiling and tiled *azulejo* floor lead to a side chapel, the **Capilla del Tercer Orden**, whose font is said to have been used to baptize the four chiefs of Tlaxcala.

▶ Toluca *158A1*

This growing town, 38 miles west of Mexico City, and the highest in the country, is famed for its gigantic, increasingly commercialized Friday market. The former site, an elegant turn-of-the-century cast-iron structure on the main Plaza Garibay, has been converted into a large botanical garden illuminated by stained-glass windows. The **Mercado Juárez** now sprawls along the southwest periphery of the city on and off Paseo Tollocán, right next to the bus station. Crafts from nearby villages are sold alongside jeans and cassettes and, for those who don't find any joy in bargaining, a government-sponsored crafts center, CASART, is located at Paseo Tollucán 900..

Peace with the Tlaxcalans
"And when we came within a mile of Tlascala these same Calciques (chiefs) who had gone ahead came out to meet us, bringing with them their sons and nephews and many of the leading inhabitants ...
There were four parties in Tlascala and their subjects came from all parts of the country, wearing their different costumes which, although made of sisal, there being no cotton to be had, were very lordly, and beautifully embroidered and decorated."
Bernal Díaz: *The Conquest of New Spain*, 1568.

Toluca's Friday market is considered one of the largest and most colorful in Mexico

The interior of Tonanzintla's church is encrusted with every conceivable decorative medium

Toltec carvings
Militarism, human sacrifice, mortality and supernatural creatures all have a high profile in Toltec carvings. The 15-ft.-high *Atlantes* at Tula, supposedly representing Quetzalcóatl as the morning star, are armed with spears and arrows, and sport feathered helmets and butterfly-shaped breastplates. More warriors and gods, prowling jaguars, human heart-devouring eagles, coyotes and incarnations of Quetzalcóatl once faced every wall or column. Legend and fact merge, even leaving in question the fate of the Toltec Quetzalcóatl, alias their king Topiltzin. Fleeing a *coup d'état* around 987 to arrive on the Gulf of Mexico, did this great king perform an act of self-sacrifice? Or did he set sail on a raft built of serpents—to return one day from the east?

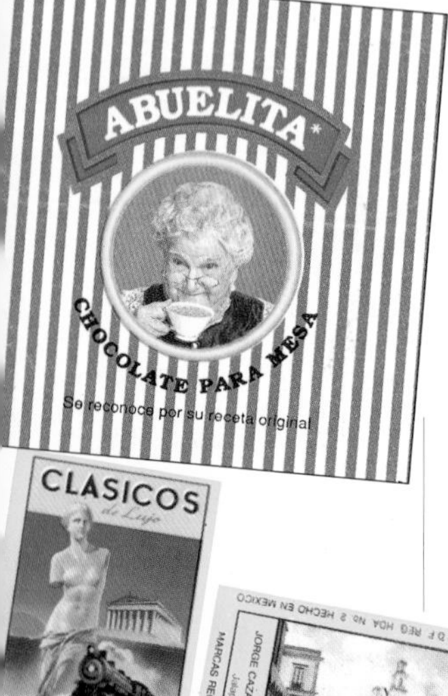

►►► Tonanzintla — 158B1

A few miles west of Puebla and south of Cholula, off Highway 190, the village of Tonanzintla boasts the remarkable **Iglesia de Santa María►►►**. Carrying 18th-century Baroque decoration to the extreme, every surface is embellished with gilded and polychrome stucco, wood and painting. What makes it unique is the fact that this is a perception of heaven created by indigenous people. Barbarous and sublime, it combines pagan atavism (winged Indian angels, vegetable offerings, naïve perspectives) with Christian symbols in a rare hybrid expression of spirituality. Further south, at Acatepec, another Baroque marvel, the **Templo de San Francisco►►►** (1788), recalls the proximity of Puebla in its riotously tiled façade and contains a richly decorated interior. Three miles farther on, the village of **Tlaxcalancingo** is home to yet another extraordinary church, ornamented with fine Talavera tiles.

►► Tula — 158A2

The ruins of the mighty Toltec kingdom of Tula lie 53 miles northwest of Mexico City. From 950 to 1150 it filled the central Mexican power vacuum between the Teotihuacán civilization and the Aztecs. The site holds more academic than real interest, as excavations are limited and the most important sculptures have been replaced by copies (the originals are exhibited in Mexico City's Anthropology Museum). The Aztecs told stories of the magnificence of Tula, and were probably also responsible for early looting.

Overlooking an arid, undulating landscape, the focal point is the **Pirámide de Quetzalcóatl** (known as the Templo de Tlahuizcalpantecuhtli) whose summit is dominated by four heavily armed *Atlantes*, giant stone warriors that once supported the wooden roof of the temple. Square columns aligned behind them are carved with relief images of crocodiles, warriors and the head of the much-venerated Quetzalcóatl. Along the northern wall of the pyramid base is the 130-ft. **Coatepantli** (Serpent Wall), a bas-relief depicting a series of snakes devouring human skeletons. Flanking the west side is the **Palacio Quemada** (Burnt Palace) with more columns, low benches and bas-reliefs. In front a roofless colonnaded hall contains two reclining *chacmools* (stone figures with bowls probably used for receiving the hearts of sacrificial victims), and opens on to a large plaza. Beyond this lies another, larger pyramid, only partially excavated. Two ball courts complete the site, all of which is explained at the entrance museum, which contains some important artifacts.

Like grim-faced sentinels guarding the past, the Atlantes of Tula form a dramatic silhouette on top of their platform

► Valle de Bravo *158A1*

The quaint little town of Valle de Bravo nestles in a wooded valley 48 miles west of Toluca. Narrow cobbled streets lined with pristine white houses create a pattern of red-tiled roofs which edge the shore of an artificial lake, Laguna de Avándaro. It is popular for its watersports, from water-skiing to sailing, as are the surrounding hills for hiking and riding. Crafts also have a high profile, and the Sunday market around the main square caters to the weekend hordes. Hotels are expensive, reflecting the resort's popularity.

►►► Veracruz *158C1*

Veracruz was the first landing-point for Cortés and his army in 1519, and for centuries was Mexico's major seaport. Perhaps more Caribbean than Mexican, this colorful, tropical port resounds to the marimba as its residents and seafaring visitors play hard and long into the night. Countless hawkers, musicians and bars cater to their needs, while adequate beaches stretch south of the center. Veracruz had the monopoly on trade between Spain and her colony despite devastating epidemics of yellow fever and pirate attacks (notably Sir Francis Drake and John Hawkins). The port was also the stepping-stone for the French in 1838 and 1861. Bombarded by the Americans in 1847, it was later occupied by them in 1914. Apart from the fort of San Juan de Ulúa, built in 1562, most public buildings date from the Porfiriato period.

Carnival

The festive atmosphere of Veracruz reaches an annual peak during the week preceding Ash Wednesday. Mexico's number-one carnival pulls in visitors from every corner of the nation so, if you are intent on joining the fun, reserve a hotel room well in advance. Every day has a special theme embodied in brilliantly colored floats and processions which wind their way through the streets, accompanied by the inevitable and very Caribbean sounds of steel drums and marimbas (large wooden xylophones). Fireworks, dances (Veracruz is particularly strong on lively traditional dances with a marked heel-tapping Spanish influence), endless food stalls and, of course, plenty of alcohol keep spirits on a permanent nine-day high.

Veracruzan beaches
Boats from the main quay leave in the mornings for the Isla de Sacrificios, the island site of an important pre-Hispanic shrine where the Spaniards first discovered traces of human sacrifice. Today's visitors should be careful not to find themselves sacrificed to the waves, as currents are strong, but the beaches are attractive. On the mainland south of town the best destinations are Mocambo (5 miles) and Boca del Río (8 miles). Both are easily reached by bus from Zaragoza. Hotels, seafood restaurants, and reasonably clean water make Mocambo a popular weekend getaway, while at Boca del Río the estuary is dotted with Veracruzan purveyors of the freshest catch.

The zócalo Most visitors make a beeline for the zócalo, the central **Plaza de Armas▶▶▶**, where shady ficus trees and porticoes create a harmonious setting both day and night. Flanked to the east by the 1627 **Palacio Municipal** (site of the tourist office) and to the south by

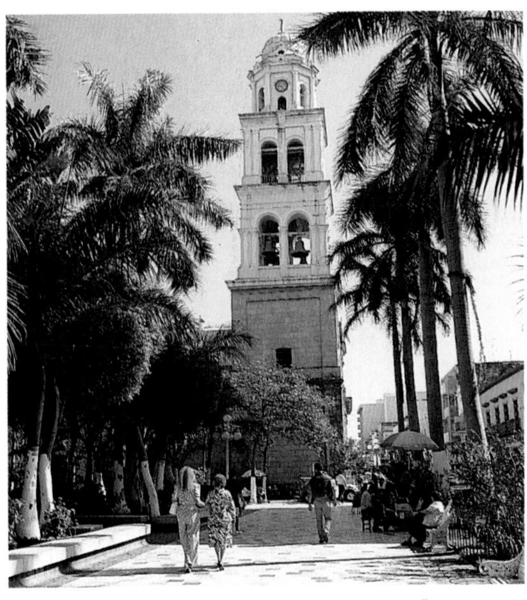

Veracruz's cathedral stands on the Plaza de Armas—said to be the oldest zócalo in Mexico

the **Catedral** (1734), the square is surrounded by hotels, bars and restaurants whose tables spill outside. As *mariachis* tune up, vendors of every age hawk hammocks or sunhats, surpassed by others staggering beneath giant model galleons, while entire families anchor themselves for the evening entertainment.

Towards the harbor A few blocks south, on Zaragoza, is the **Museo de la Ciudad▶▶** (open Monday to Saturday 9 a.m.–4 p.m.) which offers some unusual perspectives on Mexican history, notably the role of the Arab world in maritime history and the socio-economic effects of three centuries of slave-trafficking. On an opposite corner stands a fearlessly violet-colored 18th-century hospital, now the **Centro Cultural▶**, whose pretty patios are the venue for cultural events and a reasonably priced crafts shop. Two blocks east stands the **Baluarte Santiago▶** (Santiago Bastion), last survivor of nine 16th-century forts which lined a defensive wall although cannons now point (strangely) inland. The interior hosts a small museum of pre-Hispanic jewelry.

A copy of the Marigallante *in Veracruz harbor*

Down by the harbor at the lighthouse is a modest **museum▶** dedicated to Venustiano Carranza, who based his government here while formulating the Constitution between 1914 and 1915. The elegant 19th-century building is also home to the Mexican Navy High Command, and dapper naval officers in immaculate white uniforms will gladly point the way. The quay, towered over by a hideous 1960s Pemex building, is the departure point for harbor boat tours. At the town end is a covered **Mercado de Artesanías** (crafts market) which fronts a string of small shops all selling shellwork, crochet, embroidery, and souvenirs.

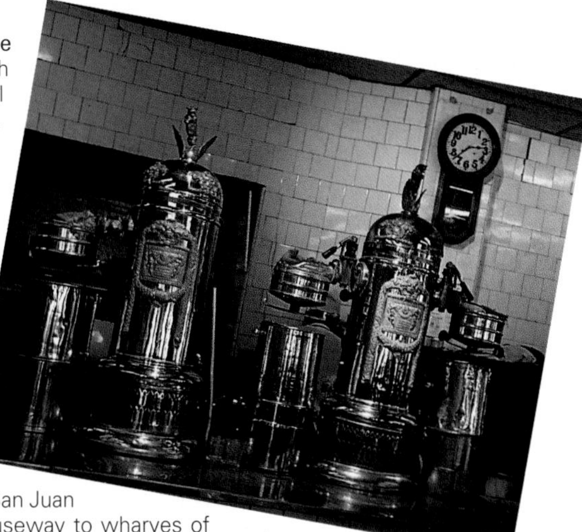

Café de la Parroquía, Veracruz

Towards San Juan de Ulúa On the seafront side of the zócalo the traffic-laden **Plaza de la República** is lined with grandiose Porfiriato buildings: the civil registry building, customs' house, post office and station. From the Aduana (customs house) buses leave for **San Juan de Ulúa▶▶▶** and the main port area north of town. Once an island fortress, San Juan de Ulúa is now linked by a causeway to wharves of containers, cranes and cargo ships. Established in 1528, but extended in the 17th and 18th centuries, its ramparts, towers and bridges create an intriguing and striking structure: some areas are still used by the National Arsenal and a small museum hides under the central arches. Across the moat are the dungeons, which were much used for Porfirio Díaz' political prisoners.

▶▶ Xochicalco *158A1*

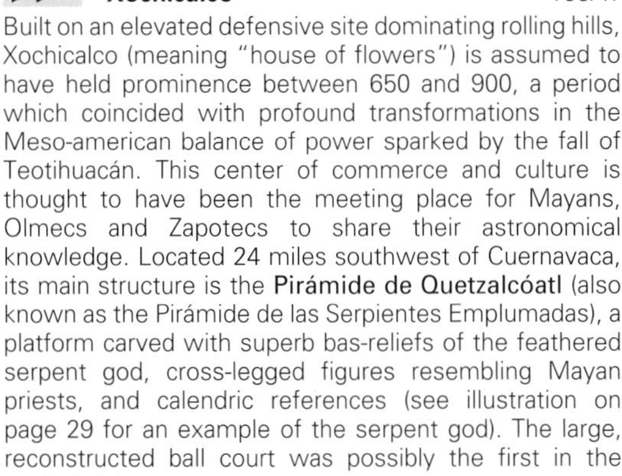

Built on an elevated defensive site dominating rolling hills, Xochicalco (meaning "house of flowers") is assumed to have held prominence between 650 and 900, a period which coincided with profound transformations in the Meso-american balance of power sparked by the fall of Teotihuacán. This center of commerce and culture is thought to have been the meeting place for Mayans, Olmecs and Zapotecs to share their astronomical knowledge. Located 24 miles southwest of Cuernavaca, its main structure is the **Pirámide de Quetzalcóatl** (also known as the Pirámide de las Serpientes Emplumadas), a platform carved with superb bas-reliefs of the feathered serpent god, cross-legged figures resembling Mayan priests, and calendric references (see illustration on page 29 for an example of the serpent god). The large, reconstructed ball court was possibly the first in the central plateau.

▶▶ Zempoala (Cempoala) *158C1*

Halfway between Jalapa and Veracruz on the Gulf Coast lies the Totonac site of Zempoala, whose gleaming white buildings, reflected in the sun, seemed to Cortés' freshly disembarked men to have been built of silver. From 1521 Zempoala was to play a key role in facilitating Cortés' victory. The excavated area stands against a mountainous tropical background with many structures scattered in nearby villages and fields. A crenelated wall encircles the **Templo Mayor**, **Templo de las Chimeneas** (named after the "chimney" form of its semi-circular columns), the **Gran Pirámide** and the adjoining **Templo del Díos del Viento**. Beyond the wall stands the **Templo de las Caritas**, once decorated with rows of little carved heads.

Number One
On the coast road between Veracruz and Zempoala the picturesque village of La Antigua was the site of the first Spanish settlement on Mexican soil in 1519, named Villa Rica de la Vera Cruz. A ruined Ayuntamiento (town hall), a restored church (Eremita del Rosario) and the ruins of the Casa de Cortés, said to have been built for the conquistador himself, are all that remain of those early years.

Cholula
17,882 ft
Popocatépetl
PUEBLA
Tonanzintla
Atlixco
Tecamachalco
Ciudad Serdán
18,696 ft
Pico de Orizaba (Citlaltépetl)
Córdoba
Orizaba
Veracruz
Bahía de
Alvardo
Punta Roca Partida
Izúcar de Matamoros
Tehuacán
Axochiapan
Chiautla
Atoyac
Acatlán de Osona
125
Tierra Blanca
Presa Miguel Alemán
Huautla
Temascal
Tlacotalpán
Cosamaloapan
Tres Valles
Tres Zapotes
San Andrés Tuxtla
Catemaco
Laguna Catemaco
Sánchez Magallanes
Agua Dulce
Coatzacoalcos
La Venta
180
Loma Bonita
Villa Azueta
Tuxtepec
Jaltipan
Acayucan
Minatitlán
Olinalá
Huajuapan de León
Cuicatlan
175
Cajones
Playa Vicente
San Lorenzo
Las Choapas
Tlapa de Comonfort
Mixteco
Grande
Lana
Trinidad
Jesús Carranza
Coatzacoalcos
Uspanapa
Tlaxiaco
Huitzo
El Tule
11,135 ft
Zacatepec
Istmo
Presa Netzahualcóyotl
Sierra
Putla
Colorado
Oaxaca
Monte Albán
Teotitlán del Valle
Zempoaltépetl
Jaltepec
de
Tebuantepec
8,374 ft
Zaachila
San Bartolo Coyotepec
Mitla
Matías Romero
Azoyú
Zimatlán
Madre
Ocotlán
Tehuantepec
Cintalapa
Ometepec
Ejutla
del
Sur
Jalapa del Marqués
Ixtepec
Zanatepec
Cuajinicuilapa
Pinotepa Nacional
Verde
Atoyac
Miahuatlán de Profirio Diaz
Unión Hidalgo
Tapanatepec
Juchitán de Zaragoza
Santo Domingo Tehuantepec
Ixhuatán
Arriaga
Punta Maldonado
Jamiltepec
Chahuites
Sierra de Miahuatlán
175
Salina Cruz
San Mateo del Mar
Parque Nacional Lagunas de Chacahua
200
Paredón
Santa María Huatulco
Puerto Escondido
Santiago Astata
Puerto Arista
Pochutla
Huatulco
El Botazoo
Golfo de Tebuantepec
Puerto Ángel
0 50 100 km
0 25 50 miles
A B C
1 2 3

THE SOUTH

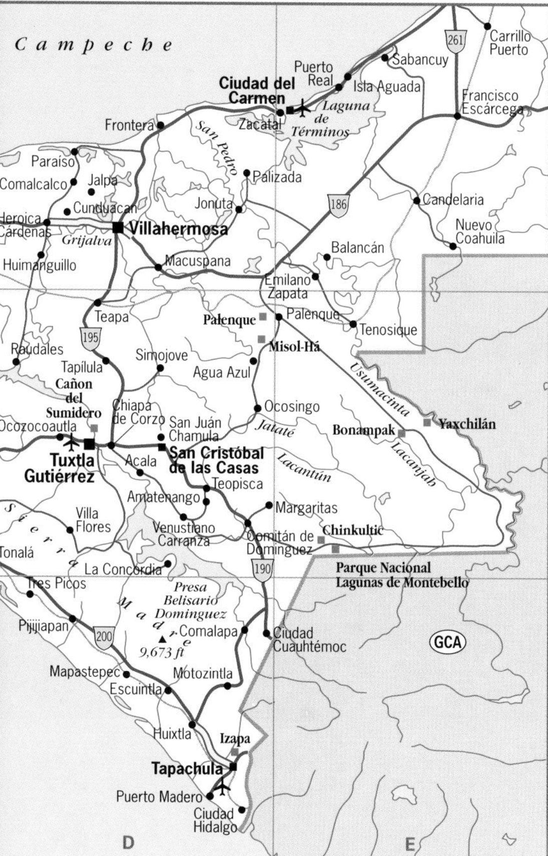

A variety of cacti flourish in the mountains of the Sierra Madre del Sur, which dominate the states of Guerrero and Oaxaca

The South The shift of gear from central Mexico to the south is very marked. Socially, economically, geographically, and historically the south (which would be more accurately described as the east) brandishes its own banner. From southern Veracruz to Oaxaca, Chiapas, and Tabasco, steamy coastlines, dry sierra, forested mountains, and tropical rain forest announce the beginning of Central America. Home to the densest concentration of Mexico's Indian population (20 percent of whom live in the state of Oaxaca alone), it breathes the souls of Olmecs, Zapotecs, Mixtecs, and Mayas, and it is their craft traditions, way of life, and spiritual beliefs that define the region's character. Decades behind the development of central and northern Mexico, the cities shrink noticeably in scale and in number and, following the same equation, poverty gains the upper hand. The exception is the more sophisticated state of Tabasco which, although the heart of Mexico's oldest civilization—the Olmecs—has made a quantum leap into the late 20th century with the discovery of rich oil deposits.

Exceptions to the rule
The south has a few geographic anomalies among its contours. In southern Veracruz the flat, hot plain suddenly breaks into volcanic sierra around San Andrés Tuxtla and Catemaco. Refreshing temperatures, lakes, and pastoral slopes have led to this region being dubbed the "Switzerland of Mexico." In Tabasco, the region bordering the Yucatán evolves into a rustic, unspoiled land of banana groves, palm trees, and estuaries. Similarly, there is a life after the rain-forest, found in the moody beauty and changing hues of the Lagunas de Montebello on the Guatemalan border.

Resistance Although most of the southern cultures were under Aztec domination when the Spanish arrived, it took several years for them to bend to new rule, and even this was not definitive as Indian revolts and land disputes have erupted sporadically up till the present. Chiapas was brought under control in 1524 by the conquistador Diego de Mazariegos, not without provoking thousands of suicides by Indians who heroically leapt into the gaping depths of the Cañon de Sumidero. One group was never conquered: by retreating into the rainforest of Chiapas the Lacandons preserved their Mayan traditions for centuries. Ruled by the Spanish colonial administration of Guatemala, Chiapas only joined Mexico in 1824, another factor which contributed to its slow development. Oaxaca, too, held out valiantly against the Spanish but the *encomienda* (land grant) system soon wrought its havoc, depriving Indians of their land and enslaving hundreds of thousands on tobacco and sugar-cane estates. Disease and deplorable conditions took their toll despite one bright light in the long dark tunnel of oppression, the Dominican bishop Bartholomé de las Casas who, in 1550, managed to have Indian slavery banned in Chiapas.

Oaxacan terrain Steamy and tropical, the coastal plains of southern Veracruz rise rapidly into the central mountainous spine, convergence of the Sierra Madre del Sur and the Sierra Madre Oriental. From Puebla and Veracruz, spectacular roads lead south through vast, empty landscapes then climb to the hot, dry region of Oaxaca where Zapotecs and Mixtecs live scattered throughout the valley. Archaeological interest is particularly strong here, whether at the sublime capital of Monte Albán, the masterfully decorated site of Mitla, the more remote ruins of Yagul or in the city museums. Nor is Baroque architecture totally absent: Oaxaca's churches more than compensate for the relative absence elsewhere. To the south the state of Oaxaca descends to the relaxed Pacific resorts of Puerto Ángel, Puerto Escondido, and the newly developing Huatulco, destined for mega-resort status with an international airport.

The Sierra Madre del Sur

Near San Cristóbal de las Casas

Like a lizard
"Before us lies the gleaming, pinkish-ocher of the valley flat, wild and exalted with sunshine. On the left, quite near, bank the stiffly pleated mountains, all the foot-hills, that press savannah-colored into the savannah of the valley. The mountains are clothed smokily with pine, *ocote*, and, like a woman in a gauze *rebozo*, they rear in a rich blue fume that is almost cornflower-blue in the clefts. It is their characteristic that they are darkest blue at the top. Like some splendid lizard with a wavering, royal-blue crest down the ridge of his back, and pale belly, and soft pinky-fawn claws." D. H. Lawrence: *Mornings in Mexico*, 1927.

Into Chiapas Moving east, Mexico narrows into the plains of the Isthmus where the Pacific is "only" 140 miles from the Gulf, a factor which once inspired thoughts of an alternative Panama Canal. From here the furrowed, pine-forested hills of Chiapas rise to San Cristóbal de las Casas and its troubled and mysterious Indian mountain villages before descending again to humid jungle around the major Mayan site of Palenque and the shrouded ruins of Bonampak and Yaxchilán. Water is abundant throughout Chiapas: reservoirs produce almost 30 percent of the nation's requirements and waterfalls such as Agua Azul offer much needed relief from the humid heat. The Río Grijalva, the main waterway artery to the Gulf, courses through Tuxtla Gutiérrez, the Cañon de Sumidero and Villahermosa to end in the flat, marshy delta of Tabasco—the last of the Mexican "south" before the country twists northwards into the Yucatán peninsula.

Zapatistas
In the early hours of New Year's Day 1994, some 2,000 armed Indians, both men and women, took over five towns in Chiapas, including San Cristóbal de las Casas and Ocosingo, in a highly organized uprising aimed at drawing attention to agrarian and human rights' issues (see page 17). Led by the charismatic but anonymous "Marcos," the Zapatista uprising was soon outnumbered by government troops, but subsequent negotiations produced some results. President Salinas awarded $250 million to Chiapas for road and infrastructure projects, while in the state of Oaxaca, where 4,000 Indians had followed Chiapas' example by taking over public buildings, social aid was increased by $64.5 million to $153 million.

Brahmin cattle, Chiapas

Agua Azul's jungle waterfalls present a dazzling display of cascades tumbling over limestone rocks

►► Agua Azul *189D2*

Deep in the jungle of Chiapas, the waterfalls of Agua Azul ("blue water") cascade down natural limestone rock terraces to create a series of turquoise pools strung out through a national park. Situated just over 38 miles south of Palenque on the road to San Cristóbal, their beauty has inevitably become a prime target for buses from Palenque. However, walk farther along upstream to smaller falls and pools and you will escape the masses as well as be able to swim in safer waters.

AGUA AZUL
N$ 5.00
CONTROL
Fecha

19___
Nº 1118

PARQUE NATURAL TURISTICO
Cascadas de Agua Azul
ADMINISTRADO POR CAMPESINOS
del Pob. Agua Azul Mpio. de Tumbalá, Chis.
La presente cuota se destinara para la protección, preservación, conservación y administración del parque Turístico, para conservar la Belleza Natural la Flora y la Fauna nuestra, ayúdenos a conservar la Ecología para nuestra futura generación, demuéstrelo.
ADMINISTRACION ENTRADA AUTOMOVIL
Fecha de Entrada ___ de 199 ___
N$ 5.00
Reg. No. 13519 S.T.
Conserve limpio el Parque
Nº 1118

► Bonampak *189E2*

Bonampak ("city of painted walls") is not easy to reach in its rainforest setting 88 miles southeast of Palenque. Access is along a severely mutilated road, built by Pemex (the national oil company) but abandoned a few years ago. Bus and camping trips are organized from Palenque, usually combining Bonampak with Yaxchilán over two days. As a pricey alternative you can charter small planes from either Palenque or San Cristóbal. Discovered in 1946, Bonampak can be a disappointment. Its limited structures hold little interest and the famed 8th-century murals deteriorated long ago, yet the 368-ft.-long images of battle, torture, and festivities are considered the most important and best conserved of the Mayan Classic period. Excellent reproductions can be seen at Mexico City's Museum of Anthropology or in Villahermosa. At the base of the temple staircase stelae are carved with images of richly attired figures.

►►► Cañon del Sumidero *189D2*

From Chiapa de Corzo the Río Grijalva winds its way 9 miles north between the sheer walls of the Sumidero Canyon to end at the Chicoasén dam. The canyon is remarkable for its grandeur, plunging to depths of over 3,200 ft. It also possesses an amazing diversity of flora and fauna. Boat trips leave (when full) from the *embarcadero* (landing place) at Chiapa de Corzo and take two to three hours to cover the roundtrip; otherwise the precipitous canyon can be viewed from look-out points on its western face, accessible by road from Tuxtla Gutiérrez.

Cast a spell
Catemaco's fame as Mexico's number-one center for witchcraft has led to a proliferation of local *brujas* (witches) and *curanderos* (healers), who offer services ranging from homemade cures for illnesses to love potions or occult predictions. Arriving in droves on weekends and holidays, Veracruzans take full advantage of their powers, a practice dating from the days of the Olmecs.

Viewed from the top or from a sightseeing boat below, the Sumidero Gorge is awe-inspiring

▶▶ Catemaco 188C3

In the southern tobacco-growing part of the state of Veracruz, 110 miles southeast of Veracruz itself, are the superb lake and sleepy town of Catemaco. Famed as a center for witchcraft, Catemaco is a bewitching and relaxed little town. The lake is surrounded by verdant volcanic hills, with waterfalls (Salto de Teoteapan), water-skiing, beaches, and islands which can easily be reached by boat from the town quay. Most popular is the **Isla de los Changos** (Monkey Island) where a troop of lively macaques has been brought from Thailand. Waterfront restaurants dish up the lake specialty, *mojarra* (a type of perch), eels and *tegogolo*, a freshwater snail. The town itself has a rundown appeal and only one sight, the charming **Iglesia de Nuestra Señora del Carmen**, which nevertheless pulls in hordes of pilgrims every mid-July. Not to be outdone, the witches convene annually on the 5,415-ft. summit of the Volcán San Martín.

▶ Chiapa de Corzo 189D2

Chiapa de Corzo is situated 12 miles east of Tuxtla Gutiérrez, just before the road climbs to San Cristóbal, and at the head of the Cañon de Sumidero. Although it is one of the most ancient sites of the South (going back to 1500BC), its pre-Hispanic ruins consist of only one small restored pyramid. However, the town possesses a certain elegance, and is redeemed by its good riverside restaurants and by the sights of the zócalo. Most curious is **La Pila**, a 16th-century octagonal fountain said to have been inspired by the shape of the Spanish crown. The **Museo de la Laca**▶▶ exhibits diverse lacquer techniques, from China to Uruapan, with strong emphasis on local lacquered gourds and masks. One block from the square stands the **Templo de Santo Domingo**, a 16th-century church which claims one of Latin America's oldest and most sonorous bells, made of silver, copper, and gold.

Lacquerware
Centuries ago, the simple gourd provided Mesoamerican hunters with essential food and water vessels. It is not known when lacquering was first developed but it already existed when the Spanish arrived. Mexico's main centers of lacquerware are at Uruapan, Olinalá, and Chiapa de Corzo. During the colonial period the latter produced a stunning range of lacquered furniture, lecterns, frames, and crosses—but today, apart from a few wooden boxes and crosses, lacquering is only applied to gourds. Alternating with the waxy fat of the *aje* insect, the craftswomen of Chiapa de Corzo fix layer upon layer of colored powder, which is finally polished and painted with a floral design.

Huatulco's nine interlocking bays with white sand beaches are set against a backdrop of dense jungle

El Botazoo
This is the name given to Huatulco's 50,000-acre nature reserve, Parque Botánico y Zoológico. Nearing completion, the reserve will be composed of an ecological center (with small inobtrusive hotels, a conference center, laboratories and other facilities designed for environmental research) and two parks. The Parque Chahue is geared towards educating and amusing children, while the Parque Copalita will remain a less structured environment. Some of Huatulco's nine bays will also remain protected nature areas.

▶ El Tule *188B2*

This gigantic tree, claimed to be the widest in the Americas, is located in the village of Santa María del Tule, 8 miles east of Oaxaca on Highway 190. At 135 ft. tall, with a perimeter of 190 ft. and diameter of 46 ft., its weight has been estimated at 636 tons. But what is more surprising is the healthy state of this *ahuehuete* tree, judged to be over 2,000 years old and still sprouting. Its gnarled, heavily ridged and whorled trunk rises majestically beside the younger, vividly painted 17th-century village church (Templo de Santa María). The village has cashed in on its oldest resident, and commercial crafts shops surround the church and main road.

▶ Huatulco *188B1*

The most recent of Mexico's government-planned mega-resorts lies 178 miles southeast of Oaxaca in a blissful jungle setting edging nine interlocking bays. In the early 1980s Huatulco, now officially known as Bahías de Huatulco, was an isolated wilderness with no water, electricity or sewage system, inhabited by 1,000 or so fishermen, and only accessible by a dirt path. With similar terrain to Acapulco, formed by the rugged Sierra Madre del Sur abutting the Pacific and breaking into endless sandy coves, it was judged perfect as a follow-up to Cancún and Ixtapa. Along came the planners and in 1983 up went the first hotels, followed shortly by an airport, a golf course, and the mandatory marina. By 2018 Bahías de Huatulco is expected to have expanded to the size of Cancún and attract two million visitors annually.

Optimistic perhaps, but at least lessons have been learned from previous mega-developments, and Huatulco already presents a more pleasingly planned face than its rivals. Building height is restricted and environmental factors are taken seriously. For the moment this exclusive, half-built resort offers boat trips to beautiful, undeveloped beaches from the main bay of Santa Cruz, good diving, horseback riding, water-sports and an extensive ecological reserve. To profit from all this, take a package deal from Oaxaca or Mexico City.

▶▶ Misol-Há *189D2*

Like Agua Azul, Misol-Há comes as a welcome relief from the often stifling heat of lowland Chiapas and is even nearer to Palenque—14 miles south of town. In a beautiful jungle setting 115 ft. of water thunder down a cliff into a large pool which is safer for swimming than Agua Azul's rushing and rocky currents. Local buses stop at the entrance path, just under 2 miles from the falls, and camping facilities, cabins and a small restaurant are now in place beside it.

▶▶ Mitla *188B2*

The fascinating archeological site of Mitla is easily reached from Oaxaca on Highway 190, 28 miles to the southeast. The village is also home to the **Frissell Museum▶▶**, an extensive private collection of Zapotec and Mixtec artifacts which is well worth visiting before the uphill climb to the red-domed church and site. Meaning "place of the dead," Mitla was occupied by the Zapotecs between AD400 and 700 and, following the decline of Monte Albán, blossomed into a major ceremonial center. Much of the rich decoration was finished by the Mixtecs who alternated with the Zapotecs in the regional balance of power until the arrival of the Spanish in 1521. Their geometric stone fretwork is remarkable for its complex inlay technique and well preserved in the priestly structures of the **Grupo de las Columnas**: up the main stairs and behind a rectangular colonnaded hall is the *pièce de résistance*, the **Patio de las Grecas** which is faced in intricate stonework friezes. A short distance downhill another large patio structure incorporates two underground cruciform tombs while, in the 16th-century church grounds to the north, the **Grupo de la Iglesia** displays the remains of Mixtec murals. The **Columna de la Vida** (Column of Life) is a large stone which, when embraced, is said to reveal how long you have to live by the distance left between your fingertips. At the site of the parking lot is a large and very commercial crafts market, and in the main village street there are small shops selling local embroidery, crochet, and weaving; there are also *mezcal* bars.

Mr. Frissell
To the left of the main square at the entrance to Mitla stands the legacy of Erwin Robert Frissell, a retired real-estate broker from Minneapolis who was bitten by the Zapotec antiquities bug in the 1940s. By 1950 Frissell had bought the Posada La Sorpresa (The Surprise). He soon filled the rooms with his vast collection of Zapotec and Mixtec artifacts from the valley. On his death, administration of the museum was transferred to the University of the Americas, which encourages donations to keep entrance free for the benefit of local Zapotecs.

Mitla's local market sells brightly colored blankets as well as many other handicrafts

Mitla's colonial church

■ **Only about one fifth of Mexico's original rainforest remains, mostly concentrated in Chiapas and the Yucatán, near the Guatemalan border. High rainfall and constant humidity create steamy jungles where howler monkeys scream from the tree-tops, but jaguars and quetzals hover on the brink of extinction.....■**

Iguana stew
Mexico boasts over 1,000 species of reptiles, more than any other country. Some of these are tried and tested gastronomic delicacies, not least the iguana. As a result, green and black iguanas, both of which are impressively large lizards with serrated dorsal crests, are becoming a rarity. However, if you see a *basilik*, you won't forget it. This prehistoric-looking creature, nicknamed the Jesus Christ lizard, possesses the extraordinary ability to walk on water—rising on to its hind legs it makes record-breaking sprints across rivers, in high contrast to the average iguana basking on the shore.

Mexico blooms in the most impossible places

Since the 1960s, deforestation has left its mark on the face of tropical forests which once stretched from the state of Veracruz through Tabasco to Chiapas, Campeche and Quintana Roo. Other environmental threats stem from the reclaiming of coastal wetlands for development, hunting and the illegal traffic in rare species—combined they are enough to put the future of this complex ecosystem firmly in jeopardy. However, regional governments have responded by creating a network of biosphere reserves which now protect some 4,200,000 acres, while allowing local inhabitants to continue a controlled rural existence within their boundaries. Montes Azules in Chiapas (part of the Selva Lacandon bordering the Río Usumacinta, and the last bastion of true rain forest in Mexico), Calakmul in Campeche (see page 233), and Sian Ka'an in Quintana Roo (see page 246) all offer the chance to enter a tangled realm of interdependent flora and fauna where flashes of vivid butterflies and the deafening racket of cicadas regularly assault the senses.

Jungle symbiosis Trees laden with epiphytes (parasitic plants) soar over 160 ft. creating a dense leaf canopy and an ideal environment for 50 species of brilliantly colored orchids. Mahogany is one of the many precious hardwoods and, like any vigorous jungle growth, a potential victim of the powerful strangler fig. In between the ant-trees, the sapodillas (provider of chicle—chewing gum), the towering guanacastes and the poisonwood trees thrives a dense mass of climbing plants and ferns whose existence depends on the shade provided by the canopy. Gracefully draped lianas such as the wild grapevine offer pure drinking water when cut open, while the gnarled bullhoof vine, if boiled and consumed, will halt internal bleeding. In this complex ecosystem, one of the richest in the world, each plant has a role and every aggressor an antidote.

From spiny anteaters to howlers The jungle is rich territory for tropical fauna, but also fertile ground for poachers. Jaguars, pumas, ocelots, and margays are favorite targets and as a result are fast disappearing. More easily spotted, and more numerous is the spiny anteater, a toothless mammal which feeds on ants by means of a its tapered nose and long, sticky tongue. Equally common are tapirs, armadillos and coatimundis (racoon-like creatures) which root around on the forest floor, but watch out for the tree-climbing porcupine, whose spines—erected at the slightest provocation—can penetrate skin and muscle. Monkeys are ever-present, crashing around in the treetops but not easily visible. Spider monkeys are the most common in the Maya rain forest and spend much of their time performing acrobatics high in the tree canopy, only descending to drink. Often audible, but rarely sighted, are howler monkeys, whose bloodcurdling screams can be heard up to 6 miles away, especially in the early morning.

Hyacinth macaw, Cuernavaca

Winged creatures From the cloud-forests of Chiapas down to the tropical rain forest there are an estimated 750 species of bird which are joined by millions of migrating northern comrades every winter. Aracaris and toucans (vividly colored, fruit-eating birds with voluminous, multi-colored bills), are still relatively common, but the magnificent turquoise-coated quetzal, despite its long-standing role in Mexican mythology, is fast approaching extinction. Still abundant are the numerous types of tiny, iridescent humming-birds which hover and dart about in search of nectar. Shrill green parakeets, amazon parrots, macaws, and king vultures (which combine a naked technicolor head with black-and-white body plumage) are all present, but spotting these elusive creatures is no easy task.

Access
Eco-tourism in southern Chiapas is still in its infancy, although there are plans for biological and tourist stations on the outskirts of Montes Azules. For the moment the possibilities are limited. The most direct way is from Palenque via the Pemex road to Bonampak, about two hours' drive and a few hours' walk, where camping and trails are in place. Near by, basic facilities are available in the Lacandon settlement of Lacanjá from where trips can also be arranged to Yaxchilán. Alternatively, boat trips can be organized from Tenosique (on the Río Usumacinta) which cuts through the heart of the rainforest. Ecogrupos de México (Mexico City tel. 661 9121 or 662 7254) offers camping/boat tours to the area.

Numbers
Together with the Petén rain forest in Guatemala, the Lacandona forms part of the largest tract of tropical rain forest north of the Brazilian Amazon. The 815,000-acre Montes Azules Biosphere Reserve forms at least half of Mexico's remaining tropical rain forest. In just one acre there are an estimated 15 species of trees, 25 of orchids, 20 of birds, 10 of mammals, 150 of butterflies and more than 2,500 of insects.

Treasure of Tomb 7
Discovered in the 1930s, the treasure of Tomb 7 is now displayed in Oaxaca's Museo Regional. Jewelry of gold, silver, turquoise, jade, seed-pearls, rock crystal, obsidian, coral and amber, cups of alabaster, beads of finely incised jaguar molars—the diversity, richness and craftmanship is astounding. Dating from the Mixtec post-Classic period (1350–1521) the treasure also includes exquisite examples of gold jewelry made with the lost-wax technique (using molds of clay and beeswax)—bird-head earrings, mask brooches, skull necklaces. The owner of the treasure was a Mixtec dignitary who was buried along with two other bodies, probably sacrificed servants.

▶▶▶ Monte Albán 188B2

The Zapotecs chose the perfect site for their capital. Leveling a hilltop which rises above the valley floor, they constructed a city commanding spectacular 360-degree views, heightened by the clear, dry air of Oaxaca. Monte Albán (meaning "white mountain") was founded around 500BC, and peaked between AD500 and 600 with an estimated population of 24,000, before being abandoned in the 8th century. During the final stages of the post-Classic period (1350–1521) the Mixtecs used the palaces and tombs for offerings and burials. Located only 6 miles west of Oaxaca, this magnificent site should be an absolute priority for any visitor to the south.

Layout From the entrance and museum a path winds up the flank of the hill to the corner of the Plataforma Norte where the breathtaking **Gran Plaza** opens up at your feet. Flanked to the east by a ball court, a palace and small temple platforms, and to the west by three large temple complexes, the plaza sweeps 984 ft. south to finish at the majestic pyramid of the Plataforma Sur. Other structures are aligned down the center, yet the sense of space remains absolute from any vantage point. Most buildings date from Monte Albán's third phase, roughly the last two centuries of its power, the final structures overlapping with the period when the Zapotecs were building their shrines in the valley below.

Structures The huge **Plataforma Norte** (North Platform) is mounted via a steep flight of stairs to a spot where immense columns once supported a roof. Beyond this lies a sunken patio (a characteristic of Teotihuacán) containing an altar, while to the west it is flanked by a structure considered to be a Mixtec addition. A fork from the main access path leads behind this elevated platform to a group of five tombs (there are nearly 190 dotted around Monte Albán), the most elaborate being **Tomb 104**. Over the entrance a clay urn represents Tláloc (the rain god), while inside are superb frescos of deities, and hieroglyphs. At the opposite end of the plaza towers the **Plataforma Sur**, offering sweeping panoramas from the summit of its second level. Beside it in the corner stands Edificio M, an echo of the tunneled structure of Edificio IV at the other end. Between these two is perhaps the most outstanding sight, the **Palacio de los Danzantes** (Building of the Dancers), named after the bas-reliefs of "dancers" carved on slabs around its base. The building consists of several tomb chambers opening on to a central courtyard.

The interconnected structures aligned down the center of the plaza terminate at **Edificio J**, an independent triangular building which is crossed by a tunnel and thought to have been an observatory due to its alignment with the star Capella. Mystery continues over the function of the other central buildings, approached from staircases on all four sides.

Example of Monte Albán's intriguing "dancers"

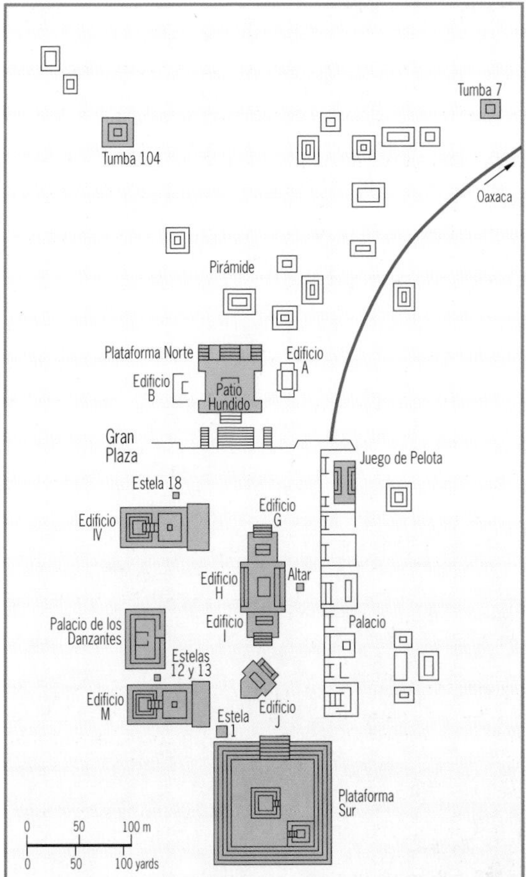

Danzantes
Still controversial are the strange subjects of the carved tablets which lined not only the Danzantes edifice but also the tunnel beneath the observatory. Deformed beings, hunchbacks and figures exhibiting odd gestures and movements, some with severely mutilated genitals, appear to dance or swim. Royal victims or sick people—for the moment debate favors the royal captives theory. Strong Olmec influence can be seen in certain Negroid features, while many are accompanied by name glyphs, bar-and-dot numerals and calendric glyphs, further evidence of Zapotec sophistication in astronomy and mathematics. The best-preserved examples are displayed in the site museum.

View north over the Zapotec ruins of Monte Albán, from the South Platform
Inset: detail of another "dancer"

Benito Juárez
Oaxaca's far-seeing political son, Benito Juárez, is commemorated in a small museum at García Vigil 609. This Zapotec Indian, who played with priesthood before becoming a lawyer, dedicated himself to improving the lot of impoverished villagers. His political career took off in 1855 when he became Minister of Justice in the new liberal government and his radical Reform Laws at last broke the stranglehold of the reactionary Church, but resulted in civil war. Elected President in 1861, Juárez closed monasteries and confiscated Church property but was soon ousted by the French invasion. On his return to power in 1866 he implemented a series of laws making free primary education mandatory and stimulating industry. He died in office in 1872.

 **Oaxaca** *188B2*

For travelers coming from the north, Oaxaca's main attraction is its tranquility—no bus fumes, no traffic snarling up the center. Ringed by beautiful forested hills to the north and west, its dry unpolluted air, low buildings and central pedestrian area make visiting the city a pleasure. These positive factors have also created a negative side: an overwhelming flow of visitors concentrated in what is basically a small town. The state of Oaxaca is not a prosperous one, and this has produced the inevitable equation of poor Zapotecs and Mixtecs mesmerized by seemingly wealthy tourists.

History and monuments Oaxaca was founded in 1486 by the Aztecs, but was renamed Villa de Antequera by the Spanish in 1526. It soon made its living from cochineal production and textiles. Although recurring earthquakes caused considerable damage over the centuries, Oaxaca still claims some major Baroque monuments, most impressive being the **Templo de Santo Domingo▶▶▶** (closed 1–4 p.m.). Located on a large plaza lined with crafts shops, the church was built by Dominicans in the late 16th century, together with an adjoining monastery. The interior stucco relief was elaborately gilded and painted by top Mexican craftsmen in the mid-17th century, and the vaulted ceiling is completely inset with 36 paintings. Other highlights include the richly gilded altar, the magnificent **Capilla del Rosario** and the famous genealogical tree with its crowned figures and cherubs which winds across the ceiling in front of the main entrance. This represents the family of Santo Domingo de Guzmán, 13th-century founder of the Dominican order. The monastery

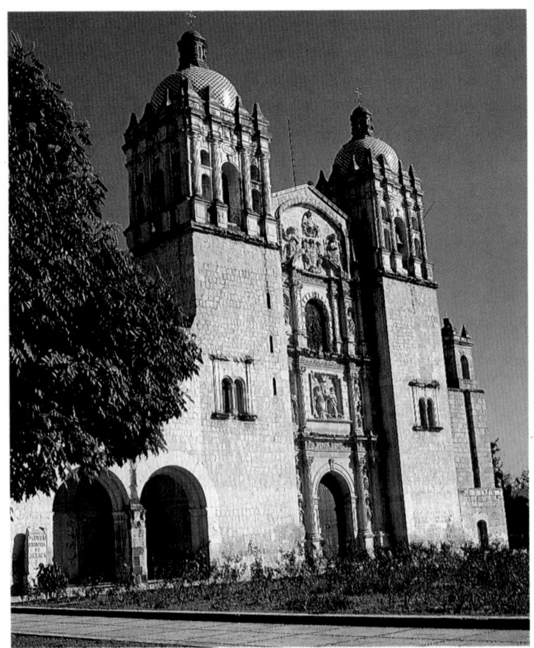

The Church of Santo Domingo, jewel of Oaxaca

Festivals
Oaxaca's lively religious festivals are legendary. Holy Week is widely celebrated but specific to Oaxaca is Lunes del Cerro (Monday of the Hill), celebrated on the last two Mondays of July, which brings together 16 different ethnic groups in a fantastic display of music and dance, the *Guelaguetza*. Most curious of all is the Night of the Radishes (December 23), when the animated zócalo is invaded by booths displaying figures and biblical scenes carved out of giant radishes. Follow tradition—eat a *buñuelos* (crisp pancake), make a wish and smash your plate to make it come true!

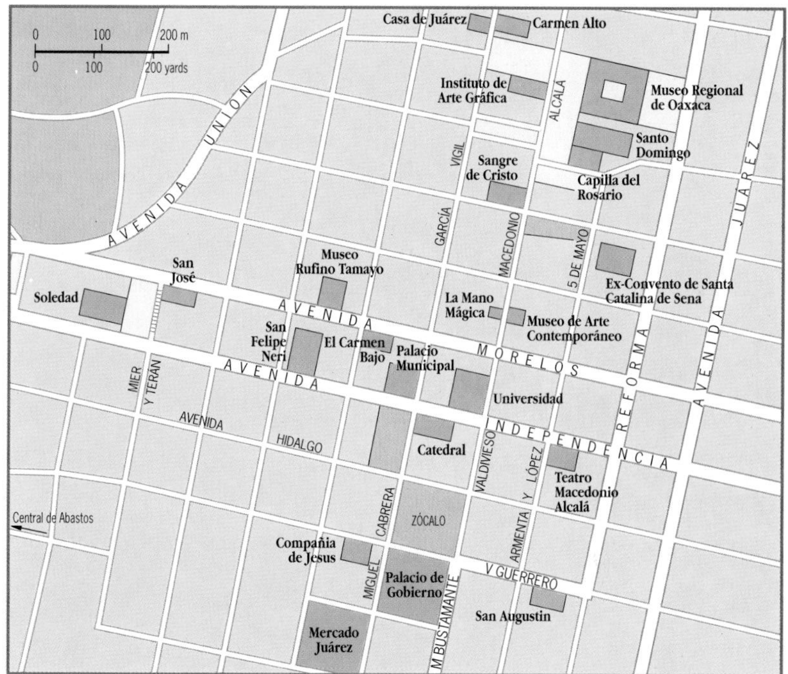

next door now houses the **Museo Regional►►►** with rooms set around a lovely central patio in which are displayed the Mixtec treasure from Monte Albán's Tomb 7 (see page 198) and Zapotec and Mixtec artifacts. The cultural pluralism of Oaxaca state (16 linguistic groups developed over a period of 12,000 years) is demonstrated in the ethnographic collection.

On the west side of town stands the imposing **Basilica de la Soledad►►** (1682), a carved green stone edifice whose rich Baroque interior contains the much-revered statue of the Virgin, resplendent in jewel-encrusted robes. Don't miss the eccentric small church museum at the back (open 10 a.m.–2 p.m. daily). Back towards the zócalo, the 1633 **Templo de San Felipe Neri►** presents another green stone Baroque façade, while one block north stands the **Museo Rufino Tamayo►►►**. Tamayo spent over 20 years collecting pre-Hispanic antiquities, and this small, select museum is the result. The rooms devoted to Olmec, Occidente, Totonac, and Maya cultures are exceptional.

Pre-Columbian artifact in the Rufino Tamaya Museum

museo de arte prehispánico de méxico
rufino tamayo
Nº 12533
precio N$ 10.00
morelos 503 oaxaca, oax.

A few minutes' peace away from the Saturday market

Village markets
Rent a car or take a bus to experience the color, bustle and aromas of a Oaxacan village market. There is a Monday market at Miahuatlán (breads, *mezcal*, leatherwork), Tuesday at Zimatlán (pottery, vegetables), Wednesday at San Pedro y San Pablo Etla (breads, cheese, flowers), Thursday at Zaachila (meat, nuts) and at Ejutla (*mezcal*, embroidered blouses), Friday at Ocotlán (flowers, vegetables, meat), Saturday at Oaxaca (everything) and Sunday at Tlacolula (ceramics, *mezcal*) and Tlaxiaco (leather, blankets and *agua ardiente*, the local liquor).

Chapulines—*edible grasshoppers*

Round the zócalo Oaxaca's zócalo pulsates with *mariachis*, shoe-shiners, beggars and tourists. At sundown the State Band dutifully tunes up and the evening entertainment gets into gear. Towering over the square is the **Catedral▶▶**, started in 1533 but not finished till two centuries later (it suffered earthquake damage in 1727). It contains an extensive collection of 16th- and 17th-century paintings. Opposite is the grandiose **Teatro Macedonio Alcalá▶** completed in *belle époque* style in 1909 and, occupying the entire southern flank of the square, the elegant **Palacio de Gobierno▶** (1882), another victim of Oaxaca's recurring earthquakes. To the north of the Catedral, on Avenida Independencia, is the **Palacio Municipal**, home to the tourist office.

Arts and crafts Two blocks south of the zócalo lies the **Mercado Juárez**, the place to go for gourmet Oaxacan specialties and crafts, but more fascinating still is the vast market at the **Central de Abastos▶▶**, located southwest of the center. Although it functions on a daily basis, every Saturday the sprawling alleys become a hub for vendors of cheese, breads of all shapes, fresh or dried giant prawns, herbs, incense, ropes, chillies, and *tortillas*. One section of this bewildering cornucopia is allocated to craft stands, where bargaining becomes *de rigueur*. For more upscale buys, the shops in the pedestrian street of **Alcalá**, which joins the zócalo to Santo Domingo, offer beautiful gold and jade reproductions of Mixtec jewelry, as well as black San Bartolo pottery, painted mythical animals (*alebrijes*), handwoven rugs, and plenty of beautiful embroidery and weavings. Calle Alcalá is also home to the **Museo de Arte Contemporáneo** at No. 202. (closed Tuesday) and, virtually opposite at No. 203, is **La Mano Mágica**, a gallery and shop offering a good range of traditional and contemporary arts and crafts. At the northern end of Alcalá the **Istituto de Arte Gráfica**, in a superb colonial house, exhibits contemporary graphic art shows. In the parallel street of 5 de Mayo more quality shops are clustered around the Stouffer Presidente, a luxury hotel housed in the beautiful 16th-century **Ex-Convento de Santa Catalina de Sena▶▶**.

Over the border

■ **Political frontiers cut through a region that shares a common Mayan heritage as well as geographical and physical characteristics. From Chiapas the Maya route continues into the rain forest and mountains of Guatemala, a nation with a troubled recent past which has spilled over the border. Winding through the Selva Lacandon, the mighty Río Usumacinta is the only stretch of the Guatemalan border that is not a straight line ruled on the colonial map. During Spanish rule, Chiapas was administered from Guatemala and after Independence, in 1823, actually joined an independent federation of Central American states.....** ■

This short-lived political union soon dissolved when 62 percent of Chiapanecos voted to join Mexico in 1824. Since 1954 Guatemala has been ruled by military dictatorships with CIA backing, a situation finally reversed by the Clinton administration, which cut off funding. After decades of military coups Guatemala now has a relatively democratic régime headed by Ramón de León Carpio, who was elected in May 1993.

Massacres In the early 1980s violence erupted between opposing groups of extreme-right army and guerrillas, with Guatemalan Indians (55 percent of the population) caught in the firing-line. Women, old people and children were massacred in a government attempt to erase all dissent. The worst trouble-spots were in the high and inhospitable sierra of Huehuetenango and Quiché near the Mexican border, and refugees were soon streaming down the slopes to escape the butchery. Initial reception was unhelpful, but the sheer mass of people finally forced the Mexican government to act. Refugee camps were set up around Comalapa and the Lagos de Montebello, while half the refugees were moved to camps in Campeche and Quintana Roo, out of range of Guatemalan soldiers who attacked across the border.

Hope By 1986 glimmers of democracy appeared in Guatemala when Venicio Cerezo was elected at the head of a "constitutional" government and started the long slow return to democracy. His *apertura* (opening) signaled a renewed popular involvement in politics. In 1991 the U.N. finally made moves to bring about the return of some 30,000 refugees, but it was in 1993 that the world became aware of what was happening. Led by Nobel prize-winner Rigoberta Menchú, a group of 2,200 Guatemalans made a symbolic and ceremonial return to their homeland. Today some 50,000 to 100,000 official and unofficial refugees remain, some having gained Mexican nationality and land, others aggravating the plight of Chiapan Indians by taking much sought-after jobs.

Crossing the border
The main entry points into Guatemala are at Tapachula and Comitán. From Tapachula there is a choice of crossing at Talismán bridge to El Carmen or, 24 miles to the south, from Ciudad Hidalgo to Ciudad Tecunumán. The other main crossing is from Ciudad Cuauhtémoc (50 miles southeast of Comitán) to La Mesilla and on to Huehuetenango along a spectacular, mountainous route which was, until a few years ago, a battle-ground between guerillas and the Guatemalan army. Visas should be obtained at Guatemalan Consulates in Mexico City, Comitán, Ciudad Hidalgo or Tapachula, although border-posts do theoretically issue them.

Palenque's Palace complex is watched over by its square tower

Palenque town
Four miles east of the archeological zone the long, straggling village of Palenque caters almost solely for the needs of visitors. Although most hotels and restaurants are located close to the zócalo (or jardín), a few more select places are situated in superb tropical grounds on the road to the ruins. Travel agencies organize trips to Misol-Há, Agua Azul and further afield to Bonampak and Yaxchilán. Two more accessible waterfalls (Motiepa and Otulum) lie off the access road to the ruins.

▶▶▶ Palenque *189D2*

The fabulous site of Palenque, shrouded in humid tropical growth, would be a moving experience were it not for the armies of tourist groups that virtually inhabit the ruins. Although not the most photogenic or climatically comfortable time of day, lunchtime seems to offer the only lull in the flow—all year round. It is the most important archaeological site in the northern Maya region, located 75 miles east of Villahermosa in the foothills of the Chiapas Highlands. Giant liana-draped trees and dense undergrowth encircle the ruins, which spread over an area of 2 square miles. At its peak between AD600 and AD800, this great city was eventually abandoned in the 10th century for reasons still unknown.

Site monuments Once brightly painted, the gray stone monuments of Palenque have been extensively restored, although only a fraction have been excavated. The first and most impressive is the **Templo de las Inscripciones** (Temple of the Inscriptions), a stepped pyramid rising to a summit temple and descending 82 ft. inside to the extraordinary tomb of King Pakal (open 10 a.m. to 4 p.m.). Hieroglyphic inscriptions (including the date AD692) are carved into three panels lining the temple, while the crypt contains a carved sarcophagus and walls decorated with fine figurative stucco reliefs. The fantastic jewelry and jade-encrusted mask found here are now exhibited in Mexico City's Museum of Anthropology. Virtually opposite this pyramid is **El Palacio**, a complex of courtyards, corridors and tunnels crowned by a tower which probably functioned as an observatory. Bas-reliefs and modeled stucco friezes stud the walls and pillars inside and out, and remarkably carved slabs were discovered in this maze. Across the stream on the hillside is a group of four temples (notably the restored **Templo de la Cruz**), some with reconstructed roofcombs and all displaying carved slabs related to their religious functions.

From this group a path follows the stream north past the **Juego de Pelota** (Ball Court) to another complex, the

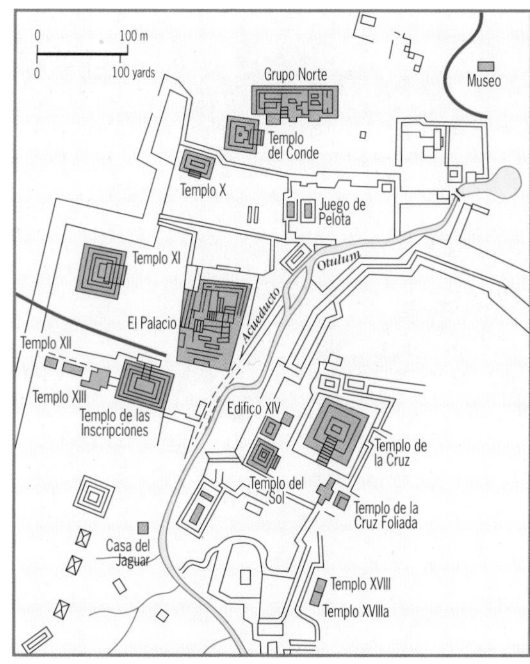

Deformations and mutilations
One of the Mayas cultural peculiarities, though also found to a lesser extent amongst the Totonacs, was their practice of mutilating the body for esthetic ends. Foreheads were deformed from birth by binding a baby's head between concave wooden tablets: this produced their much admired sloping forehead. The Maya also filed and encrusted their teeth with obsidian and jade, perforated their lobes for earrings, and painted and tattooed their bodies, although the latter practice was probably reserved for priests and nobles. Many of Palenque's superb sculptures depict the results of these practices.

Mayan stone carving in the courtyard of the Palace

Grupo Norte (Northern Group) and the **Templo del Conde** (Temple of the Count) where three tombs were found. The Grupo Norte is composed of five temples built at different periods but presenting a beautiful architectural unity. From here a path leads east, past maintenance buildings and downhill through thick jungle. A small group of ruins stands evocatively in a forest clearing and, beyond a pyramid, the path veers left to a bridge across a rushing waterfall (good for a dip). The exit to the main road lies a short distance downhill, emerging near the excellent museum. The main entrance is a hot 1-mile uphill walk from here, so make sure you have organized return transportation from the museum itself.

Museum This airy, well-designed museum opened in 1993 with exhibits of some of the most important artifacts found on the site, so should not be missed. Hieroglyphic panels (notably the Tablet of the Palace covered with 262 glyphs), pots, intricately sculpted plaster and clay heads and figures (some with deformed foreheads) are exhibited beside the celebrated Tablet of Slaves (7th- to 8th-century) which depicts priests and priestesses making offerings to a central deity. Restoration workshops, a gift-shop and open-air cafeteria complete this new complex.

Set in mountainous jungle scenery, the Lagunas de Montebello are popular for fishing and diving

Danger!
Visitors arriving on Oaxaca's beautiful Pacific coast are often so bewitched by its relaxed veneer and superb setting that they forget basic survival tactics. Remember that despite a booming tourist industry, certain regions of Mexico remain severely impoverished and crime thus becomes a very real problem. Both Puerto Ángel and Puerto Escondido are notorious for theft, particularly the latter where visitors tend to be more well-off. Muggings are on the increase, so beware, particularly after dark. Other threats lie in the fierce undertow, prowling tarantulas, and relentless mosquitoes.

►► Parque Nacional Lagunas de Montebello *189E2*

The Lagunas de Montebello lie 25 miles east of Comitán, on the border of Guatemala, on the edge of the Lacandon rain forest. Strewn across a hilly, forested region are dozens of lakes of all sizes and colors, ranging from a delicate pale blue to emerald and shades of violet, each hue created by the different mineral deposits present and the physical surroundings. Some basic accommodation and a camp site are available, and public transportation serves the park regularly from Comitán. The beautiful park is crossed by tracks which offer lovely walks as they wind past the various lakes, rocky outcrops, orchid-topped trees, the Mayan site of Chinkultic and a few remote villages. A number of Guatemalan refugee camps have been set up here, but recent political changes may change this.

► Parque Nacional Lagunas de Chacahua *188A2*

On Oaxaca's south coast, halfway between Puerto Escondido and Pinotepa Nacional, the lagoons of Chacahua make a great birdwatching destination. Reached from the village of Zapotalito (off Highway 200), the lagoons and their mangrove-edged islands can only be toured by boat: aim for early morning or late afternoon for good sightings of ibis, egrets and cormorants, as well as deers and alligators. Bring your insect repellent, as mosquitoes thrive in this swampy land.

►► Puerto Ángel *188F1*

The superb protected beaches and tropical setting around this relatively undeveloped fishing port have kept nude sunbathers, swimmers and snorkelers happy for years (with the notable exception of Playa Zipolite, which is plagued with deadly currents). However, time and Fonatur (Mexico's tourist development agency) march on, and with Huatulco mushrooming some 30 miles to the east, the port's low-key atmosphere may soon disappear. For the moment visitors can enjoy the balmy evenings watching the sunset from under the coconut palms, sleeping in basic hotels, cabins or hammocks.

The fishing village, with basic amenities (tourist office,

bank, hotels, seafood restaurants), lies at the east end of the mountain-ringed bay, and its main beach, the **Playa del Panteón**, offers easy swimming in shallow water. A prettier setting can be found just over a mile east of here around **Estacahuite**'s delightful creeks and blissful beaches. Two-and-a-half miles west of Puerto Ángel, accessible by a winding path or by taxi, **Zipolite** unfolds its charms in hammock-hotel splendor. Palm-fringed white sands stretch a couple of miles to end at a rocky headland invaded by more beach-huts and cabins. A farther 30 minutes on is San Agustín, where tourists are practically nonexistent. Puerto Ángel's hazards are legendary: contaminated tap water, mosquitoes, theft and Zipolite's dangerous undertow, but despite this it has a certain appeal.

Puerto Ángel has long been a favorite hideaway for those seeking a quiet existence

▶▶ Puerto Escondido *188A1*

Forty-four miles west of Puerto Ángel, by a twisting, mountainous road, the coastal resort of Puerto Escondido has much to offer the comfort-seeking tourist, but is still far from competing with the Pacific's mega-resorts. Originally visited for its world-class surfing, its attraction lies in the string of beaches stretching out from the bay in both directions. The hub of this former fishing village radiates from the main bay, which is edged by a pedestrian promenade, the heart of a relaxed tourist zone. Uphill behind this area lies a more authentic, animated quarter where cheap lodging and restaurants can be found. To the east of the central fishermen's haunt is **Playa Marinero**, but beyond the rocky headland stretches the long sandy beach of **Zicatela**, a surfers' paradise, although its strong undertow can make it dangerous for swimming.

To the west lies the beautiful cove of **Puerto Ángelito**, accessible by boat or taxi from downtown, and a popular weekend destination. Beyond the headland is **Playa Carrizalillo**, overlooked by a trailer park, and the cliffs of **Playa Bacocho**, at the foot of a new development of condominiums and related services.

Puerto Escondido — "hidden port" in Spanish

Chamulan belief
Independent-minded San Juán Chamula, site of strong anti-Spanish resistance and a major rebellion in 1869, now functions with its own political, civic and religious structure, represented by the crosses facing the church. Draped in pine branches, they are the earthly symbols of Mayan cosmic forces as well as the starting point for Christ's embodiment as the sun. Inside the gloomy church row upon row of flickering candles, clouds of incense and chanting worshippers reinforce this intense spiritual belief. However, all is not rosy. San Juán's strange atmosphere derives partly from the dichotomy of tourism versus local poverty, but more so from religious persecution and expropriation of land by local drug syndicates. This is another region where visitors should be wary of solitary wandering: attacks are on the increase.

►► San Andrés Tuxtla *188C3*

About 90 miles southeast of Veracruz the flat coastal plain rises into the fertile rolling green hills of Los Tuxtla, a volcanic region which was once Olmec territory and is now the last bastion of agriculture and fishing before the Gulf Coast plunges into industrialization and oil at Minatitlán. San Andrés is known, above all, for its *puros*, cigars made from the tobacco which grows nearby, and makes a good, economical base for visiting the Olmec site of **Tres Zapotes►**, the **Laguna Encantada►►** (Enchanted Lagoon) in the crater of an extinct volcano and, farther afield, Lake Catemaco (see page 193).

► San Bartolo Coyotepec *188B2*

Located 8 miles southeast of Oaxaca, this small village is renowned for its black pottery which is made using an ancient Zapotec technique. Water-jars, *mezcal* containers, perforated sieve pots, toy whistles shaped like fish or birds, and bells and flutes are still baked in sealed-off, circular underground kilns. The black sheen is created by the soot and smoke that impregnates and colors the clay, and a final luster and deeper tone is achieved by subsequent staining and polishing. The pieces sold at the artisans' market here are generally cheaper than in Oaxaca.

►►► San Juán Chamula *189D2*

High in the Chiapas Highlands, 6 miles north of San Cristóbal, the Chamulan village of San Juán Chamula, sometimes just called Chamula, offers an extraordinary vision of an ethnic group (one of 22 Tzotzil villages in the area) still clinging fiercely to its unique traditions in the face of overwhelming odds. This religious and commercial hub for over 65,000 Chamulans scattered around the mountains, is invaded by tour groups from San Cristóbal on Sundays when a huge market occupies the central square. Apart from the colorful costumes of the proud Chamulans, the main interest is the church, focal point for extraordinary worship which combines Christian and ancient Mayan spiritual practices. A ticket to enter the church must be obtained from a small office across the square, and photography is strictly forbidden.

San Juán Chamula's parish church, with its painted portal, is special to the local Indians

Lacandon indians

The Lacandons, the last pure survivors of the Mayas, live in the heart of the Mexican rain forest where they are thought to have fled from colonial invaders. This tiny ethnic group offers a unique window on the traditional beliefs of the ancient Maya. Only "discovered" about a century ago, today's Lacandons number about 400 and, despite attempts to preserve them from the march of the 20th century, the younger generation is now only too aware of what modern life has to offer.....

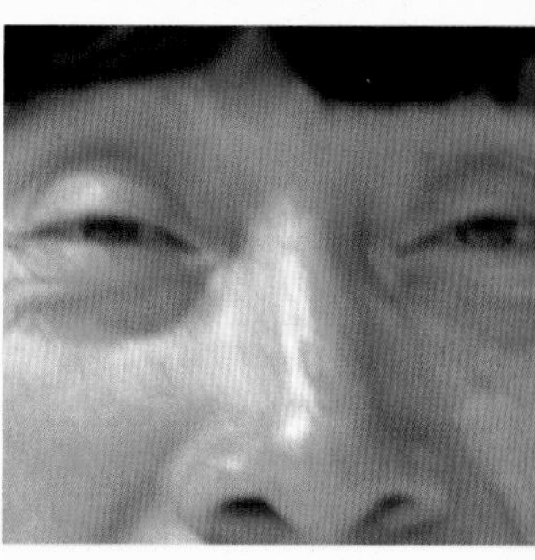

Mostly untouched by Christianity, apart from a few converts by American missionaries, many Lacandons continue to worship at the temple site of Yaxchilán where their gods include Metsaboc, god of rain and of the heavens, and his opposite, Kisin, god of the underworld and bringer of sickness. Ceremonial dates are calculated using the 260-day cycle, harking back to the Maya lunar calendar (see pages 228–229). However, their cosmological view of the world as doomed to destruction may soon apply to their own ethnic group: the proximity of 150,000 relocated farmers is doubtlessly announcing the end of their purity.

Lifestyle Based around the lakes of the Selva Lacandon between the rivers Usumacinta and Jacate, the Lacandons make their living from hunting, fishing, gathering wild jungle fruits, and cultivating crops. These highly distinctive, diminutive Indians wear their hair long with bangs, and dress in unbleached cotton *huipils* (tunics). Men may sport nose-rings, and women necklaces of berries or beads, but precious metals are nonexistent: they are a primitive people who still use digging-sticks for sowing seeds and, when clearing land for farming, start their fire by rubbing sticks together in an ancient ritual.

Lacandon houses are simple structures consisting of four posts supporting a palm-leaf roof which is tied down with lianas. Created for single families which have completely supplanted former clan villages, these units raise the problem of inbreeding, something which is difficult to measure. A good source of information on the Lacandon is the institution of Na-Bolom in San Cristóbal de las Casas (see page 211) which even makes accommodation permanently available to them.

Lacandon origins
Linguistically the Lacandons have no connection with any other Chiapan Indian group, something which has given rise to long speculation on how and when they arrived in the rain forest. Their own name for themselves is *masswal* (meaning "low class"), probably an Aztec word related to their primitive lifestyle. What is certain is that they are a Mayan group, probably from the Yucatán peninsula, as their language bears strong similarities to an archaic Yucatecan dialect.

The Church of Santo Domingo is an excellent example of the Mexican high-Baroque style

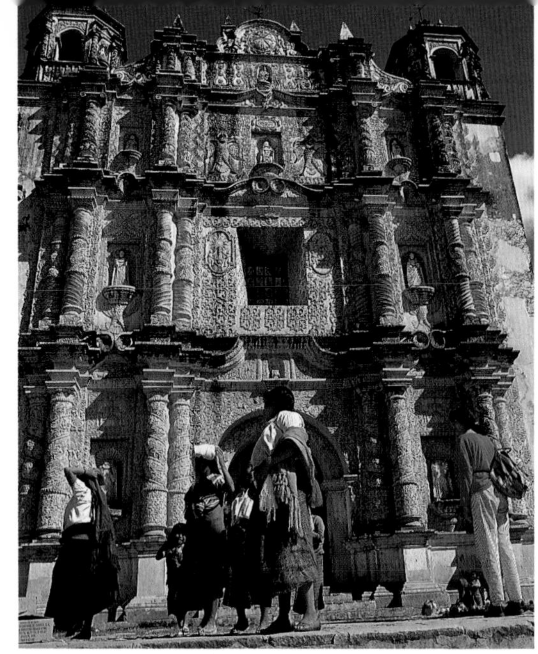

Out and about in Chiapas
San Cristóbal makes the ideal base for exploring nearby villages known for their fine, varied textiles and fiercely guarded ethnic traditions (particularly San Juán Chamula, Zinacantán, and Amatenango). There is no shortage of organized tours by bus, horseback or on foot, some going as far as Yaxchilán. Volunteer work is also possible and can involve a few hours' labor in a tree nursery or several weeks in a Guatemalan refugee camp. Notice-boards pop up all over town: those outside the tourist office at Casa Margarita and El Puente are particularly good sources of information about what is on offer.

►►► San Cristóbal de las Casas *189D2*

No longer the remote, picturesque mountain town that it was 20 years ago, San Cristóbal attracts an increasing number of visitors and much of its center is dedicated to catering to them. Past travelers have left a legacy of restaurants, bars, and charming hotels which, together with very visible ethnic traditions give San Cristóbal a unique and upbeat character. Colorful buildings, cool mountain air, a wealth of local handicrafts, a handful of fascinating institutions and the interest of nearby Tzotzil and Tzeltal villages all combine to make a stimulating stay.

Resistance and persecution Named after the Dominican bishop of Chiapas, Bartholomé de las Casas, San Cristóbal's inhabitants put up fierce resistance to the con-

San Cristóbal de las Casas lies high in pine-forested mountains

quistadors but were subsequently forced into the Spanish *encomienda* (entrustment) system. De Las Casas' valiant championship of Indian rights in the 1540s freed Tzotzil slaves, but as recently as the 1960s there was still a curfew on Indians in town after dark. San Cristóbal's progress has been slow, with agriculture as the main money-earner: regular flooding of farmland in the valley was only stopped in the 1970s by installing a drainage system. Other problems stem from religious persecution and the power of drug syndicates, all of which has resulted in an estimated 20,000 Chamulans swelling San Cristóbal's population over the last decade.

Layout and sights A grid of streets surrounds San Cristóbal's zócalo, dominated by the remodeled 16th-century **Catedral▶** and the **Palacio Municipal**, home to the tourist office. Two parallel streets running east, Real de Guadalupe and Madero, form a concentrated area of hotels, restaurants, and endless Aladdin's caves. Insurgentes, the main street south, leads past churches, more hotels and restaurants to the bus station on the Panamerican highway. Uphill to the north stands the **Templo de la Caridad▶** (1712), but far more striking is San Cristóbal's oldest church, **Santo Domingo▶▶▶**, which rises beside it. Started in 1547, the church was substantially transformed in the 18th century, leaving a fine lacy façade of vine-draped columns and vegetal motifs. The interior walls integrate paintings and statues with gilded, Baroque altars, equalled in ornamentation by the carved pulpit. On the terraces surrounding the two churches a colorful **crafts market** springs to life daily, manned by squatting Indian women and children and a few foreign residents who specialize in jewelry made of local amber. Santo Domingo's monastery now houses the **Museo Regional▶** which concentrates on San Cristóbal's history, together with a rich collection of local costumes and textiles. Across the street from the monastery is the weavers' cooperative, **Sna Jolobil▶▶** (meaning "the weavers' house" in Tzotzil), founded to revive and perpetuate the ancestral weaving traditions of Chiapan villages and now claiming 800 members. More handicrafts can be seen in the labyrinthine **Mercado**, a couple of blocks farther north. This is also the best place to admire the local costumes worn by families on shopping sprees: tiny in stature, poor in purse, but proud by nature, they should only be photographed with prudence.

Na Bolom A living institution, **Na Bolom▶▶▶** ("house of the jaguar") is a fascinating destination for anyone interested in the Lacandon Indians and the rain forest. Located 10 blocks east of Santo Domingo along Calle Comitán, the sprawling colonial mansion was, from the 1950s, the social and professional hub for countless anthropologists, writers and artists (including Diego Rivera), thanks to its owners, the Danish explorer Frans Blom and his Swiss photo-journalist wife Trudy. It now functions as an artifact-packed cultural guest-house, library (with 14,000 books on Chiapas), botanic garden, and introduction to local environmental and ethnic issues. The house can be visited daily, except Monday, with guided tours in English and Spanish at 4:30 p.m.

Village uniforms
Chiapan costumes are renowned for their intricate embroidery and weaving, skills which have always had a ritualistic significance. Tzotzil and Tzeltal villages differentiate themselves by colors, motifs, and even the cut of their clothing. *Huipiles* (tunics), *quechquemitls* (shoulder-capes) and *rebozos* (shawls) are often predominantly red and white—looking pink from a distance—or blue, but many other fine distinctions come into play. Tassels, pompons and ribbons appear on men's flat palm hats or swinging from their tunics, while women's looped braids are tied up with vivid bows. More sober, certain Chamulans dress in belted cream wool tunics over white pants—a style imposed by the Spaniards who were shocked by the Indians' tasseled loincloths.

The courtyard of Na Bolom

Natural dyes
Fast disappearing, the natural dyes used by Mexican weavers produced an astonishing palette of subtle tones. Roots, bark, berries and leaves created soft reds and browns, while blue was derived from mixing acacia leaves with black clay or, more often, with the indigo plant. Yellow came from dahlia flowers or the mora tree. Animal dyes were chiefly obtained from the cochineal, a tiny parasite found on cacti which, when crushed, yields a dense crimson color. Sea-snails were another important dye source: their secretion turns a brilliant lilac on contact with the air, and families would camp out on Oaxacan beaches dipping their yarn into the precious liquid.

► Tapachula 189D1

Tucked away in the southeast corner of Mexico, only 10 miles from the border with Guatemala, Tapachula is little more than a stopping point in or out of Mexico. Visas can be obtained from the Guatemalan Consulate and the town buzzes with their citizens, formerly refugees and now shoppers. The main attraction is the archaeological site of **Izapa►►**, located 6 miles east of town on the road to the border. The incredibly hot but fertile surrounding plain was home to a flourishing civilization in the last two centuries BC and shows a distinctive art style. Numerous temple platforms have revealed carved stelae (stone slabs) which create the vital link in time and space between the Olmecs and the later Maya. Artifacts from the site can be seen at the **Museo Regional,** which is located on Tapachula's zócalo near the cathedral.

►► Tehuantepec 188B2

Tehuantepec is situated near the south coast of Mexico's narrowest point, the Isthmus, and claims a unique matriarchal society as well as descent from African slaves who were brought to Mexico from the 16th century onwards. Still clinging to tradition, Tehuantepec's women, known for their beauty, wear elaborately embroidered gold and red *huipiles* (tunics) over long, gathered skirts, heavy gold necklaces and large fanlike headdresses of stiff white

Women play a dominant role in many aspects of daily life in Tehuantepec

lace. Local transport is the *motocarro*, a motor-tricycle attached to a back platform on which passengers stand, holding on to a rail. Industrialization may continue its relentless crawl, leaving its mark on the nearby port of Salina Cruz and, to the north, on Juchitán, but for the moment Tehuantepec retains its red-roofed, riverside charm heightened by countless joyful *fiestas*.

Motocarro *in Tehuantepec*

►► Teotitlán del Valle 188B2

No visitor to the state of Oaxaca can fail to notice the heavy, patterned wool rugs and blankets which are mostly woven in the village of Teotitlán, 18 miles east of the state capital. Teotitlán's weaving tradition goes back to pre-Hispanic times. The wool was once dyed using the natural colors of indigo, moss or cochineal, but synthetic dyes are now used, producing less appealing tones which sometimes verge on the downright garish. However, the oldest village in the Oaxaca Valley deserves a visit, even if it means an overdose of *serapes* (blankets) and rugs. The **Mercado de Artesanías** (artists' market) displays a vast choice of designs, and many workshops are open to visitors.

► Tlacotalpán *188B3*

In the flat lagoons and marshes of southern Veracruz, 62 miles southeast of Veracruz itself, the large village of Tlacotalpán is the ideal spot for a quiet day out. Located beside the Río Papaloapan its main offerings are river trips, fishing, and swimming, but the pretty streets and plazas also hold a passing interest. A small museum, the **Museo Salvador Ferrando**, displays a private collection of furniture from the late 19th century, *objets d'art* and costumes, and there are several basic hotels on the main street. From here Highway 175 takes off through spectacular landscapes into the state of Oaxaca.

► Tuxtla Gutiérrez *189D2*

The state capital of Chiapas, 183 miles south of Villahermosa, is the center of a thriving coffee-growing region and source of Mexico's famed marimba music. Its steamy heat is all-enveloping, but little more than an hour away and a mile higher lie the cool mountain villages around San Cristóbal. Relatively modern and prosperous, Tuxtla's zócalo is a revamped square awash with marble fountains and dominated by the modern **catedral**. The **Museo Regional**►► in the Parque Madero, one of Pedro Ramírez Vázquez' innovative designs, displays Olmec and Mayan artifacts together with colonial and ethnographic exhibits. A botanical garden and Orquideario (orchid garden) complete the park offerings. However, the main claim to fame is the **zoo**►►► (open Tuesday to Sunday, 8:30 a.m. to 5:30 p.m.), located south of town and best reached by taxi. An enlightened approach to animal captivity has resulted in large enclosures apparently housing every native species of Chiapas. You will see ocelots, jaguars, pumas, howler monkeys, and the Vivario's unappealing community of spiders and insects. The tropical park setting is magnificent, with cedars and huge hardwoods weighed down by epiphytes and orchids.

Fruit-throwing
Each *barrio* (quarter) of Tehuantepec celebrates its patron saint over several days to the tunes of the marimba, but most telling of all is the local custom called *tirada de frutas* which takes place at numerous *fiestas* throughout the year. The first sign of this is a Tehuana woman staggering under lacquered gourds piled high with sweets, toys and mangoes which she distributes to the crowd. If only to show who wears the pants (or *huipil* in this case), women dressed in dazzling finery then climb on to the rooftops and throw fruit at the inferior males in the streets below.

Doll wearing local costume in Tuxtla Gutiérrez

Transportación Fray Matías de Córdoba S.A. de C.V.
☆☆☆☆☆
Transportes Terrestre Aeropuerto
Terán - Tuxtla
R.F.C. TFM-920122-JDO
Rel. Ext. No. 09002372
N$ 10.00
ZONA ORIENTE
Nº 04438
TUXTLA GUTIERREZ, CHIAPAS. TEL. 5-31-95
USUARIO

Indian costumes

■ Brilliantly colored, woven and embroidered clothes are an enduring tradition of Indians all over Mexico. Oaxaca and Chiapas, home to the highest proportion of Indians, continue weaving techniques bestowed on them by none other than Quetzalcóatl.....■

The rhombus
The rhombus, a recurring motif in Chiapan embroidery, represents the Maya universe. Its four sides denote the limits of time and space, while smaller rhombuses in each corner symbolize the four cardinal points. Mitla-style "Greek" hooks (a motif which was used in ancient Greece), which fill the margins of the rhombus, are stylized butterflies.

Mixtec woman weaving, Lake Chapala, Jalisco

Separation of the secular and the sacred is impossible in Mexico. Through craftwork the Indians express their highly personal view of the world, of life and death, and of the forces of nature. Never static, Indian costume has developed over the centuries by assimilating outside influences. The arrival of the Spaniards brought new techniques and symbols imbued with Arab skills imparted by the Moors, an injection which greatly stimulated creative potential. With the opening of Mexico's gate to the Orient through direct trade with the Philippines a subtle synthesis of world cultures came about. Far more negative is the impact of 20th-century synthetic dyes and machines, which in extreme cases have reduced what was once a spiritual exercise into a mechanical industry aimed at tourist purses. However, the geographical isolation and low standard of living in parts of Oaxaca and Chiapas have perversely maintained certain weaving and embroidery traditions in a state of suspended animation.

Cloth For the Aztecs, weaving was an art invented by Xochiquetzal, goddess of flowers and patroness of weavers, and every self-respecting girl was expected to lend her hand to the spindle and the loom. In their hierarchical society, costume variations distinguished the privileged from the poor as well as symbolizing the wearer's tribe and origin, something that still holds despite the passage of over 400 years. Although clothes made of rabbit fur or twisted feathers disappeared long ago, certain Chiapan villages (Zinacantán for example) still interweave downy feathers into ceremonial *huipils* (tunics), while Tzotzil and Tzetzil costumes are heavily decorated with swinging pompons, tassels and flowing satin ribbons. Cotton remains the predominant cloth, although wool, introduced at the time of the Conquest and mainly used for striped *serapes* (blankets), is rapidly being replaced by acrylic. In Chiapas rough wool is beaten to give it a felt-like texture and care is taken not to remove the natural oils during the cleaning stage: waterproof garments for the cold and damp highlands are thus assured. Back-strap looms (attached to the back by a belt) are commonly used by women who make their own and their family's clothes, often weaving complex designs without diagrams or models and relying entirely on intuition, memory, and imagination.

Dress styles Indian women still favor the *enredo*, a wrap-around skirt which is held in place by a separate waist sash, a highly decorative and essential element. Over this, or tucked inside, is the tunic-like *huipil* which displays

most of the intricate weaving patterns and/or embroidery and thus becomes the most personalized garment in a woman's wardrobe. Finally, the versatile *rebozo* (a rectangular shawl introduced during the colonial period) serves as a wrap or baby-carrier. Male dress has evolved even more radically, with the loin-cloth (banned from settlements by the Spaniards) replaced by pants, while bare, once-painted torsos are now covered in shirts, topped with a *serape*, and belongings carried in shoulder-bags woven from cotton, wool or vegetable fibres. In the Chiapan villages near San Cristóbal many Tzotzils and Tzeltals wear richly embroidered and trimmed tunics, yet another sign of their proud sense of identity—and among the richest, most varied and elaborately worked textiles in Mexico. A variation is the typical Chamulan male outfit of wide hat, shirt, belted natural wool tunic and pants—a dashing Spanish legacy.

Design motifs Seemingly abstract, yet symbolic stylized snakes, deer, butterflies, birds, flowers and foliage are combined with pre-Hispanic geometric forms—chevrons, triangles, zigzags, rhombuses and squares. Astutely aware of the tourist market, many local embroiderers have copied designs from archaeological sites such as Mitla or Yaxchilán, although in some cases these may have genuinely survived. Entire zoos invade the colorful Mixtec embroidery of Oaxaca, even offering exotic, non-indigenous animals such as lions, but more likely to be crocodiles, iguanas, or scorpions.

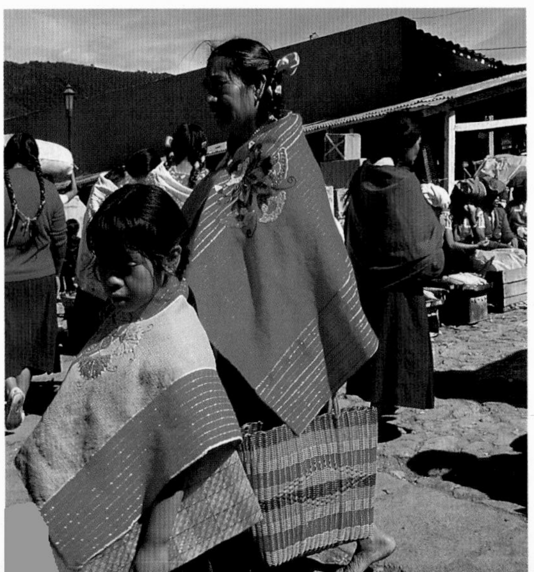

China Poblana
A well-entrenched legend regarding Mexican costume highlights the Asian input which followed the Spanish galleons plying the Pacific between Manila, in the Philippines, and Acapulco. The story goes that in the 17th century a Chinese princess was captured by pirates, then rescued by gallant Spanish mariners who brought her to Acapulco. Abandoned to her fate, she made her way to Puebla where she spent her life helping the poor. Scorning the elegant Spanish fashions of the day, she wore simple, full skirts and a loose, frilly blouse covered with a shawl, thus innovating a colorful, peasant-chic style. *China Poblana* (Chinese-Pueblan) is now Mexican national costume.

Colorful Indian costumes, San Cristobal de las Casas

A group of school children investigates an Olmec head at La Venta

Colossal heads
The American archaeologist Matthew Stirling first uncovered the Olmec mystery, the massive carved basalt heads which reach heights of nearly 10 ft. and weigh over 25 tons. Throughout the 1930s and '40s Stirling and his wife excavated three major Olmec sites: Tres Zapotes, La Venta, and San Lorenzo and became convinced that these civilizations predated the Maya. Vehemently opposed by Mayan specialists, Stirling was subsequently proved right by carbon-dating. However, the secret of the heads remains: how were they created? how were they moved? where did their Negroid features originate from? and are they warriors or kings?

▶▶ Villahermosa *189D3*

The steamy capital of Tabasco flourishes as a booming metropolis at the heart of the state's oil industry. The layout of this industrialized city follows the course of the Río Grijalva, which carries much of the trade to the interior of Chiapas and out to the port of Frontera. Not the most appealing of cities, Villahermosa's main interest lies in **Parque la Venta▶▶** to the northwest of town. This archaeological park is an outdoor museum of the original Olmec site of La Venta, some 75 miles west of the city, which was unearthed by oil engineers in the 1940s. Roughly dating from 900 to 300BC, La Venta is now represented by numerous stone artifacts, including three colossal sculpted heads which have been transferred to this beautiful lush jungle setting. Roaming deer, monkeys, a children's playground and a lagoon complete the attractions. More Olmec masterpieces can be seen at the excellent **Museo Regional de Antropología▶▶**, part of the CICOM (Centro de Investigaciones de las Culturas Olmeca y Maya) complex situated south of the center.

▶▶▶ Yaxchilán *189E2*

Nestling in thick rain forest on the Guatemalan border, in a loop of the Río Usumacinta, the extensive Mayan site of Yaxchilán would be a major highlight of southern Mexico were it easier to reach. Adventurous souls arrive by local bus and boat via Lacanja and Frontera Central, but most people visit Yaxchilán by bus or plane tours from Palenque or San Cristóbal. The main buildings, remarkably preserved, display intricately carved lintels, statues and walls inscribed with glyphs that have been deciphered to reveal Yaxchilán's secrets. Its heyday was in the mid-8th century when it was ruled by the Bird Jaguar (*Pájaro Jaguar*) but, like all Mayan cities, it declined and by 900 was abandoned. The most important building is the richly decorated **Edificio 33**, a monumental temple on a leveled-off hilltop behind the riverside structures of the main plaza. Apart from glyphs and carved mythological creatures, its main feature is a towering roofcomb framing a 23-ft. niche which once contained an enthroned statue of a god. This is now kept inside the temple and still forms part of an annual ritual performed by the Lacandons.

■ Ritual *pulque*-drinking bouts were an important part of pre-Hispanic culture, depicted in friezes and on murals in many archaeological sites such as El Tajín (see page 165), but it was the Spanish who brought the distilling techniques which produced *tequila* and *mezcal*.....■

Three alcoholic drinks dominate the *cantinas* and *pulquerías* (male-only bars) of Mexico: *tequila, mezcal,* and *pulque*. All are distilled from species of the agave or maguey (century plant) but there is a vast difference in strength—*pulque* is like a mild beer while *tequila* and *mezcal* are hard liquor (over 40 percent alcohol). Only one type of maguey produces true *tequila*, several produce *mezcal* (thriving in warm, lowland climes, particularly Oaxaca) and over six will yield the basic juice for *pulque* (suited to cool, dry central highlands). *Tequila* is named after the Jaliscan town of Tequila (see page 132), center of *agave tequilana* plantations and distilleries which by law are restricted to this area. Along the Gulf Coast tastes swing to rum or *agua ardiente* (a local liquor made from sugar-cane), while in the Yucatán peninsula the regional drink is based on honey fortified with the bark of the *balché* tree.

Production To obtain *pulque*, 10- to 12-year-old maguey hearts are punctured over a period of six months to yield a liquid which is transferred to the vats of the processing plant. Yeast speeds up the natural fermentation agents and within seven to 14 days the frothy, milky *pulque* is ready for the market. Perfect timing is essential as over-fermentation turns it sour.

Mezcal and *tequila* production are more complex processes. The pulpy spikes of the maguey are hacked off to obtain the solid *piña* (pineapple-type heart) which is then roasted in huge steam ovens before being shredded and the juice extracted. Sugars are added and the mixture fermented for four days, followed by two distillations. Average (and rough) *tequilas* are colorless, while smoother, matured *tequila añejo* turns a golden color after up to seven years of aging.

Tehuana

EHUANA is a word to identify the voman was born in the region of EHUANTEPEC in Oaxaca state. 'hat's why this authentic and excelent MEZCAL has deserved this vorthy name.

ocktails:

Zapoteca" coffee

cup of tehuana mezcal
cup of Coffee liquor
innamon
hake with pecked ice use cognac
up

"Xochitl" cocktail

/2 cup of Tehuana mezcal
/2 cup pf cane syrup
/2 cup of orange liquor
/2 cup of lemon juice
/4 cup of pecked ice
shake
use champagne cup frosted with salt

"Huatulco"

cup of Tehuana mezcal

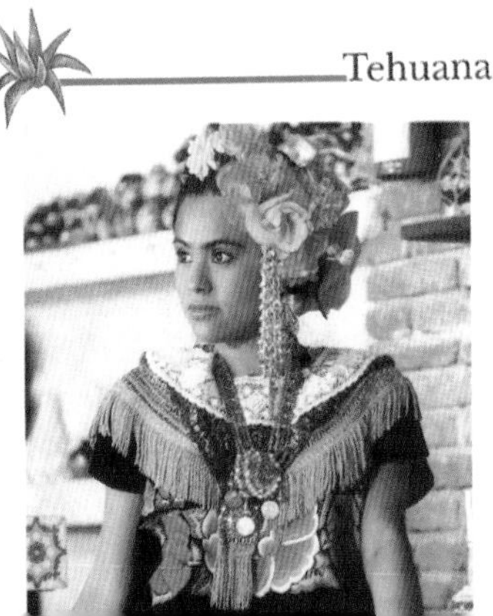

Tequila accessories
Often found at the bottom of a bottle of *tequila* or *mezcal* is a *gusano de maguey*, the worm which inhabits the maguey and is added for good measure. It is sometimes reduced to a powder, mixed with salt and wrapped in a packet, attached to the bottle. More common is the ritual which accompanies *tequila*-drinking: salt is sprinkled on the hand then licked with the juice of a lime—followed by a shot of *tequila*. Another alternative is the chaser *sangrita* ("little blood"—a spicy cocktail of chillies, tomato and orange juice) which should be alternated with each shot of *tequila*.

Universal *tequila*
Since 1940, the first year that *tequila* exports were of any consequence, business has multiplied 2,000-fold. Some 40 countries have caught the habit, with 87 percent going directly to the U.S., followed, in order of consumption, by Germany, Belgium, and France. Forecasts for future production indicate an annual production of 83 million liters, offering a rosy future to the 32 registered factories in Jalisco.

Enjoying a glass of tequila

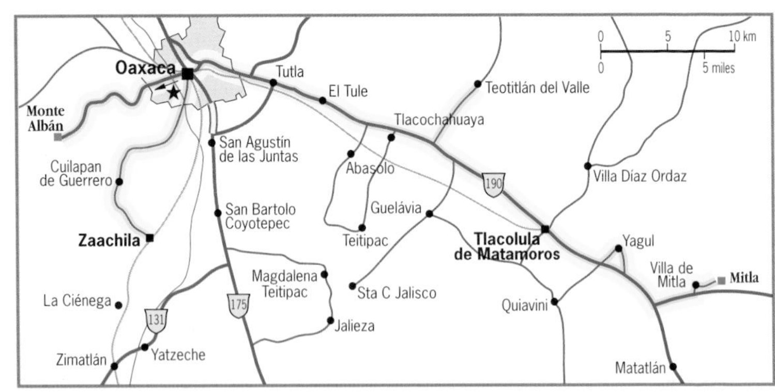

Drive Oaxaca's valleys and Zapotec sites

From Oaxaca, roads radiate through the valleys but do not join up. This drive follows several spokes but means back-tracking through Oaxaca to drive east to Mitla. Allow a full day.

El Tule, a giant ahueheute tree outside Mitla, has a circumference of 187 ft. and is believed to be over 2,000 years old

Drive south out of town following signs to Mexico DF until you reach MEX 175, where signs indicate Monte Albán. Cross a railroad track and follow a winding road for 6 miles to the hilltop site of **Monte Albán** (see pages 198–199) , exceptional in the clear early morning light. Allow two hours to explore the site. Retrace your route to the railroad track, after which immediately turn right towards Zaachila. Six miles farther the road passes **Cuilapan de Guerrero**, a rare Mixtec town in this predominantly Zapotec area. Unmistakable are the roadside ruins of a beautiful 16th-century **Dominican church** and **monastery**, part of which stands open to the elements, although the two-story Renaissance-style cloister is being restored. Here some rare murals survive, while the roofless colonnaded **chapel** is a marvel of graceful proportions.

Continue for 3 miles through flat farmlands to **Zaachila**, the last capital of the Zapotec empire and now a sleepy market town with a good selection of restaurants serving traditional Oaxacan dishes. Its busiest market day is Thursday, although villagers bring produce daily on mules. The town's main historic interest lies up the road behind the pink and yellow church in its *zona arqueológica.* Here stand the grassy tombs of ancient Mixtec royalty. From Zaachila drive back to Oaxaca's traffic circle, keep to the central lane and follow signs to Istmo or Tehuantepec which lead through the outskirts to link up with MEX 190, the main road east.

The first stop here is at **El Tule** (see page 194) to see what is claimed to be the world's largest tree, easily visible from the road, right in front of the church. Four miles beyond is a turn-off to the right to **Tlacochahuaya**, a small village in undulating pastures. Follow the main road through the village and turn left at the end to reach a magnificent 16th-century **church**. This important Dominican monastery complex is notable for the church interior, entirely decorated in vivid floral murals by local artists, an ornately painted 16th-century organ and a portrait of San Jerónimo by the Indian Juan de Arrué.

Back on the main road continue east to a turn-off on the left to **Teotitlán del Valle** (see page 212), the oldest village in the Oaxaca valley and famed for its woollen rugs woven on domestic handlooms. This is also the beginning of a lofty sierra which follows the road to Mitla and beyond. Another stop can be made at **Tlacolula**, famed for its *mezcal*, a few miles farther on the right of MEX 190. Turn off at the Pemex station and drive straight ahead as far as the market area.

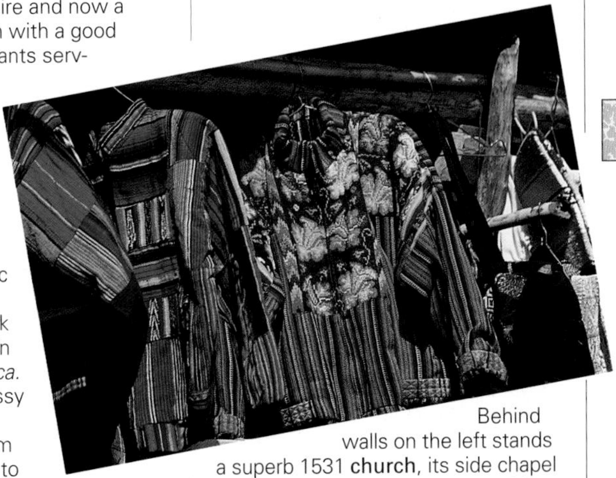

Brightly colored woven clothes at Mitla's local market

Behind walls on the left stands a superb 1531 **church**, its side chapel rich in early Baroque carvings, with a unique wrought-iron pulpit. From here drive straight out to **Mitla** (see page 195), an astonishing sight with its impressive Zapotec structures merging into the church precinct. Frequently visited by tourist buses, the locals have set up a large crafts market at the entrance to the site. This lies uphill at the back of the village, while the **Frissell Museum** is beside the main square on the road in. The end of this drive should take you back 6 miles on the road to Oaxaca to the little-visited Zapotec site of **Yagul**, magnificent in the late afternoon light as it commands a strategic hilltop position with 360-degree views over the Tlacolula valley. Explore the large ball court, palace patios, fortress and temple ruins in their verdant and panoramic setting of cacti before returning to Oaxaca on MEX 190.

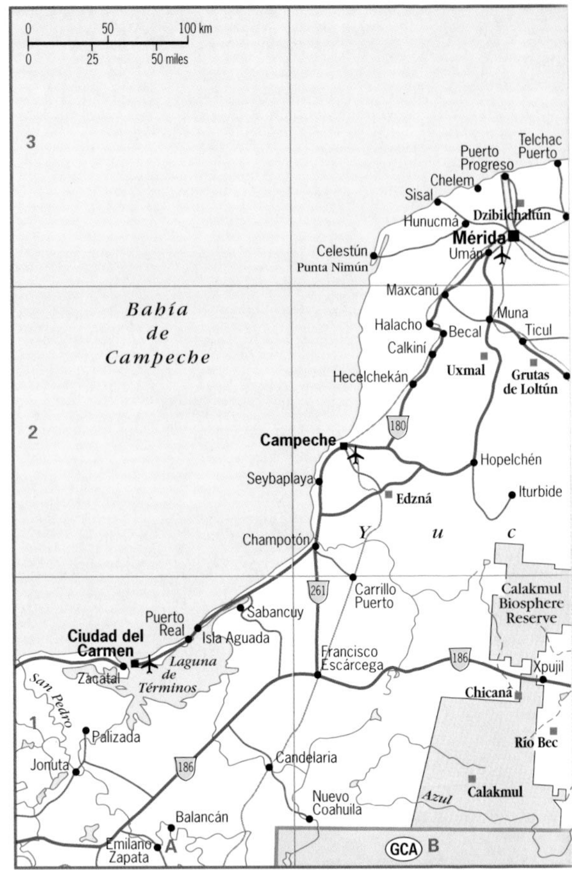
0 50 100 km
0 25 50 miles
3
2
1
Telchac Puerto
Puerto Progreso
Chelem
Sisal
Dzibilchaltún
Hunucmá
Mérida
Celestún
Umán
Punta Nimún
Maxcanú
Bahía de Campeche
Muna
Halacho
Becal
Ticul
Calkiní
Uxmal
Grutas de Loltún
Hecelchekán
180
Campeche
Hopelchén
Seybaplaya
Edzná
Iturbide
Champotón
Y u c
261
Carrillo Puerto
Calakmul Biosphere Reserve
Sabancuy
Puerto Real
Isla Aguada
Ciudad del Carmen
Francisco Escárcega
186
Xpujil
Laguna de Términos
Zacatal
Chicaná
San Pedro
Palizada
Río Bec
Jonuta
186
Candelaria
Azul
Calakmul
Nuevo Coahuila
Balancán
Emilano Zapata
A
GCA B

THE YUCATÁN

Left: Monument on the waterfront at Chetumal, in Quintana Roo, on the border with Belize

The Yucatán No longer the tropical paradise that it was 20 years ago, the Yucatán peninsula is, in some parts, rapidly turning into a Mayaland theme park, providing a large percentage of the state's revenue. Vastly improved communications with Florida and New Orleans combine with charter flights from Europe directly to Cancún to create a steady influx of visitors thirsting for the sun and the sea, and the Yucatán's exemplary archaeological sites. However, tourism tends to be concentrated on the Caribbean coast, but it takes little—a rented car being the basic necessity—to escape inland or along to the Gulf of Mexico coast.

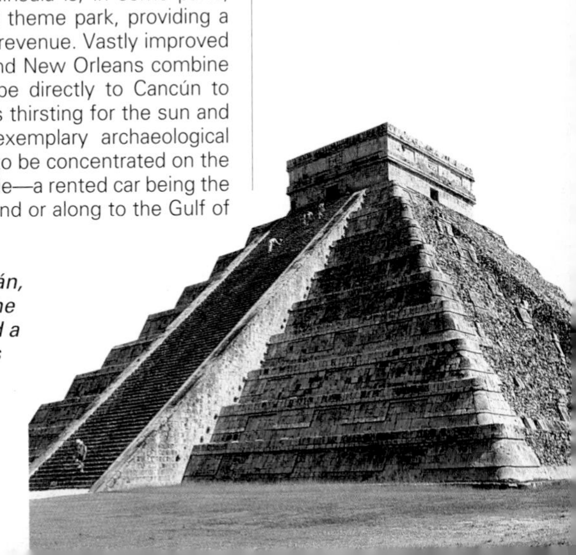

Right: The Pyramid of Kukulcán, Chichén Itzá, also known as the Castillo, has nine terraces and a square temple on the top. It is possible to climb up it, but extreme care is needed as the steps are very steep

Water, water nowhere
"The peninsula of Yucatán ... is a vast plain. The soil and atmosphere are extremely dry; along the whole coast, from Campeachy to Cape Catoche, there is not a single stream or spring of fresh water. The interior is equally destitute and water is the most valuable possession in the whole country. During the season of rains, from April to October, there is a superabundant supply, but the scorching sun of the next six months dries up the earth, and unless water were preserved man and beast would perish, and the country be depopulated."
John Lloyd Stephens: *Incidents of Travel*, 1841.

History The Mayan civilization extended into Belize, Guatemala, Honduras, and El Salvador, and dates from over 2,500 years ago. Great cities and ceremonial centers developed over the centuries until they suffered a cataclysmic decline in the 10th and 11th centuries. By the time the Spaniards arrived the Maya had abandoned the main centers and returned to subsistence farming, but this did not lessen their resistance. In 1528 Francisco de Montejo began a prolonged and painful campaign to subdue them, finally achieved by his son, "El Mozo," in 1542. As a result Mérida, then Campeche and Valladolid were founded and the once-proud and independent Maya became mere *peons* (serfs) at the mercy of the Spanish landowners. Independence in 1821 sparked Yucatecan separatist moves and, more iniquitous, the long and bloody War of the Castes (1847) which decimated the population. The Mexican Revolution brought reforms which finally returned the land to its Maya inhabitants—four centuries on.

Terrain The Yucatán peninsula, a giant peninsula jutting out between the Gulf of Mexico and the Caribbean Sea, is divided into three states: Campeche in the southwest, Quintana Roo in the east and Yucatán itself, which occupies a good chunk of the north and center. For centuries this region was isolated from the rest of Mexico by dense jungle and vast swamps, only opening up in the 1950s with rail and road links. Formed by a flat limestone shelf honeycombed with underground rivers, caves and *cenotes* (sinkholes), the dry countryside is covered with savannah, jungle, and agave and has poor soil and little rain. The Puuc Hills, just south of Mérida, provide the only topographical relief.

A Mayan village in the Yucatán

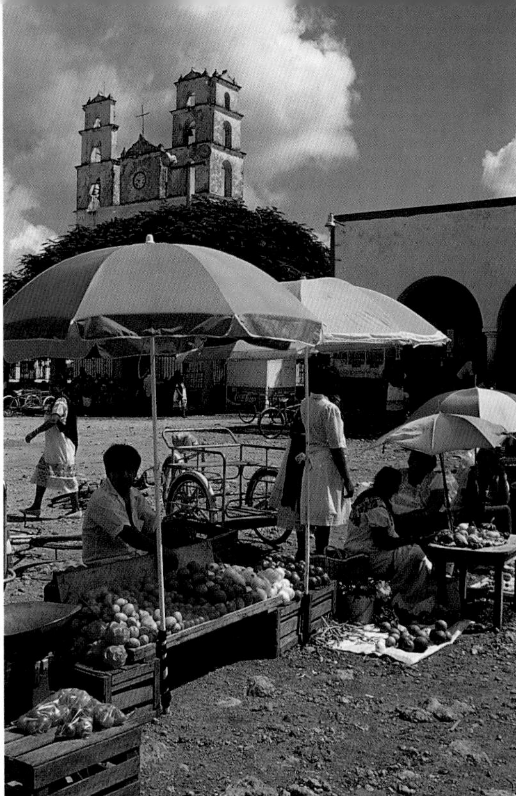

Fresh produce for sale at the local market

Produce
The Maya traded jade, salt, feathers, obsidian, cotton and pottery in an area extending from central Mexico to Costa Rica, with cacao (cocoa) beans used as currency. Under Spanish rule, the Yucatán was divided into vast creole *haciendas* which, by the late 19th century, profited from the boom in world demand for *henequén* (sisal—used for ropes) before a decline due to the discovery of synthetic materials in the 1920s. Some of these onceglorious, now decaying, partly derelict monuments to slave labor can be visited: San Bernardo (near Maxcanú off Highway 180), Yáxcopoil (south of Umán on Highway 261) and Teya (8 miles east of Mérida on Highway 180).

Sophistication or not Those seeking an upbeat holiday should head for the coast of Quintana Roo, starting in the north with Isla Mujeres, continuing through artificial Cancún and down the so-called "corridor," a coastal highway which ends at Tulúm. Originally a favorite destination for divers who came for the limpid Caribbean waters, thick with coral reefs and wrecked galleons, this stretch is now a prime target for developers who have dotted the island of Cozumel with a high-rise horizon and international airport. But all is not lost. Wildlife and biosphere reserves at Isla Contoy, Sian Ka'an, Río Lagartos and Calakmul preserve the last jaguars, toucans and rain forest. The perfect base for exploring this region is Mérida, a handsome colonial city which cleverly mixes culture with pleasure.

Sites Virtually every Mayan village has a crumbling pyramid looming somewhere behind a colonial church, but the obvious archaeological sites to visit in the Yucatán are those of Chichén Itzá, Uxmal, Tulúm, Cobá, Edzná and the many smaller excavated ruins in the Puuc hills (see pages 250–251), as well as the Río Bec group between Chicaná and Kohunlich. Hundreds of early settlements still await excavation, while picturesque villages of traditional thatched Mayan huts dot the interior, a reminder that today's Yucatecans have not forgotten their illustrious and still mysterious forebears.

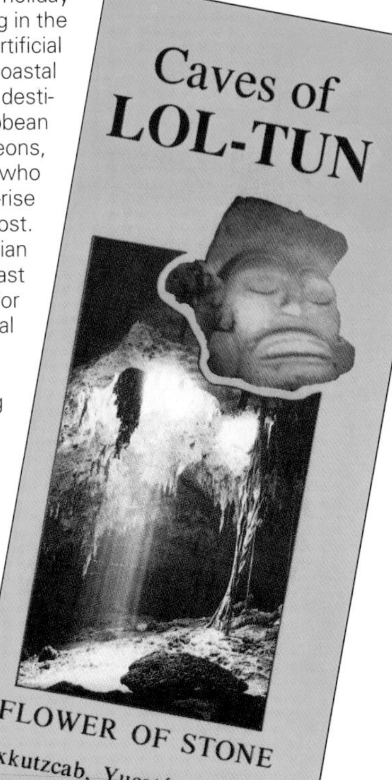

The sparkling turquoise waters off Akumal beach

Swashbuckling
Sixteenth-century Campeche became the principal port on the Yucatán peninsula as shiploads of timber and *chicle* (gum) were sent back to Spain, along with vast quantities of silver, gold and other precious minerals. Such wealth attracted the covetous attention of pirates, who started attacking the city only six years after it was founded in 1540. Swash-buckling buccaneers included such infamous characters as Laurent Graff, El Brasileño, Diego the Mulatto, John Hawkins and peg-legged Pato de Palo. In 1663 the pirates united for a particularly murderous attack on Campeche, slaughtering the citizens and sacking the city. This inspired the building of the famous city ramparts.

▶▶ Akumal *221D2*

Akumal, "the place of the turtles," lies some 22 miles north of Tulúm on the languid Caribbean coast. From May to August loggerhead, green, and hawksbill turtles drag themselves on to the powdery sands to lay their eggs, but year-round divers and snorkelers are drawn to the outstanding coral formations of Akumal reef and a sunken Spanish galleon. Low-rise hotels and exclusive guesthouses nestle in the protected bays, imparting a distinctly upscale atmosphere. Those with a less flexible budget can still take advantage of the marine offerings, particularly at the superb and less-developed lagoon of Yalkú, just over 1 mile north.

▶▶ Campeche *220B2*

The state capital of Campeche on the west coast of the Yucatán peninsula combines its image of a modernized port with its rich colonial history. Encircling the old town are the remains of a sturdy 1.5-mile wall, built between 1668 and 1704, and reinforced by *baluartes* (bastions) to protect the population from deadly pirate attacks. Seven of the original eight forts remain, best seen by following Avenida Circuito Baluartes. Overlooking the reclaimed sea-front area on one side and the Plaza Principal on the other are the ramparts of the **Baluarte de Soledad** which houses the **Museo de Estelas Mayas▶▶**. Mayan relics from Edzná are exhibited beside a substantial section covering colonial history and anti-pirate mechanisms. Opposite stands the Yucatán's first church, the **Catedral de la Concepción**, dating from the 1540s, which faces the arcades of the 19th-century Palacio Municipal. Two blocks down Calle 8, beyond the very 20th-century **Palacio de Gobierno**, is the **Baluarte San Carlos▶▶**, with cannons aligned on its ramparts, a small fortifications museum and a network of tunnels. At the northern end of Calle 8 the courtyard of the **Baluarte de Santiago** is ablaze with the lush tropical plants of the **Jardín Botánico Xmuch Haltún**, while directly inland the **Baluarte de San Pedro** houses a handicrafts collection. Last stop on the history tour is the **Museo Regional▶▶** (Calle 59, No. 36) where a fine collection of Olmec and Mayan artifacts is displayed in a lovely colonial mansion.

Gate in the old town walls of Campeche, a target for pirates

▶ Cancún *221D3*

The only reason for coming to Cancún is for an economical vacation of sun, sea, rock-music and *piña coladas*. This artificially planned resort, its fate sealed by computer in the early 1970s, is the ultimate in Mexican mega-resort blandness. Glitzy high-rise hotels tower over the Caribbean from the shores of a 14-mile-long sandspit which is connected to the mainland at both ends by bridges, thus creating a vast lagoon (Laguna Nichupté). The island **Zona Hotelera** is set up to cater to every hedonistic need—from theme park to golf course, deep-sea fishing, parasailing or diving—and the luxury hotels carry on a dazzling battle to outdo each other. Some outstanding contemporary architecture has developed as a result (don't miss the pool of Ricardo Legorreta's Hotel Conrad-Cancún, opened in 1991, or his landmark Stouffer Presidente which got the luxury ball rolling in 1975), rivaling the attraction of the talcum-powder consistency of Cancún's beaches. Cancún makes an ideal base for visiting many of the area's outstanding archaeological sites—Tulúm, Cobá and Chichén Itzá—as well as the smaller, local ones.

The mainland **Ciudad Cancún** (Cancún City) is home to 250,000 residents who are mainly immigrant workers, and is also where hotels and restaurants offer normal Mexican prices. Dissecting the town, Avenida Tulúm leads to Puerto Juárez in the north and the Cancún–Tulúm "corridor" to the south. With the relaxation of foreign trade agreements U.S. capital poured in, spawning hotel chains and giant shopping-malls. Over 20,000 hotel rooms cater for nearly 2 million annual visitors, who generate 20 percent of Mexico's total tourist revenue.

Cruising Cancún
What it lacks in authenticity, Cancún attempts to make up for in entertainment. At the Hyatt Regency Hotel the Tradicion Mestiza stages a folkloric ballet nightly (except Sunday) at 8:15 p.m., to be enjoyed while indulging in a buffet dinner. Or visitors can slip into pirate gear and cruise to "Treasure Island" on a galleon, dining, dancing and drinking all the way—boats leave the dock at Playa Langosta at 6 p.m. Sunset cruises, which throw in a lobster dinner, leave from the pier at the Royal Mayan Marina daily at 4 p.m. and 7:30 p.m. However, first prize for virtual reality goes to *The Sub Sea Explorer* which offers a hermetic, air-conditioned submarine trip around Cancún's offshore reefs.

Cancún's hotels line the beach overlooking the Caribbean

Pink flamingos

■ Flocks of flamboyant pink-feathered flamingos have chosen the shores of the Yucatán peninsula as their habitat, offering a brilliant spectacle which, from a distance, creates the impression that the water itself is a blushing, rosy liquid.....■

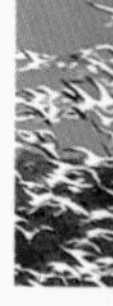

Flighty flamingos
Four species of flamingo exist in the world, most common being the greater flamingo, the Caribbean race of which occurs in Mexico. All have elongated, webbed feet, and sinuous necks, and obtain food by filtering plankton through their beaks. Known for their powerful flight and preference for warm climes, they choose to live in India, Africa, South America, the Caribbean, and the South of France.

Four hours from Cancún on the north coast of the Yucatán lies the 124 sq mile nature reserve of Río Lagartos, nesting and breeding ground for thousands of pink flamingos. Named by Spanish explorers after the alligators which infested the area, it is not a river at all but an area of eight ecosystems where salty coastal waters have eaten into flat marshes to create a network of estuaries and lagoons. Alligators can still be tracked down by the more adventurous (although hunting has greatly reduced their population), but the outstanding natural feature is the sheer number of pink flamingos drawn to the macrobiotic algae and aquatic life of the lagoon. From April to early July they join 270 other bird species (ducks, egrets, herons, ibises storks, cormorants, pelicans and plovers), which in winter include migratory birds from the north. Among the latter are sandpipers, scarlet tanagers, black-and-white warblers and ovenbirds—best spotted in the early morning.

Nesting An estimated 15,000 flamingos nest in the muddy shallows of estuaries which extend west from Río Lagartos to beyond San Felipe and east past El Cayo. Official rangers patrol the area during the breeding season to ensure that visitors do not disturb the flamingos, and the only way to see anything more than a distant pink haze is to indulge in a boat-trip of five to six hours. This will bring you to their favorite nesting-haunts deep in the marshlands, although flamingos are fast to take flight—however isolated they are. Outside this season the best place to spot these graceful creatures is in the fish-laden lagoon of Celestún, southwest of Mérida on the Gulf of Mexico, where they spend the winter months.

Caribbean flamingo

▶▶ Celestún

220B3

The small fishing port of Celestún, 58 miles west of Mérida, is famed for its colony of flamingos in the Parque Natural del Flamenco Mexicano, whose vivid pink bellies impart a rosy tinge to the waters of a beautiful inner lagoon. Birdwatching is best in the winter season when migratory birds wing in from North America to this mild corner. Boats can be rented to tour the mangrove-edged lagoon, and there are plenty of sandy (though windy) beaches between the port and Sisal, 25 miles farther north. Seafood is the other attraction here, and a handful of hotels caters for more long-term needs.

▶▶ Cenote Azul

221C1

The flat limestone terrain of the north and central areas of the peninsula is criss-crossed by a series of labyrinthine caves and *cenotes* (freshwater sinkholes caused by the collapse of cavern roofs). Cenote Azul, located on the southwestern shore of Laguna Bacalar (see page 241), towards the Belize border, is estimated to have a depth of 300 ft. Its famous brilliant blue water teeming with fish makes an inviting stop for swimming, snorkeling or diving, while those with less energy can admire the colors from a *palapa*-roofed restaurant on the *cenote* rim.

▶ Chetumal

221C1

Relaxed, but with a mounting crime rate, the capital of the state of Quintana Roo is tucked away in the southeast corner on the Belize border, isolated from the main Yucatán masses. A frequent victim of hurricanes, Chetumal has become a mainly modern port of wide avenues interspersed with a more Caribbean-style of beaten-up clapboard houses with porches and tin roofs. Its special tax status has resulted in stores brimming with imported electronic goods and a transient population of Belizeans in town on shopping sprees, while the regular influx of sailors has inspired a string of cheap bars and related amusements. The *malecón* (Boulevard Bahía) runs 4 miles north to Calderitas, a palm-fringed fishing village edged by a rocky beach and a few *palapa* stands. To the southwest lie the jungle-shrouded ruins of Kohunlich (see page 241) and, beyond, the Río Bec group.

Dark days

After conquering northern Yucatán in the 1540s, Francisco de Montejo's son—"El Mozo"—sent an expedition south under Lieutenant Gaspar Pacheco. Men and women were pressed into service as the Spanish advanced, burning abandoned settlements and countering any guerrilla resistance with instant death. Prisoners were garrotted or dismembered by dogs, and women were thrown into lagoons with weights attached to them. During the march Mayan porters were chained together by their necks and those who slackened were simply removed by decapitation. By 1544 resistance around Chetumal had collapsed and Pacheco had established a provincial capital on Laguna Bacalar.

Pelican, Chetumal

The Mexican/Belize border crossing, near Chetumal

Mayan astronomy

■ Brilliant mathematicians and creators of a calendar that was more accurate than our Western Gregorian one, the Mayan obsession with planetary movements governed not only religious rituals and mythology but also daily life. Understanding the complexities of their numerological achievements has become an obsession for Mayanists, bent on uncovering the truth about this advanced civilization.....■

Top: Mayan codex from the Museum of Anthropology in Mexico City

To assure their place in the cosmos, pre-Columbian Americans developed elaborate rituals based on their observations of the sun, the moon and the stars. Perceived as personifications of the gods, planetary movements were carefully observed with the naked eye, usually by trained shamans or priests who built up detailed records over the generations. The earth was conceived as four segments, each with its own color and deity, and the sun was pictured as circling around it. Predictions were made concerning the fates of kings and empires or the right days for rituals, while the rainy season and planting times could be forecast according to precise records.

Chronological coercion
According to American Mayanist Sylvanus Morley, Mayan belief in the repetitive nature of their almanacs was such that they underwent "chronological coercion." At the end of each cycle of 13 *katuns* (256.5 of our years) they "went beneath the trees, beneath the bushes, beneath the vines, to their misfortune" as the books of *Chilam Balam* put it. For example the Itzá Maya claimed to have founded Chichén Itzá in the 5th to 6th centuries before, being driven out and settling elsewhere a century or so later. Precisely 256.5 years later they claim to have returned to Chichén, possibly bringing with them Kukulcán and other Toltec influences.

Archeoastronomy Cities were laid out, pyramids were built and openings were positioned in precise relation to planetary or astral positions, whether the point where the Pleiades set behind the mountain of Cerro Colorado as in Teotihuacán, the cave-shaft at Xochicalco oriented to receive the sun's rays at its first passage through the zenith, or the Governor's House at Uxmal aligned to face the southern rising of Venus as the morning star. Interest in this domain has stimulated an emerging field of study named archeoastronomy which brings together astronomers, archaeologists and anthropologists to examine relationships between astronomical knowledge and religion, mythology and daily life.

Mayan calendars Mayan codices (ancient manuscripts) and ruins offer rich but confusing sources of information on the subject. Their earliest calendar was based on the long-count system, starting with a date that is the equivalent of August 10 3113BC, the beginning of a huge cycle of 13 *bakhtuns* (394.5 years) cheeringly forecast to end on December 24 2011 with the destruction of the world. By the time of the Conquest they had abandoned this system to adopt the short-count, a confusing calculation which placed history and prophecies in recurring cycles of time which firmly governed their lives, predicted eclipses and even planned pyramid construction. Two parallel calendars coexisted: a sacred almanac (the *tzolkin*) of 260 days, and the 360-day year to which five unlucky days (considered bad omens, when it was thought best not to venture out or undertake anything not strictly necessary) were added on to create a third system, the *haab* or 365-day solar calendar. A complete cycle contained 13 *katuns*

(256.5 years of our calendar): each *katun* consisted of 20 years of 360 days, subdivided into 18 months of 20 days, plus the five unlucky days. From these complex divisions emerged a dual calendar wheel which contained 18,980 days, the cycle of 52 years which was necessary for the two calendars to coincide.

Venus and the sun Mayan legend recounts the story of twin heroes Hunahpu and Xbalanque who, after overcoming countless obstacles in the underworld, finally emerged as gods themselves. Echoing the astronomical progress of Venus which, in fraternal harmony, precedes the sun at dawn or sets later at dusk, Hunahpu became Venus and Xbalanque the sun, creating a partnership common in Mesoamerican celestial society (see pages 180–181). The complete orbit of Venus takes 584 days: multiply 584 by 5 and 365 by 8 and you have the same total. The eight-year almanac constructed to interlock the Venus-sun cycles is thought to have served to determine propitious dates for ritual combat, sacrifice or war, since for the Maya this planetary god represented warfare and blood. More important still was the passage of the sun, whether at the spring equinox (March 20), 60 days later at the first zenith passage, the summer solstice on June 21, the autumn equinox (September 23) or the winter solstice of December 23. The most celebrated indication of this is at Chichén Itzá's Pirámide de Kukulcán which, when the sun's rays descend at the spring or autumn solstice, is mounted by a serpentine shadow—a homage to Kukulcán, the Mayan plumed serpent, or mere chance?

Observatories
Chichén Itzá's observatory (or Caracol) is a unique example of the significance of astronomy for the Maya as it was built with the sole purpose of tracking celestial movements. The circular construction stands on a platform at the top of a wide stairway and encloses an inner spiral staircase. The windows of the upper chamber (not open to the public) are aligned with the positions of the setting sun at the equinox and the solstice, while others indicate the four cardinal points. Alignments between other doorways and openings have been analyzed as related to the cycles of the moon and Venus.

Chichén Itzá's Observatory, known as El Caracol (The Snail) because of its spiral staircase

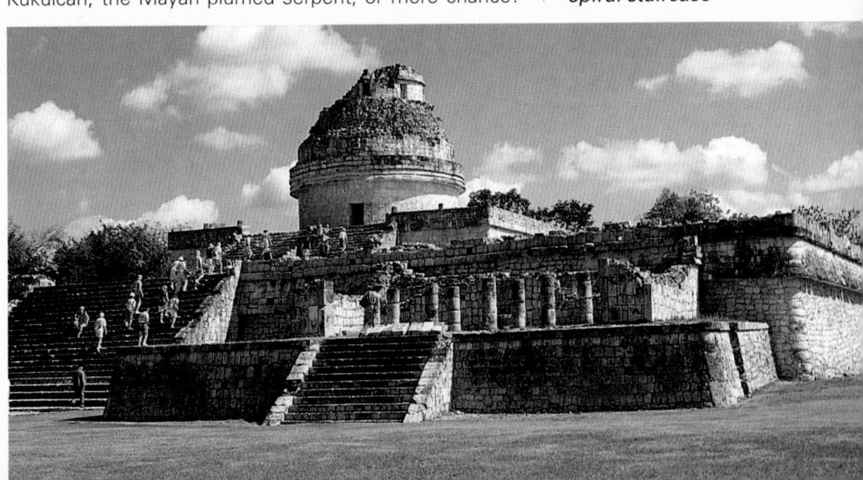

Cenote de los Sacrificios Chichén's largest *cenote*, the Cenote de los Sacrificios, lies about 984 ft. to the north of the plaza along a *sacbé* (sacred Mayan path—see page 232). Over 130 ft. deep and with a diameter approaching 200 ft., this perfectly circular sinkhole probably served as a sacrifical site. Soon after the foundation of the city, around 650, offerings to the rain god Chac consisted of objects—statues, vessels, gold discs, jade or incense—but later human sacrifice was introduced. Victims were first purified in an adjacent steam-bath, then richly dressed before being cast into the well from a platform on its southern edge.

▶▶▶ Chichén Itzá 221C2

Overwhelming in its scale, architectural beauty, and violence, Chichén Itzá is the most visited of the Yucatán peninsula's Mayan sites. Composed of three distinct zones, the ruins spread across a plain 75 miles east of Mérida. To visit them in relative peace it is advisable to stay at one of the many hotels nearby and arrive early. The sound-and-light show takes place in Spanish at 7 p.m. and in English at 9 p.m., while the entrance museum gives a good background to the site's complexities. Founded in the 6th century, the ceremonial center experienced two peaks: from 600 to around 900 and again from the late 10th century till 1196, subsequently traversing almost three centuries of civil wars and cultural stagnation before finally collapsing in 1441.

Chichén Nuevo (New Chichén) Soaring over the central plaza is the astonishing **El Castillo** (or Temple of Kukulcán—the Mayan feathered serpent) which embodies the solar year in the total number of steps (365) and in the 52 panels lining each side of its base; twice a year, at the spring and autumn equinoxes, serpentine shadows are thrown down the north staircase to join the carved snake heads at the bottom. In the northern flank a narrow stairway leads inside to a dank **tomb** (open 11 a.m. to 1 p.m. and 4 to 5 p.m.) which contains a *chacmool* (a reclining statue used to receive sacrificial offerings) and an extraordinary red jaguar throne studded with jade and shell. To the northwest of the pyramid a group of temples is clustered around the **Juego de Pelota** (Ball Court), the largest yet discovered in Mexico, whose walls are lined with reliefs of ball players—some being decapitated. Overlooking this is the **Templo de los Jaguares** (Temple of the Jaguars), its walls carved with eagles and jaguars devouring hearts in Maya-Toltec style, as well as an image of Quetzalcóatl. Immediately east stands the macabre **Tzompantli** (Platform of Skulls) which once served to display the heads of sacrificial victims.

Towering over the opposite side of the plaza is the richly decorated **Templo de los Guerreros** (Temple of the Warriors), a stepped structure built around the older

Temple of the Warriors with the Court of the Thousand Columns below. At the top of the stairs stands the famous chacmool

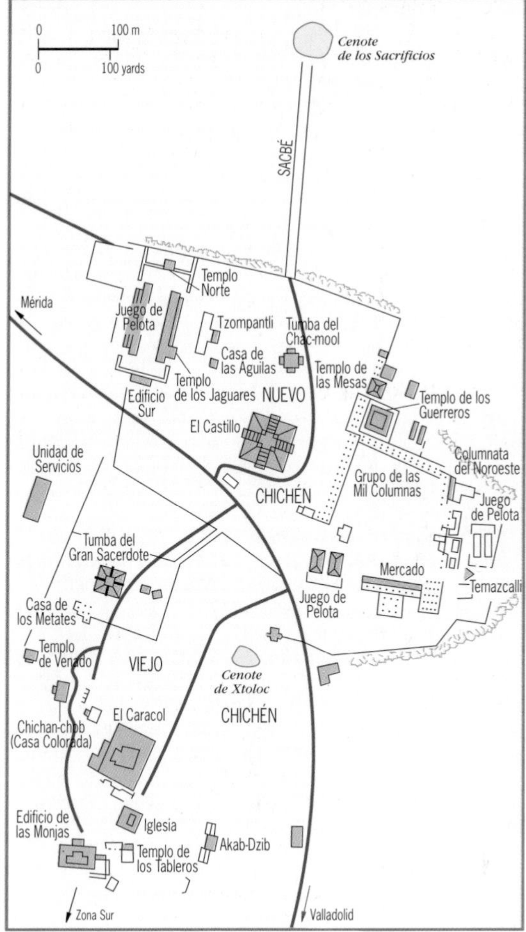

Templo del Chacmool, named after the *chacmool* that surveys the site from the temple platform. Serpentine columns, Atlantean pillars and an extensive colonnade below, **Grupo de las Mil Columnas** (Court of the Thousand Columns), now roofless, are among the controversial elements recalling Toltec Tula.

Chichén Viejo (Old Chichén) From the plaza a path winds south to another, older cluster of monuments: the **Tomb of the High Priest**, **Chichan-chob** (red house) and **El Caracol**, an elevated, circular building which was used for astronomical observations. Facing this to the south is the imposing palace complex, the **Edificio de las Monjas** (nunnery), its façades decorated with cut stone forming a Puuc-style mosaic. Between the two is the so-called **Iglesia**, remarkable for its roofcomb and frieze adorned with masks of the rain god Chac and mythological creatures. A path from behind the nunnery leads off to a third group of ruins, the largely unrestored **Zona Sur** (south zone) whose structures are best understood with the help of a guide.

Detail on the façade of the Temple of the Warriors

Sacbeob
The longest known *sacbé* (singular) in the Mayan world begins at the base of Cobá's Nohoch Mul and runs southwest for nearly 65 miles to Yaxuná near Chichén Itzá. The function of these numerous "white roads," built of limestone and surfaced with cement, is debatable: they could have been used for transportation (yet the Maya did not use the wheel) or for ceremonial purposes. Maya legend recounts *sacbé* construction ... The devout King Ucan unrolled the roads like a ribbon from a stone on his shoulder until one day a beautiful princess appeared. Refusing her advances, he turned away, only to be repeatedly blocked by her. At last he dropped his stone and made love to her. His magic power vanished and he could no longer pick up his stone!

▶ Chicaná *220B1*

Chicaná is the first of a string of archaeological ruins lying halfway along Highway 186 between Escárcega and Chetumal, the last being Kohunlich (see page 241). Still under excavation and shrouded in the remains of Quintana Roo's rain forest, these little-visited Mayan sites are collectively known as the Río Bec group and offer the rare chance of being alone with time. Their regional style of architecture is characterized by long, low buildings with giant serpents' mouths as doorways. Built in a combination of the Puuc and Río Bec styles, Chicaná reached its peak in the late 7th century when the eight-roomed palace—the main structure so far excavated—was probably built. Its central serpentine entrance represents the open mouth of the rain god Chac. Becán (once encircled by a moat) and Xpujil (famous for a lattice-towered pyramid) are also easily visited from the road, but **Río Bec▶▶** itself and **Calakmul▶▶▶**—thought to have been one of the largest Mayan cities and claiming a colossal pyramid—lie in the heart of the jungle so require guides from the village of Xpujil.

▶ Ciudad del Carmen *220A1*

This important fishing and oil town sits on the elongated western tip of Isla del Carmen, joined to the mainland by a causeway and enclosing the large Laguna de Términos, a favorite with anglers. Some 145 miles south of Campeche, it is the Gulf of Mexico's chief shrimp fishing port and an important oil center. During the 17th century it was a major pirates' base, vying with Isla Mujeres on the Yucatán's Caribbean coast for notoriety. Well off the main tourist circuit, the town now makes a peaceful, pleasant stop-off, characterized by palm-shaded plazas, fishing nets drying in the sun, good beaches, and excellent seafood restaurants.

▶▶ Cobá *221C2*

Situated about 25 miles inland from Tulúm along a good road, Cobá (meaning "wind-ruffled waters") is an easily accessible site which remains refreshingly unexploited. Its pretty lakeside setting encircled by jungle has spawned a few restaurants, hotels and craft shops, but if you come here after Chichén Itzá or Tulúm the atmosphere is decidedly low-key. Excavations began in the 1970s, and to date only an estimated five percent of this enormous Mayan city

Deep in the jungle, Cobá was never discovered by the Spaniards: Ca Iglesia —one of the many structures found at the site

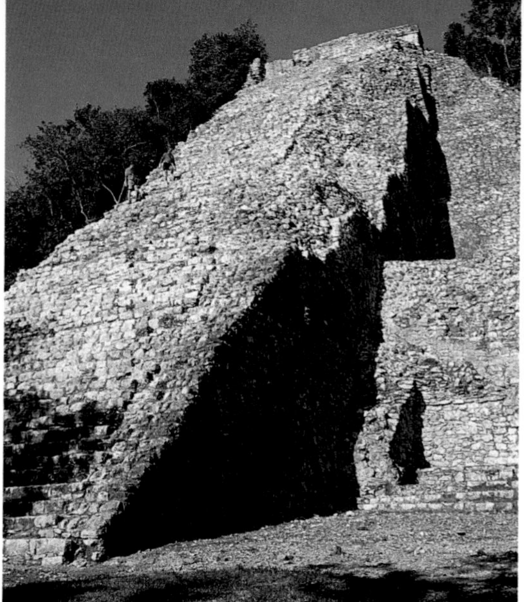

Cobá's Nohuch Mul, at 138 ft., is the tallest pyramid in the northern part of the Yucatán peninsula

Calakmul Biosphere Reserve
A vast area to the north and south of Chicaná has now been established by UNESCO as a biosphere reserve in order to save what little remains of the Petén rain forest. Calakmul's jungle, the densest on the peninsula, is rich in flora and fauna, with 300 species of birds, rare orchids and jaguars, howler monkeys and tapirs still prowling through the undergrowth. To the south the reserve joins Guatemala's Maya Biosphere Reserve (north of Tikal) and to the west Belize's Río Bravo conservation area.

has been uncovered. Distances between each ruin are great—so come prepared with good shoes, water and insect repellent. Covering a total area of over 23 sq miles, Cobá flourished between 600 and 900 when thousands of homes huddled around the forested shores of five lakes, and monumental structures were built in a style that curiously resembled Guatemala's Tikal rather than other northern Yucatán sites. A further enigma are the 45 wide *sacbeob* (plural), thought to be ceremonial avenues, which radiate from Cobá for distances of nearly 65 miles to other ancient settlements.

Following the main path and forking to the right, the first significant complex is the **Grupo de Cobá**, whose narrow but steep pyramid rises 80 ft. above the tree-tops and offers a fabulous view south towards Lago Macanxoc and east to Nohoch Mul—the great pyramid. At its base is a vaulted tunnel with traces of murals, and beyond here tracks lead through the jungle, past countless unexcavated structures, underground Mayan homes and tunnels to reach the lake. Back on the main path, the next turn-off leads to the **Conjunto de Las Pinturas** (Temple of the Painted Lintels) where a four-tiered temple displays badly deteriorated murals. Close by are some beautifully carved stelae (stone slabs) and circular altars known as the **Grupo Macanxoc**.

All Cobá's *sacbeob* converge on **Nohoch Mul**, an easy, but hot, mile-and-a-half walk from Las Pinturas. Tapirs, butterflies, snakes, fire-ants and the occasional toucan will make the going more interesting. Towering 138 ft. high, Cobá's great pyramid offers sweeping panoramas over the surrounding jungle from a small temple decorated with descending god figures. Thought to be connected with the God of Honey, they stress Cobá's vital role as a trading center for cocoa and honey.

Mayan carving at Cobá

Browsing in the shops lining Cozumel's pedestrianized main street is a favorite occupation with visitors

Pre-diving days
For the early Maya, Cozumel was a pilgrimage destination favored by women who visited the shrine dedicated to Ixchel, the goddess of the moon and fertility. When the Spanish ships captained by Juan de Grijalva arrived on the horizon from Cuba in 1518, the reception was timid and Cozumel was left in peace. The following year, along came Cortés and the first brush with Catholicism. In Bernal Díaz' words: "It seems that a number of idols of most hideous shapes were kept in a prayer-house in Cozumel to which the natives of the country habitually offered sacrifices at that season." Cortés didn't flinch in his actions and Cozumel's shrines were soon destroyed and replaced by crucifixes.

▶▶ Cozumel *221D2*

Cozumel incorporates both extremes of the Yucatán's moods. Just 12 miles off Playa del Carmen and only 30 miles south of Cancún, it has become a prime target for cruise-ships, island-hoppers and Cancún beach fanatics. However, first and foremost it was discovered by divers, drawn to its shores to follow in the wake of Jacques Cousteau, who filmed the fabulous Palancar Reef in 1961. Teetering on the shelf of a mighty 3,280-ft. drop which teems with brilliantly colored fish and spectacular coral formations, the reef is considered one of the world's top diving destinations. Altogether there are more than 8 miles of reefs lying in the limpid waters off Cozumel's west coast, all of which have been protected as a marine reserve since 1972.

The island Ten miles wide and 28 miles long, Cozumel boasts one road (the Transversal) which circles the southern half of the island, leaving the north to scattered ruins and much of the east coast to spectacular rocky headlands, rare hotels and some dangerous surf. Ferries from Playa del Carmen and Puerto Morelos dock on the west coast at **San Miguel**, a pedestrianized, commercialized town entirely governed by tourism. Cruise-ships land their glazed passengers a few miles south of town, and international flights do the same at the airport to the north. Cozumel is certainly not the destination for lovers of unadulterated atmosphere or those on a budget, although campers can escape the crowds by heading for the east coast.

Reefs and beaches Cozumel is a paradise for divers: San Miguel's dive-shops outnumber the reefs, but those with less experience can also enjoy themselves. Six miles south of San Miguel is the heavily structured **Laguna Chankanab**▶ where botanic gardens, a small museum, restaurants, and a man-made beach line a bay which offers prime snorkeling—as well as gear for rent. Avoid the middle of the day, when cruise passengers pour in

Best dives
Divers head off in droves for the reefs of Palancar, Paradise, Santa Rosa, Colombia, and Tormentos, where average visibility ranges from 115 to 165 ft. and silver bait fish, eels, angelfish, grouper, technicolor parrot-fish, sergeant majors and four-eyed butterfly fish swim by. Experienced divers should head for the reefs bordering the southern point of the island (Colombia and Maracaibo) which, although requiring an hour's boat-trip from San Miguel, offer spectacular natural environments. The famed wall of Maracaibo is formed by coral covered tunnels which descend to depths of over 130 ft., while in the 65-ft. shallows there is a dazzling wealth of reef and marine life.

and access to the water becomes nightmarish. Three miles farther, **Playa Maya** is a quieter, sandy beach backed by jungle but beaten in the popularity stakes by the seemingly endless **Playa San Francisco▶▶** where *palapa* restaurants, bars and pleasure-seeking sunlovers set the tone. Next along the coast is the lovely **Playa Escondida▶▶**, reached via a rough turn-off from the main road about 12 miles south of San Miguel, and frequented mainly by locals. Only three beaches are practicable on Cozumel's east coast: **Punta Chiqueros**, a beautiful beach protected by a headland; the small cove of **Chen Río**; and **Punta Morena**, a rocky beach partly frequented by fishermen.

Fundación de Parques y Museos de Cozumel, A. C
Parque CHANKANAAB
Cozumel, Q. Roo, México
R.F.C. FPM-870331-Q13
ADMISSION
CHANKANAAB
$12,000.00
N$ 12.00
Nº 352286

The reef off Palancar Beach is excellent for fishing and diving

Rest of the island From Punta Morena a 15-mile sandy track, only accessible with four-wheel drive or motorcycle, winds north past minor Mayan ruins to **Punta Molas**, where a lighthouse and the ruins of **Aguada Grande** announce the tip of Cozumel. Better restored but not particularly enthralling is the site of **San Gervasio**, accessible along a dirt-track off the east–west Transversal. Much of the rest of the island is swathed in jungle or edged by mangrove swamps and can only be reached on foot. This is in high contrast to the Manhattan-type skyline fast developing along Playa San Angel, a few miles to the north of San Miguel.

■ Colorful algae, sponges, spectacular coral formations and shoals of technicolor fish are not the only sub-aqua visions of the Yucatán's Caribbean coast. Sunken galleons add to the deep-sea thrills, while a vast inland network of underwater caves and *cenotes* offers an enthralling world of sculptural rock formations.....■

Beyond the Yucatán
Mexico's diving delights are not monopolized by the Yucatán. Although much of the Gulf of Mexico is polluted, Veracruz claims a sunken vessel at Isla Verde and, south of town, off the coast from Anton Lizardo, the protected reef of La Blanquilla where shelves and grottos descend to 165 ft. and teem with marine life. Another spectacular sea is the Mar de Cortés where deep underwater trenches reach depths of 2 miles. On the southern tip of Baja California, Los Cabos makes a fabulous destination for over 800 species of reef fish (including the unique Cortés angelfish, Clarion angelfish and Cortés rainbow wrasse), and is famous for its underwater sandfalls.

From the tiny Isla Contoy lying off Yucatán's northern tip to the port of Chetumal on the Belize border stretch 438 miles of limpid, turquoise-green water lapping the world's second largest barrier reef. With their epicenter on Cozumel, divers have flocked to the area since the 1960s after oceanographer Jacques Cousteau revealed the glories of the now-legendary Palancar Reef. With the advent of Cancún and the over-development of Cozumel, parts of this delicate underworld ecosystem have suffered, and more time and money are now necessary to reach pristine, less accessible coral reefs. Parallel to this popularity comes a new sport, that of closed-water diving through *cenotes* (sinkholes) to underground rivers and caverns that riddle the limestone shelf of the peninsula.

Reef diving Serious divers head for the remote promontory which ends at Xcalak, from where trips can be made to the fabulous Banco Chinchorro, a ring of islands edged with reefs about 15 miles offshore. Far easier to reach is the coastline between Cancún and Punta Allen: Akumal, Puerto Aventuras and Xel-Há all offer numerous structures geared to experiencing sub-aquatic delights, including sunken galleons and night-dives.

Off Cancún itself good beginners' dive spots include the underwater garden of Punta Nizuc, Los Cuevones and the shallow Chitales Reef. Experienced divers head for open-sea sites such as El Tunel, San Toribio and San Miguel, where depths range from 50 to 65 ft. and strong currents may bring with them dolphins, sea-turtles or sleeping sharks. These lethargic and normally dangerous creatures (bull, black-tip, lemon or nurse sharks), overdosing on oxygen bubbles from fresh-water undersea springs, favor, above all, the isolated Sleeping Shark Caves north of Isla Mujeres. Close by lies the 1980 wreck of *El Frío* (*Ultrafreeze*), now a refuge for stingrays, green morays, giant jewfish and brilliant yellowjacks. Midway between Isla Mujeres and Cancún, the elongated reef of La Bandera (averaging depths of 40 ft.) is topped with elkhorn coral and slashed with ledges and overhangs. Schools of barracuda and pompano swarm over it, while clustered beneath the overhangs are large crabs, spotted moray eels, lobsters and angel fish.

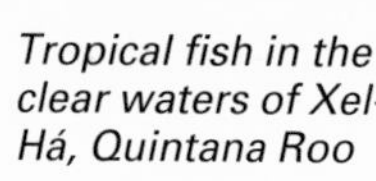

Tropical fish in the clear waters of Xel-Há, Quintana Roo

Nearly 20 miles of marine park make Cozumel the third most popular dive destination in the world. Exceptionally clear and nutrient-filled currents have nourished spectacular coral formations (including black coral), and abundant marine life, and maintain an unmatched underwater visi-

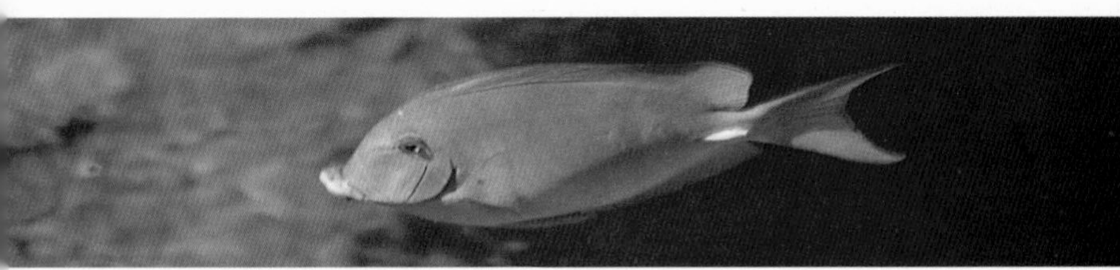

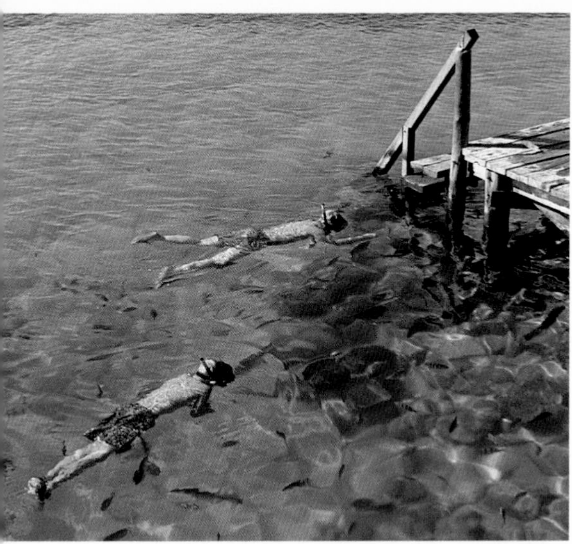

Snorkeling at Xel-Há—come early or late to avoid the crowds

bility. Fifteen dive spots with depths of 50 to 130 ft. are scattered across the massive southeastern reefs of Palancar, Santa Rosa and Colombia, while at the majestic Maracaibo Reef (off the southern point) coral-covered tunnels descending to over 150 ft. swarm with grouper and yellowjack.

Cave diving Only developed in the Yucatán in the last decade, cave diving is a highly specialized and dangerous sport that has already claimed hundreds of lives. Over 80 cave systems have so far been registered along the Cancún–Tulúm Corridor, of which Nohoch (just southwest of Akumal) is the father of them all, its 12 miles of interconnected underwater passages and caverns making it the longest underwater cave system in the world. Vast water-filled limestone caves, resplendent with gnarled columns, stalagmites, stalactites and radiating tunnels, were sealed by rising water some 10,000 years ago at the end of the Ice Age and now offer a dramatic environment for advanced divers. Aquatic life consists mainly of crustaceans, occasionally joined by blind-fish and eels. For snorkelers and inexperienced divers, the *cenote* entrances to these networks (notably at Nohoch, Xcaret and Dos Ojos) offer unique glimpses of these recently discovered underworlds.

Car-wash
No, this is not an enterprising Maya initiative but the name of a *cenote* located about 4 miles along the Tulum-Cobá road. Like most *cenotes* of the Yucatán it is much used by local inhabitants as a fresh water source—and in some cases for a quick car-wash. The immense natural pool of clear water is an open invitation to snorkelers, swimmers and divers.

Punta Xpu-há
Ideal for snorkelers, the cenote of Xpu-há is one of the most extensive of the Akumal region, with a length of over 1,600 ft. and depths never exceeding 20 ft. Located between Akumal and Puerto Aventuras, it can be reached on foot from the beaches of Xpu-há or Rancho Viejo. A few miles south lies another superlative underwater spot around the inlets of Xaac and Xaac Chico, still relatively secluded due to their inaccessibility from the highway. With depths of up to 130 ft. and easily reached from the shore, the coral reefs here offer brilliant formations and fluorescent fish.

Caste War
Mexico's independence from Spain, signed and sealed in 1821, did not mean relief for Mayan Indians, most of whom were enslaved by mounting debts to the great landowners. However, the Yucatán's wealthy ruling classes, aspiring to their own independence from Mexico, set about arming their *peons*. This was a great mistake as the Maya soon turned against their masters, initiating the War of the Castes in Valladolid in 1847. Exorcizing centuries of oppression, they pillaged and murdered, their cause spreading throughout the peninsula. Suddenly, when all seemed lost for the whites, the rebels turned tail and fled to their fields—the sowing season had arrived and everything else took second place. White vengeance was terrible—between 1848 and 1855 the Mayan population was halved.

► Dzibilchaltún *220B3*

Dzibilchaltún, meaning "place of inscriptions on flat stones," is no longer the glorious Mayan city which was occupied continuously from 800BC to AD1250. Located 10 miles north of Mérida, just off the road to Progreso, the site starts at a derelict Spanish church built of stones salvaged from Mayan temples. From here a *sacbé* (sacred Mayan road) runs east to the main restored structure, the **Templo de las Siete Muñecas** (Temple of the Seven Dolls), crowned by an unusual pyramidal roofcomb and decorated with masks of Chac. Clay dolls were found at its altar, each with a different physical deformity, and are now exhibited at the entrance museum. Countless other unexcavated buildings hide beneath the surrounding vegetation, and the Cenote Xlacah, when dredged by archaeologists, revealed numerous offerings. Soon to crown Dzibilchaltún's role as the Yucatán's oldest Mayan site is an important new museum of the Mayan culture.

►► Edzná *220B2*

The most fully excavated ruins in the state of Campeche lie 40 miles east of the state capital off Highway 261 and see far fewer visitors than sites further north. Edzná ("the house of grimaces" in Mayan) was settled in 600BC and reached its zenith between AD550 and 810. Its architectural style incorporates Puuc stone mosaic friezes into buildings of classic proportions. The most striking feature is the main plaza dominated by the **Templo de los Cinco Pisos** (Temple of Five Levels), a vast tiered platform with rooms at each level, once faced in stucco and paint but

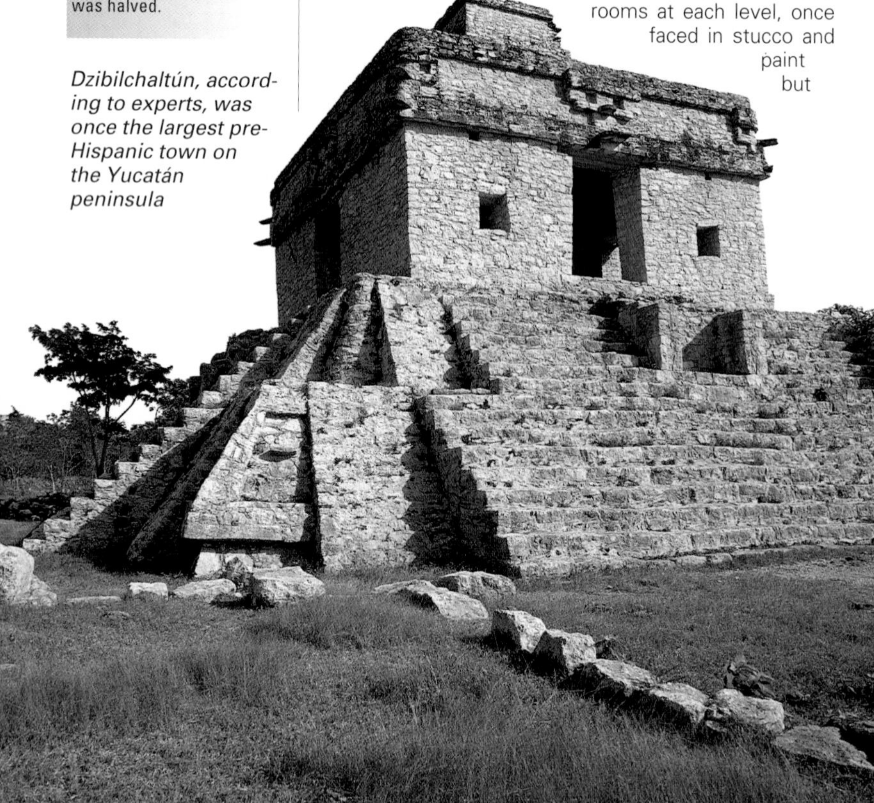

Dzibilchaltún, according to experts, was once the largest pre-Hispanic town on the Yucatán peninsula

now revealing only a few serpent and jaguar heads. Opposite this stands the **Casa de la Luna** (Temple of the Moon). The entire site is riddled with a network of tunnels believed to have been used for irrigation.

►► Grutas de Balankanché *221C3*

A 4-mile drive east from Chichén Itzá along Highway 180 brings you to this impressive network of caves, once the site for Mayan ceremonies honoring the rain god Tláloc, the Toltec version of Chac. Narrow passageways lead to three of the seven cave chambers open to the public, revealing stunning stalagmites and stalactites which in one case have mysteriously formed the shape of a *ceiba*, the sacred Mayan tree. Around the chamber are numerous *metates* (maize-grinding stones) and 1,000-year-old clay vessels, while another cavern is filled with a glassy pool. A small museum adjoins a botanical garden at the entrance, and visits include a "sound-and-light" guided tour (in Spanish at 9 a.m., noon, 2 p.m., 4 p.m.; in English at 11 a.m., 1 p.m., 3 p.m.).

►►► Grutas de Loltún *220B2*

Even more impressive than Balankanché are the vast caves of Loltún which lie in the heart of the pastoral Puuc Hills, just over 62 miles south of Mérida and 11 miles east of Labná. Stumbled upon in 1888 by an American, they were not charted until 1959 when the giant "Loltún head," reminiscent of the Olmecs, was uncovered. Carbon-dating has confirmed that the caves were inhabited over 2,500 years ago, and possibly much earlier. Apart from the extraordinary natural formations of this 1¼-mile network, the caves have revealed rock-carvings, wall-paintings, ceremonial and pottery-making areas as well as hollow stalactites which create musical notes, natural air-vents providing fresh, cooled air and natural cisterns of filtered rainwater. The largest chamber—the **Cathedral**—soars 150 ft. high and its tunnels were still used during the Caste War of the mid-19th century by rebellious Mayas seeking refuge from *Creole* landowners. Visits are by guided tour only at 9 a.m., 11 a.m., 1 p.m. and 2 p.m.

►► Isla Holbox *221D3*

This tiny island lies off the northeastern point of the Yucatán and is reached by ferry from the village of Chiquilá. A real getaway, the fishing village offers few services (one modest hotel for the moment), but opens on to endless sandy beaches which attract campers and those seeking the wilder aspects of the Yucatán. Shells are abundant along the shore, the water, although not a classic Caribbean turquoise, is clean and calm, and wildlife is prolific.

Isla Contoy
Another island situated off the northern point of the peninsula, between Isla Holbox and Isla Mujeres, provides rich rewards for birdwatchers. Protected as a wildlife sanctuary, the miniscule Isla Contoy is inhabited by over 60 species of birds, including brown pelicans, snowy egrets, boobies, cormorants, frigatebirds, flamingos and spoonbills. Its exquisite white beaches attract day-trippers from Cancún, Isla Mujeres and Cozumel, and the surrounding waters are also great snorkeling territory. Although trips to Isla Contoy were suspended in 1993 to enable an ornithological study, they should soon resume.

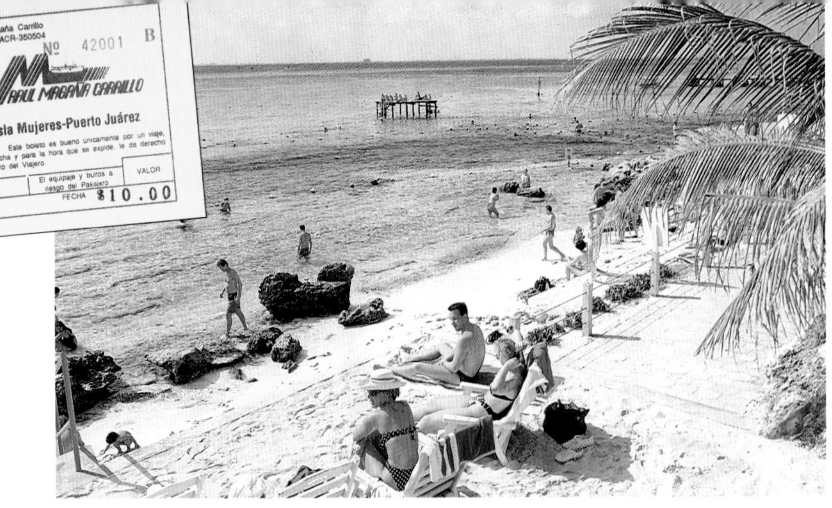

The coral reef is close to the fine white sand beach at El Garrafón, Isla Mujeres

A rare chance to see nature close-up—shark at Isla Mujeres

►► Isla Mujeres *221D3*

Just 7 miles north of Cancún, Isla Mujeres has a decidedly different rhythm, more laid back, more Caribbean, in keeping with its pirate past. Less than 2 miles wide and only 5 miles long it is a typical palm-fringed tropical retreat, discovered in the 1950s when Cozumel and Cancún were mere figments of developers' imaginations. Today it is still a favorite destination for egg-laying turtles and exhausted travelers, but is increasingly frequented by day-trippers from Cancún.

Ferries from Puerto Juárez and pleasure boats from Cancún dock at the main village, its harbor dotted with colorful fishing boats and its cobblestoned lanes lined with a jumble of shops, outdoor cafés and restaurants. Immediately north lies Isla's best beach, **Playa Los Cocos►►**. Calm, aqua-jade waters, gently sloping sands, watersports, a rare topless bathing area and a few *palapa* restaurants make it a popular haunt, though Hurricane Gilbert ripped out most of the palm trees in 1988. **El Garrafón National Park►**, on the southern tip, is an underwater paradise for snorkelers, although most of the coral is now dead. Equipment can be rented on the beach, whose facilities include a marine museum and restaurant, but avoid going around in the middle of the day when the water swarms with Cancunites. Experienced divers can head further out to numerous sunken wrecks, the reefs of Los Manchones or the "sleeping sharks caves" with diving trips organized from the port diving shops.

Escape the hordes by walking a short distance from El Garrafón up a rocky windswept point to the ruins of a **Mayan temple►** dedicated to Ixchel (the Mayan goddess of fertility) and a lighthouse, both of which have fabulous sea views. More history lies in the center of the island at the **Hacienda Mundaca►**, an early 19th-century estate, built by a slave-trader and imbued with legends, gently rotting in its jungle environment.

►► Izamal *221C3*

Izamal is a striking brilliant yellow market town situated 44 miles east of Mérida, which combines crumbling Mayan pyramids with the gigantic **Convento de San Antonio.** Incorporating Mexico's largest atrium and built with the stones of a Mayan temple, this huge structure dates from 1553, although the church was rebuilt in 1795. A corridor and staircase to the left of the church leads to an inner sanctuary where a statue of the Virgin of Izamal (the patroness of the Yucatán) is wheeled in and out of

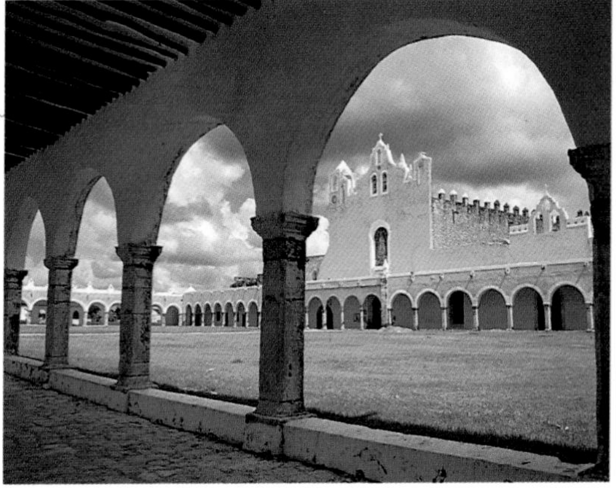

the front altar on rails. The Franciscan monastery still functions and recalls a visit by the Pope in August 1993—souvenirs and photos abound. The relaxed atmosphere of the town is heightened by horse-drawn buggies and the market which occupies the main square below the monastery.

What's in a name?
Theories abound about the origin of the name Isla Mujeres, the "Island of Women." Some say it came from the pirates who left their women here while they plundered the high seas. Others say that the island was a sanctuary for sacred Mayan virgins. The most probable explanation is that it was given the name by the Spanish conquistadors who, on landing on the island in 1519, found sculptures of female figures in the temple dedicated to Ixchel, the goddess of fertility.

Left: monastery, Izamal
Below: Kohunlich

▶▶ Kohunlich *221C1*

Deep in pristine tropical forest, some 35 miles west of Chetumal, Kohunlich offers superb wildlife and vegetation as well as little-visited ruins mainly dating from AD300 to 600. Two hundred or more mounds await excavation and for the moment the chief sight is the **Pirámide de los Mascarones** (Pyramid of the Masks), suggesting a strong Olmec influence, which stands just behind the Gran Plaza and a grove of cohune palms—sacred to the Maya. Its central stairway is flanked by two intricately carved masks which depict the sun god, Kinich Ahau: they are unique in the Yucatán for their prominent features and height of nearly 7 ft.

▶▶ Laguna Bacalar *221C1*

About 25 miles northwest of Chetumal, Highway 307 runs past this brilliant palette of blues, a lake sometimes referred to as the "lagoon of seven colors," the result of a mixture of freshwater and the sea. Visually leaping out of the scrubby jungle, the lagoon's attractions lie in its *balneario* (bathing resort) and the imposing **Fuerte San Felipe Bacalar**, a stone fort erected in 1729 against pirate attacks which now houses a small museum of colonial arms and uniforms (open mornings only). The lake shore is lined with white sands, open-air restaurants and private villas surrounding the *balneario*, a modest structure which livens up considerably on the weekends.

Isla legend
Isla Mujeres' Hacienda Mundaca was built in the early 1800s by the Spanish pirate and slave-trader Fermín Mundaca after he had fallen hopelessly in love with an island girl. Renouncing his lawless occupations he set about creating the hacienda and an impressive tomb, but she spurned him for a younger and poorer island man, much to the chagrin of Mundaca, who spent the rest of his heartbroken days in Mérida where he eventually died. The epitaph on his tombstone touchingly reads: "What I am, you shall be; what you are, I was."

Cultural agenda
Mérida's authorities ensure that tourists are never short of free entertainment. The following are held daily at 9 p.m.
Monday—regional Vaquería with dances and costumes harking back to hacienda days, Palacio Municipal.
Tuesday—1940s big-band music and dance in Parque Santiago, Calle 59 and 72.
Wednesday—string quartet music at the Casa de Artesanías, Calle 63 and 64.
Thursday—lively Yucatán dances and music at the Parque Santa Lucía, Calle 60 and 55.
Friday—students' serenade in the courtyard of the Universidad de Yucatán, Calle 60 and 57.
Saturday—English mass at the Iglesia de Santa Lucía, Calle 60 and 55 at 6 p.m.
Sunday—all-day *fiesta* and street market between the zócalo and Parque Santa Ana.

▶▶▶ Mérida

220B3

Mérida, the capital of the state of Yucatán, with a population approaching one million, makes a relaxed base for exploring the surrounding Mayan ruins and villages, as well as offering plenty of charm and interest itself. Mérida's fortunes changed from those of a decaying Mayan city called T'ho to a grand colonial "white city," which by the early 20th century was the hub of a burgeoning sisal industry, attracting French investors who bequeathed a *belle époque* architectural imprint. Geographically isolated from their compatriots, Mérida's inhabitants had more contact with the U.S., Cuba and Europe, and also attracted Syrian and Lebanese settlers. This independent, cosmopolitan flavor only changed in the 1950s when road and railroad links were finally established with Mexico City.

Historical sights Founded by Francisco de Montejo in 1542, Mérida soon saw the south side of Plaza Mayor lined with the conquistador's residence, the **Casa Montejo▶▶▶** (1549). Until recently this magnificent Plateresque building, with sculpted busts decorating the façade, was still inhabited by descendants of the Montejo family, but is now a branch of Banamex, the National Bank of Mexico. Soon after, Mérida's massive **Catedral▶▶** (1561–98) was built with the stones of dismantled T'ho. The beautifully proportioned interior was stripped during the 1915 Revolution but this gives it a striking purity and reinforces the impact of a 23-ft. statue of Christ. Across the large plaza stands the elegant **Palacio Municipal▶** (1735) and, on the northern flank, the **Palacio de**

One of Mérida's handsome colonial mansions on Paseo de Montejo

Gobierno▶ (1892) whose interior contains 27 murals by Fernando Castro Pacheco depicting the complex history of the Maya, Spaniards and Mexicans.

The main road north from Plaza Mayor, Calle 60, continues the parade of Merida's history at the **Parque Hidalgo**, a favorite social hub dominated by the **Iglesia de la Tercera Orden▶▶** (1618), whose interior contains some lovely frescos. Rising beyond this Jesuit church is the grandiose **Teatro Peón Contreras▶▶** (1900), a wildly ornate building with a Carrara marble staircase, Rococo boxes and a frescoed dome. The city tourist office is located in its southwestern corner. Passing the Universidad de Yucatán, Calle 60 continues to the arcaded **Parque Santa Lucía**, site of a Sunday morning crafts market and a stirring folk dance performance every Thursday evening, before reaching **Parque Santa Ana** four blocks further.

Paseo de Montejo One block east of Parque Santa Ana the broad, tree-lined Paseo de Montejo, Merida's answer to the Champs Elysées, takes off. Built by the wealthy *henequen* (sisal) *hacienda* owners of the late 19th century, the palatial homes and a few modern intrusions are now the focus for Mérida's banks, hotels, nightclubs and restaurants. At the corner of Calle 43 stands the Palacio Cantón, erected between 1909 and 1911 at the behest of the state governor by the Italian architect responsible for the Teatro Peón, which now houses the **Museo de Arqueológico e Historia▶▶**. In an interior of Doric columns and chandeliers, dripping with decorative stuccowork and heaving under marble, the state archaeological collection runs the risk of paling into insignificance. However, it is a clearly laid-out history of the Yucatán, its Mayan sites and culture, juxtaposing panels and photographs with artifacts which include a rare display of carved jade offerings recovered from the *cenote* (sinkhole) of Chichén Itzá.

South of Plaza Mayor Despite Mérida's multitude of itinerant hammock-sellers, a stroll round the sprawling municipal **market** located on Calle 56 and Calle 67 is essential. *Guayaberas* (men's tucked white shirts), *huipils* (embroidered tunics), Panama hats, hammocks of every size and color, baskets, belts, and much more are sold in tiny stalls or rambling stores, in between the chillies, limes, *tamales,* and chickens. For an idea of high-quality handicrafts and fixed prices check out the official **Casa de Artesanías**, located just behind a former convent on Calle 63, between 64 and 66.

Of hammocks...
Compulsory purchases for visitors to the Yucatán are hammocks, and Mérida is by far the best place to buy them. The finely threaded, colorful cotton webs made locally are the coolest way to have a siesta or even to spend the night on the beach, but the quality varies considerably. Make sure you get the right size: *sencillo* (single), *doble* (double), *matrimonial* (large double) or *matrimonial especial* (kingsize). Impress the street vendor by counting the knots at each end—90 should be the minimum and threads should be triple. Recommended is La Poblana, Calle 65 No. 492.

An excellent way to see the sights of Mérida is to take a calesa *(horse-drawn carriage)*

Playa del Carmen is chock-full of beautiful beaches

Yucatecan cuisine
One of the Yucatán's great pleasures, after the tribulations of northern *tortilla* diets, is its imaginative food, partly due to long isolation from the rest of Mexico and close contact with Europe (especially France), New Orleans and Cuba. Common dishes include *sopa de lima,* a delicious chicken broth cooked with shredded chicken, *tortilla* and lime juice; *pollo* or *cochinita pibil,* chicken or pork marinaded in spices and sour orange juice then baked in banana leaves; and *poc-chuc,* pork fillet marinaded in sour orange juice and served with pickled onions. A common ingredient is wild turkey (*pavo*), which can be shredded, wrapped in *tortillas* (*salbutes*), pickled (*escabeche*), or stewed in soups.

►► Playa del Carmen 221D2

Situated opposite the island of Cozumel, Playa del Carmen was for years merely a launching-pad to ferry across to the island. Today it is gaining a name for itself as a small resort town with a grid of pedestrian streets around the jetty area entirely devoted to visitors. Located 43 miles south of Cancún and only 30 minutes by ferry from Cozumel, it attracts day-trippers for its infinitely less sophisticated and still half-built setting. Edged by a palm-lined beach, Playa's sands extend north around a point to a wide, empty beach with clean waters and gentle waves much favored by the topless brigade. Discreet hotels are creeping in here, too. South of the jetty a gigantic new structure of hotel, marina, shops and condominiums may set the tone for the future, but there are still some atmospheric *cabañas (cabins)* along the seafront or tucked away down side-streets. Fishermen work off the beaches and at dusk a fleet of *triciclos* speeds hundreds of crates of fresh eggs to be ferried across to Cozumel for divers' breakfasts. Mellow and fun-loving, its beach bars blasting 1970s rock music and mixing endless *margaritas,* Playa makes an easy and relatively economical stop-off on the Caribbean trail.

► Puerto Morelos 221D3

Just over 18 miles south of Cancún on Highway 307, this small, nondescript fishing village is mainly frequented for its car-ferry service to Cozumel. Escaping the coastal development that continues elsewhere along the Cancún–Tulúm corridor, Puerto Morelos retains a low-key atmosphere with beach-front seafood restaurants, limited accommodation and uncrowded beaches, as well as an enormous offshore reef for snorkelers and divers. Near the highway turn-off leading to Puerto Morelos are the **Palancar Aquarium** with exhibits on all aspects of the area's marine environment, **Croco Cun**, a crocodile farm and, further south, the **Jardín Botánico Dr Alfredo Barrera Marín▶**, a delightful park featuring local flora, a nature trail, and a small archaeological site.

▶ Puerto Progreso *220B3*

Progreso, 20 miles due north of Mérida, is a sprawling port town periodically invaded by Yucatecans looking for sea and seafood. Its main features are a jetty jutting nearly 4 miles out beyond the shallows into the Gulf of Mexico and a gently sloping sandy beach bordering the town. Seafood is prepared in abundance in the cheap open stalls and the pricier, air-conditioned restaurants, and the constant sea breeze makes a welcome change from the heat of the interior. However, the buildings lining its *malecón* are mainly charmless and there is no particular reason to stay here rather than in Mérida—only 20 minutes away by bus. Eat and swim, then head on! Much more attractive beaches lie less than 5 miles west and east, at Chelem and Chicxulub respectively.

▶▶ Punta Bete *221D3*

Isolated from the main "corridor" by a rough 3-mile dirt road winding through tangled jungle and banana palms, Punta Bete makes a scenic getaway only 33 miles south of Cancún. Two-and-a-half miles of palm-fringed sands edged by typically transparent water until recently offered little apart from camping, hammocking or a handful of beach *cabañas* and relaxed *palapa* restaurants. Inevitably, progress now looms on the northern horizon in the shape of a large condo resort.

▶▶ Río Lagartos *221C3*

This swampy lagoon area situated 65 miles north of Valladolid was once a haven for pink flamingos. No longer. The ravages of Hurricane Gilbert are still felt, and many of the 30,000 flamingos that once built their nests here have departed to more welcoming shores (see Celestún on page 227). However, the 89,000-acre wildlife refuge offers plenty of other sights, from spider monkeys to white-tail deer, a rare type of alligator, and 212 different species of birds. Boat trips through the wetlands are easily arranged in the fishing village and can take you as far as Orilla Emal, the flamingos' nesting area between April and July. Other abundant birdlife can be spotted around the lobster-fishing village of San Felipe, 6 miles west, or at Punta Holohit, just across the estuary from Río Lagartos.

Of Panama hats...
These famous hats are woven from *jipijapa* palm leaves. The Yucatán's center of production is at Bécal, a small town on Highway 180, 53 miles south of Mérida. The best-quality hats are the finest in fiber and weave. If made under optimum, humidified conditions, they obtain their springy resilience and can be rolled up, stashed away then reopened to their former glory. Not exactly the ultimate in fashion, but a practical, cool necessity in a Yucatecan wardrobe.

Unilateral ecology
Punta Laguna is a rare exercise in village self-determination. Situated in semi-evergreen forest menaced by logging concerns, the villagers took the initiative and declared their surroundings an ecological reserve. Spider monkeys and an abundant birdlife are what the tiny Maya community is trying to protect, and visitors are welcome to observe them. Contact Serapio Canul in the village, the man responsible for the movement, or the ecology group Pronatura Yucatán in Mérida, which advises the community (tel. 44 22 90).

► Sian Ka'an Biosphere Reserve *221C2*

South of Tulúm and away from the V.W. Beetle car-rental crowds, this vast 1,235,000-acre wildlife reserve stretches south of Tulúm to **Punta Allen**, a lobster-fishing village of limited attraction, and curves around two bays east of Highway 307. Patchy tropical forest, mangrove swamps, grassy savannah and the world's second-longest ocean reef join in a protected environment for the remaining fauna of Quintana Roo—from jaguars and pumas to white-tail deer, crocodiles, howler monkeys and an astonishing 300 species of birds—but you are unlikely to spot any of them from the road. All-day treks, which include a three-hour boat-trip, can be arranged through the Amigos de Sian Ka'an (which in Mayan means "where the sky is born") in Cancún, tel. 84 95 83 or 87 30 80.

►►► Tulúm *221D2*

Magnificently situated, teetering on a craggy cliff overlooking the Caribbean, the walled ruins of Tulúm have become the meeting point between sunworshippers and archaeological enthusiasts. From the clifftop site a path winds down to a perfect beach; other coves dot this stretch of coastline and this makes it a favorite day-tripping target. The approach from Highway 307 leads from the main village east to the coast, where the archaeological site is located, and from here a secondary road hugs the coast as far as Punta Allen.

Thought to have been settled during the post-Classic period (AD900–1500) when Mayan civilization was on the decline, Tulúm was an important trading port and its fortress was still occupied when the Spaniards arrived in 1518. Fortified walls enclose palaces and temples, with the sheer cliff face creating the fourth side. From the entrance, walking towards the Castillo which dominates the cliff edge, you pass the ruins of a small royal palace before arriving at the **Templo de los Frescos**►►► (Temple of the Frescos) to the right. The façade of the former features carved reliefs of the descending god, a

The walled city of Tulúm overlooks the dazzling turquoise waters of the Caribbean from its magnificent clifftop vantage

winged figure plunging earthwards (also depicted at Cobá and thought to be the god of honey), while faded interior murals depicting the three levels of the Mayan universe include one god astride a horse—evidence that the last Mayan inhabitants had already had contact with the conquistadors.

The next complex is that of **El Castillo▶▶▶**, Tulúm's watchtower landmark fronted by serpent columns, which was built in several stages and which can be climbed for superb views seawards and landwards. To the left stands the **Templo del Dios Descendente** (Temple of the Diving or Descending God), decorated with a stucco carving of the god above its entrance and housing mural fragments. Several other ruined structures are dotted around the small site, but its main interest lies in the dramatic coastal setting.

Four-legged myth
One of the reasons for the success of the Spanish conquistadors was their beast of burden—the horse. Completely unknown to the indigenous people, the mere sight of it convinced them of the Spaniards' god-like superiority. Only 16 were brought by Cortés' first expedition, but the vision of mounted soldiers gave rise to a belief that man and animal were firmly one, a mythical four-legged beast with a man's torso.

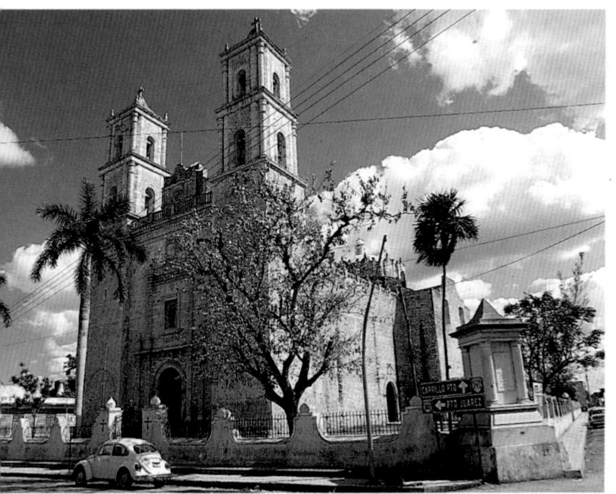

Left: Valladolid's Church of San Bernardino was built by Franciscans

The entrance to Cenote Zací, on the outskirts of Valladolid

▶▶ **Valladolid** *221C2*

Often treated as a halfway stage between Mérida, Chichén Itzá, and Cancún or Tulúm, the town of Valladolid itself merits attention. Founded in the mid-16th century, its aristocratic old center is dotted with Spanish mansions and churches as well as two impressive *cenotes* (wells). Scene of the bloody massacre of its white élite by the Maya during the 1847 War of the Castes, Valladolid now offers a pleasant, provincial atmosphere. Of the many churches, the oldest is the **Iglesia de San Bernardino de Siena▶**, attached to the **Ex-Convento de Sisal**, six blocks west of the zócalo on Calle 41. Built in 1552 and set behind thick fortified walls, it was twice a target for attack by Maya Indians; as a result the church interior is bare apart from a statue of the Virgin of Guadalupe. Of the two *cenotes*, **Dzitnup▶▶▶** is the more beautiful and less visited. Located 4 miles southwest of town, its crystaline waters make one of the peninsula's best freshwater dips. In a cultural park off the town center, the vast **Cenote Zací▶▶** (Calle 36, between 37 and 39), inside a large limestone cave, is a spectacular, stalactite-studded sight, but the algae-coated water is less inviting.

BIENVENIDOS
Al Restaurant Turistico
"CENOTE ZACI"
H. Ayuntamiento 1991-1993
Valladolid, Yuc.
ADULTOS N$ 4.00 Nº 210

The Pyramid of the Magician rises majestically before you as you enter Uxmal

Uxmal's dwarf-king
Legend has it that Uxmal was erected by a dwarf with magical powers. Hatched from the egg of a sorceress, the young boy one day struck a forbidden gong, thus alluding to a prophesy which said that when the gong rang the ruler would be replaced by a boy "not born of woman." The ruler wanted the boy dead but he was offered a reprieve if he could accomplish three seemingly impossible tasks, one of which was building the Pyramid of the Magician in a single night. This he achieved, but the ruler still demanded his execution. After a trial of strength, the ruler was killed and so the dwarf boy came to govern Uxmal.

▶▶▶ Uxmal *220B2*

Meaning "three times built," Uxmal was developed in stages from around AD600, and its fine Puuc architecture (named after the surrounding hills) makes it, in the eyes of some experts, superior to Chichén Itzá, although the layout lacks Chichén's impact. Occupying a broad plateau in the Puuc Hills, 50 miles south of Mérida on Highway 261, Uxmal was at one point one of the largest Mayan cities of the Yucatán with 25,000 inhabitants, but by 900 had been abandoned, either due to drought or the magnetism of Chichén Itzá. First excavated by Frans Blom (of San Cristóbal fame) in 1929, much of the site has now been restored and a museum with tourist facilities stands at the entrance. Sound-and-light shows are held in Spanish at 7 p.m. and in English at 9 p.m.

Main structures The first and largest monument is the **Pirámide del Adivino** (Pyramid of the Magician), a smooth, elliptically-shaped structure which rises 115 ft., offering a steep but rewarding climb. Composed of five successive temples, its western entrance is formed by the mouth of a gigantic mask of Chac, a relic from the fourth temple. Immediately west of the pyramid lies the extraordinary **Cuadránglo de las Monjas** (the Nunnery) whose elaborately crafted inlaid stonework exemplifies pure Puuc tradition but whose original function remains a mystery. Chac reappears constantly on the façades of four multi-roomed edifices facing inwards on to a central courtyard. Intertwined snakes (possibly forerunners of the plumed serpent), jaguars, seated figures and stylized thatched Mayan huts can be distinguished on the façades, while the south building is embellished with a remarkable lattice design and corbelled arches.

To the south, beyond a ball court, lies an elevated complex dominated by the superb 328-ft.-long **Palacio del Gobernador** (Governor's Palace), considered the zenith of the Puuc style. Its upper façade boasts a remarkable frieze of intricate stone mosaic, creating geometric patterns interspersed with over 200 stylized faces of Chac and glyphs of the planet Venus. Arched entrances lead into 24 rooms.

On the northwestern corner of this platform the **Casa de las Tortugas** (House of the Turtles) is adorned with carved turtles whose tears were believed to bring rain

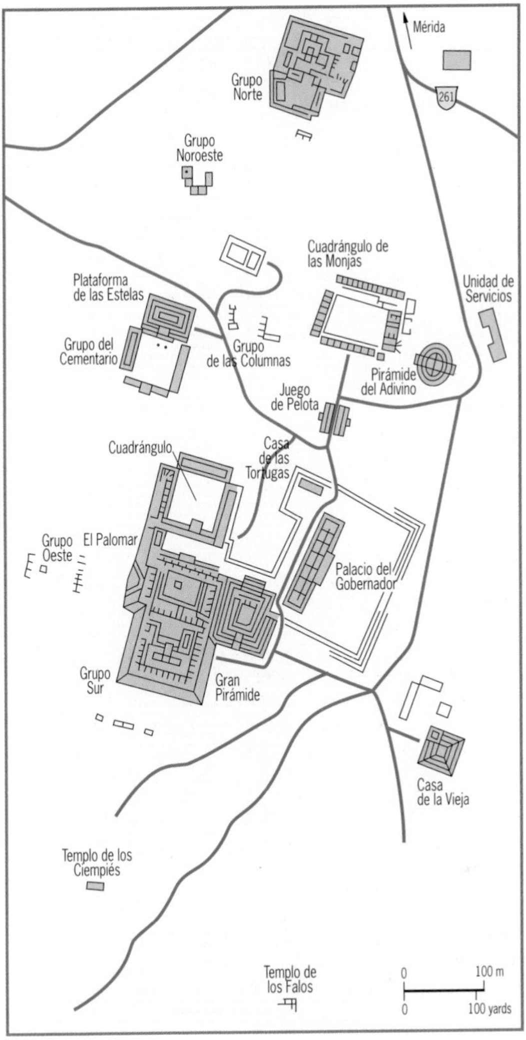

Mérida
261
Grupo Norte
Grupo Noroeste
Cuadrángulo de las Monjas
Plataforma de las Estelas
Unidad de Servicios
Grupo del Cementario
Grupo de las Columnas
Pirámide del Adivino
Juego de Pelota
Cuadrángulo
Casa de las Tortugas
Grupo Oeste
El Palomar
Palacio del Gobernador
Grupo Sur
Gran Pirámide
Casa de la Vieja
Templo de los Ciempiés
Templo de los Falos
0 100 m
0 100 yards

Stephens and Catherwood Images of the Mayan world burst on to public consciousness in the mid-19th century when American archaeologist John Lloyd Stephens and British illustrator Frederick Catherwood published their remarkable *Incidents of Travel*. Their first trip to Central America in 1839 followed in the footsteps of Count de Waldeck to Palenque, but proved such an endurance test of local climate and insects that, when they finally reached Uxmal, they beat a hasty retreat to New York. Eighteen months later they valiantly returned and Catherwood produced his masterpiece, a highly detailed, panoramic drawing of the Governor's Palace.

during periods of drought. On the other side of the palace is the partly excavated **Gran Pirámide** which faces **El Palomar** (The Dovecot), a beautiful, crumbling structure crowned by nine roofcombs.

Other structures From the Governor's Palace, a path leads southwest to two unrestored edifices, the **Casa de la Vieja** (House of the Old Woman) and, further still, the **Templo de los Falos** (Temple of the Phalli). The latter is named after its numerous sculpted phalluses, some of which served as rainwater spouts, which curiously indicate a phallic cult otherwise unknown among the Maya. In the northern section of the site, the **Grupo del Cementerio** (Cemetery Group) is decorated with skulls, a rare reference to death in Uxmal, a factor which sets it firmly apart from militaristic Chichén Itzá.

Masks of the rain god Chac adorn the Pyramid of the Magicians

Drive Puuc Hills

South of Mérida lies the Yucatán's only hilly region, home to picturesque Mayan villages and lesser archaeological sites. For a better insight into today's Mayan traditions it is advisable to spend the night on the way, although most of the route can be covered in a long day.

From **Mérida** drive west out of the center to the traffic circle and follow signs to Campeche on MEX 180. At Umán the road branches: follow MEX 261 to Muna, stopping for a short visit to the 16th-century domed **Church of San Francisco de Asis**. About 8 miles further stands the atmospheric hacienda of **Yaxcopoil**, once an important hemp factory which is still equipped with original family furniture and machinery which functioned as recently as 1987. Drive due south through a flat green landscape hiding a wealth of *cenotes* (sinkholes) to Muna, where the Puuc Hills start.

Follow signs to **Uxmal**, 10 miles farther, one of the largest and best preserved Mayan sites in the peninsula (see pages 248–249) and well

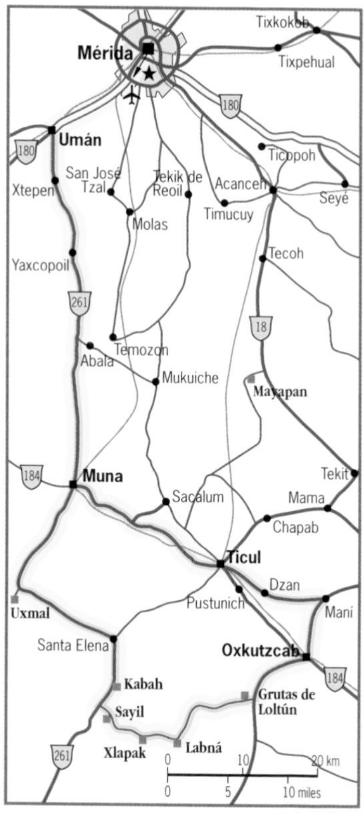

Mérida's colorful market, in the Yucatán

frequented by tourist buses from Mérida. From here the road winds south through **Santa Elena** (known for its hand-embroidery) to the site of **Kabah**, a Mayan ceremonial center whose main structure, the **Codz Pop** (which in Mayan means "rolled straw sleeping-mat"), is adorned with masks of the rain god Chac. The **Casa de la Bruja** and the **Templo de las Columnas** complete the excavated areas to the east of the road, but walk west to see an important arch structure in a vast unexcavated area.

About 3 miles farther south follow the left-hand branch off MEX 261 leading to **Sayil**. Here in a clearing stands an outstanding palace structure on three levels, finely carved in the Puuc style, which once contained 100 rooms. The next archaeological stop, 3 miles farther, is at the small site of **Xlapak** where a relatively modest edifice with carved masks of Chac stands in pretty woods set back from the road. Last on this Puuc loop is **Labná**, 2½ miles beyond, where an elegant arch marks the limits of a ceremonial area once inhabited solely by priests and other high ranks. El Palacio and El Mirador are the most important structures in this complex.

Some 11 miles east along often surprisingly straight roads, lie the fantastic **Grutas de Loltún** (see page 239) which can only be visited with a guide (aim for the 3 p.m. tour). There is also a small restaurant at the caves' site. After a farther, sometimes potholed 6 miles lies the important market town of **Oxkutzcab** (meaning "land rich in turkeys"). The church façade displays an interesting representation of the sun and moon, and inside a valuable altarpiece is flanked by ridged columns. The market, indoors and out, is the center of town activity, full of Mayan women in embroidered *huipiles* (tunics) and the Mayan taxi—the *triciclo*, a form of rickshaw. From here, depending on the time of day, drive to the pretty town of **Mani**, which claims a *cenote* and the 16th-century San Miguel Arcángel with an open-roofed chapel. If time is short take MEX 184 directly to **Ticul** (from behind the market), a small town with hotels and other services, mainly known for its shoe industry. At Muna the road rejoins MEX 261 which leads north to Mérida. If staying overnight at Ticul, return to Mérida through the picturesque Mayan villages of **Chapab**, **Mama**, **Tekit**, **Tecoh** and **Acanceh**.

The Nun's Quadrangle, Uxmal, decorated with carvings of Chac

Diana's bathing-place

"What a cenote was we had no idea ... I came to a large opening in the ground, with a broad flight of more than fifty steps; descending which, I saw unexpectedly a spectacle of extraordinary beauty ... It was a large cavern or grotto, with a roof of broken, overhanging rock, high enough to give an air of wilderness and grandeur, impenetrable at midday to the sun's rays, and at the bottom water pure as crystal, still and deep, resting upon a bed of white limestone rock. It was the very creation of romance; a bathing-place for Diana and her nymphs. Grecian poet never imagined so beautiful a scene."
John Lloyd Stephens: *Incidents of Travel*, 1841.

▶ Xcalak 221C1

End of the world? It is certainly the end of the Yucatán before Belize takes over. At the southern point of a desolate 40-mile peninsula traversed by dirt road, Xcalak is a reminder of what Quintana Roo was before Cancún was thought of. The tiny community exists on water from *cenotes* (sinkholes) and electricity from private generators, its clapboard houses offering nothing of historic interest. However, Xcalak is known to divers for its proximity to the fabulous **Banco Chinchorro▶▶▶**, an island-rimmed reef where the sea floor is littered with wrecks. Diving facilities are provided by a few dive resorts and *cabañas* hotels.

▶ Xcaret 221D2

Forty-five miles south of Cancún, a short distance from Playa del Carmen, this pricey leisure park (open daily 8:30 a.m. to 5 p.m.) has been developed around what was once a Mayan ceremonial center and seaport. Gone are those days, including the days when lone travelers could roll up for a dip in the fabulous *cenote* or snorkel in the beautiful *caleta* (inlet). Today the entire area targets Cancunites, its structured environment announced by a giant fake Maya pyramid on Highway 307. This said, Xcaret's main feature is spectacular: over 1,600 ft. of underground river wind through *cenotes*, caves and tunnels lit by natural light shafts.

▶ Xel-Há 221D2

This natural aquarium is a designated national park (open daily 8 a.m. to 6 p.m.), but being only 6 miles north of Tulúm, its restaurants, gift shops, and cafés are firmly geared towards tourists. Landscaped grounds edge a pretty lagoon which is fed simultaneously by subterranean springs and by the salty Caribbean, thus providing a perfect environment for a fabulous variety of exotic tropical fish. Snorkeling is allowed in specified areas—however, aim to get here early or late to avoid the crowds. Some rather undistinguished ruins lie across the main road, and a small marine museum displays items recovered from off-shore wrecks.

Xel-Há's warm, transparent waters

TRAVEL FACTS

By air Americans can fly direct to the airports at: Acapulco, Cancún, Cozumel, Guadalajara, Huatulco, Ixtapa/Zihuatanejo, Los Cabos, Manzanillo, Mazatlán, Mérida, Mexico City and Puerto Vallarta. To reach the city center take the metro (station: Terminal Aerea) or buy a taxi voucher outside the terminal. Some resort airports (Acapulco, Los Cabos) run collective taxi services (*transporte terrestre*); look for their signs in the arrival terminals. All international airports have car-rental offices and duty-free and money-changing facilities.

By sea Cruise ships regularly stop at Mexico's ports, from Cozumel to Acapulco or Puerto Vallarta: contact travel agents for schedules and itineraries. For ferries between Baja California and the mainland see page 260.

By train There are no direct trains from the U.S. into Mexico. However, Amtrak serves two American border towns, which offer easy on-going connections: from Laredo (Texas) cross to Nuevo Laredo where *The Aztec Eagle* departs every morning (arriving in Mexico City about 25 hours later); from El Paso (Texas) cross to Ciudad Juárez for connections to Chihuahua and beyond. From Mexicali and Nogales there are connections with the main Pacific coast railroad to Guadalajara. For information, contact Ferrocarriles Nacionales de México, Estación Buenavista, Avenida Insurgentes Norte, 06358 México DF, tel. (5) 547 3190/5819).

By car If traveling by car or camper, insure yourself at the border. No other national insurance is valid within Mexico, so sign up with one of the many 24-hour insurance offices at main border towns. Proof of car ownership, current registration documents, and a valid driver's licence are necessary to obtain a 90-day vehicle entry permit (for a small fee). You cannot leave Mexico without the permit, so in case of an accident make sure you have a police report/declaration to show at the border. U.S. and Canadian drivers' licences are recognized, but any other nationality should bring an international

The reservations center at Mexico City's Terminal Norte bus station, which serves the north, the north-east, and the northwest

Cabo San Lucas—a popular Pacific destination for cruise ships

license. Unleaded gas (*magna sin*) is now more readily available in Mexico: look for road signs announcing it.

By bus Some U.S. border towns offer direct service into Mexico, but these cost more than the Mexican buses that start across the border. There are bus connections between Guatemala City and destinations in Chiapas, as well as between Flores and Chetumal (Yucatán peninsula). Frequent buses connect Belize City with Chetumal.

Customs regulations Incoming travelers can bring personal photographic, radio, and sports equipment up to a value of $300, 3 liters of liquor, 200 cigarettes, and unlimited foreign currency. After submitting your customs declaration form you are asked to push a red or green button. If the red light flashes you will be searched.

Travel insurance Buy a travel insurance policy before leaving home. Travel agents usually offer reliable policies.

Visas and tourist cards Citizens of the U.S., Canada, Australia, New Zealand and the U.K. do not need visas. Check with your Mexican embassy for other national requirements. All non-visa holders need a tourist card, issued free of charge at Mexican consulates, airlines, or border towns. This is validated on entry and must be kept throughout your visit to surrender on exit. Tourist cards are issued for 90-or 180-day periods; if including Guatemala and Belize in your itinerary, ask for a multiple-entry card. Visits of less than 72 hours to border towns and the north of Baja California do not require tourist cards.

Passports U.S. citizens need a passport to enter Mexico for stays up to three months. You may renew your passport in person or by mail. First-time applicants must apply in person at least five weeks before departure; applications are accepted at the 13 U.S. Passport Agency offices and at county courthouses, many state and probate courts, and some post offices. You'll need a completed passport application; proof of citizenship; proof of identity (e.g., a valid driver's license;) two recent, identical, 2-inch-square photographs; and $65 in check, money order, or cash for a 10-year passport ($40 for a five-year passport, issued to those under 18). Passports are mailed 10-15 business days from receipt of application. Contact Department of State Office of Passport Services (tel. 202/647–0518) for specifics.

Departing Tourists must surrender their cards and vehicle permits on leaving Mexico—do not overstay your time limit. An airport tax (payable in US $ or *pesos*) is required from air passengers.

Climate
Mexico's climate is as diverse as its many latitudes and altitudes. Generally, the rainy season lasts from June to October, peaking in July and August, although Baja California has more rain during the winter months and flash-floods all year.

In the central highlands and plateaus the climate is temperate, while the arid northern plains experience extremes of stifling hot summers and cool winters.

Move toward the Pacific, Gulf and Yucatán coasts and you enter tropical zones, where temperatures and humidity are high and summer rains diluvial.

Complete contrasts can be found in the northwest Sierra Tarahumara and the Chiapas highlands of the south, where it remains cool and damp except in late spring. A final factor is the coastal hurricane season, which starts in June but favors September.

The best time to visit is in the dry season, November to May, when you should encounter pleasant temperatures in most areas.

National holidays
Mexico's public holidays are legion, but minimal in comparison to countless local *fiestas*. The following are celebrated nationally:

January 1	**New Year's Day**
January 6	**Epiphany (Day of the Three Kings)**
February 5	**Constitution Day**
March 21	**Benito Juárez Day**
March/April	**Easter (Maundy Thursday, Good Friday, Easter Sunday)**
May 1	**Labor Day**
May 5	**Battle of Puebla**
September 16	**Independence Day**
October 12	**Day of the Race (Columbus Day)**
November 2	**All Saints Day (Day of the Dead)**
November 20	**Revolution Day**
December 12	**Festival of the Virgin of Guadalupe**
December 25	**Christmas Day**

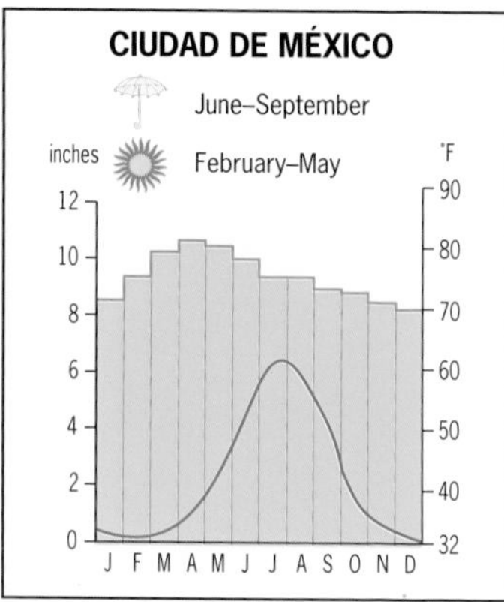

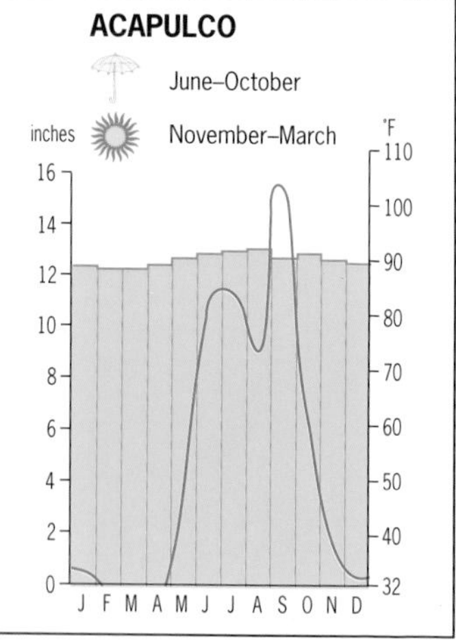

Time differences
Most of Mexico runs on Central Standard Time. The northern states of Sinaloa, Sonora, Baja California Sur, and parts of Nayarit are on Mountain Standard Time, while Baja California Norte is the same as U.S. Pacific Standard Time. In line with California and British Columbia, this region also observes Daylight Saving's Time in summer.

Opening times
Time is a Mexican hang-up. Whatever the clichés, things are improving and travelers can rely on archaeological sites being open daily from 8 a.m. to 5 p.m. National museums close on Mondays and usually Sunday afternoons. Their hours are generally 9 a.m. to 6 p.m., with closures for

siesta usually from 2 to 4 p.m., although these are being abandoned, particularly in major towns.

Government offices are open Monday to Friday 8 a.m. to 2 p.m., banks 9 a.m. to 1:30 p.m. and post offices 8 a.m. to 6 p.m. Shops open 9 a.m. to 8 p.m. Monday to Saturday, with siestas from 2 to 4 p.m. outside Mexico City.

Money matters
Mexico's currency is the *peso*, divided into 100 *centavos*. Since devaluation in January 1993 new coins and notes marked *nuevo peso* (new *peso*) are in circulation, but you may still encounter old currency with three extra zeros (e.g., 100,000 old *pesos* are now worth 100 new *pesos*). The new *peso* is written as N$, but beware of certain large resorts where prices may be posted in U.S.$—written $. Coins are in denominations ranging from 5¢ to N$10, and bills N$10 to N$100: always hoard small change for taxis, buses, and tips.

Foreign currency and travelers' checks can be changed at banks, but this can often take a long time. Rates offered by *casas de cambio* (exchange bureaus, open Mon. to Sat. 9 a.m. to 5 p.m.) in large towns are generally equivalent to banks, so use them whenever possible. Hotels and tourist stores offer the worst rates.

Credit cards are widely accepted in mid- to top-range restaurants and hotels: make sure you fill in the *propina* (tip) and "total" sections on the voucher to avoid subsequent surprises! Cash can be withdrawn with MasterCard and Visa at automatic teller machines outside Banamex and Bancomer banks.

Tips are generally expected in hotels and restaurants—from N$5 for a porter to 15 percent for waiters. Taxi drivers do not expect tips, unless they have been particularly helpful in some way.

Mexican pesos*—old and new*

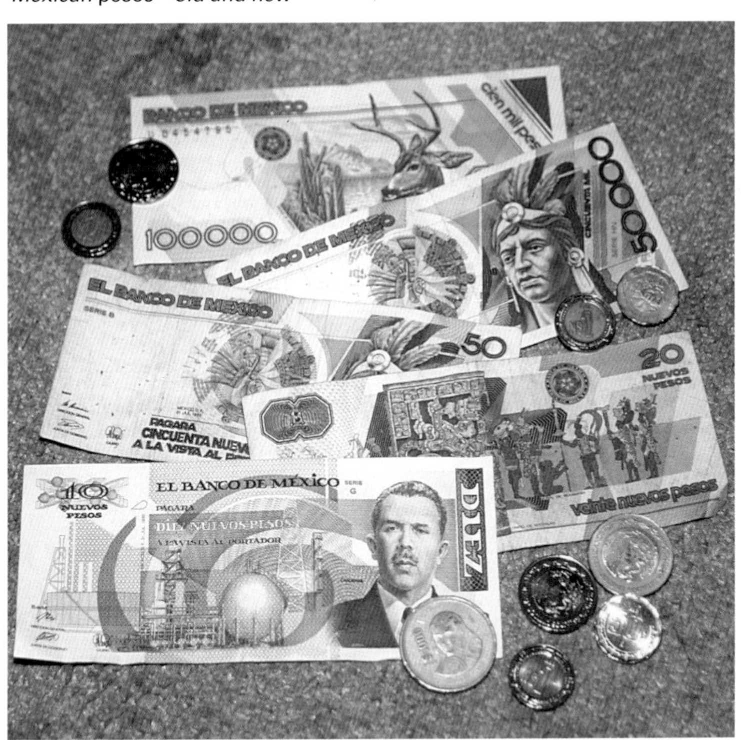

Public transportation

Air Price wars are heating up between Aeromexico, Mexicana and Taesa, all now private companies juggling for the domestic market. Travel agents are well informed about special offers and will generally find you the best deal. Subsidiary airlines operate short-hop flights: the south is covered by Aerocaribe and Aviacsa, the center by Aeromar and Aeromorelos, and the north by Aerocalifornia and Aerolitoral. For longer flights Aeromexico remains the most reliable and generally most expensive, operating 40 domestic routes. Prices fluctuate considerably, depending on the opposition, but Mexicana offers good deals on routes such as the Maya archaeology trail or colonial cities if reserved outside Mexico. An airport tax is charged for every flight: this is added to tickets bought in Mexico but not necessarily to those bought abroad.

Buses By far the best way of getting around most regions economically is by bus. Mexico has over 700 companies that offer a bewildering choice of routes and schedules, making time spent in the *Central Camionera* (bus terminal) an integral part of your journey. Prices, classes of bus, and schedules are posted behind each bus-company counter: it is up to you to compare and choose. Bus stations are increasingly modern and efficient: all have baggage check facilities, rest rooms, snack bars, stores and international telephone call facilities. As they are often on the distant outskirts of town, check onward bus schedules when you arrive. In some cases there is no *Central Camionera,* so you need to trek around scattered terminals or make phone inquiries.

Avoid *segunda* (2nd-class) buses except for short trips; they can be bone-shaking and crowded, and they make frequent stops. *Primera* (first-class) buses are the standard, reliable, and economical way of covering hundreds of miles in relative comfort. All have air-conditioning, a rest room, videos, and sometimes drinks. *Directo* first-class buses make very few stops. Luggage is usually checked into the outside lockers—keep the receipt to collect it on reaching your destination, and keep your valuables on you.

At the top of the league are the luxury buses (*de lujo*), which compete with airlines for comfort: plush reclining seats, hostesses, in-"flight" magazines, snacks, complimentary drinks, and videos all boost the price to almost twice that of first-class. Bus services deteriorate rapidly in comfort and frequency the farther south you go. For any trip over five or six hours, reserve a day or so in advance—refunds are made for cancelations made at least three hours before departure.

Trains Some 15,000 miles of railroad connect Mexico's major cities, but this is not a popular method of traveling. Trains are slow and not particularly safe, and are only worth while for long overnight journeys in sleeping-cars (Mexico City to Veracruz, Oaxaca, Guadalajara, Zacatecas, Nuevo Laredo, or Monterrey).

Trains in the south (Chiapas and Yucatán) are notorious for thefts and delays and are best avoided. *Segunda clase* (second-class) is often dirty, dangerous, and uncomfortable; *primera general* (regular first-class) is one step up and sometimes air-conditioned. At the top, *primera especial* offers reserved reclining seats, air-conditioning, and relative security. Sleeping-car supplements are charged on top of the first-class ticket (obligatory reservations) and can be for a *camarín* (small private berth with basin and toilet), the roomier *alcoba* (for up to four adults), or a simple curtained-off bunk (*cama*). Tickets can be purchased in Mexico City at the Estación Buenavista from 7 a.m. to 9:30 p.m., tel. (5) 547 3190/5819.

Taxis Every city has its own system, but the only place you are likely to see a meter is in Mexico City. Elsewhere you must establish the fare beforehand; short town trips are generally cheap, but journeys to airports can be steep. For any out-of-town destination check on *colectivos*

Train travel is the cheapest form of transportation in Mexico, but it is often slow and unreliable

(often V.W. vans seating up to 14 people plus the occasional animal), which cover set routes, usually scrawled in white paint on their windshields. Modest fares are set for each route, and ground is covered much faster than in a normal urban bus.

If you want a taxi ask for the nearest sitio *(cab stand)*

Ferries Three car ferries ply the Mar de Cortés between Baja California and Mexico's west coast. All are operated by SEMATUR (Paseo de la Reforma 509, Mexico City, tel. (553) 7957), which will supply schedules and prices. Daily overnight services run between Mazatlán and La Paz with first-class (private cabin and bath), salon and tourist classes. In Mazatlán contact the ferry terminal, tel. (69) 817020; in La Paz tel. (682) 53833. Between Guaymas and Santa Rosalía ferries leave at 8 a.m. and arrive at 3 p.m. in both directions: tourist and salon classes are available. Contact the Muelle Fiscal in Guaymas, tel. (622) 23390 and in Santa Rosalía, tel. (685) 20014. The Topolobampo–La Paz route leaves La Paz daily at 8 p.m., arriving at 6 a.m.; from Topolobampo it leaves at 10 a.m. and arrives at 6 p.m. In Topolobampo (Los Mochis) contact the Muelle Fiscal, tel. (686) 20141, in La Paz tel. (682) 53833. On the Caribbean coast there are frequent ferries to Cozumel from Puerto Morelos or Playa del Carmen, and to Isla Mujeres from Puerto Juárez or Punta Sam.

Car rental

The only way to get around some of Mexico's more obscure and more rewarding places is with your own four wheels. Unfortunately car rental costs are very high everywhere except in the Yucatán, where competition and demand keep rates reasonable. Special offers occasionally crop up, and it is always worth bargaining (try reducing their monstrous drop-off rates, for example). Very often it is more advantageous to reserve and pay for car rental through your travel agent. The basic V.W. beetle is excellent for rough terrain and heavy rain, as it is high off the ground and remarkably resilient. Before accepting a car, check the lights, windows, brakes, windshield-wipers, spare tire and tools, and make sure every existing dent is noted on the contract. All you need is to be over 25, have a valid driver's license and a major credit card.

Mexico City head offices of international car-rental companies with branches all over Mexico include:
Budget, Atenas 40, tel. 5 566 6800; toll-free: 91 800 70017.
Dollar Rent-a-Car, Avenida Chapultepec 322, tel. 207 3838/208 0473; toll-free: 91 800 90010.
Hertz, Versalles 6, tel. 5 566 0099; toll-free: 91 800 70016.
National, Marsella 48, tel. 5 533 0375; toll-free: 91 800 90186.

In Mérida good rates are offered by:
Better Car Rental, Calle 57, No. 491, tel. 239648.
Mexico Rent-a-Car, Calle 62 No 483E, tel. 274916/233637.

In Baja California:
Amca, Calle Madero 1715, La Paz, tel. 682/30335 (US toll-free: 800/832 –9529).

Driving tips

Driving in Mexico requires constant alertness, as dangers come from the road itself (cavernous potholes) or unexpected hazards—drunks and cattle figure prominently. Night driving supplements these with unlit breakdowns, oncoming vehicles without headlights, and invisible pedestrians or bicycles. In poorer, rural regions there is also the threat of *bandidos* (bandits) who favor the cloak of darkness.

Never stop unless you are confronted with what seems a genuine accident: in this case do not touch any injured passengers as you may be liable for prosecution. Instead, drive straight to the nearest police station to report the accident.

Another Mexican specialty to watch out for are the ubiquitous *topes* or *vibradores* (sleeping policemen) that are strategically laid across the road before every village or town and impose radically reduced speeds. Very "awake" policemen make occasional spot-checks: be polite and produce all the car documents plus your passport. If for some reason a fine is demanded ask for a receipt (*recibo*): if this is not forthcoming a little *mordida* (unofficial tip) may speed you on your way.

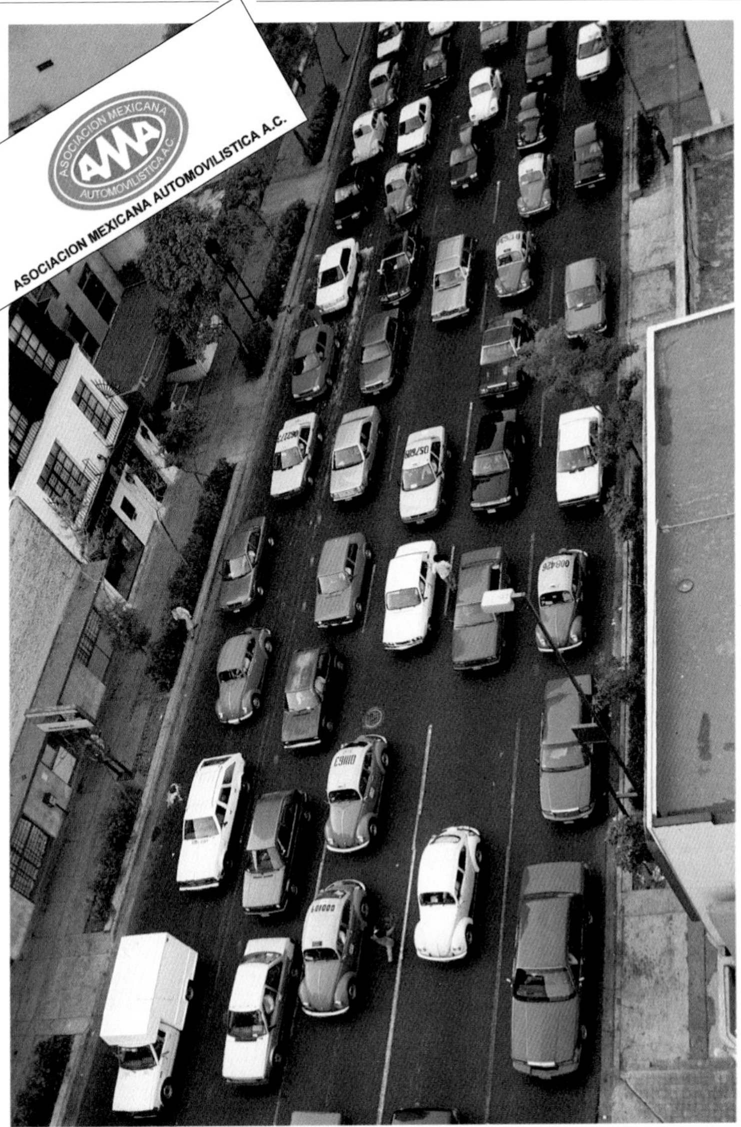

Driving in Mexico City is not recommended. Fortunately the city is well provided with public transportation

Avoid street parking at night: always use locked hotel or private lots.
On a brighter note, Mexico possesses a unique road service, the Green Angels (*Angeles Verdes*), who patrol major highways in search of stranded tourists. Manned by English-speaking mechanics, this service can provide emergency assistance, administer first aid and carry spare parts, gas, and oil charged at cost price.

Student and youth travel
There is little available in the way of student discounts for those not enrolled in a Mexican educational institution. Domestic flights offer 33 percent reductions for children under 12.

Newspapers Mexico has a burgeoning local and national press as well as its own English-language daily, the *Mexico City News*. This is published in the capital and distributed in other major cities (where its price rises considerably). News coverage is U.S. oriented, but it includes good articles on Mexican affairs as well as useful listings for the capital's cultural activities. *The New York Times*, *USA Today*, and the *International Herald Tribune* are available in large cities, but Europeans will only find a limited choice (branches of Sanborn's carry the best selection). Of the many national dailies, *El Tiempo* and *Excelsior* offer mainstream news and opinions, *El Financiero* business news, while *La Jornada* represents a more independent left-wing intellectual viewpoint.

Television and radio Despite the extreme poverty of the majority of the population, 60 percent possess a TV. Targeting this mass audience, Televisa's four channels churn out vacuous entertainment including the seemingly endless *telenovelas* (soap operas). Televisa also rebroadcasts American channels (NBC, CBS, ABC, etc.) by cable and owns the powerful Spanish International Network in the U.S. All large hotels have satellite television.

Radio stations are privately owned and generally operate on a regional basis. Mexico City's Radio XEVIP (AM 1560) broadcasts in English all day, and major resort towns always include a few hours of English-language programs. American radio stations can be picked up on AM in some regions, while BBC World Service can be found on 11.75 MHz.

Post offices Although no longer functioning by mule-back, the Mexican postal service is notoriously slow, but it is reasonably reliable. Allow at least 10 days for airmail post to the U.S., and three flexible weeks for Europe. Always mail letters at a central post office (*agencia de correo*). For anything vital use a private courier service (DHL, Federal Express, etc.) or Mexpost, which operates from within post offices. Stamps can also be bought at hotels. Mailboxes *(buzones)* are mainly yellow.

Telephone and fax At last in the throes of modernization, the newly privately owned (rather than state-run) Mexican phone service (Telmex) is confusing to say the least, and requires much patience at times. Several different pay-phone systems are in operation (using old or new coins) and you are lucky if you find a phone that functions with your available coins or phone card (*tarjeta de teléfono*).

Some new Ladatel phones function with international credit cards. Ladatel (*larga distancia*/long-distance) booths are found in bus stations, airports, railroad stations, and city centers, and offer direct-dial service worldwide.

International and long-distance calls are phenomenally expensive and should be avoided in hotels: surcharges and taxes are added on. Calls are discounted outside business hours, but the cheapest method is, of course, a collect call (*llamada por cobrar)* made through the operator.

Prefixes: 91 for long-distance calls in Mexico; 92 for Mexican long-distance person-to-person or collect; 95 for U.S. and Canada; 96 U.S. and Canada person-to-person and collect; 98 for other international calls; 99 for other international calls person-to-person and collect.

Fax machines are easy to find in most public places (post offices, bus stations, airports) as well as in private fax offices in all towns. Charges are slightly higher than telephone calls.

Which way out? A few words of Spanish are useful

Language

It will make a vast difference to your visit if you can speak some Spanish. In resort towns, English is widely spoken, but the moment you enter small-town Mexico it is essential, and only courteous, to communicate in Spanish, however limited. These are a few basic phrases to survive:

buenos días	good morning
buenas tardes	good afternoon
buenas noches	good evening/ night
adíos	goodbye
(muchas) gracias	thank you (very much)
por favor	please
si/no	yes/no
perdone	sorry/excuse me
como está/están?	how are you? (singular/plural)
muy bien gracias	very well thank you
cuánto vale ...?	how much is ...?
quiero /quisiera	I want/I would like
tiene ...?	do you have...?
hay ...?	is/are there ...?
no entiendo	I don't under stand
habla inglés?	do you speak English?
no hablo español	I don't speak Spanish
dónde está ...?	where is ...?
el central camionera	bus station
la gasolinera	gas station
el sanitario	bathroom
la taquilla	ticket office
la casa de cambio	money exchange office
á qué distancia está ...?	how far is ...?
cuánto tiempo se necesita?	how long does it take?
tiene un cuarto sencillo/doble?	do you have a single/double room?
con baño	with bathroom
con cama matri monial	with a double bed
con dos camas	with twin beds
con aire acondicion-ado	with air-conditioning
con ventilador	with fan
puede hacer un descuento?	can you make a discount?
qué hora es?	what time is it?
hoy	today
mañana	tomorrow
mañana por la mañana	tomorrow morning
por la tarde	in the afternoon
por la noche	in the evening
me voy ...	I'm leaving ...
salida	exit

Crime and police

As in most countries, care should be taken on crowded public transportation and in markets, Mexico City being the worst spot. Always stay vigilant, don't flaunt cameras, jewelry, etc., avoid carrying large amounts of money, and never leave your car parked overnight on the street.

Pickpocketing is the most common crime that affects visitors, although in the south knife attacks have been known: be careful about walking in remote areas, and stick to central and well-lit places for walking in the evenings.

Mexican police are not known for their helpfulness and have a penchant for *mordidas* (small bribes), so unless you need a theft report for insurance purposes, there is little point in contacting them. Drugs, although widely cultivated, are illegal, so should be given a wide berth.

Embassies and consulates

- **Australia:** Plaza Polanco Torre B, Jaime Balmes 11, Colonia de los Morales, 11510 México DF (tel. (5) 395 9469/9988)
- **Canada:** Avenida Schiller 529, Colonia Polanco,11550 México DF (tel. (5) 254 3288)
- **New Zealand:** Homero 229, 8th floor, 11570 México DF (tel. (5) 250 5999)
- **U.K.:** Río Lerma 71, Colonia Cuauhtémoc, 06500 México DF (tel. (5) 207 2089/2149)
- **U.S.:** Paseo de la Reforma 305, 06500 México DF (tel. (5) 211 0042).

The U.S. State Department operates a Citizens' Emergency hot line for information on health, political unrest, or for locating travelers abroad in emergencies: tel. (202) 647–5225.

Emergency phone numbers

Police 06
Fire department (5) 768 3700
Ambulance (5) 588 5100
Emergency information 07
***Angeles Verdes* (Green Angels tourist patrol)** (5) 250 8221
Highway patrol (5) 684 2142
24-hour tourist hot line (5) 250 0123/0151
Tourist harassment/complaints (5) 250 0493
Missing persons (5) 658 1111
American British Cowdray Hospital (ABC), for emergencies (5) 515 8359

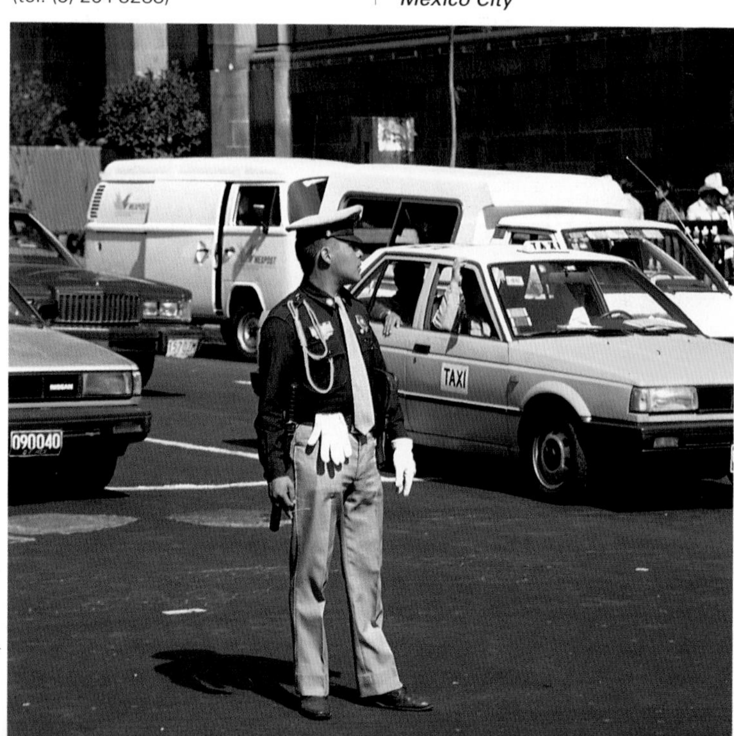

Traffic cop on duty, Mexico City

Lost property
If you lose essential items such as a passport or travelers' checks, report them to your embassy and to the issuing bank (always keep check numbers separate). Other losses—cameras, etc.—can be reported to the local police station for insurance purposes, but you will need to speak good Spanish. If lost items are returned to you it is common courtesy to give a token reward.

Vaccinations, health, and pharmacies
Vaccinations There are no health requirements for entering Mexico unless you have been in a yellow fever or cholera-infected country, in which case you need proof of these inoculations. Make sure your typhoid, polio, and tetanus vaccinations are up to date. Cholera shots are no longer effective. A new vaccination against Hepatitis A (Havrix) replaces the old gamma-globulin: this requires two injections over two weeks' time before departure, followed by two boosters a year later.

Health hazards Mexico's main health hazards come from its polluted water: never drink tap water (unless in upscale hotels, which have their own filtering systems), and in restaurants or street stalls always stick to *agua mineral/purificada*. Ice cubes should be avoided unless made from *agua purificada* (purified water), which is luckily becoming increasingly common.

Much is said about *turista*, also poetically known as "Montezuma's Revenge" or more universally as diarrhea, but this need not be inevitable. Don't eat fruit, salads, or uncooked vegetables that are not peelable, and avoid *ceviche* (marinated raw fish) in dubious places. A tip to remember that many long-term residents swear by, is to make liberal use of the lime slices served with most dishes—apparently effective deterrents against bacteria. If you do undergo the dreaded Aztec revenge, drink lots of fluids (water with squeezed lime, weak tea, and even Coca Cola) and only eat dry toast and bananas until it clears.

Malaria is not a major danger in Mexico, but if you intend to trek through southern rain forests it is advisable to take preventative treatment. Mosquitoes are omnipresent throughout the country, and a good repellent is essential.

Dehydration and sunburn are the least obvious hazards but can be debilitating: the Mexican sun is powerful and precautions should be taken. Always drink plenty of non-alcoholic liquids and use sun-blocks at least for the first few days. When visiting archaeological sites take a large bottle of *agua purificada* and wear a hat.

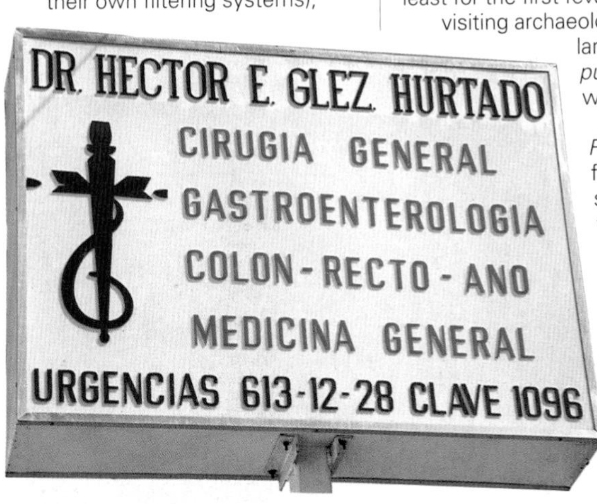

Pharmacies *Farmacias* can be found in every small town and will supply all basic medication. Many prescription items are sold over the counter here.

Every town has a clinic or hospital for emergency treatment, but doctors vary considerably in their expertise. For anything serious contact your embassy, which will put you in touch with a reliable, English-speaking doctor.

Camping

Organized campsites are rare in Mexico, but no permits are required for camping in nature parks or on beaches. Be careful of where you pitch your tent in terms of safety: it could be an easy target for thieves. Trailer parks are abundant in Baja California and down the Pacific coast and, although not the most picturesque of settings, offer safe, low-cost havens with facilities.

Visitors with disabilities

Mexico is not particularly geared to travelers with disabilities. In some cases modern, upscale hotels are adapted for their needs. Inbound tour operators, such as Grey Line Tours, can provide services on request, but otherwise facilities are very limited. An exception is Guadalajara where the revamped city center abounds with ramps; your own transportation remains an absolute necessity.

Places of worship

There is obviously no shortage of Catholic churches with regular daily masses in Spanish. Services in English are only held in cosmopolitan cities such as Mexico City, Guadalajara, Cuernavaca, Acapulco, and Monterrey. The *Mexico City News* lists times of services in its Friday edition. The following offer English-language services in the capital:

- Beth Israel Synagogue, Boulevard Virreyes 1140, Lomas de Virreyes.
- Capital City Baptist Church, Bondojito and Calle Sur 138, Las Americas.
- Christ Church Episcopal, Montes Escandinavos 405, Lomas de Chapultepec.
- Christian Science Church, Dante 21, Colonia Anzures.
- Lutheran Church, Palmas 1910, Lomas Barrilaco.
- St. Patrick's Roman Catholic Church, Bondojito 248, Tacubaya.
- Union Evangelical Church (interdenominational), Reforma 1870, Lomas de Chapultepec.

CONVERSION CHARTS

FROM	TO	MULTIPLY BY
Inches	Centimeters	2.54
Centimeters	Inches	0.3937
Feet	Meters	0.3048
Meters	Feet	3.2810
Yards	Meters	0.9144
Meters	Yards	1.0940
Miles	Kilometers	1.6090
Kilometers	Miles	0.6214
Acres	Hectares	0.4047
Hectares	Acres	2.4710
Gallons	Liters	4.5460
Liters	Gallons	0.2200
Ounces	Grams	28.35
Grams	Ounces	0.0353
Pounds	Grams	453.6
Grams	Pounds	0.0022
Pounds	Kilograms	0.4536
Kilograms	Pounds	2.205
Tons	Tonnes	1.0160
Tonnes	Tons	0.9842

MEN'S SUITS

U.K.	36	38	40	42	44	46	48
Rest of Europe	46	48	50	52	54	56	58
U.S.	36	38	40	42	44	46	48

DRESS SIZES

U.K.	8	10	12	14	16	18
France	36	38	40	42	44	46
Italy	38	40	42	44	46	48
Rest of Europe	34	36	38	40	42	44
U.S.	6	8	10	12	14	16

MEN'S SHIRTS

U.K.	14	14.5	15	15.5	16	16.5	17
Rest of Europe	36	37	38	39/40	41	42	43
U.S.	14	14.5	15	15.5	16	16.5	17

MEN'S SHOES

U.K.	7	7.5	8.5	9.5	10.5	11
Rest of Europe	41	42	43	44	45	46
U.S.	8	8.5	9.5	10.5	11.5	12

WOMEN'S SHOES

U.K.	4.5	5	5.5	6	6.5	7
Rest of Europe	38	38	39	39	40	41
U.S.	6	6.5	7	7.5	8	8.5

Toilets
Public toilets (variously described as *baños, sanitarios* or *servicios*) can be found in all restaurants, bus stations, airports, large archaeological sites, and—usually the cleanest—in museums. Keep your own supply of paper and follow signs for *damas* (women) or *caballeros* (men).

Photography
Color film is easily obtainable in camera shops, pharmacies, and hotels all over the country, but slide film is harder to find and there is rarely a choice of ASA or make. Prices are significantly higher than in the U.S. and slightly more than in Europe, so if you're an avid photographer it's worth bringing rolls of your preferred film with you. When buying film in Mexico, always check the expiration date. If your trip involves several domestic flights, carry exposed and unexposed film separately to avoid excessive passages through X-ray security machines.

Electricity
110 volts, 60 cycles AC. From Europe you will need an adaptor for two-prong flat plugs, U.S.-style.

Etiquette and local customs
Mexicans are, on the whole, a formal, conservative people, generally courteous and helpful. *Para servirle* (at your service) is a little phrase that will follow you around whenever you utter *gracias,* even if the next most common phrase is *ahorita* (meaning "in a short while" but not necessarily the case). The most sensitive area in terms of etiquette is in churches: don't interrupt worshippers and show respect in the way you dress (no shorts or miniskirts). When a sign says "no flash," observe it and if, as in the churches of the Chiapas Highlands, photography is forbidden, observe that too. Indians are not always happy about being photographed, so be sensitive to their feelings, respect their dignity, and ask first. Topless bathing is unheard of except on specific Yucatán and Oaxacan beaches, and care should be taken even in seemingly deserted areas.

Women travelers
Women traveling alone in Mexico will find traditionally *macho* Mexicans ever ready to help out, not always welcome but sometimes useful in explaining the complexities of internal travel. Needless to say, the younger you are the more attention you get, and it is always advisable to have some command of Spanish in order to avoid difficult situations.

Precautions
Attacks on tourists (both male and female) do happen and great care should be taken before embarking on any solitary rural walks or treks. It goes without saying that nocturnal wandering in large cities is not a good idea.

Outside Mexico

Canada
Montreal: 1 Place Ville Marie, Suite 2409, Montreal, Quebec H3B 3M9, tel. (514) 871–1052.
Toronto: 2 Bloor Street W, Suite 1801, Toronto, Ontario M5H 3M7, tel. (416) 925–0704/1876.
Vancouver: 999 West Hastings, Suite 1610, Vancouver BC, V6 C2 W2, tel. (604) 669–2845.

U.K.
60–1 Trafalgar Square, London WC2N 5DS, tel. (0171) 734–1058.

U.S.
Chicago: 70 E Lake Street, Suite 1413, Chicago, IL 60601, tel. (312) 565–2778.
Houston: 2707 North Loop West, Suite 450, Houston, TX 77008, tel. (713) 880–5153.
Los Angeles: 10100 Santa Monica Boulevard, Suite 224, Los Angeles, CA 90067, tel. (213) 203–8191.
New York: 405 Park Avenue, Suite 1402, New York, NY 10022, tel. (212) 755–7261.
Washington D.C.: 1911 Pennsylvania Avenue N.W., Washington D.C. 20006, tel. (202) 728–1750.

State tourist offices

Aguascalientes: Palacio de Gobierno, 20000 Aguascalientes (tel. 49 164286).
Baja California Norte: Edificio Plaza Patria, 3rd Floor, Boulevard Díaz Ordáz s/n, 22000 Tijuana (tel. 66 819492).
Baja California Sur: Carretera Norte Km 5, Edificio Fidepaz, 23000 La Paz (tel. 112 21190).
Campeche: Avenida Ruíz Cortines 61, 24000 Campeche (tel. 981 66767).
Chiapas: Boulevard Belisario Domínguez 950, 29000 Tuxtla Gutiérrez (tel. 961 24535/25509).
Chihuahua: Calle Libertad 1300, 1st Floor, CP 31000 Chihuahua (tel. 14 162436).
Coahuila: Boulevard Los Fundadores Km 6.5, Centro de Convenciones, 25000 Saltillo (tel. 84 300510/ 300695).
Colima: Portal Hidalgo 20, 28200 Manzanillo (tel. 331 24360).
Distrito Federal: Amberes 54, 06600 México DF (tel. 5 5334700).
Durango: Hidalgo 408 Sur, 34000 Durango (tel. 181 12139).
Guanajuato: Plaza de la Paz 14, 36000 Guanajuato (tel. 473 20086/21574).
Guerrero: Costera Miguel Alemán 4455, 35359 Acapulco (tel. 74 843780).
Hidalgo: Carr México-Pachuca Km 93.5, 42000 Pachuca (tel. 771 41150).
Jalisco: Morelos 102 Plaza Tapatía, 44100 Guadalajara (tel. 3 6131196).
Michoacán: Nigromante 79 Palacio Clavijero, 58000 Morelia (tel. 43 128081).
Morelos: Avenida Morelos Sur 802, 62050 Cuernavaca (tel. 73 143872).
Nayarit: Avenida México 34 Sur, 63000 Tepic (tel. 321 29545).
Nuevo León: Zaragoza 1300 Sur, Edificio Kalos Nivel A-1, 64000 Monterrey (tel. 83 444343).
Oaxaca: Independencia esq García Vigil, 68000 Oaxaca (tel. 951 67700).
Puebla: 5 Oriente 3, 72000 Puebla (tel. 22 461285).
Querétaro: Avenida Constituyentes 102, 76000 Querétaro (tel. 42 138512).
Quintana Roo: Palacio de Gobierno, 77000 Chetumal (tel. 983 20855).
San Luis Potosí: V Carranza 325, 78000 San Luis Potosí (tel. 48 129906).
Sinaloa: Paseo Olas Altas 1300, 82000 Mazatlán (tel. 69 851847).
Sonora: Tehuantepec y Comonfort Palacio Administrativo, 83000 Hermosillo (tel. 62 170076).
Tabasco: Edificio Administrativo, 86000 Villahermosa (tel. 93 163633).
Tamaulipas: 16 Rosales 272, 87000 Ciudad Victoria (tel. 131 21057).
Tlaxcala: Avenida Juárez esq Lardizabal 18, 90000 Tlaxcala (tel. 241 20027).
Veracruz: Avenida M Avila Camacho 191, 91000 Jalapa (tel. 281 87402).
Yucatán: Calle 59 No 514 X 62 y 64, 97000 Mérida (tel. 99 248013).
Zacatecas: Prol G Ortega Edificio Marzes s/n, 98600 Zacatecas (tel. 492 40552).

HOTELS AND RESTAURANTS

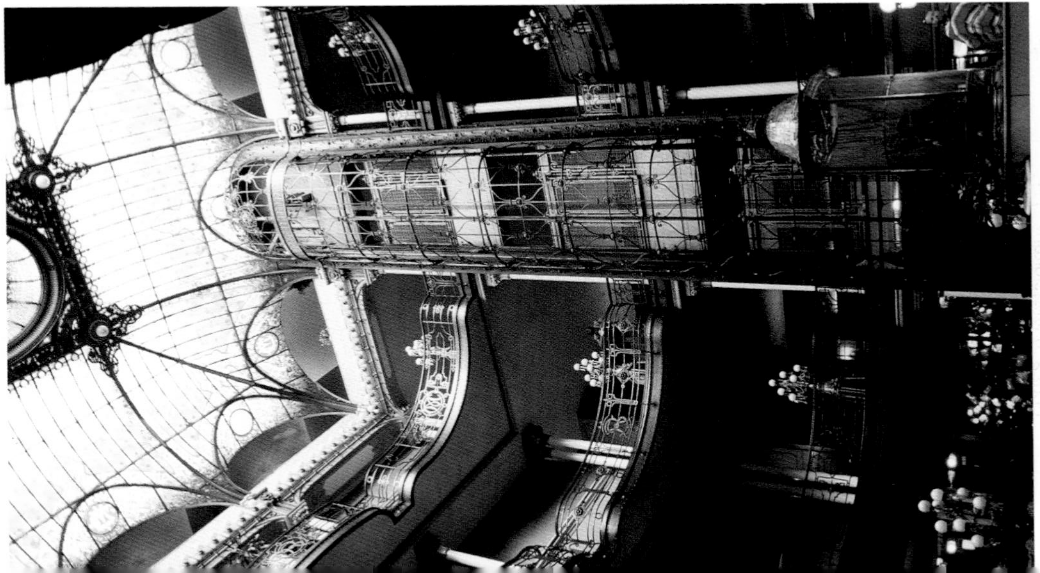

The hotels listed below have been been divided into three price categories:
- budget ($): simple adequate hotels within the U.S.$20–40 range;
- moderate ($$): well-appointed hotels with good facilities in the U.S.$40–70 range;
- expensive ($$$): luxury hotels offering top amenities and comfort costing upwards of $70.

MEXICO CITY

Camino Real ($$$) Mariano Escobedo 700 (tel. 5 203 2121). A 1960s architectural landmark belonging to a chain of luxury modern hotels. No fewer than 10 restaurants, 720 rooms and excellent service make it one of Mexico's top hotels.
Emporio ($$) Paseo de la Reforma 124 (tel. 5 566 7766). Newly renovated, well-located 124-room hotel.
Galeria Plaza ($$$) Hamburgo 195, Zona Rosa (tel. 5 211 0014). Part of the Westin hotel group, a quiet and well-appointed place with a popular nightclub and international restaurants.
Holiday Inn ($$$) Paseo de la Reforma 80 (tel. 5 705 1515). Giant modern building with over 600 rooms and dependable though unexciting facilities. Lively evening entertainment.
Hotel Antillas ($) Belisario Domínguez 34 (tel. 5 526 5674). Friendly, basic 100-room hotel in lively neighborhood northwest of the Zócalo. TV and bathroom.
Hotel Canada ($) Avenida 5 de Mayo 47 (tel. 5 518 2106). Spacious, clean rooms in a centrally located modern hotel with reasonable rates.
Hotel Casa Blanca ($$) La Fragua 7 (tel. 5 566 3211/705 1300). A modern 270-room hotel with rooftop pool, restaurants, bars, just off Reforma.
Hotel Catedral ($) Donceles 95 (tel. 5 518 5232). Some rooms actually have views of the Cathedral in this modernized 140-room hotel just north of the Zócalo. Pleasant and comfortable rooms with TV and bathroom.
Hotel de Cortés ($$) Hidalgo 85 (tel. 5 518 2181/2). A national monument, this 18th-century former hospice makes an atmospheric choice to soak up colonial atmosphere. Pretty dining patio used for Saturday night *fiestas*. Rooms can be dark and/or noisy but the location is excellent.
Hotel Majestic ($$) Madero 73 (tel. 5 521 8600). Colonial-style hotel with panoramic terrace restaurant and attractive rooms. Unbeatable central location overlooking the Zócalo.
Hotel Marquis Reforma ($$$) Paseo de la Reforma 465 (tel. 5 211 3600). With good views of Chapultepec Park, this is the capital's latest deluxe modern hotel offering good business facilities and art-deco inspired rooms.
Hotel Monte Carlo ($/$$) Uruguay 69 (tel. 5 518 1418/521 2559). Legendary for having housed D. H. Lawrence, this former monastery, now a 60-room hotel offers a wide price range depending on facilities. Great location near the Zócalo, but choose rooms on the interior patio to avoid noise.
Hotel New York ($) Edison 45 (tel. 5 566 9700). Small, unpretentious mid-range hotel a few blocks northwest of Alameda and Reforma. Basic, clean rooms, small restaurant, garage.
Hotel Nikko Mexico ($$$) Campos Eliseos 204, Polanco (tel. 5 280 1111). One of the luxury Japanese high-tech giants offering predictably pricey but reliable fitness and business facilities, as well as a good gastronomic selection.
Howard Johnson Gran Hotel ($$) Avenida 16 de Septiembre 82 (tel. 5 512 9275/510 4040). Art Nouveau splendor and central location just off the Zócalo makes this 125-room hotel a classic. Comfortable rooms.
Krystal Zona Rosa ($$$) Liverpool 155, Zona Rosa (tel. 5 228 9928). A towering glass-fronted hotel with all amenities and comfortable though uninspired rooms, popular with groups.
María Cristina ($$) Río Lerma 31 (tel. 5 703 1787). A favorite with budget-conscious romantics, this charming 156-room colonial hotel offers gardens, patio, piano bar, a reasonable restaurant, plenty of atmosphere and good value. Reserve well ahead.
Sheraton María Isabel Hotel and Towers($$$) Reforma 325 (tel. 5 207 3933). Right in front of the Angel monument and across Reforma from the Zona Rosa, an excellent luxury base with spacious modern rooms, popular with business guests.
Stouffer Presidente ($$$) Campos Eliseos 218 (tel. 5 327 7700). Popular luxury high-rise hotel with bars, restaurants, discos and shops. Overlooking Chapultepec Park.
Vasco de Quiroga ($) Londres 15 (tel. 5 546 2614). Small, friendly family hotel on less action-packed east side of the Zona Rosa, with 50 well-furnished, colonial-style rooms, restaurant.

BAJA CALIFORNIA AND THE NORTH

Barranca del Cobre/Copper Canyon

Casa Margarita ($) Avenida López Mateos 11, Creel (tel. 145 60045). Creel's backpacking institution, now with over 70 rooms and dormitories. Family-run guest house on main square opposite the station. Good value. Organizes tours.
Hotel Misión ($$) Cerocahui (contact Hotel Sta Anita, Los Mochis (tel. 681 57046). Fabulous orchard and canyon setting for comfortable,

wood-beamed old hotel. Great horseback riding, treks and tours from here.
Hotel Paraiso del Oso ($) Cerocahui (tel. 14 124344). Primitive log cabins often without electricity in spectacular canyon setting, 7½ miles from Bahuichivo station. Tours.
Parador de la Montaña ($$) Avenida López Mateos 41, Creel (tel. 14 104580/ 155408). Comfortably well-appointed hotel on Creel's main street. International restaurant/bar, local tours, off-season discounts.
Pension Creel ($) Avenida López Mateos 61, Creel (tel. 145 60071/62). Rustic wood cabins and stone house (once Pancho Villa's H.Q.) located on the edge of town overlooking a pine forest.

Cabo San Lucas

Hotel Dos Mares ($) Calle E Zapata (between Hidalgo and Guerrero) (tel. 114 30330). Close to the marina and the action. Reasonably-priced rooms with cable TV or self-catering studio-apartments. Discounts for long stays.
Hotel Finisterra ($$$) Boulevard Marina (tel. 114 30000). Perched high on a cliff overlooking the Pacific with 110 well-appointed rooms, bars, pools, restaurant, spectacular views.
Hotel Mar de Cortés ($/$$) Lázaro Cárdenas y Guerrero (tel. 114 30232). Intimate colonial-style hotel just a short walk from the marina. Restaurant and bar.

Chihuahua

Hotel Apolo ($) Avenida Juárez 907 (tel. 14 161100/01). Astonishing 1900s hotel with original ornate lobby, but most rooms are in modern, upstairs extension. Well-appointed, central, parking lot.
Hotel San Francisco ($$$) Victoria 409 (tel. 14 167770). Modern 140-room hotel behind the cathedral. All top hotel amenities, bar, restaurant, parking.

Durango

Hotel Posada Durán ($) Avenida 20 de Noviembre 506 (tel. 181 12412). Atmospheric old colonial mansion just off the zócalo. Reasonably comfortable with low rates.
Hotel del Prado ($$) Avenida 20 de Noviembre 257 (tel. 181 10480). Attractive 100-room hotel with pool and restaurant, east of the zócalo.

Ensenada

El Cid Motor Hotel ($$) Avenida López Mateos 993 (tel. 667 82401). Small hotel close to the bay with a strong accent on Mexican crafts and flamenco music. Restaurant, bar, some Jacuzzis.
Hotel Bahía ($$) Avenida López Mateos (tel. 667 82101/03). Popular, well-established place with large pool, great bay views, bar, restaurant.

Guaymas

Hotel Rubi ($) Avenida Serdán y Calle 29 (tel. 622 40169). Clean, pleasant air-conditioned rooms in center near the harbor.
Playa de Cortés ($$$) Bahía Bacochibampo (tel. 622 40131). Ten minutes out of town, Guaymas' original luxury resort built in discreet colonial style around a patio. Pool, restaurant, bar, tennis, trailer park.

Hermosillo

Calinda Hermosillo Quality ($$$) Avenida Rosales y Morelia (tel. 62 172430). Well-appointed modern hotel in central location. Pool, bar, restaurant.
Hotel Montecarlo ($) Juárez y Sonora (tel. 62 123354). Clean air-conditioned rooms at reasonable rates which fill up fast.

La Paz

Hotel Los Arcos ($$) Avenida Alvaro Obregón 498 (tel. 682 22744). Upscale, 130-room hotel overlooking the bay with *cabañas*, pools, fishing facilities.
Hotel Perla ($$) Avenida Alvaro Obregón 1570 (tel. 682 20777). Pleasant, breezy central hotel overlooking the seafront, with well-kept rooms at reasonable rates.
Hotel Posada San Miguel ($) Calle Belisario Domínguez 1510 (tel. 682 21802). Extravagant arabesque exterior for a modest but adequate hotel in the town center.

Loreto

Hotel Misión de Loreto ($$) Boulevard López Mateos 1 (tel. 683 30048). Attractive, spacious, colonial-style hotel overlooking the seafront. Pretty patio/garden with pool and verandas, bar, restaurant.
Hotel Plaza Loreto ($$) Paseo Hidalgo 2 (tel. 683 30280). Opposite the old mission and central plaza. Shady patio, cleanly designed with bar and restaurant.

Los Mochis

Santa Anita ($$$) Leyva y Hidalgo (tel. 681 57046). The only breath of style in town and useful for organizing trips to the Copper Canyon. All first-class hotel amenities.

Monterrey

Gran Hotel Ancira Radisson Plaza ($$$) Hidalgo y Escobedo (tel. 83 451060). A real grand old hotel dating from 1912: Pancho Villa once tethered his horse in the lobby. Pool, shops, live jazz bar and general elegance. Rates drop considerably on weekends.
Hotel Quinta Avenida ($) Madero Oriente 243 (tel. 83 756565). Reasonable air-conditioned rooms with T.V. at moderate rates.
Motel Chipinque ($$) Meseta de Chipinque (tel. 83 781100). Friendly resort motel on outskirts of town with a panoramic view of Monterrey's skyline. Bar, restaurant, pool, tennis.

Mulegé

Hotel Las Casitas ($) Madero 50 (tel. 685 30019).

Cheerful cabin-style rooms opening on to verdant patios. Restaurant, bar.
Hotel Serenidad ($$) N Lincoln 345 (tel. 685 30111). Situated on the river by the airstrip. Well-appointed rooms, bar, restaurant, fishing trips.
Punta Chivato Resort ($$/$$$) Apartido Postal 18 (tel. 685 30188). Fabulous, isolated location on the headland north of Mulegé. Pool, restaurant, fishing and diving facilities.
Vieja Hacienda ($) Madero (tel. 685 30021). Historic, atmospheric *hacienda* with a superb courtyard where John Wayne once sipped *margaritas*. Bar, pool, restaurant, inspired tours around the region.

Saltillo

Hotel Urdinola ($) Victoria Poniente 207 (tel. 841 40940). Eccentrically decorated, friendly hotel uphill from Plaza Acuña. Spacious, clean rooms around a courtyard at back.
Imperial del Norte ($$) Boulevard V Carranza 3800 (tel. 841 50011). An 86-room motor hotel and trailer park with restaurant, bar and pool.

San Felipe

El Capitán ($$) Avenida Mar de Cortés 298 (tel. 657 71307). This 42-roomed hotel offers good facilities at a more reasonable rate than neighboring giants.

San José del Cabo

Hotel Ceci ($) Zaragoza 22 (no phone). A last outpost budget dinosaur in developing, luxury San José. Simple rooms with fan and bathroom at rock-bottom rates.
Posada Real ($$$) Malecón c/o Cerrada de Nicolas San Juan 16, Col del Valle, Mexico 03100 DF (tel. 114 20155). Low-rise 150-room hotel superbly sited in cactus garden leading to beach. Excellent sports and fishing facilities.

Tijuana

El Conquistador ($$$) Boulevard Agua Caliente 1777 (tel. 66 817955). Colonial-style, 110-room hotel with good middle-range facilities, gardens, pool. Located south of town near the racetrack.
Hotel Nelson ($) Avenida Revolución 503 (tel. 66 854302). Long-standing, reasonably comfortable budget hotel in the town center. Restaurant.

PACIFIC COAST

Acapulco

Boca Chica ($$) Gte Miguel Angel Muñoz (tel. 74 836741). Superb secluded location on Playa Caletilla. Somewhat delapidated but warm atmosphere. Restaurant with Japanese and Mexican dishes, very popular with locals.
Hotel Los Flamingos ($$) Avenida López Mateos (tel. 74 820690). Tranquil old 1930s hotel once favored by Cary Grant, Errol Flynn, etc. Lovely garden, sea views, great food.
Hotel Misión ($) Felipe Valle 12 (tel. 74 822076/ 823643). A gem of an old hotel in downtown Acapulco. Spanish-style rooms overlooking verdant patio with restaurant. Friendly, reasonable rates.
Hotel Royal Elcano ($$$) Avenida Costera Miguel Alemán 75 (tel. 74 841950). Well-located opposite the golf course at the eastern end of Costera, overlooking the bay. Excellent restaurant, bars, pool, good service.
Las Brisas ($$$) Carretera Escénica 5255 (tel. 74 841580). Break your bank account at this established rendezvous for the rich and famous with 300 *casitas* (bungalows) dotted around the hillside offering superb bay views.

Barra de Navidad

Hotel Barra de Navidad ($) M López de Legazpi 250 (tel. 333 70303). Rooms with balconies overlooking the beach, slightly delapidated pool.
Hotel Delfín ($) Morelos 23 (tel. 333 70068). Pretty, modestly scaled place on the lagoon side of town. Terrace breakfasts, German beer garden, pool.
Hotel Sand's ($) Morelos 24 (tel. 333 70018). Rambling hotel in wooden rustic style with patios and terraces overlooking the lagoon. Tropical garden, pool, parrots, monkeys. Off-season discounts.
Posada Pacifico ($) Avenida López de Legazpi 206 (tel. 333 70910). Large, clean rooms around a patio. Low rates, friendly, family-run.

Careyes

Club Med Playa Blanca ($$$) Playa Blanca Cihuatlán (tel. 333 20005). Self-contained resort in beautiful site for package deals only. Every possible amenity, sport and activity.
Costa Careyes Resort ($$$) Careyes (tel. 333 70050). Huge, revamped villa resort on picturesque horseshoe bay. All luxury amenities plus riding, watersports, spa.
El Tecuan Hotel ($$) Km 33.5, Highway 200 (tel. 333 70132). About 12 miles south of Careyes through mango plantations. Hilltop hotel overlooking the ocean, favored by Mexican families. Pool, water-skiing on the lagoon.

Colima

Gran Hotel Flamingos ($) Avenida Rey Coliman 18 (tel. 331 22525). Centrally located, 50-room hotel with clean, modern rooms, some air-conditioned. Small pool, garage.
Hotel Ceballos ($$) Torres Quintero 16 (tel. 331 24444). Historic 19th-century building, right on the zócalo, with 70 elegant, spacious air-conditioned rooms. Reasonable prices.

Ixtapa

Hotel Dorado Pacifico ($$$) Boulevard Ixtapa (tel. 753 32025). Good beach location, spectacularly designed with spacious, landscaped gardens. All luxury facilities.
Posada Real Ixtapa ($$$) Boulevard Ixtapa (tel. 753

31625). Pleasant, colonial-style, 110-room beach hotel with large pool, gardens and good fishing amenities. Slightly cheaper than other luxury choices.

Manzanillo

Fiesta Mexicana ($$) Km 8.5, Carretera Manzanillo Santiago (tel. 333 32180). Concrete tower, 200-room hotel in the thick of beach-front family action. Well-decorated rooms, restaurant, bar, pool.

Las Hadas ($$$) Avenida de los Riscos y Vista Hermosa s/n (tel. 333 30000). Now-legendary Arabian Nights fantasy hotel with hanging gardens, cobblestone streets, marble-floored rooms, gourmet restaurants, bars, pools and more. Very expensive.

Mazatlán

Costa de Oro ($$$) Camarón Sábalo (tel. 69 135113). Design-conscious, oceanside hotel in Zona Dorada with rooms set round gardens and paths. Open-air restaurant, bar, pool, tennis.

Hotel Santa Bárbara ($) Calle B Juárez y 16 de Septiembre (tel. 69 22120). Very basic but cheap, clean rooms with fans and shower. Close to the beach.

Hotel Siesta ($) Paseo Olas Altas 11 (tel. 69 812640). Atmospheric tropical courtyard hotel in Old Mazatlán, above the famed Shrimp Bucket restaurant on cliff boulevard.

Playa Mazatlán ($$$) Rodolfo T Loaiza 202 (tel. 69 134444/55). Semi-circular low structure with 424 rooms, right on the beach in the center of Zona Dorada. Casual atmosphere and frequent *fiestas*.

Playa Azul

Hotel Delfín ($) Calle V Carranza (tel. 753 60007). Friendly small-scale hotel with comfortable rooms surrounding a small pool. Restaurant.

Hotel Playa Azul ($$) Calle V Carranza (tel. 753 60024). The best place in town with a wide range of rates. Pleasant patio restaurant beside the pool.

Puerto Vallarta

Camino Real ($$$) Playa Las Estacas (tel. 322 30123). Five minutes south of the center on Highway 200, one of Vallarta's most luxurious hotels monopolizes an exquisite secluded cove. Beautiful pool, tropical gardens. All rooms have ocean views.

Hotel Rosita ($) Paseo Díaz Ordáz 90 (tel. 322 21033). Large 90-room 1950s hotel on the beach where the lively esplanade begins. Wide range of prices, fan or air-conditioned rooms, pool, restaurant. Somewhat worn at the edges but friendly and good value.

Los Cuatro Vientos ($$) Matamoros 520 (tel. 322 20161). Peaceful retreat high up in the cobble-stoned streets of Old Vallarta. Sixteen rooms surround a flowery patio, with a small pool, excellent restaurant and great views from the rooftop bar.

Molino de Agua ($$) Vallarta 130 (tel. 322 21907/57). Delightful tropical garden hotel centrally located by Río Cuale and the beach. Simple, air-conditioned bungalows with terrace rocking-chairs or more luxurious ocean-view suites. Pools, bar, restaurant, parking lot.

Quinta Maria Cortez ($$/$$$) Playa Conchas Chinas, Apartitdo 356 (tel. 322 15317/21184). Most eccentric and spectacular American-owned guest-house with five self-contained suites. Superb beach location south of town; artist-designed rooms with European antiques.

San Blas

Hotel Los Flamingos ($) Avenida Juárez 121 (no phone). Opposite the Old Customs House, an atmospheric old hotel with rooms around a lovely central courtyard. In the process of renovation, some rooms with air-conditioning.

Las Brisas ($$) Paredes Sur s/n (tel. 321 50480/50307). Prettily designed 42-room family hotel with gardens, pool, excellent restaurant. Comfortable, spacious rooms, well-screened against the local insect population. Close to the beach, parking lot.

Zihuatanejo

Catalina-Sotavento ($$) Playa La Ropa (tel. 753 42032). Spectacularly located beach resort on the cliff edge with 124 spacious rooms, Mexican décor, restaurant. Stairs down to the beach. Off-season discounts.

Hotel Tres Marías ($) Juan N Alvarez s/n, Col Lázaro Cárdenas (tel. 753 42191/42591). Small family-run hotel, excellent value, clean rooms with flowery terraces and sea-views. Popular with budget travelers.

CENTRAL HIGHLANDS

Aguascalientes

Hotel Francia ($$) Avenida Madero y Plaza Principal (tel. 49 156080). An elegant 80-room establishment overlooking the main square, with restaurant, bar and well-appointed rooms. Parking lot.

Hotel Maser ($) Juan de Montoro 303 (tel. 49 163562). Centrally located hotel with reasonably priced rooms enclosing a covered patio. Garage.

Guadalajara

Hotel Frances ($$) Maestranza 35 (tel. 3 613 1190). Popular historic old hotel (1610) a few yards from Plaza de la Liberación. Inside patio, antique furniture, restaurant, bar, comfortable modernized rooms.

Hotel San Francisco ($) Degollado 267 (tel. 3 613 8954/71). Undergoing renovation and upgrading. A superb mansion with a large inner courtyard and fountain on the edge of the historic center.

Hyatt Regency ($$$) López Mateos Sur y Moctezuma (tel. 3 622 7778). Stunning glass pyramidal design for 346 deluxe rooms in the city's Zona Rosa, across from Plaza del Sol. All luxury amenities, lively bars, restaurants, pool, parking.
Posada Regis ($) Avenida Corona 171 (tel. 3 613 3026). Eccentric first-floor hotel retaining many of its early 19th-century features. Slightly worn but clean, helpful and good value for central location. Avoid noisy front rooms.

Guanajuato

Hacienda de Cobos ($) Calle Padre Hidalgo 3 (tel. 473 20143/20350). At the western end of Avenida Juárez, down a side alley. Bougainvillaea-shrouded courtyard with parking. Reasonable rooms. Restaurant.

Hosteria del Frayle ($$) Sopena 3 (tel. 473 21179). Atmospheric old hotel just east of the Jardín de la Unión. Spacious wood-beamed rooms at very reasonable rates.
Hotel San Diego ($$) Jardín de la Unión 1 (tel. 473 21300). Central location. Well-appointed, tasteful rooms, restaurant, roof terrace.
Posada Santa Fe ($$) Plaza Principal (tel. 473 20084). An elegant 19th-century national monument on Guanajuato's lively main square, with colonial décor and antiques. Suitably stylish rooms. Excellent restaurant with outside tables.

Laguna de Chapala

La Nueva Posada ($$) Donato Guerra 9, Ajijic (tel. 376 61333). Small colonial-style inn facing the lake with 12 spacious suites and pool. Restaurant and bar popular with local expatriates.
Real de Chapala ($$) Paseo del Prado 20, Ajijic (tel. 376 60007/14/21). Colonial-style, 85-room hotel set in lovely gardens overlooking the lake. Restaurant, piano bar, tennis, pool.

Morelia

Hotel Casino ($$) Portal Hidalgo 229 (tel. 43 131003). Very reasonably priced hotel on the zócalo overlooking the cathedral. Colonial architecture, good facilities and popular outdoor bar under arches.
Hotel El Carmen ($) Eduardo Ruíz 63 (tel. 43 121725). Modest, centrally located hotel opposite the Ex-Convento del Carmen. Basic rooms with shower and T.V. at budget prices.
Hotel Virrey de Mendoza ($$) Avenida Madero 310 (tel. 43 124940/120633). Historic 18th-century hotel on the zócalo with lofty atrium restored to former glory. Friendly service and comfortable rooms. Restaurant, bar, shops.

Pátzcuaro

Hotel Los Escudos ($) Portal Hidalgo 73 (tel. 454 20138/21290). Elegant 30-roomed colonial hotel on Plaza Vasco de Quiroga. Well-appointed rooms, some with fireplaces, surround verdant patios. Popular restaurant.
Hotel Mansion Iturbe ($) Portal Morelos 59 (tel. 454 20368). Shadowy 17th-century mansion on Plaza Vasco de Quiroga. Bike rental.
Posada la Basílica ($) Arciga 6 (tel. 454 21108). Small, old-fashioned hotel facing the Basilica, popular with pilgrims. Pretty, clean, spacious rooms with fireplace, T.V. Excellent restaurant.
Posada de Don Vasco ($$) Calzada de las Americas 450 (tel. 454 20227). Pátzcuaro's top hotel, situated just outside town on the highway. Best Western management, colonial décor, tennis, pool, restaurant, parking lot.

Querétaro

Hotel Hidalgo ($) Madero 11 Poniente (tel. 42 120081). Simple, central hotel set back from street on courtyard used as parking lot. Friendly, reasonable rooms, budget rates. Cheap restaurant.
Hotel Impala ($$) Colon 1 (tel. 42 122570). Modern 102-room hotel overlooking Parque Alameda. Nothing special but well located and good, basic facilities. Avoid noisy front rooms.
Meson de Santa Rosa ($$$) Luis Pasteur 17 (tel. 42 145623/145993). Magnificent converted colonial mansion on Plaza de la Independencia with 21 suites opening on to galleries above the courtyard. Excellent restaurant/bar inside and out.

San Luis Potosí

Hotel Jardín Potosí ($) Los Bravos 530 (tel. 48 23152). Charming pastel-colored hotel. Clean rooms with private showers arranged around a patio.
Quinta Real ($$$) Real de Lomas 1000 (tel. 48 250125). Recently built luxury hotel in style of local colonial architecture. Superb central courtyard with pools and garden. All possible amenities, 15 minutes from town center.

San Miguel de Allende

Casa de Huéspedes ($) Mesones 23–7 (tel. 465 21378). Small first-floor family guesthouse brimming with plants. Clean, old-fashioned rooms at bargain prices.
Casa de Sierra Nevada ($$$) Hospicio 35 (tel. 465 20415/21895). Swiss-managed luxury hotel, discreetly located near main square in restored 1580s mansion, with 18 individually decorated suites, flowery patio, antiques, recommended gourmet restaurant.
Hotel Sautto ($) Hernandez Macías 59 (tel. 465 20251). Rambling old hotel in lovely large garden with range of room prices. Discounts off-season and for long stays.
Posada Carmina ($) Cuna de Allende 7 (tel. 465 20458). Lovely converted colonial mansion beside Parroquia off main square. Pleasant, spacious rooms. Courtyard restaurant.

Posada de las Monjas ($$) Calle Canal 37 (tel. 465 20171). Converted monastery with 65 rooms, restaurant, bar, roof-terraces, parking. Comfortable rooms, choice of rates.

Sierra Gorda

Mesón de San Nicolás ($$) Jalpan-Río Verde Km 32 (tel. 42 22556). Beautiful rural sierra setting by the river. Clean, well-kept rooms with T.V. Pool, restaurant, bar.

Uruapan

Hotel Plaza Uruapan ($$) Ocampo 64 (tel. 452 33599). Relaxed, elegant 124-room hotel overlooking the zócalo. Inexpensive for its range of facilities and comfort. Restaurant, disco, parking.
Mansion del Cupatitzio ($$) Parque Nacional s/n, Col la Quinta (tel. 452 32100). Magnificently sited 56-room hotel on the edge of the Parque Nacional Eduardo Ruíz. Colonial charm, large pool and garden, restaurant with views.

Zacatecas

Hotel Posada de la Moneda ($$) Avenida Hidalgo 413 (tel. 492 20881). Great location by the theater and cathedral. Reasonably priced, comfortable rooms, some with balconies. Restaurant.
Paraiso Gami ($) Boulevard López Mateos 309 (tel. 492 28005). Basic comforts at this cheap 60-room hotel not far from the central sights.
Quinta Real ($$$) Rayón 434 (tel. 492 29104). Extraordinary, unique luxury hotel arranged around a 17th-century bullring with 50 suites not excessively priced for quality and amenities. Generously scaled splendor, antiques, fine restaurant.

CENTRAL VALLEYS AND THE GULF

Cholula

Hotel Calli Quetzalcóatl ($$) Portal Guerrero 11 (tel. 22 471533). Well situated on the zócalo. Modernized rooms, restaurant and bar opening on to a courtyard. Reasonable rates.
Villa Arqueologica ($$) Pirámide de Cholula (tel. 22 471966). Well-run Club Med hotel at the foot of great pyramid and views to Popocatépetl. Shops, restaurant, pool, tennis.

Cuautla

Hotel Hacienda Cocoyoc ($$$) PO Box 300 (tel. 735 62211). Beautiful 16th-century hacienda in extensive landscaped grounds, with 300 colonial-style rooms, pools, restaurants, tennis, golf, riding.

Cuernavaca

Hacienda de Cortés ($$) Plaza Kennedy, Atlacomulco (tel. 73 158844). Historic hacienda built for Cortés in the 16th century, just outside Cuernavaca with 22 deluxe rooms, lovely gardens, pool.
Hotel Casino de la Selva ($$) Avenida Vicente Guerrero (tel. 73 124700). Sprawling 200-room hotel where Malcolm Lowry once hid out. Pools, riding, restaurant, disco. Popular with families.
Hotel Iberia ($) Rayón 9 (tel. 73 126040). Friendly old hotel in central location. Spartan but clean rooms with showers opening on to a terrace above a flowery courtyard.
Hotel Las Hortensias ($) Hidalgo 22 (tel. 73 185265). Very central location. Modest but clean rooms opening on to a pretty garden-courtyard.
Hotel Las Mañanitas ($$$) Ricardo Linares 107 (tel. 73 124646). A Cuernavaca luxury institution. Lovely old converted mansion in well-tended grounds with pool and peacocks. Gourmet restaurant and garden bar.

Ixtapan de la Sal

Hotel Spa Ixtapan ($$$) Boulevard San Roman (tel. 724 30021). Giant 250-room spa hotel with all-in facilities from diet menus to thermal pools, gym, golf, tennis, riding.

Jalapa

Hotel Salmones ($) Zaragoza 24 (tel. 28 175433). Gloomy but atmospheric old hotel on the main street. Excellent value rooms with T.V. and phone, quieter on the garden side. Restaurant, bar.
Meson del Alfarez ($$) Zaragoza y Sebastian Camacho (tel. 28 120403). Interestingly converted 18th-century townhouse. Tasteful décor, rustic furniture, tiled bathrooms, T.V., phone. Restaurant and bar.
Posada del Cafeto ($) Canovas 12 (tel. 28 170023). Prettily decorated little hotel down a peaceful side-street. Cheerful, whitewashed rooms but service not so joyful.

Pachuca

Hotel Noriega ($) Matamoros 305 (tel. 771 25000). Centrally located and good value. Attractive, rambling colonial hotel with comfortable rooms and good restaurant.

Papantla

Hotel Tajín ($) Calle José de Nuñez Domínguez 104 (tel. 784 21062/20121). A few yards up from the main square to the east of the church. Spacious old hotel. Clean, large rooms with T.V., phone and balcony. Some with air-conditioning. Restaurant.
Hotel Premier ($$) Enríquez 103 (tel. 784 20080/22700). On the main square opposite the church. Modernized, reasonably priced, comfortable hotel, air-conditioned throughout. Restaurant.

Puebla

Hotel del Portal ($$) Maximino Avila Camacho 205 (tel. 22 460211). Recently modernized, old colonial hotel on the northeast corner of the zócalo. Small but pleasant rooms.
Hotel Imperial ($) 4 Oriente 212 (tel. 22 424980). Upper corridors reminiscent of a prison but rooms are spacious and clean. Central location convenient for sights.

Hotel Lastra ($$) Calzada Los Fuertes 2633 (tel. 22 351501). Well-appointed rooms, pretty garden, pool, restaurant, views.
Hotel Royalty ($$) Portal Hidalgo 8 (tel. 22 424740). Moderately sized and priced, comfortable rooms in colonial-style hotel in plum zócalo location. Friendly service. Good restaurant/bar.

San Juan del Río
Hotel Colonial ($$) Juárez 28 Poniente (tel. 467 22991/24406). Upscale hotel with pool, restaurant, parking. Air-conditioned rooms with TV, phone, and some with poolside terraces.

Taxco
Hotel Agua Escondida ($$) Plaza Borda 4 (tel. 762 20726/36). Well situated on the zócalo with terrace views of the cathedral. Colonial-style rooms, rooftop pool, good children's facilities, parking. Relaxed atmosphere.
Hotel Montetaxco ($$$) Lomas de Taxco (tel. 762 21300). Sprawling 156-room resort hotel with fabulous views from the hilltop over the town and mountains. Popular with families, lots of sports facilities, restaurants.
Hotel Posada San Javier ($) Estacas 1/Ex-Rastro 4 (tel. 762 20231). Blissful palm-shaded garden with rustically furnished rooms with balconies. Small pool, garage, very central.
Posada de la Misión ($$$) Cerro de la Mision 32 (tel. 762 20063). An attractive 150-room hotel at the bottom of the main slope, whose pool claims a mural by Juan O'Gorman. Restaurants, bars, garden.

Tepoztlán
Hotel Mesón del Indio ($) Avenida Revolución 44 (tel. 739 50238). Modest little hotel with garden. Pleasant rooms with baths.
Hotel Posada del Tepozteco ($$) Paraiso 3 (tel. 739 50010). Beautifully sited hacienda-hotel with pools, gardens and terraces overlooking the valley. Exclusive atmosphere. Rates rise with private spa-baths.

Tlaxcala
Albergue de la Loma ($) Guerrero 58 (tel. 246 20424). Spacious, pleasant rooms with bathrooms, two blocks south of the zócalo.
Misión Park Plaza Resort ($$) Highway to Apizaco (tel. 246 24000). A 102-room resort hotel with spa in large grounds adjacent to the canyon and waterfall. Pool, tennis, restaurants.

Toluca
Hotel Plaza Morelos ($) Serdán 115 (tel. 72 133929/159200). A reasonable, well-maintained hotel and restaurant. Convenient for central sights and action.

Veracruz
Gran Hotel Diligencias ($$) Avenida Independencia 1115–1129 (tel. 29 322967/312116). Rambling 1950s hotel overlooking the zócalo. Rooms with T.V., some with balconies. Bar, restaurant, coffee-shop.
Hotel El Faro ($) 16 de Septiembre 223 (tel. 29 316176/316538). Excellent value, family-run hotel a few streets back from the harbor. Clean rooms with T.V. and air-conditioning or fan.
Hotel Emporio ($$$) Paseo del Malecón 244 (tel. 29 320020). Towering modern hotel facing the harbor, with 202 air-conditioned rooms and suites, three pools, tennis, restaurants, bars, roof garden.
Hotel Mocambo ($$) Carretera Veracruz-Mocambo (tel. 29 220205). Longstanding favorite on Mocambo Beach, about 6 miles south of town. Decent-sized rooms, some overlooking the gardens and beach beyond.
Hotel Ruíz Milán ($$) Insurgentes Veracruzanos 432 (tel. 29 326707). Rather battered "modern" hotel overlooking the harbor. Spacious air-conditioned rooms with T.V., phone, balcony. Cheaper ones with fans. Convenient and relatively quiet location.

SOUTH

Catemaco
Hotel del Lago ($) Paseo del Malecón s/n (tel. 294 30160). Reasonable air-conditioned rooms with T.V., right on the town's lakefront. Modest pool, restaurant.
Hotel La Finca ($$) Carretera de Golfo Km 147 (tel. 294 30322). Air-conditioned hotel on the edge of the lake just outside town. Pleasant rooms with balconies and lake views.

Huatulco
Hotel Flamboyant ($$) La Crucecita (tel. 958 70113). On the main square of Huatulco's service town. Colonial-style hotel with 70 air-conditioned rooms, pool and restaurant.
Marco Polo ($$$) Benito Juárez 4, Balcones de Tangolunda (tel. 958 10202). Clifftop setting with fabulous views. Exclusive small hotel with 25 large, well-appointed suites, pool, restaurant.
Sheraton Huatulco ($$$) Bahía Tangolunda (tel. 958 10055). Six-story luxury beachfront complex with 346 spacious and comfortable rooms and suites and all amenities.

Oaxaca
Hotel Antonios ($) Avenida Independencia 601 (tel. 951 67227). Medium-sized, well-located hotel just off the zócalo. Recently renovated rooms.
Hotel Monte Albán ($$) Alameda de León 1 (tel. 951 62777). Lovely old colonial mansion opposite the cathedral with a restaurant in a covered courtyard. Reasonably-priced, comfortable rooms.
Hotel Principal ($) Cinco de Mayo 208 (tel. 951 62535). High-ceilinged, wood-beamed rooms, impeccably maintained, opening

on to a lush courtyard. Four blocks northeast of the zócalo.
Parador Plaza ($$) Murguia 104 (tel. 951 42027). Close to the zócalo. Colonial-style hotel with pleasant rooms built around an interior patio.
Posada San Pablo ($) Fiallo 102 (tel. 951 64914). A bargain for longer stays: minimum 3 days for small apartments with cooking facilities surrounding atmospheric old courtyard. Central location.
Stouffer Presidente ($$$) Cinco de Mayo 300 (tel. 951 60611). Stunning 16th-century convent converted into a charming luxury hotel. Banquets and folk-dance shows in a vaulted chapel. Excellent restaurant, pool, piano bar. Secluded gardens.

Palenque
Chan-Kah Resort ($$$) Km 3, Carretera Ruinas (tel. 934 51100). Beautifully sited bungalows in lush jungle grounds very close to the archeological site. Good *palapa* restaurant, *cenote*-type pool, entertainment, tours.
Hotel la Cañada ($$) Calle Merle Green 13 (tel. 934 50102). Legendary bungalow accommodation in jungle setting at the entrance to town. Air-conditioned or fan-cooled. Good, lively restaurant.
Hotel la Croix ($) Hidalgo 104 (tel. 934 50014). A budget hotel opposite the zócalo garden, with a pretty courtyard. Rooms with fan and bath but no hot water.
Hotel Mision Palenque ($$$) Rancho San Martín de Porres (tel. 934 50300). At the eastern end of town in extensive landscaped grounds with 160 air-conditioned rooms, pool, good open-air restaurant/bar and panoramic views.

Puerto Ángel
Pension Buena Vista ($) no phone. Living up to its name (fine view), a small village hotel with terrace restaurant (plus hammocks), tasteful rooms with balconies, fans and insect screens.
Posada Cañon De Vata ($) Playa del Pantéon (no phone). A cluster of bungalows, 500 yards from port in a peaceful, tropical hillside setting. Good wholefood restaurant.

Puerto Escondido
Hotel Arco Iris ($) Playa Zicatela (tel. 958 20432). Favorite surfers' haunt. Friendly 20-room hotel on beach. Clean rooms with fans, bathrooms, and balconies.
Hotel Paraíso Escondido ($$) Calle Unión 10 (tel. 958 20444). Lovely old whitewashed hacienda-style hotel, two blocks from the beach, with 20 air-conditioned rooms, pool, gardens, open-air restaurant.
Hotel Santa Fe ($$) Playa Marinero (tel. 958 20170). Between Playa Zicatela and Marinero, a superbly designed hotel laid out around terraces, pool and gardens. Air-conditioned and/or fan-cooled rooms. Panoramic restaurant.
Posada Real ($$$) Boulevard Benito Juárez (tel. 958 20133). A 100-room Best Western hotel perched above the ocean in magnificent gardens, offering useful tourist information, car-rental, tours. Easy access to the beach.

San Andrés Tuxtla
Hotel De Los Perez ($) Rascón 2 (tel. 294 20777). Conveniently located just off the zócalo. Reasonable, clean air-conditioned rooms with T.V.

San Cristóbal de las Casas
Casa Margarita ($) Real de Guadalupe 34 (tel. 967 80957). A budget travelers' favorite in a lively street. Pretty, open courtyard dining, spartan rooms, communal bathrooms. Good tours and general information.
Hotel Capri ($) Avenida Insurgentes 54 (tel. 967 83018). Friendly little hotel/restaurant south of the center towards the bus station. Most rooms have external windows and views. Parking.
Hotel Flamboyant ($$) Calle 1 de Marzo 15 (tel. 967 80726/80045). Elegant and newly redecorated colonial-style hotel in central location, with 50 well-appointed rooms with T.V. and fireplace off flowery patio. Restaurant, bar, solarium, gym.

Tapachula
Hospedaje Colonial ($) Avenida 4 Norte 31 (tel. 962 62052). Central, budget hotel with pleasant rooms above a lush courtyard garden.
Hotel Don Miguel ($) Calle 1 Poniente 18 (tel. 962 61143). Bright, clean rooms with air-conditioning and T.V. Restaurant.

Tehuantepec
Hotel Posada Donaji ($) Calle Juárez 10 (tel. 971 50064). Overlooking the Amado Chinas park. Front rooms can be noisy, those opening on to the central courtyard are quieter.

Tuxtla Gutierrez
Gran Hotel Humberto ($) Avenida Central Poniente 180 (tel. 961 22080). Well located near the zócalo. Spacious air-conditioned rooms with T.V., though some a bit gloomy. Popular nightclub.
Hotel Flamboyant ($$) Boulevard Belisario Domínguez Km 1081 (tel. 961 32101). Excellent facilities at reasonable rates in Moorish-inspired modern, 118-room hotel. Large pool, tennis, restaurants, live music, video bar.

Villahermosa
Hotel Madero ($) Avenida Madero 301 (tel. 931 20516). Charming old hotel in the town center close to the river. Rooms with fan or air-conditioning, very reasonable rates.
Hotel Maya Tabasco ($$) Boulevard A Ruíz Cortines 907 (tel. 931 21111). 160-

room hotel close to park and museums. Air-conditioned rooms with TV, pool, gym, tennis, disco, restaurants.
Hotel Miraflores ($$) Reforma 304 (tel. 931 20022). Modernized hotel in central pedestrian zone. Pleasant air-conditioned rooms. Restaurant, travel agent and car-rental.

YUCATÁN

Akumal

Hotel Akumal Cancún ($$$) Km 104, Carretera Cancún–Tulúm (tel. 987 22453). Well-designed modern wings in carefully tended gardens on a sweep of Akumal's main beach. All luxury facilities including diving, riding, fishing, disco, tennis.

Las Casitas Akumal ($$) Apartido 714, Cancún (tel. 987 22554). Air-conditioned self-catering bungalows with direct access to the sea. Reasonable value for four people.

Campeche

Hotel América ($) Calle 10 No 252 (tel. 981 64588). 52-room hotel converted from an old colonial mansion in the city center. Spacious rooms with T.V., phone, fan, and bathroom.
Hotel Baluartes ($$) Ruíz Cortines 51 (tel. 981 63911). Facing the bay two blocks from downtown, a comfortable 102-room hotel with restaurant, pool, nightclub, parking.

Cancún

Club Lagoon ($$) Boulevard Kukulcán, Km 5.8, Zona Hoteleres (tel. 98 831111). Mediterranean-style architecture, patios, gardens facing Laguna de Nichupté, with 70 rooms and 19 suites. Pretty restaurant.
Hotel Hacienda Cancún ($) Avenida Sunyaxchén 39, Ciudad del Carmen (tel. 98 841208). Central location in the main town. Pleasant air-conditioned rooms with TV and bathroom, pretty patio and pool. Top end of budget category.
Hotel Margarita ($) Avenida Yaxchilán 4, Ciudad Cancún (tel. 98 849333). A new 96-room hotel in the town center, with restaurant, pool, beach-club. Air-conditioned rooms with T.V., phone, large bathrooms, balconies. Baby-sitting, car-rental.
Hotel Conrad Cancún ($$$) Boulevard Kukulcán, Km 20, Punta Nizuc (tel. 98 850086). State-of-the-art 390-room luxury hotel at the southern end of the hotel zone next to Club Med.

Chetumal

Hotel El Dorado ($) Avenida 5 de Mayo 42 (tel. 983 20315). Good central location for 25 clean, spacious rooms with fan or air-conditioning, T.V.
Hotel Caribe Princess ($) Avenida Alvaro Obregón 168 (tel. 983 20520). Right in the town center. Rather drab décor but airy rooms with T.V., phone, shower, and air-conditioning.
Hotel Los Cocos ($$) Avenida Héroes de Chapultepec (tel. 983 20544). Modern 80-room hotel with pool, restaurant, bar.

Chichén Itzá

Hotel Dolores Alba ($) Km 122, Carretera Cancún (tel. Mérida 99 285650). About 2 miles east of the ruins on the Cancún highway. Charming, family-run hotel, well-maintained with small pool and reasonable restaurant.
Misión Chichén Itzá Park Inn ($$$) Piste (tel. 985 62671). A two-story modern hotel in colonial style set in extensive gardens, about 1 mile west of ruins. Local fauna. Pool, pretty restaurant and bar.
Villa Arqueólogica ($$$) Chichén Itzá (tel. 985 62830). One of Club Med's "cultural" hacienda-style hotels, five minutes from the ruins, with 43 air-conditioned rooms, good restaurant with French and regional food, pool, bar, disco, library, movies.

Ciudad del Carmen

Hotel Isla del Carmen ($) Calle 20A No 9 (tel. 938 21246). Reasonably priced modern hotel/restaurant. Rooms with air-conditioning, phone, T.V.
Hotel Del Parque ($$) Calle 33 No 1 (tel. 938 23066). Modest 24-room establishment with well-appointed rooms, restaurant, bar, pool.

Cobá

Restaurant El Bocadito ($) Apartido Postal 56, Valladolid (no phone). Situated on the right of the main road leading down to the lake. A low-key place with eight decent rooms, each with fan and bathroom.
Villa Arqueólogica ($$$) Cobá (tel. 987 42087 or Mexico City 5 203 3833). Beautifully sited hotel by Cobá's main lake close to the ruins. Air-conditioned rooms, pool, good restaurant and excellent library for Maya-addicts.

Cozumel

Casa del Mar ($$) Carretera Sur (tel. 987 21900). Upscale 106-room hotel 3 miles south of town on coast, with scuba facilities, restaurant/bar and own submarine.
Hotel Suites Elizabeth ($) Calle Adolfo Rosado Salas 44 (tel. 987 20330). Close to the harbor, good value and well-maintained self-catering suites. Hotel rooms too.
Hotel Pepita ($) Avenida 15 Sur 120 (tel. 987 20098). Three blocks from the port, a friendly family hotel with basic but adequate rooms opening on to a patio, all with bathroom.
Hotel Vista del Mar ($/$$) Avenida Rafael Melgar 45 (tel. 987 20545). On the seafront looking across to the mainland. Overpriced rooms (a Cozumel habit), some with balconies. Restaurant, car-rental.

Isla Mujeres

Hotel Berny ($) Juárez y Abásolo (tel. 988 20025).

Simple rooms with fan and bathroom surrounding courtyard. Video-bar and small pool.
Hotel Rocamar ($$) Guerrero y Bravo (tel. 988 70101). Fabulous perch overlooking the Caribbean on Isla's eastern coast above the main town square. Slightly aging rooms but with acceptable nautical spirit, fan, bathroom and views. Good restaurant.
Maria's Kan Kin ($$) Carretera El Garrafón (tel. 988 20015). A superbly secluded spot on a private beach, 5 miles south of the port. Excellent though overpriced restaurant. Only nine rooms/suites.
Posada del Mar ($$) Calle Medina y Morelos (tel. 988 20044). A delightful hotel with 41 comfortable rooms or bungalows four blocks from the pier below a lighthouse. Sea views, pool, garden, restaurant.

Mérida

Gran Hotel ($$) Calle 60 No 496 (tel. 99 247730). Great location on Parque Hidalgo just off the zócalo. Magnificent "grand hotel" with restaurant/bar in a flowery courtyard. Slightly overpriced rooms with air-conditioning or fan.
Hotel Casa del Balam ($$$) Calle 60 No 488 (tel. 99 248130). Large, stylish, central hotel, part 19th-century and part modern. Antiques, spacious atrium/bar, comfortable air-conditioned rooms. Parking, pool, travel agent. Gourmet restaurant.
Hotel Posada Toledo ($) Calle 58 No 487 (tel. 99 232256). Superb old family mansion recently converted leaving memorabilia intact. Ornate interior, particularly the very French-style suite but some rooms are dark, dingy, and overpriced.
Hotel Trinidad ($) Calle 62 No 464 (tel. 99 213029/ 232033). Rambling, artist-owned hotel filled with bric-à-brac and art. Wide range of basic but clean rooms around patios with fountains and much foliage. Friendly and well located. Annexe at Calle 60 456 (tel. 99 232463) with slightly higher rates, pool, coffee-shop and further extremes of eccentricity.
Montejo Palace ($$$) Paseo de Montejo 483-C (tel. 99 247644). Modern hotel with colonial décor on Mérida's Champs Elysées. Sixty rooms, 30 suites, restaurants, bar, pool, nightclub. Cheaper rates at its sister establishment across street, the Hotel Paseo de Montejo ($$) (tel. 99 239033).

Playa del Carmen

Banana Cabañas ($) Avenida Quinta (tel. 987 30036). Clean, friendly place with selection of bungalows or fan-cooled rooms with bathrooms in tropical garden on Playa's main pedestrian street, one block from the beach.
Blue Parrot Inn ($$) Calle 12 (tel. 987 30083). The hippest hotel in Playa on the beach to the north of the center. Rooms or thatched *cabañas*, some with small kitchens. Beach bar and restaurant. Relaxed, fun atmosphere.
Posada Sian-Ka'an ($) Avenida Quinta (tel. 987 30203). Oldish building in the central Playa. Fan-cooled rooms with sea views, bungalows in garden.
Shangri-La Caribe ($$) Km 69.5 Carretera Tulum (tel. 987 22888). Seventy beachfront bungalows at the secluded northern end of the beach, accessible by separate turn-off from corridor highway. All fan-cooled or air-conditioned, with terrace. Restaurant, bar, pool.

Progreso

Sian Ka'an Hotel and Beach Club ($$) Calle 17 s/n (tel. 993 54017). Small beachfront hotel with 11 suites in Mexican colonial décor. Pool, restaurant, bar.

Río Lagartos

Hotel Nefertiti ($) Calle 14 No 123 (tel. 986 1415). The only hotel in town! Boasts a statue of Egyptian Queen Nefertiti herself. Basic but adequate rooms with fan and bathroom. Helpful with organizing boat tours of the lagoons.

Tulúm

Cabañas Tulúm ($) Carretera Tulúm-Boca Paila (no phone). The last of the scattered *cabañas* hotels down the Boca Paila road. Fairly battered, concrete huts among palm trees on the beach.
Gato's Bar & Cabañas ($) c/o Aldea Dzib-ak-tum, Apartido 100, Tulúm (no phone). On the coast road a few miles south of the ruins. Lovely *palapa*-roofed *cabañas* clustered round tiny coves in coconut palms. Shared bathroom. Suspended beds, hammocks, solar-lights. Superb, breezy open-air restaurant with Baroque decorative inspiration.
Hotel Acuario ($) Carretera Tulúm (tel. Cancún 98 844856). At the intersection for the Tulúm turn-off from Highway 307, convenient for the ruins and/or those without a car. Reasonable rooms with fan, bathroom, T.V. Pool.
Sian Ka'an Osho Oasis ($$) c/o Apartido 99, Tulúm (no phone). At the edge of the biosphere reserve on the coastal road. New Age spirited group of *cabañas* with vegetarian restaurant. Well-equipped diving shop, reef and *cenote* trips. Morning meditation sessions on beach.

Valladolid

Hotel Mesón del Marqués ($$) Calle 39 No 203 (tel. 985 63042). Valladolid's top hotel, a 16th-century colonial mansion on the main plaza. Tastefully decorated, reasonably priced for its setting. Air-conditioned rooms with T.V. and phone. Good restaurant, pool, parking.
Hotel San Clemente ($) Calle 42 No 206 (tel. 985 62208). Large, pleasant hotel built around a spa-

cious courtyard, with a pool. Large rooms with air-conditioning or fan, cheap restaurant, parking.

Xcalak

Costa de Cocos ($$) Carretera Xcalak (tel. USA 800 443 1123). Up-market *palapa*-roofed *cabañas* literally at the end of the road, about 30 miles south of Majahual. American-Mexican owners assure all basic comforts. Divers' haven as spectacular reefs lie only 10 minutes away.

RESTAURANTS

In smaller towns the best restaurants are often found in hotels. Refer to the hotel listings for these. Other establishments listed below have been divided into the following categories:

- budget ($)
- moderate ($$)
- expensive ($$$)

MEXICO CITY

Bar l'Opéra ($$) 5 de Mayo 10 (tel. 5 512 8959). Ornate *belle époque* institution. Average food but a fabulous setting close to Bellas Artes. Go just for a drink.

Café El Parnaso ($) Felipe Carrillo 2 (tel. 5 554 2225). Best people-watching spot on Coyoacán's Jardín Centenario. Bookshop and café for whiling away weekend hours.

Café Tacuba ($$) Tacuba 28 (tel. 5 535 2704). Famous old Mexican restaurant dating from 1912. Endless *enchiladas, chiles rellenos* (stuffed peppers) and *mole* dishes. Lively atmosphere with entertainment on Friday and Saturday nights.

Carrousel International ($$) Nizza 33 (tel. 5 533 6417). Bar/pub/restaurant spiced up by vociferous *mariachis*. Drinks and copious snacks served noon till midnight daily.

Champs-Elysées ($$$) Amberes 1 (tel. 5 514 0450). Parisian-style restaurant with five dining-rooms and a roof-garden overlooking the city's grand boulevard. Gourmet French cuisine. Reservations essential. Weekdays only.

El Hijo del Cuervo ($$) Jardín Centenario 17 (tel. 5 658 5306). Lively evening watering-hole on Coyoacán's main square. Wide range of drinks and snacks in friendly atmosphere. Closed Monday.

Fonda Don Chon ($$) Regina 159 (tel. 5 522 2170). An exceptional place near La Merced market, specializing in pre-Hispanic dishes (maguey worms, iguana, grasshoppers, vipers, ant-soup!). Friendly, popular, unpretentious with wide price range.

Fonda El Refugio ($$) Liverpool 166, Zona Rosa (tel. 5 525 8128). Award-winning Mexican restaurant, reservations advisable. Fun atmosphere and décor, excellent traditional dishes. Closed Sunday.

Fonda San Ángel ($$) Plaza San Jacinto 3 (tel. 5 548 7566). A few steps from San Ángel's Bazar Sabado. Traditional Mexican dishes in relaxed atmosphere. Open till midnight.

Hostería de Santo Domingo ($$) Belisario Domínguez 72 (tel. 5 526 5276). Atmospheric old *hosteria* in interesting downtown area. Typical Mexican dishes include divine *chile en nogada* all year round. Weekend entertainment and *mariachis*.

Hosteria Santa Caterina ($) Jardín Sta Caterina 6. Rustic old restaurant in Coyoacán, right next to small theater. Great weekend buzz, friendly. Good range of typical Mexican dishes: try the excellent *nopales* (cactus-leaf) salad.

La Gondola ($$) Genova 21 (tel. 5 514 0743). An established Zona Rosa favorite serving delicious Italian cuisine. Sidewalk tables and live classical music on weekend evenings. Open daily till 1 a.m.

Lago Chapultepec ($$$) Lago Mayor, Bosque Chapultepec (tel. 5 515 9585/6). Reservations and ties essential at this formal lakeside restaurant. Spectacular modern setting, outstanding wine list, smoochy music and dancing in the evenings. Good Sunday brunches.

Las Lupitas ($) Jardín Sta Caterina, Francisco Sosa (tel. 5 554 2875). Popular Coyoacán neighborhood place on charming square. Typical, unpretentious Mexican food, great breakfasts. Open till 11 p.m.

Les Moustaches ($$$) Río Sena 88 (tel. 5 533 3390). Pretentious restaurant off Reforma in a beautiful restored mansion. Continental cuisine includes snails, sea bass with almonds, pepper steak and lavish desserts. Jacket and tie. Weekdays only.

Los Irabiens ($$) Avenida de la Paz 45 (tel. 5 660 2382). Piano music, smart Mexican décor, antiques and paintings. San Angel's most inventive menu and discreet service, much favored by the upwardly mobile.

Prendes ($$) 16 de Septiembre 10 (tel. 5 521 5404/1878). Crowded lunchtime place in historic center, more memorable for its murals and atmosphere than its menu. Seafood specialties and good Sunday paella. Closes daily at 6 p.m. Another branch at Frontón México, Plaza de la República (tel. 546 0487) is open till midnight.

Restaurant Centro Castellano ($) Uruguay 16 (tel. 5 510 1461). Vast restaurant with good value *comida corrida*. Endless choice of typical local dishes such as roast kid and seafood – octopus and red snapper – as well as copious paella. Open daily till 10 p.m.

San Ángel Inn ($$$) Diego Rivera 50, Altavista (tel. 5 548 6746). Fabulous restored 18th-century mansion, an institution in San Ángel. Patio or indoor dining for international or Mexican gourmet food.

Sanborns ($) Calle Madero 4 (tel. 5 512 9820). Eat in Moorish-style palatial splendor at the Casa de los Azulejos, close to Alameda. Average food but pleasant atmosphere and reasonably priced.

Tenampa ($) Plaza Garibaldi (tel. 5 526 6176). Touristy but still amusing for soaking up *tequila* and *mariachi* music. Open daily till 3 a.m.

VIPS ($) Hamburgo 126 (tel. 5 514 5541). You don't come here for the décor but for an economic haven in the Zona Rosa. Good, filling Mexican dishes, salads and sandwiches with adjoining bookstore.

BAJA CALIFORNIA AND THE NORTH

Cabo San Lucas

Da Giorgio ($$$) Km 25, Highway 1, Misiones del Cabo (tel. 114 21988). A superb Italian restaurant high on a headland with fabulous ocean views, offering homemade pasta, *focaccia* bread and pizzas baked in a wood-fired oven. Open daily till midnight.

El Delfin ($$) Playa del Medano (tel. 114 30901/32988). A glassed-in *palapa* restaurant on the main town beach, serving large portions of Sonora beef, lobster and ultra-fresh fish. Open all day.

Mi Casa ($$) Serdán y Lázaro Cárdenas (tel. 114 31933). A rare authentic Mexican restaurant on the main square behind the marina. Colorful décor, wide choice of typical dishes. Open till 10 p.m.

Ensenada

El Rey Sol ($$$) Avenida López Mateos 1000 (tel. 667 81733). Award-winning seafood restaurant serving French Provençal and Mexican dishes and homegrown vegetables. Elegant, colonial-style setting.

Loreto

Caesar's ($$) Emiliano Zapata y Benito Juárez (tel. 113 30203). Top seafood restaurant founded over 20 years ago. Mega-portions of delicious lobster, red snapper and much more. Friendly service.

Monterrey

El Pastor ($) Madero Poniente 1067 (tel. 83 425084). *The* place to sample all cuts of charcoal-grilled kid (*cabrito*) in an unpretentious setting. Near the market and the bus station.

El Tío ($$) Avenida Hidalgo 1746 Poniente (tel. 83 333559/460291). Landmark restaurant over 60 years old in downtown area. Roast kid and steaks in lively indoor bullfight-theme décor or in calmer garden patio.

La Paz

La Costa La Paz ($$) Navarro y Bahía de La Paz (tel. 682 28808). Seafront restaurant with good bay views. Imperial shrimp, fish and grilled meats.

San José del Cabo

Café Fiesta ($) Boulevard Mijares 14 (tel. 114 22808). Good breakfast café with tables under shady trees situated on the plaza. Moderately priced dinner menu.

Damiana ($$) Boulevard Mijares 8 (tel. 114 20499). Elegant little restaurant tucked away beside San José's main square in an old town house. Romantic patio dining. Excellent seafood – giant prawns, abalone, lobster, shrimp, steak or châteaubriand, with discreet service.

Tijuana

Tía Juana Tilly's ($$) Avenida Revolución y Calle 7 (tel. 66 856024). The most popular *gringo* hang-out in Tijuana, located next to the Jai Alai stadium. Mexican specialties, fun atmosphere. Another branch across street called Tilly's Fifth Avenue.

PACIFIC

Acapulco

Carlos 'n Charlie ($$) Costera M Alemán 999 (tel. 74 40039). Another of the Anderson's chain and one of Acapulco's "in" places. Old photos, loud rock, and long lines of potential customers for seafood and meat dishes.

La Granja del Pingüe ($) Benito Juárez 10 (tel. 74 835339). Also known as the Fat Farm. Friendly, relaxed place offering good breakfasts, snacks, pasta, salads and pastries all day. Cool patio setting in an old farmhouse a few blocks west of the zócalo.

Tio Alex ($$) Avenida Costera Miguel Alemán 111 (tel. 74 843656). In the thick of the beachfront action overlooking Playa Condesa. Open-air dining, cheerful service. Seafood, steaks, and soups with booming rock music from the nextdoor Taboo bar.

Manzanillo

Willy's ($$) Crucero Las Brisas (tel. 333 31794). Highly reputed French-owned restaurant with a lovely beach view. Dinners only – get there early for a table.

Mazatlán

El Shrimp Bucket ($$) Olas Altas 11 (tel. 69 816350). The original Anderson chain restaurant, open all day but more fun with the evening marimba band. Good seafood in picturesque courtyard.

Señor Frog's ($$) Avenida del Mar 225 (tel. 69 851109). Heavily marketed chain of young, lively restaurants. Barbecued ribs or Madrazo oysters, omnipresent rock music. Open till 1 a.m.

Tres Islas ($$) Camarón Sábalo (tel. 69 135932). Popular *palapa*-roofed beach bar/restaurant/disco with views to outlying islands. Try the *parrillada* (grilled mixed seafood).

Puerto Vallarta

Chez Elena ($$) Matamoros 520 (tel. 322

20161). An intimate colonial-style atmosphere, established in the 1950s, offering Continental menu. Views over the city.
Le Bistro Jazz Café ($$) Isla Río Cuale (tel. 322 20283). Lush, riverside setting with cool jazz to escape Vallarta's tropical heat. Open all day for delicious crêpes, *tampiqueña* (marinaded beef), seafood. Elegant but informal, indoor and outdoor eating.
Mr Gallo ($) Basílio Badillo y Pino Suárez (no phone). Normal Mexican prices in what is rapidly turning into Old Vallarta's gastronomic H.Q. near Playa Los Muertos. Lofty *palapa*-roofed place serving excellent barbecued meat or fish. Open till 11 p.m.

Zihuatanejo
Casa Elvira ($) Paseo del Pescador 16 (tel. 753 42061). Long-established restaurant facing the beach near the pier. Quaint interior, good seafood and authentic Mexican dishes.
Pepper's Garden ($$) Ignacio Altamirano 46 (tel. 753 43767). Superbly prepared Mexican dishes (stuffed peppers, chicken in banana leaves) generous portions, great *margaritas*.

CENTRAL HIGHLANDS

Guadalajara
El Abajeño ($$) Minerva, Avenida Vallarta 2802 (tel. 3 630 0307). Smart courtyard bar/restaurant at the city's western end. Traditional Mexican fare, friendly service and *mariachis*.
La Fragata Azteca ($$) López Cortilla 2120. Favorite long-lunching place in giant tent-like structure. Good fish and meat dishes, bustling atmosphere and local *mariachis*.
Portal San Angel ($) Edificio Progreso 102 (tel. 3 617 8199). Breezy café/restaurant with outside tables opposite Instituto Cabañas. Typical Mexican snacks at reasonable prices. Open till 8.30pm.
Río Viejo ($$$) Avenida Americas 302 (tel. 3 616 5321). Beautiful old colonial *hacienda* owned by a former bull-fighter and antiques dealer. Selective menu of fine Mexican cuisine.

Guanajuato
El Trujo ($) Calle del Trujo 7 (tel. 473 28374). Design-conscious café/bar/restaurant in a side-street behind the cathedral. Lively atmosphere. Good background music. Open till midnight.
Restaurant 4 Ranas ($) Plazuela San Fernando 24 (tel. 473 20301). Simple Spanish-style place on beautiful, shady square. Breakfasts, snacks and late-night Mexican food. Open till 1 a.m.

San Miguel de Allende
Mamma Mía ($$) Umarán 8 (tel. 465 22063). Popular courtyard restaurant with good all-round menu and copious breakfasts. Live music in evenings, open till midnight.

Zacatecas
Acropolis ($) Avenida Hidalgo y Tacuba (tel. 492 21284). Lofty old café-restaurant adjacent to the Cathedral. Favorite Zacatecan meeting-place for *quesadillas*, ice-creams, cakes, coffee and juices.

CENTRAL VALLEYS AND GULF

Cuernavaca
La India Bonita ($$) Morrow 106B (tel. 73 125021). Located in the former residence of U.S. Ambassador Dwight Morrow. Traditional Mexican atmosphere and food including some pre-Hispanic dishes and grilled meats.
La Strada ($$) Salazar 3 Centro (tel. 73 186085). Secluded, verdant patio with fountain and pomegranate tree, candle-lit at night. Copious Italian pasta, pizza, fish or meat dishes. Next to Palacio de Cortés.

Jalapa
La Casona del Beaterio ($$) Zaragoza 20 (tel. 28 182119). Restaurant/coffeehouse of great character. Tasteful rooms thick with old photos, patio, good breakfasts and lengthy lunch or dinner menu.
Restaurant Casino Español ($) Gutiérrez Zamora 14 (tel. 28 175593). A budget-traveler's delight. Vast, echoing old restaurant serving delicious *corrida comida* in faded splendor.

Puebla
Fonda Santa Clara ($$) Avenida 3 Poniente 307 (tel. 22 422659). Rather overrated but still as popular with locals as tourists. Friendly service and long menu of Pueblan specialties.
Restaurant El Cortijo ($$) 16 de Septiembre 506 (tel. 22 420503). Spanish-style restaurant with heavy wood-beamed décor located just south of the cathedral. Excellent *mole* and other Pueblan specialties.

Taxco
Paco's Bar Grill ($$) Plaza Borda 12 (tel. 762 20064). Its outdoor terrace is a great vantage point opposite the cathedral. Get there early for a good table and *queso cilantro*.
Restaurant Santa Fe ($) Miguel Hidalgo 2 (tel. 762 21170). Friendly family-run place with moderately priced fish and chicken dishes.

Veracruz
Café de la Parroquia ($) Independencia 105 (tel. 29 323584). One of Mexico's most famous cafés, founded in 1810. Always bustling and full, the place to linger and people-watch. Tap your glass for a coffee refill. Good, basic dishes served from 6 a.m. till midnight. Another, less atmospheric version is by the harbor at Insurgentes Veracruzanos 340.

La Paella ($) Zamora 138 (tel. 29 320322). On the quiet side of the zócalo, a small attractive place serving good value seafood.
Pardiños ($$) Zamora 40, Boca del Rio. Vast and well-frequented by locals, particularly for Sunday seafood lunch. Try the *vuelve a la vida* (return to life) seafood cocktail.

SOUTH

Oaxaca

Antijitos Regionales ($) Alcala 301 (no phone). Delicious *quesadillas, tamales* and *molotes* at rock-bottom prices. Assorted tables in plant-filled courtyard, much frequented by local families. Open till 11 p.m.
Restaurant Catedral ($$) García Vigil 105 (tel. 951 63285). Smart but relaxed place a block from the zócalo. Rooms lead off an open patio where live music is played nightly. Oaxacan meat specialties.
Restaurant Del Vitral ($$$) Guerrero 201 (tel. 951 63124). Elegant mansion setting two blocks from the zócalo. Sophisticated Oaxacan dishes combined with international cuisine.

Palenque

Restaurant Virgos ($) Calle Hidalgo 5 (tel. 934 50883). Breezy terraced first-floor restaurant. Pleasant setting near the zócalo for salads, pastas, fish and endless *antojitos*.

San Cristóbal de las Casas

El Puente ($) Calle Real de Guadalupe 55 (tel. 967 82250). New multi-activity center, cheap coffee shop and restaurant, bookstore, workshops, tours, etc. Contact for Guatemalan refugee apprentice programs.
La Galería ($) Hidalgo 3. Rambling bar/café/restaurant in tastefully converted mansion off the zócalo. Plants, paintings and live Latino music. Inventive fresh salads and chicken dishes.
Na Bolom ($) Avenida Vicente Guerrero 33 (tel. 967 81418). For a cultural lunch or dinner with researchers, students or anthropologists. Large communal table and conversation assured.

YUCATÁN

Campeche

Restaurant Miramar ($$) Calles 8 y 61 (tel. 981 62883). One of Campeche's many excellent seafood restaurants in the central zone near the port. Copious seafood platters and relaxed atmosphere.

Cancún

Carlos 'n Charlie's ($$) Paseo Kukulcán, Km 5.5 (tel. 98 830846). Sprawling lagoonside restaurant with usual cheerful atmosphere and menu. Adjoining disco-bar in the marina complex.
La Dolce Vita ($$$) Avenida Cobá 87 (tel. 98 840461/841384). Romantic candlelit Italian restaurant with delightful pergola patio in main town. Exquisite combinations of fresh pasta and seafood, discreet service. A change from Cancún's usual brashness.

Chetumal

Restaurant La Ostra ($$) Calle Efraim Aguilar 162 (tel. 983 20452). Air-conditioned restaurant just off Avenida de los Heroes. Typical Mexican dishes and hearty breakfasts for reasonable prices.

Cozumel

Café del Puerto ($$) Avenida Rafael Melgar (tel. 987 20316). Upstairs harbor-front location with wide windows on both sides. Lobster, snail, crab, prime rib and soup specialties. Live guitar and piano music. Dinner only.
Casa Denis ($$$) Calle Primera Sur (tel. 987 20067). Intimate restaurant in converted old residence in the main town. Freshly prepared menus change daily and feature seafood and/or delicious Yucatecan cuisine. Dinner only, reservations essential.
La Choza ($) Avenida 10 Norte y Calle Salas (tel. 987 20958). Simple, family-run *palapa* place serving traditional Yucatecan home-cooking.

Isla Mujeres

Restaurant Gomar ($$) Calle Hidalgo (tel. 988 70142). Touristy but colorful hacienda-style indoor and outdoor dining. Fresh seafood and meat dishes.
Restaurant Miramar ($) Avenida Rueda Medina Sur. Right beside ferry pier, a popular local spot for grilled fish, *sopa de lima* and fish *tacos*.

Mérida

Amaro ($) Calle 59 No 507 (tel. 99 282451). Cool courtyard vegetarian restaurant in birthplace of poet Andres Quintana Roo. Try the emerald-green *chaya* soup. Open all day till 11 p.m.
La Bella Epoca ($$) Parque Hidalgo, Calle 60 (tel. 99 281928). Delightful *fin-de-siècle* setting overlooking the square. International, Mexican and Lebanese dishes. Attentive service.
Portico del Pelegrino ($$) Calle 57 between 60 & 62 (tel. 99 286163). Charming intimate patio or indoor air-conditioned dining. Divine Yucatecan specialties and international cuisine. Excellent service.
Restaurant La Casona ($$) Calle 60 No 434 (tel. 99 238348). Italian cuisine in a fine old Mérida mansion: elegant interior or leafy patio. Fresh pasta, seafood, grilled meats. Open till midnight.

Ticul

Los Almendros ($$) Calle Principal 23, no. 207 (tel. 997 20021). Rustic, slightly beaten-up setting acclaimed for some of the Yucatán's best traditional dishes. Reasonably-priced, air-conditioned.

Index

285

Picture credits

The Automobile Association would like to thank the following photographers and libraries for their assistance in the prepartion of this book:
FIONA DUNLOP 15 Crafts, Tzintzuntzán, 41 Mitla church, 86, 87a Chihuahua, 87b Cañon del Cobre, 88, 101b Sierra Tarahumara, 130 Guadalajara, 136b Templo de la Compania de Jésus, 155a Independence Day, Zacatecas, 170a Papantla, 222 Mayan village, 223 Yucatán village, 241a Izamal monastery
MARY EVANS PICTURE LIBRARY 29b Hernando Cortés, 39 Moctezuma II, 43 Maximilian, 44 Porfirio Díaz, 45 Juárez 1911
RONALD GRANT ARCHIVES 90a 'The Alamo', 90b 'The Lives and Times of Judge Roy Bean'
ADI KRAUS 11 dancers, Zócalo, 23 car restriction sign, 51 Mexico City, 60b Mexican Museum of Anthropolgy, 144b displays for the Day of the Dead, 196 flora
NATURE PHOTOGRAPHERS LTD 226b Caribbean flamingo (PR Sterry), 236b lemon-peel angel fish (SC Bisserott)
R NOWACKI 100a, 100c, 101 Tarahumara Indians, 209a Man, 246 Tulúm, 250 Mérida market
PICTURES COLOUR LIBRARY Cover Mayan statue, Mitla, Oaxaca 138b Mariachis
PLANET EARTH PICTURES/SEAPHOT LTD 93b gray whale
REX FEATURES LTD 24 Carlos Salinas de Gortari
SPECTRUM COLOUR LIBRARY 238 Mayan temple, Yucatán
F SPOONER PICTURES LTD 46 Carlos Salinas de Gortari

The remaining photographs are held in the Automobile Association's own photo library (AA PHOTO LIBRARY) and were taken by Rick Strange, with the exception of pages 2, 6/7, 18/9, 20/1. 20, 24/5, 26, 27, 40/1, 78, 80a, 80b, 81, 82, 84a, 85a, 85b, 89b, 92b, 93a, 95a, 96, 98a, 98b, 102a, 102b, 103, 104, 105a, 105b, 118a, 119a, 255, 259b, which were taken by R Holmes, and pages 3, 83, 84b, 92a, 94, 99, 135, 143, 167, 169, 206, 232, 247a, 251, which were taken by P Wilson.

Contributors

Series advisor: Christopher Catling **Designer:** Leigh Jones
Joint series editor: Susi Bailey **Indexer:** Marie Lorimer
Copy editor: Karen Bird **Verifier:** Mona King